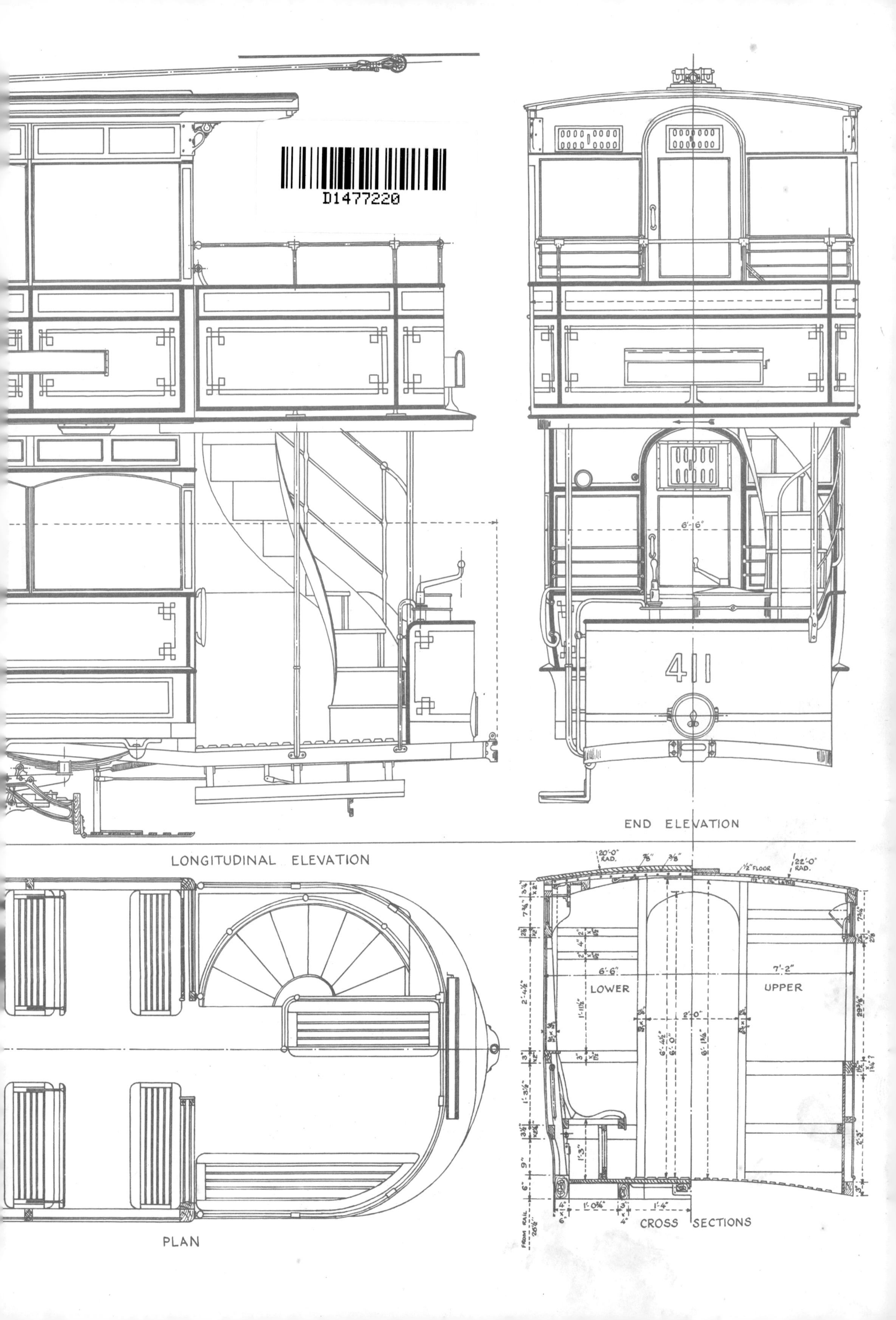
LONGITUDINAL ELEVATION
END ELEVATION
411
6'-6"
PLAN
LOWER
UPPER
6'-6"
7'-2"
2'-0"
CROSS SECTIONS

46 Bath Street was Glasgow Corporation Transport Department's Head Office. This is where decisions were taken, orders placed for equipment from nuts and bolts to complete trams and orders given to staff. Note the etched glass at street level with pictures of (1938) modern trams and buses in full colour. These have been restored and are now displayed in the tearoom of Glasgow's excellent Museum of Transport. *G.C.T.*

THE GLASGOW TRAMCAR

by IAN STEWART

King George VI drove Glasgow tramcar 38 when he was Duke of York on 2nd September 1924. The occasion was the opening of Glasgow Corporation Tramways' Recreation Ground at Helenvale. Note the General Manager, James Dalrymple, on the platform (left) watching his motorman somewhat apprehensively. *G.C.T.*

A

PUBLICATION

To Struan, your help in all things over the past twenty years has been very much appreciated.

FOREWORD

Whilst much thought and attention has been given to the subject of developing towards a comprehensive and co-ordinated system of public transport throughout Strathclyde during the 1970s, it is interesting to observe that by as early as the 1920s the Glasgow tramway system had been developed into a comprehensive system in accord with the vision of James Dalrymple, General Manager of the then Glasgow Corporation Transport.

The variety of design of the tramcars inherited from the former Paisley and Airdrie systems, together with the range of experimental types of cars, portrays the reason why the Glasgow tramcar fleet has provided such interest over the years. The experience gained from such a range of experimental cars culminated in the design and production of the Coronation class of car, which characterised the modern efficient image of the Glasgow tramway system, considered to be one of the best in Europe.

This unique and detailed account of the Glasgow tramway fleet by Ian G. McM. Stewart will not only be of extreme interest to all tramway enthusiasts but will act as an excellent reference for students of the history of public transport in Glasgow.

Alan R. Westwell
M.Sc., ACT(Hons.), C.Eng., M.I.Mech.E., M.I.Prod.E., F.C.I.T.
Director General
Strathclyde PTE.

INTRODUCTION AND ACKNOWLEDGMENTS

This book has been a long time in coming, just as the Glasgow trams were a long time in dying—if indeed they have succumbed even now. Many people have gathered together information on Glasgow trams over a lifetime. This publication attempts to collate all the detail available, combining official and unofficial records and correcting—in some cases—the former.

The late Maurice Marshall's excellent workmanlike history on Stockport's trams has been an inspiration and if this effort is half as good the Editor will be more than pleased. Would that Glasgow only had around a hundred trams to be documented! At least they never renumbered trams in Glasgow . . . or did they . . . ?

In 1977 the task commenced in sifting through all available data. Some was conflicting and had to be resolved without offending the contributors. Gaps in detail from one source were often filled by another. Sometimes mysteries of long-standing were solved and this was most satisfying. Sometimes they have remained unsolved to be entered in an enigma file. Many have been the myths which have been exploded. Where doubt still exists this is highlighted in the Chapters which follow. It is hoped the tabular form adopted will be clear. The story of the evolution of the Standard Car, at least, could not have been related in any other way.

The Glasgow Tramway fleet was second in size only to London County Council's. Because of this the history of the system really has to be split into three sections. That on the Horse Cars has been researched separately and will form the basis of a later volume. The development of Services in the widest sense will also provide the nucleus of another study at a later date. The Rolling Stock of the electrified era from 1898-1962 is meantime as completely documented as it ever will be and this book confines itself to that subject.

I would like to express my gratitude to all those who have assisted in the compilation and collation of material for this publication. Most of all, a personal 'thank you' must go to Doctor Struan Robertson who handed over his volumes covering years of patient research around which this book has been written. Had he not spent so much of his time caring so unselfishly for others he would surely have written it himself years ago.

By way of recognition which he would never seek, this book is dedicated to Struan.

Next, thanks must go to Strathclyde Passenger Transport Executive and Brian Longworth whose access to restricted information, reports and records has confirmed much conjecture and opened up other avenues of exploration. The move of Strathclyde Passenger Transport Executive from the former Glasgow Corporation Transport premises at 46 Bath Street to Consort House caused many long forgotten cupboards and their contents to be opened up and examined—to the benefit at least of this publication. The remainder of the contributors is listed below. Without them, individually and collectively, there would be no Glasgow Tramcar Rolling Stock Book.

Dr. Neil A. MacKillop	John H. Price
Dr. J. Morrison Ritchie	W. D. McMillan
Ian L. Cormack, MA	Charles C. Hall
Ian Hamilton, MMPA	Dr. J. A. Emslie
Brian T. Deans, BA, MSc	David A. Young
W. Tuckwell	Hamish Stevenson

Photographers, and suppliers of photographs, whose efforts are acknowledged throughout this book.

Lastly, any queries which result from this book on any aspect of the Glasgow Tramway system should be addressed to the Scottish Tramway Museum Society, PO Box 78, Glasgow G3 6ER and not the Strathclyde Passenger Transport Executive.

Ian G. McM. Stewart, FCIBS, MASHRAE,
Newton Mearns, Glasgow.
March, 1983.

CONTENTS

CODING AND ABBREVIATIONS USED THROUGHOUT THIS BOOK

EQUIPMENT SUPPLIERS:—

BT-H = British Thomson-Houston
CP = Crompton Parkinson
CW = Crompton-West
EEC = English Electric Co. Ltd.
EMB = Electro-Mechanical Brake Co. Ltd.
GCT = Glasgow Corporation Tramways or Transport
GEC = General Electric Co. Ltd.
HN = Hurst Nelson
LCC = London County Council
M&T = Maley & Taunton
MV = Metropolitan Vickers
REGEN = Regenerative Braking
RYP = R. Y. Pickering & Co. Ltd.
WH = Westinghouse
WIT = Witting Brothers
McF = Macfarlane Bros.

DEPOTS:—

'b' = Langside (Battlefield)
'c' = Coatbridge (Jackson St.) formerly Airdrie & Coatbridge Tramways
'd' = Dennistoun
'e' = Elderslie formerly Paisley District Tramways
'k' = Parkhead (replacing original 'Whitevale' depot)
'l' = Govan (Lorne School, replacing original 'Kinning Park' depot)
'm' = Maryhill
'n' = Newlands (replacing original Pollokshaws depot)
'p' = Possilpark (replacing original Springburn-Keppochill Rd. depot)
'r' = Renfrew formerly Paisley District Tramways
's' = Springburn (replaced by Possilpark)
't' = Partick
'x' = Dalmarnock
'y' = Barrland St. permanent way yard.

COLOUR DIFFERENTIATION OF SERVICES:—

'R' = Red
'G' = Green
'Y' = Yellow
'B' = Blue
'W' = White
'S' = Standard (or 'bus')—Green if applied prior to 1942.

Where details in the fleet tables are shown in brackets ( ) this is deduction.

GENERAL INFORMATION:—

Track Gauge 4' 7¾". Nominal Voltage 575v d.c.

First published September 1983.

Published by the Scottish Tramway Museum Society.

Design and Artwork by W. Tuckwell
Typesetting by K & N Studios, Glasgow
Separations by Reproscan, Glasgow
Printed by M & M Press, Glasgow

ISBN 0 900648 21 X

CHAPTER 1

The
Early Single Deckers
665~685

THE 'ROOM AND KITCHEN' CARS Nos. 665-685

The lease of the tramways by Glasgow Tramways and Omnibus Company expired on 30th June 1894. The Corporation decided in 1890 that it would take over operation. It was actually as early as 1892 that it first began to consider widespread use of mechanical traction in place of horses and even at that early date the Springburn route was considered for experiments in this respect. In April 1896, a Report upon Mechanical Tramway Motors based upon investigations on the Continent of Europe was presented to the Subcommittee of the Tramways Committee on Tramway Motors by Councillor Crawford and the General Manager, John Young. These gentlemen had inspected installations in Brussels, Hanover, Hamburg, Berlin and Dresden and various examples of open and closed conduit and overhead systems were critically compared. The overhead system was that recommended. A follow-on Report was submitted in June 1896 by the Subcommittee as a whole. They covered almost identical ground although also taking in Coventry and Bristol. Their recommendation was the same: the route from Mitchell Street to Springburn should be equipped for overhead electric traction.

It had been hoped at one time that this route would be ready before the Corporation took over in 1894, but if progress had been slow since 1892 due initially to legal restrictions on operations prior to expiry of the lease and intervention from the City Fathers on successive occasions, the time delay was fortuitous. Electric traction advanced from 1892 to such an extent that Glasgow's adoption of the overhead system was undertaken at the very end of its experimental period.

The Corporation had played safe by retaining horse traction when it did. Perhaps a change of operator simultaneously with a change of traction would have been too traumatic. The chosen Springburn service was selected as it formed a detached line suitable for demonstration purposes and was complete with its own depot. In September 1896 both Mr. John Young and Mr. William Clark, Engineer were directed to sail to America to investigate practices there. This they did at once, but it was May 1897 before authorisation was granted by the Council to equip the Springburn route. Indeed the Council had been very reluctant to vest any authority in its Committees, Subcommittees or Sub-Subcommittees—a classic case of non-delegosis thrombosis!

The route along Springburn Road passed beneath a low railway bridge carrying a goods line to St. Rollox Mineral Depot. This dictated the use of single deck cars before it was found possible to lower the road underneath. On 25th August 1897 the General Manager reported to the Subcommittee on Electric Traction that the single deck car which he and his engineer had worked out was practically ready and it was inspected by the Subcommittee on 1st September at Coplawhill Carworks. Here was 665 showing decided signs of American influence, numbered consecutively above the highest numbered Horse Car, 664. A mock-up of the St. Rollox bridge was erected to illustrate the limited clearance available.

665 was a 33'-6" long single decker with two saloons and a central entrance. One saloon had two large fixed windows per side and longitudinal seats while the other had three windows, also with fixed sashes. Accommodation was provided for 50 passengers. The car had hand and electric brakes and is believed to have had 2 x No. 39B Westinghouse motors of 30 h.p. and Westinghouse controllers. The bogies were to Glasgow Corporation Tramways Department design constructed by the Metropolitan Railway Carriage & Wagon Co. Van Dorn couplers were located beneath the dashes to permit the hauling of trailer cars. A handsome clerestory roof was provided, with pivoting half-lights each incorporating the city coat of arms in etched glass. 665 introduced Glasgow's famous cadmium yellow

The very first electric tramcar for Glasgow was 665 constructed in 1897 and seen here undergoing its official inspection standing on ground later used to build the Coplawhill erecting shop. Note the car's 'off centre' entrance. The side number '665' was later replaced with the City Coat of Arms. **STMS Collection**

on the body side panels. This superseded the horse car brown and silver lining replaced the former gold. Rotating destination boards painted in the white route colour were provided above each driver's platform and above each door.

One week after the inspection of 665, the General Manager submitted to his Subcommittee the draft specification for the production cars which were to be numbered 666-685. He stated that these cars would be along the lines of the sample car 665, but with some detail improvements. And so they were. 666-685 also employed the centre entrance but each saloon had three windows. One was glazed and fitted with red plush longitudinal seating while the other was totally unglazed along the sides. Instead, there were spring-loaded waterproof blinds. This saloon was slightly widened to permit installation of transverse wooden seating with rotating backs and fixed bases. The bogies were similar to those on 665 built to GCT specification by the Metropolitan Railway Carriage & Wagon Company. Electrical equipment was identical to that on 665. The dash plates were manufactured from two longitudinal plates bent to shape and flanged together in line with the rubbing strake. All cars had wireplough lifeguards and lattice gates to the centre platform. This latter feature promoted the unofficial nickname given to these single-deckers, namely, 'Room & Kitchen' or 'But & Ben' cars.

On 3rd March 1898 the decision to create additional headroom below the St. Rollox bridge was approved by the Corporation after considering the use of conduit at this location and at a stroke this ensured that these single deckers would not be the Glasgow Standard Tramcars. Even while under construction, their centre entrances were suspected of causing danger to intending passengers.

The 'Railway World' for 13th October 1898 listed the rolling stock for the new electric service as twenty one single deck cars with two bogies (665 and 666-685), two double deck four-wheel cars (686 and 687, see Chapter 3) and 'two double deck bogie cars'(?). What their numbers were or their subsequent fate is not known for sure and remain the major unsolved mysteries of Glasgow Corporation Tramways. Several possibilities and facts must be considered:

(1) A drawing was definitely prepared to show a double deck bogie tramcar. A copy of this drawing is in the collection of the Glasgow Museum of Transport. The General Manager had been instructed to prepare this design, incorporating end entrances, for evaluation alongside the other trams before bulk construction.
(2) Two sets of J. G. Brill maximum traction bogies were ordered and delivered on 4th August 1898.
(3) Dr. J. Morrison Ritchie of Kirriemuir catalogued the early period of the Glasgow tramcars most meticulously and clearly recalls seeing unused four-window double deck cars consigned to the Barrland Street Permanent Way Yard from passing commuter trains. The cars were inscribed 'Mitchell St.-Springburn' on the upper side panels.
(4) Another possibility was that the bogies were used under Standard Cars 688 and 689 which could have accommodated them although they would have been rather tightly compressed beneath their 17' 0" saloon underframes. However, only 686 was ready for the opening date.
(5) 36 maximum traction bogie brake blocks were sold in April 1909 as being obsolete.
(6) A letter was received by the Transport Department in August 1962 from a surviving employee enclosing a photograph taken at Springburn terminus in 1899 when the service had been extended to the Cross. The 'But and Ben' tram was mounted (he said) on maximum traction bogies. It is possible of course that the single motored bogies were confused with unequal wheeled maximum traction ones. Would that the photograph could come to light now!

It is possible that the 'Railway World' based their reports on inaccurate information or speculation but out of phase with actual developments but this will probably never be known now. Intriguing. Make of it what you will . . .

Whatever the facts of the matter, the 'Room & Kitchen Cars' were not an unqualified success. The bogies did not incorporate offset king-pins as on conventional maximum traction cars and the unmotored wheels and axles had a tendency to climb out of the rail grooves on curves. After a spell on the Mitchell St. service which was progressively extended to Glasgow Cross and Govanhill, the cars were transferred to the Springburn-Shawlands service with red route colour. A specially-formed team was on permanent stand-by to perform re-railing techniques at well-known black spots. Understandably, the single deckers ended their active days on the comparatively straight London Road-Clydebank service. Latterly the dash panels were repainted from ivory to brown as on the contemporary open-topped double deckers. The fleet numbers were re-sited from the corners of the dashes to the centre above the dash lamp and became yellow, edged red. The destination boards were also altered from white to red, when the red Shawlands service was electrified in 1901 and extended to replace the Mitchell St. service. The Van Dorn couplers were also replaced by standard Glasgow coupler pockets mounted on a lowered section of the collision fenders.

Originally housed at Springburn Depot in Keppochhill Road, these cars spent most of their lives in storage. The Standard car was omnipotent and omnipresent. The unreliable lower capacity single deckers did not last long in passenger service beyond 1905. In 1906, eleven were in storage at Langside Depot with nine at Dalmarnock. They had the armatures, controllers and other material removed to stores in that year and were written down to £10 value in August 1907 only to be further written off to scrap value (15 of them) in September 1910. Twenty pairs of Westinghouse 49B motors (ex 666-685) and Westinghouse type 90 controllers were thus salvaged. Bogies, underframes and other remaining mechanical equipment were periodically removed for use by the Permanent Way Department and Mains Department from 1906 until 1924.

665 departed very early on from service use although the body was not dismantled until 1924. 672 became the Mains Testing Car No. 3 and thus survived to be rebuilt for the Glasgow Museum of Transport to near original condition thanks to the intervention of the Scottish Tramway Museum Society. In this condition it had been given four motors to enable it to transport its heavy load of electrical testing equipment. In this form the

Photographs of Room & Kitchen cars are few and far between–particularly if quality is required. Although well-known, this view of 667 displays their features most clearly. The motors were mounted on the inside axles. Soon the dash panels were painted brown and the Van Dorn couplers replaced by fixed brackets. *G.C.T.*

The ceremonial closing procession of trams passes Bridgeton Cross and features the restored 'Room and Kitchen' car 672. Despite receiving a great deal of advice to the contrary, the Coplawhill paintshop staff insisted on painting 672's dash panels orange. This had to be corrected later. *Beaverbrook Newspapers*

derailment problem was simply cured!

Paisley District Tramways purchased two trams, complete, which became static accommodation at the Company-owned Queen Mary Tea Gardens, Rouken Glen. One of these was 671 which was photographed inside Renfrew Depot. Some Room & Kitchen car bogies were used by the Paisley Company as the basis for trailers but whether these were off the two bodies purchased for the Tea Gardens or a separate purchase is not confirmed.

The only alterations carried out to the mechanical equipment were to offset the bogie king-pins but this was only applied to the Permanent Way Department's conversions. No passenger car was given this treatment.

The last remaining Room & Kitchen car in its original form had been thought to have been scrapped at Newlands Depot in 1925 but an interesting and *confirmed* entry in GCT's official records refers to the scrapping of '678—Old Springburn Car' at Newlands on 5th December 1938. This had languished in Renfrew Depot until 1936 and one wonders if it had been set aside for some GCT preservation scheme like Horse Car 543. Either way, there was clearly a duplication of stock numbers in the period 1923-38 following the entry to service of the new Hexagonal Dash Standard trams 665-685.

This early view of the interior of an early single decker shows the original pattern of transverse seating soon substituted with more conventional wooden backs. Note the spring-loaded waterproof blinds and absence of glazing. ***G.C.T.***

Dimensions of Cars. 33'-6" long. Interior height of saloons 7'-9½'.

Car No.	*Built*	*Depots*	*Colour*	*Disposed of Written off*	*Remarks*
665	1897	s/x	WR	5/1900	Non-standard saloons: Body dismantled 1924
666	1898	s/x	WR	3/1907	Motors out 3/07: Dismantled at 'n', 1924
667	1898	s/x	WR	?	
668	1898	s/x	WR	2/1925	Dismantled at 'n'
669	1898	s/x	WR	3/1924	One bogie to PW Dept. for carrying Jib. 5/15, remainder dismantled 1924
670	1898	s/x	WR	5/1917	Body became shelter at Auchinairn Rd. Bogies to PW dept. sand wagon
671	1898	s/x	WR	—/1921	Sold to Paisley District Tramways
672	1898	s/x	WR	8/1907	Became Mains Testing Car No. 3. Preserved as 672
673	1898	s/x	WR	2/1913	One bogie to Glasgow University: Body dismantled 1924
674	1898	s/x	WR	3/1924	
675	1898	s/x	WR	4/1925	Dismantled at 'n'
676	1898	s/x	WR	4/1925	Dismantled at 'n'
677	1898	s/x	WR	?	
678	1898	s/x	WR	12/1938	Dismantled at 'n'
679	1898	s/x	WR	5/1915	Became mineral wagon. Body dismantled 1925
680	1898	s/x	WR	4/1907	Bogies out 4/07. Body dismantled at 'n' 4/1925
681	1898	s/x	WR	3/1924	
682	1898	s/x	WR	4/1925	Dismantled at 'n'
683	1898	s/x	WR	2/1908	One bogie out 2/08. Body dismantled 1924
684	1898	s/x	WR	3/1924	
685	1898	s/x	WR	1/1910	One bogie out 1/10. Body dismantled 1924

When Glasgow Cross service extended to Govanhill (11/99) some cars may have been based at Coplawhill Depot.
Equipment from 8 No used to construct Permanent Way Wagons 1906-20.
Two bodies sold to Paisley District Tramways with bogies.
Three bodies noted in use as sheds in builder's yard, Airdrie, 1920s.
Two sets of bogies (not accounted for above) removed 3/1914.
Motors and controllers eventually standardised on Westinghouse 49B and '90' respectively but also quoted as '39B'
One body remained extant until 1970s at farm in Carnbroe, Coatbridge.

If this really was electrified horse car No. 4, the digit '4' would not be visible in this photograph taken at the back of Coplawhill. This is the first conversion retaining short underframes and the original number (664). The Brill 21E truck must have required some surgery to enable it to be accommodated within the restricted length available. On the original photograph the Govanhill and Springburn panel is a fake, covering the inscription 'Mitchell St. and Springburn'. G.C.T.

The Tramways Department commissioned a series of photographs in 1914 to promote road safety. Included in the series was this view showing the perils of bravado when this open top Converted Horse Car encountered the then brand new Hex-dash Standard Car 141. G.C.T.

CHAPTER 2

The Electrified Horse Cars 1~120

THE ELECTRIFIED HORSE CARS Nos. 1-120

Such was the expansion of the electrified tramway system in its earliest years and the need for a large number of trams to operate it that it created a need for new rolling stock beyond the capacity of the Coplawhill Car Works. It will be seen later that 80 cars were built by outside contractors. The Tramways Department also looked to its fleet of horse trams. The last horse-drawn trams were withdrawn in 1902, the oldest of which had been constructed in 1894.

Being of such recent origin, it seemed an obvious decision to upgrade them for electric traction. During careful inspection it was found, however, that their ash timber construction used exclusively for all framing had reached an advanced stage of decay in nearly 75% of the cars at the side framing and consequently they had to be broken up. This was to influence the choice of timber for all future construction. As a result teak became the first and practically only choice for side and end framing, longitudinal rails and underframing.

that this was Car 4. Further close scrutiny shows, however, that the digit '4' is not located in the correct position dead centre above the dash lamp and it shows that it must have been Horse Car 664, recorded as being the first conversion retaining its original number before renumbering in a new series. When the electric cars reached 1000 from 665, they recommenced at 665 downwards and the electrified horse cars were numbered in ascending numerical order from '1' upwards.

Later converted Horse Cars were mounted on new extended teak underframes to provide lengthened platforms and fitted with new quarter-turn staircases similar to those on the Phase I Standard trams. Car 664 was altered to conform during 1903. The canopies on the converted cars were, however, extended on the nearsides over the platform areas but left the stairwells open. 6'-0" wheelbase J. G. Brill 21E trucks were provided with 2 x 30 h.p. motors conforming to the Phase I standard of the time. Motors were of Westinghouse 49B pattern then

Electrified Horse Car (apparently car 6) in white route colour shows the greater protection to platform staff afforded by the lop-sided canopy design compared with the Phase I Standard trams. *G. E. Langmuir*

Progress in electrifying the Horse Tram bodies can be detected from the Annual Reports.

Year ending	31st May 1899:	1 Converted Horse Car
,,	31st May 1900:	1 ,,
,,	31st May 1901:	3 ,,
,,	31st May 1902:	69 ,,
,,	31st May 1903:	120 ,,

120 was the maximum number rebuilt although running gear was re-used in the construction of 42 salt trailers. In 1902, the remaining disused Horse Trams were written down to scrap value.

The first conversion retained its short platforms and canopies. Examination of the photograph taken at the rear of Coplawhill Depot on the occasion of an official inspection would indicate—at first glance—

almost universal in Glasgow but many of the Witting Bros. motors purchased by the Tramways Department at the time found their way to the converted horse tram fleet as did a few British Thomson-Houston GE52 examples also acquired. Controllers were of types WH210, B18 or B13 which could also be found on contemporary standard trams. Lifeguards ultimately became Tidswell pattern and the outside spring trolley standards were supplied by Blackwell.

It is not known which horse cars took which numbers in the electrified series nor has it been possible to verify which builders' products were used in the conversion process. However, the following table summarises the situation as it existed in January 1903.

Just one month before curtailment of services within Renfrew, 57, 672 and 143 were caught simultaneously by the camera lens at Porterfield Road.
W.D. McMillan

The arch of the bridge over the Monkland Canal can be detected quite clearly with lots of transport interest around. 231 leads a Lawsons' Bristol Lodekka past a three-axle London type trolleybus complete with rear destination display and green blinds.
W.D.McMillan.

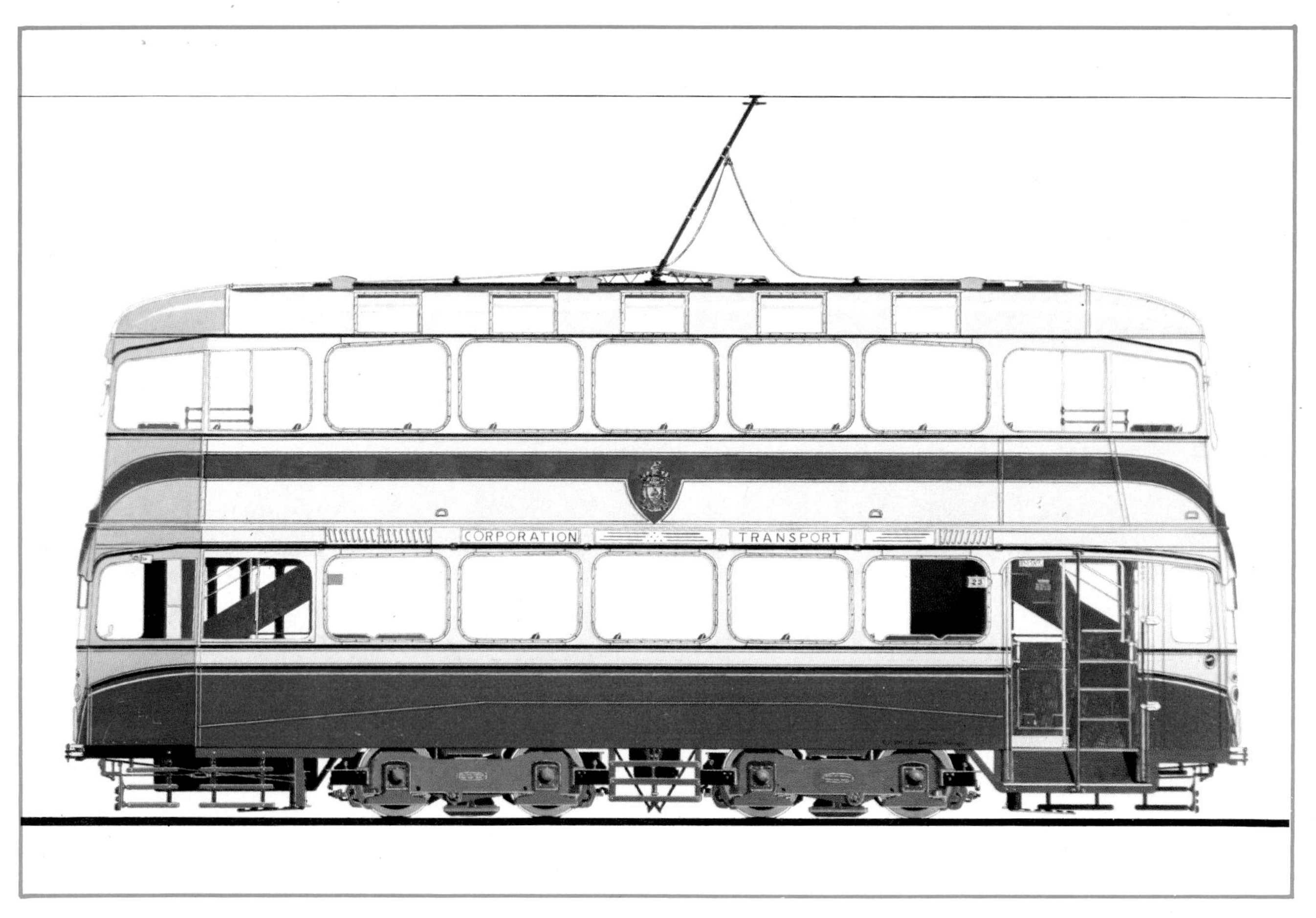

1142's livery for the 1937 Coronation was spectacular to say the least, taking full advantage of the lines of the bodywork. It was the lasting impression made by this car which embossed the name "Coronation Car" for evermore in the minds of the Glasgow travelling public to be applied henceforward to all modern cars. *Drawing: Author.*

1005's livery fulfilled the purpose for which it intended — it had to be distinctive. Various alternatives were discarded before opting for the three shades of blue. These included red and cream, green and cream and red and orange in various styles. *Drawing: Author.*

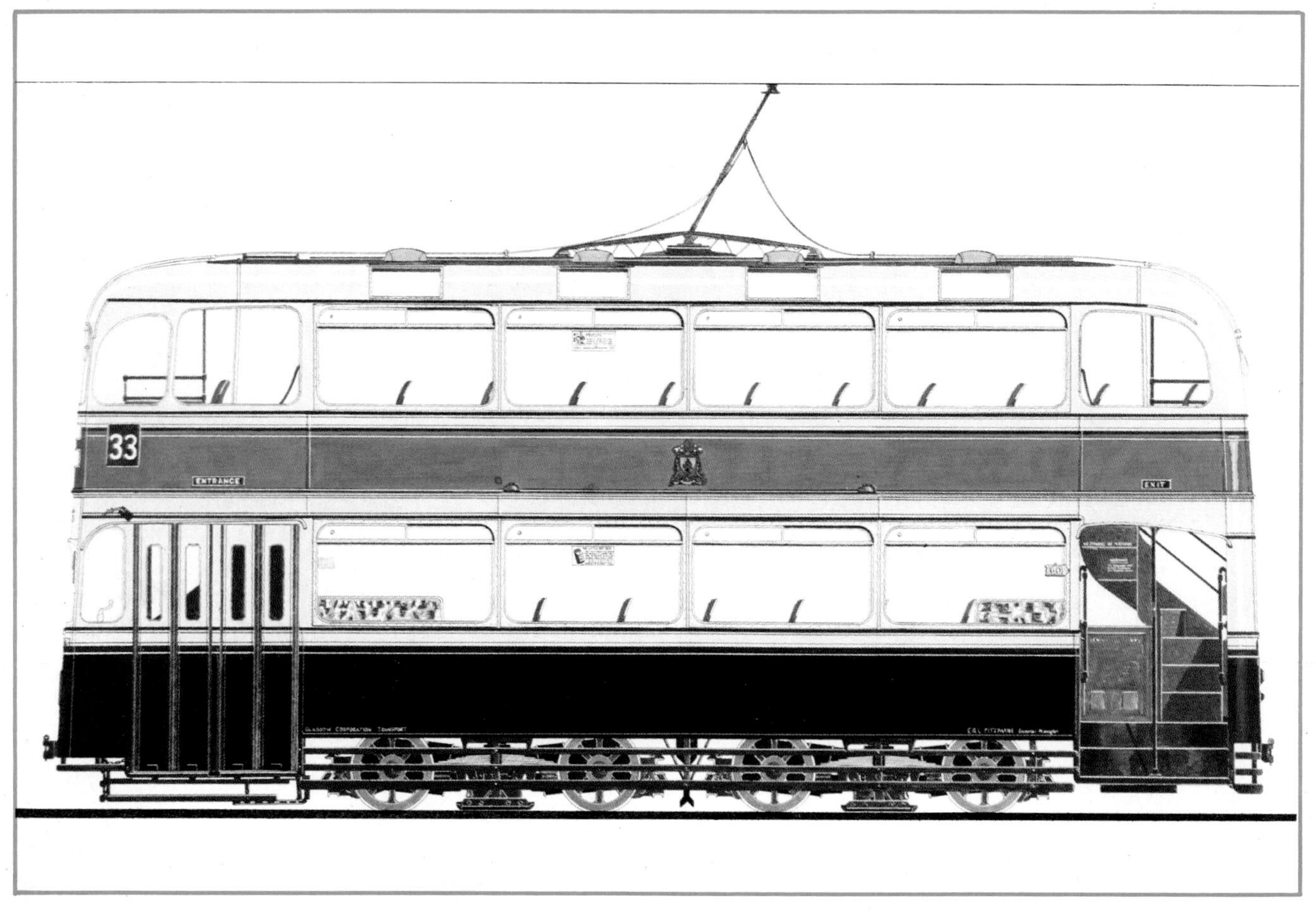

Makers	Number Built	Electric Conversions	Salt Trailers	Sold	On Hand
Brown Marshall	135	8	13	9	105
Midland	80	18	15	4	43
Metropolitan	115	47	14	6	48
Samples	5	1	—	—	4
GCT	29	29	—	—	—
GT & OC	21	—	—	15	6
Totals	385	103	42	34	206*

*17 of these remained to be converted.

Apart from Car 1 which retained its original short underframes, the only other non-standard car was No. 11 whose canopy end sheeting extended around the car to enclose the stairwells. The end decency panels were originally neutral cream but soon acquired the same colour as the side panels to differentiate the route colour information. At first, the route information was painted directly on to the sides of the cars, but this was later superseded by detachable slip-boards listing three 'via' places.

Each depot had its share of converted horse trams and at one time the Sinclair Drive service, which is best remembered for its association until the early 1920s with the 'Unobtrusive' covered top Standard trams, had a predominance of electrified horse trams. Each was licensed to carry 50 passengers. From 1908, the 117 then remaining in service had the top deck railings heightened similarly to the open top Standard trams. In that year, it was also necessary to renew the corner pillars. As can be seen, scrapping began quite early and some interchange of mechanical and electrical equipment took place between the electrified horse cars and Standard cars.

In May 1911 it was decided to provide top covers and vestibules for all except the ex-horse cars which, until then, had received all other improvements awarded to Standard trams. In the following year it was reported that 100 Hexagonal-dash Standard trams would be constructed to replace the remaining ex-horse cars.

When these appeared, some acquired the motors, controllers and running gear from the ex-horse cars which they replaced. The new 7'-0" wheelbase Brill 21E trucks provided for the new trams at first incorporated re-usable components where these were compatible. Only in the case of late survivors did the replacing Hexagonal-dash Standard cars taking up the vacated numbers also adopt the same route colour.

Disposal dates for each car are noted in the Fleet Table as are subsequent fates where of interest. The parcels cars mentioned were the basis of an experimental service from St. Vincent Place which lasted only six months. The cars were painted dull red with brown dashes, having had the seats removed from the upper deck.

The last examples were scrapped in 1920, their lives prolonged by the 1914-18 War. Only Car 92 remained and survived until 1938 but this had been substantially altered for special use.

The shuttle service from the top of Finnieston Street to the Stobcross Ferry was very short in length and doubtless lightly loaded. It lent itself ideally to operation with a one-man crew. 92 was converted for this purpose in May 1910 and had the top deck seats and fittings removed, extended canopy roofs added and the dashes reversed so that the motorman-conductor could observe passengers boarding or alighting. Folding steps were also fitted. 92 was

The extended underframe on this electrified horse car can clearly be seen although this example with full length canopies was non-standard. Car 11 later had the neutral cream upper dashes repainted red to match the side decency boards. The trolley standard has been heavily retouched and was unlikely to have featured inside springs. ***G.C.T.***

stabled at Partick Depot and remained there until the service was withdrawn in 1925 and it was transferred to Renfrew Depot for use on the semi-rural service to Abbotsinch. Although vestibules had been added within a year of its conversion, it was the mid 1920s before the brown dash panels were repainted in the standardised cadmium yellow. Seating for 24 was provided.

Most interesting, however, was the adoption of the Continental pattern plain bow collector on 92—the only one in the fleet at the time. This was later repeated on the second one-man car, 1013 in 1924 and both employed plain bows without the sliding plate contact later to become standard. The bow collector was no doubt thought to be less prone to dewirement than with a trolley. This was important on a tram where such an occurrance would have resulted in its having no crew left on board while the trolley was put back on the wires. Latterly 92 did acquire a standard Fischer bow collector with extended legs in 1928 prior to the policy to adopt them as standard in November 1930.

When the Abbotsinch service was replaced by Glasgow Corporation buses in May 1932, 92 was put in store at Renfrew Depot until 1936 and scrapped from Newlands in December 1938, long outliving her 119 sister cars.

Converted Horse Car No. 92 in original condition as a One Man Operated car on the Finnieston Street shuttle serving the Stobcross passenger ferry. *STMS Collection*

A short-lived parcels delivery service was operated by G.C.T. from St. Vincent Street to Uddingston after the 1914-18 War. Converted electrified horse cars were used, painted dull red with brown dashes. *G. E. Langmuir Collection*

Converted Horse car 92 in its latter days as a one man operated car on the rural Abbotsinch service. Note the conventional extended arms bow collector and cadmium painted dashes. *STMS Collection*

Car Number	To Service	Depot(s)	Colour(s)	Motors	Controllers	Disposed of	Remarks
1	1899	b/m	WR	49B	WH210	5/13	Ex-Horse Car 664: Short underframes
2	1901	b	R	49B	WH210	5/13	Ex-Horse Car 663
3	1901	b/m	R	49B	WH 90	5/10	
4	1901	b/m	RWR	49B	WH210	5/13	
5	1901	b/m	BRWR	49B	WH210	5/13	
6	1901	b	YR	49B	WH210	1/14	
7	1901	b/m	R	49B	WH210	5/13	
8	1901	b	Y	49B	WH210	1/14	
9	1901	b	YR	49B	WH210	1/14	
10	1901	d/l	Y	49B	WH210	1/14	
11	1901	b/m	YR	49B	WH210	5/13	Full length canopies
12	1901	d/l	RY	49B	WH210	1/14	
13	1901	?	?	49B	WH210	1/14	
14	1901	d/l	Y	49B	WH210	11/13	
15	1901	d/l	RY	49B	WH210	9/13	
16	1901	d/l	YB	49B	WH210	11/13	
17	1901	d/l	Y	49B	WH210	5/13	
18	1901	?	?	49B	WH210	5/13	
19	1901	?	?	49B	WH210	11/13	
20	1901	?	W	49B	WH210	1/14	
21	1901	?	?	49B	WH 90	5/10	Body sold 4/21 to Springwell Tennis Club
22	1901	?	?	49B	WH210	5/13	
23	1901	?	B	?	?	5/20	Became Parcels Car
24	1901	?	?	?	?	3/09	Sold to Dumbarton Tramways
25	1901	?	G?	49B	WH210	11/13	
26	1901	d	B?	49B	B13	5/13	
27	1901	?	G	49B	WH210	1/14	
28	1901	?	?	49B	WH210	1/14	
29	1902	?	R	BT-H	B13	5/13	
30	1902	?	?	49B	WH210	5/13	
31	1902	k/l	G?	?	?	1/06	Converted to PW Dept. Tool Van No. 22(i)
32	1902	k/l	G?	?	?	3/09	Sold to Dumbarton Tramways
33	1902	k/l	G?	49B	WH210	5/13	
34	1902	k/l	G?	49B	WH210	1/14	
35	1902	k/l	G	49B	WH210	1/14	
36	1902	k/l	G?	49B	B13	5/13	
37	1902	k/l	G	49B	WH210	1/14	
38	1902	k/l	G	49B	WH210	1/14	
39	1902	k/l	G	49B	B18	11/13	
40	1902	?	?	49B	WH210	1/14	
41	1902	d/l	Y	49B	WH210	1/14	
42	1902	b	WY	49B	WH210	1/14	
43	1902	b/x	YW	WIT	B18	5/13	
44	1902	d/l	Y	49B	WH210	1/14	
45	1902	?	?	WIT	B18	1/13	
46	1902	b	Y	49B	?	5/20	
47	1902	d/l	Y	?	?	3/09	Sold to Dumbarton Tramways
48	1902	?	?	49B	WH210	1/14	
49	1902	d	G	49B	WH210	5/13	
50	1902	?	R	49B	WH210	9/13	
51	1903	?	W	WIT	WH210	1/14	
52	1903	t	RG	49B	WH210	5/13	
53	1903	?	?	49B	WH210	4/12	
54	1903	?	?	WIT	B18	4/12	
55	1903	t	Y	WIT	B18	10/12	
56	1903	d	B	49B	WH210	9/13	
57	1903	?	?	49B	WH210	9/13	
58	1903	?	R	WIT	WH210	9/13	
59	1903	?	W	WIT	B18	10/12	
60	1902	b/m/t	R	49B	?	5/20	WH49B motors 6/18 ex-175: Formerly BT-H motors
61	1902	b/m	R	WIT	B18	10/12	
62	1902	b/m	R	49B	B18	9/13	
63	1902	b/m	R	WIT	B18	10/12	
64	1903	b/m	R	WIT	B18	10/12	
65	1903	b/m	R	49B	WH210	9/13	

Car Number	To Service	Depot(s)	Colour(s)	Motors	Controllers	Disposed of	Remarks
66	1903	b/m	R	?	B18	1/13	
67	1903	b/m	R	BT-H	WH210	5/13	
68	1903	m	R	49B	WH210	9/13	
69	1903	b/m	R	WIT	B18	11/13	
70	1903	?	?	WIT	B18	1/13	
71	1903	?	GW	WIT	B18	10/12	
72	1903	?	?	WIT	B18	10/07	
73	1903	b/m	R	49B	WH210	5/13	
74	1903	?	?	49B	WH210	5/13	
75	1902	?	R	WIT	B18	11/13	
76	1903	t	GWG	WIT	B18	11/13	
77	1903	t	GWG	49B	WH210	11/13	
78	1903	p	G	WIT	B18	11/13	
79	1902	?	?	WIT	B18	10/12	
80	1902	?	?	WIT	B18	1/13	
81	1903	m	W	49B	?	5/20	WH49B motors 10/18 ex-?: Formerly BT-H motors
82	1903	t	G	WIT	B18	11/13	
83	1903	?	?	49B	?	1/14	
84	1903	?	?	BT-H	WH210	5/13	
85	1903	m	R	WIT?	?	5/20	Scrapped 4/24
86	1903	?	?	WIT	B18	4/13	Became PW Dept. Tool Van No. 23(i)
87	1903	b/x	YW	WIT	B18	10/12	
88	1903	?	?	WIT	B18	10/12	
89	1903	?	W	49B	WH210	9/13	
90	1903	b/m	WR	WIT	B18	10/12	
91	1903	b	Y	WIT	B18	11/13	
92	1902	t/x/t/r	B	WIT	?	12/38	Rebuilt Single Deck One Man Car 5/10
93	1902	b/m	R	WIT	B18	1/13	
94	1902	t	Y	WIT	B18	4/12	
95	1902	t	RY	WIT	B18	10/12	
96	1902	t	Y	WIT	B18?	1/14	
97	1902	t	Y	WIT	B18	10/12	
98	1903	m	W	49B?	?	5/20	Scrapped 4/25
99	1903	?	R	WIT	B18	11/13	
100	1903	b/m	R	WIT	B18	10/12	
101	1903	b/m	R	WIT	B18	4/12	
102	1901	b/m	R	49B	WH210	1/14	
103	1902	b/m	R	WIT	B18	5/13	
104	1902	t	GWG	49B	WH210	9/13	
105	1902	p	GWG	WIT	B18	2/11	Body sold to private buyer 2/12. Truck to 856
106	1902	p	G	?	?	5/20	Became Parcels Car. Sold 9/22
107	1902	p	B	49B	?	5/20	WH49B motors 4/19 ex- 981, Formerly BT-H motors
108	1902	p	B	BT-H	B13	5/13	
109	1902	p	B	WIT	B18	5/13	
110	1902	p/l	WB	WIT	B18	1/13	
111	1902	b/m	R	WIT	B18	5/13	
112	1902	t	Y	WIT	B18	10/12	
113	1902	p	RB	WIT	B18	11/13	
114	1902	p	B	WIT	B18	5/13	
115	1902	p	B	WIT	B18	5/13	
116	1902	p	B	?	?	3/09	Sold to Dumbarton Tramways
117	1902	p	B	WIT	B18	1/13	
118	1903	p	B	BT-H	?	5/20	Became Parcels Car, then Ticket Box Car Sold to Luton 5/23
119	1903	?/p	YB	49B	WH210	1/14	
120	1902	?	R	BT-H	B13	5/13	Became Mains Dept. Tool Van No. 2

Code: 49B = Westinghouse 49B Motors
WIT = Witting Bros. Motors
BT-H = British Thomson-Houston GE52 Motors
} All 30 hp — Equipment listed is as at scrapping date

Numbers quoted for Tool Van conversions are those ultimately carried

These were the only Horse-Car bodies in good enough condition to warrant expenditure on conversion to electric traction.

CHAPTER 3

The Glasgow Standard Cars

THE GLASGOW STANDARD TRAMCAR

Inevitably, the Chapter dealing with the Glasgow Standard Tramcar must be the longest. The class was the biggest, with over one thousand constructed and reconstructed over a sixty-three year period. In Great Britain, they were second in number only to the London County Council 'E' and 'E1' class cars. Before examining the detail of the various subclasses within this, the best remembered of the Glasgow trams it is important to assess the situation which produced them and the conditions under which they entered service.

The early single deckers were destined not to become the Standard cars for Glasgow when it was found possible to create sufficient clearance beneath most of the railway bridges in the city. Mr. John Young, the General Manager, was adamant that at least one double decker should be available for the opening procession of electric cars in October 1898 and craftsmen worked round the clock to make No. 686 available. Early construction featured ash framing because good supplies remained from horse car days but this was found to decay rapidly and a decision was made to use teak despite its price being 100% above the price of ash. The compensation, however, was that it could be sawn to almost the finished size with little wastage other than the sawdust, whereas ash warped after cutting. The result was that ash had to be cut from planks considerably in excess of the size of the finished piece and—moreover—it had to be re-stacked for further drying or shaving.

The very first Standard car was 686, photographed in 1898 when new. Note the very low slung platform accommodating the Van Dorn coupler. How the motorman was able to see where he was going remains a mystery! ***G.C.T.***

Early in 1899 it was determined that 500 fully-equipped cars should be produced in just over two years to be available for the 1901 Exhibition at Kelvingrove Park. The Tramways Department laid down its own machinery and plant in the purpose-built Coplawhill Carworks. The Department received much criticism of this policy that they would become their own tramcar builders as some felt that the plant would not be used once the construction of trams was complete. The demand for new trams was such that the Tramways Department felt unable to rely on deliveries from outside sources. Despite this resolve and the maintenance of considerable pressure on the staff at Coplawhill, it still became necessary to resort to contracting out the supply of 80 car bodies. A sample car was produced for inspection by prospective tenderers. One of the largest car builders declined to quote because it was felt that the price for such a highly specified vehicle would be unacceptable. The Chief Engineer, Mr. John Ferguson, was to admit some years later that the firm which inspected his sample car *before* estimating put in the highest price, while that which quoted and *then* inspected won the contract! The Gloucester Carriage & Wagon Company was the successful tenderer. Unfortunately, their products were the subject of some criticism in Glasgow due to rather inferior woodwork which had to be put right after the expiry of the warranty period and—particularly—the poor quality of painting. This attitude persisted towards those cars until the end, reinforced by the 'we didn't build them' syndrome. The Gloucester cars all had to be repainted within two years of entering service, whereas by 1908 only No. 686 had needed such attention due to the speed at which it had been prepared for service. Until the First World War, trams were only 'flatted' and varnished unless the subject of accident damage.

Gloucester-built Phase I Standard car 930 was provided with trolley standard, controllers, truck and lifeguards when it arrived at Coplawhill. The builder's plate can be detected on the sole-bar below and between the 'C' and 'O' in 'Corporation'. 930 did not enter service as a red car. ***STMS Collection***

The timber specification to which Glasgow tramcars rigidly conformed was as follows:—

Moulmein teak for main framing, mahogany for end and side panels, mouldings and side boards, red pine for floors and platforms, ash for side ribs and roof sticks, oak or pitch pine for underframing, mahogany and teak for inside finishing, larch for lathing, birch for platforms and steps and bird's eye maple veneer for roof panels.

By 1908, the cost of a Standard car without a top cover was £550 and the cost of cars with top covers amounted to £632 7s 5d, including an oncost on wages of approximately 33⅓%.

Prototype Standard Cars Nos. 686 & 687

Built: Coplawhill Works 1898 (authorised February 1898)

Trucks:

686 Brill 21E, 6'-0" wheelbase, without extension trusses.

687 Peckham Cantilever, 6'-0" wheelbase.

Specification: 17'-0" long 5 window saloons with perforated strip ventilator and internal monitor roof. The windows had bow tops. The platforms were 5'-0" in length with 90° turn stairs. The floor level of the platforms was kept exceptionally low to accommodate Van Dorn coupler rods beneath the stairs. 686 had the controller located flat against the dash plate beneath the staircase while 687's was

All three Standard cars visible in this view, 926, 827 and 975 employ the angled wooden blade lifeguard used for a while before standardisation on the gate and tray pattern. This is Argyle St.-Union St. in 1902. ***Tramway Museum Society Film Archive***

centred on the platform behind the foot of the stairs. No lifeguards were installed in either car.

Adjustments were made to 686 and 687, and the next dozen or so cars constructed were also subject to modifications to the extent that all of these should be regarded as experimental towards the evolution of the Phase I Standard specification. These included changing the dash colours from ivory to Vandyke brown (699 was the first), alteration to tow gear, inclusion of lifeguards and fitting of truck extension trusses. Following the opening of the inaugural electrified service, the success of 686 and 687 dictated the authorisation of a further twelve to be implemented on 19th October 1898 for an extension from Parliamentary Road to Glasgow Cross. Twelve more were needed for the extension from Glasgow Cross to Govanhill and these were authorised in December of that year.

Later alterations made to the early cars and standardised in later deliveries were the raising of the platform floors when the tow gear was redesigned and the introduction of roller blind destination indicators attached to radiussed upper deck end panels. 687's controller position became standard. The earliest lifeguards consisted of wire mesh aprons, soon superseded by vee-shaped wooden ploughs, although many cars had Tidswell angled wooden blades. These variants eventually bowed to the Hudson & Bowring 7-bar gate tray pattern. In 1903, the Westinghouse-Newell electromagnetic track/wheel power brakes were fitted and this culminated in

The Phase I Standard Car

Built: 1899-1903 and 1909-10

Numbers of cars: 686, 687, 688-1000, 665(II), 664-440 and 316-287 (total 571 cars. Constructed roughly in ascending or descending order as indicated.) Note that 665(II) existed alongside 665(I) but the latter was by this time written off.

Specification: Open top double deck cars with short canopies, 17'-0" long saloons as in 686/7, 6'-0" wheelbase Brill 21E trucks with 31¾" wheels, British Westinghouse 30 hp Type 49B motors. 50 cars did have Witting Bros. motors—most of these had been in the electrified horse car fleet and many found their way into Standard cars of this and later Phases. Controllers were either Westinghouse Type 90, 90M or 210 or British Thomson-Houston Type B18. Track/wheel brakes were Westinghouse-Newell electromagnetic pattern from 1903 onwards, in addition to the basic hand and rheostatic braking.

All were built at Coplawhill Carworks except 901-980 which had bodywork by the Gloucester Carriage & Wagon Company in 1900/01. These received

The blue Phase I tram in the foreground within the original Coplawhill Depot merits a second glance. This is prototype car 687 still retaining the original Peckham track. ***G.C.T.***

An odd production car in the Phase I Standard series was 770 which had full length canopies and reversed stairs; it was photographed outside the original Springburn Depot. The reversed stairs were unsatisfactory but did enable the controllers to be situated ideally. ***G.C.T.***

trucks and equipment at Coplawhill. The order for these cars had been placed in October 1899. The very early trams probably had their route distinguishing decency boards detached and thus route colours were fluid for a little while to meet the demands of the rapidly expanding system. Unless otherwise stated, where information is given in the fleet tables it refers to the stabilised period.

All earlier cars were altered to this specification. The disposal date for the sole Peckham truck from 687 has not come to light but it was certainly prior to 1904.

This photograph of 893 in early form is interesting in that it was taken at Hayburn Street, Partick, before the depot was reconstructed with covered accommodation extending to the pavement and all pointwork giving access to the various lyes located on the street. ***B. M. Longworth collection***

562 at Phase I stage was used for experiments with an angled lifeguard which looked more appropriate for sweeping snow clear of the tracks than for any other purpose. ***STMS Collection***

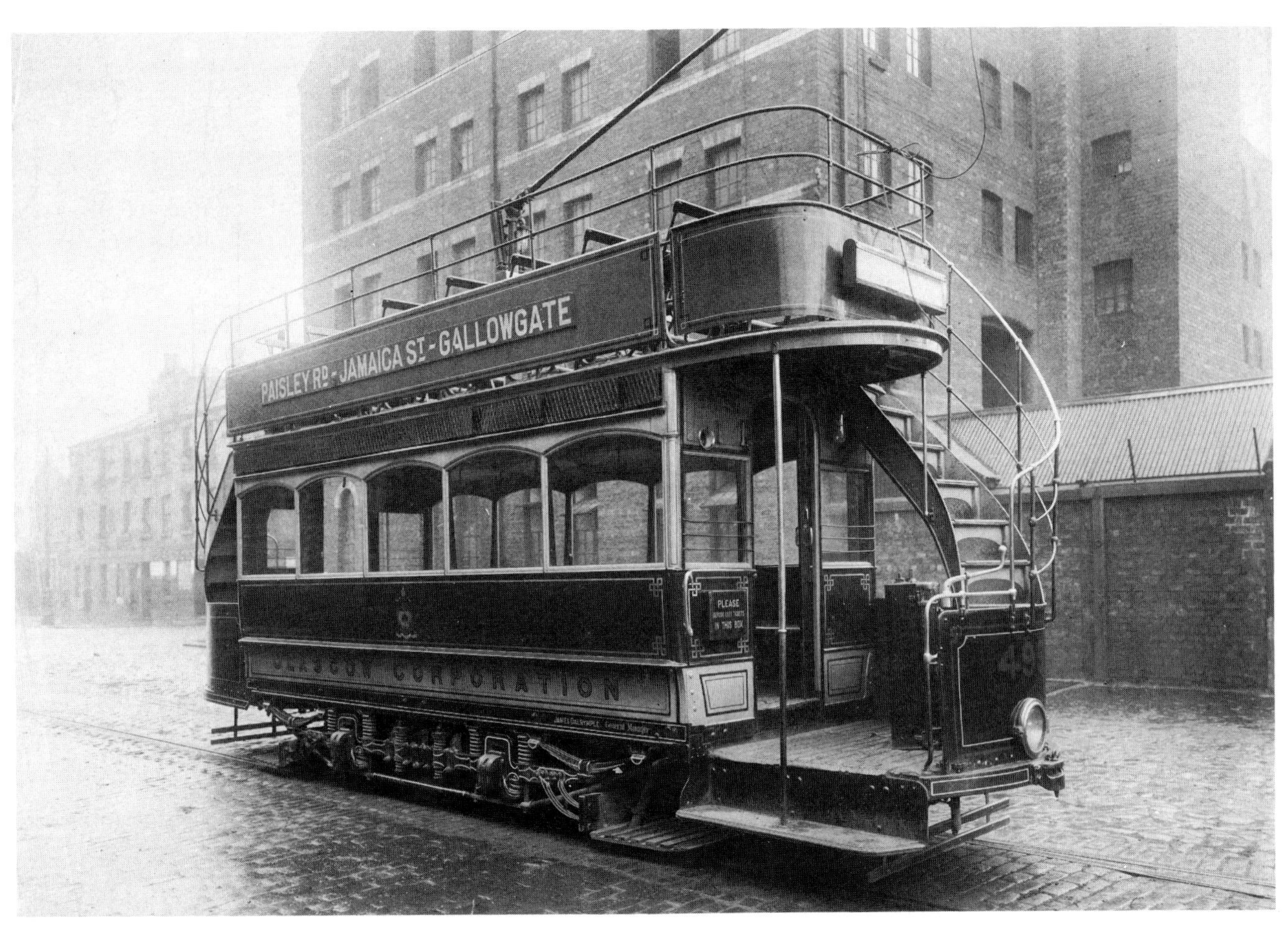

An example of the Phase I louvred ventilator cars is 495. The height of the top deck railings has been increased and the route colour illuminating bullseye has been repositioned to the lower saloon bulkhead. The outside spring trolley standard was non-standard for these cars. 495 was photographed outside Kinning Park Depot. *G.C.T.*

The first Motor School Car was 729. In most respects it was a completely Standard Phase I car but was dedicated to Motor School use only. At one time it had wireplough lifeguards at one end and the gate and tray pattern at the other. Note the louvred ventilators – non standard for this type of car. 729 was released for normal service in 1924. *STMS Collection*

Two sets of Brill Maximum Traction bogies are known to have been ordered and a decision to construct two double deck bogie cars was taken in February 1898. A drawing was prepared showing a double deck version of 666-685 but construction was not implemented. The bogies are thought to have been fitted, for a time, to Standard cars 688 & 689 but confirmation would be welcome. (see Chapter 1).

Lower deck seating was longitudinal of the 'lath-and-space' variety. Top deck seating was transverse. The wide lath seat pattern of the earliest cars was superseded by narrow lath 'dry' seats in cars built from 1902 onwards.

These are three main subclasses within Phase I:

(i) **Phase I/1**

Features:
Narrow bodies, perforated strip ventilators, outside trolley springs.

Numbers:
686-728, 730-1000, 665(II) and 664-510 (total 470 cars)

(ii) **Phase I/2**

Features:
As per Phase I/1 but with louvred ventilators and enclosed trolley springs. Both patterns of ventilator strips were removed each time cars were repainted and became somewhat interchanged. The louvred variety tended to disappear during the 1930s although that on 444 remained until c1947.

Numbers:
509-440 and, for a time 578, and 729 (allocated to the motor school from 1911 until car 1017 was specially adapted for driver training

(iii) **Phase I/3**

Features:
As per Phase I/1 but with the later design of glass ventilators and crown roofs to the lower saloon. these were 'late construction' open toppers built in 1909 just before the top covering programme resumed. The lower saloon design came from cars 437-338 built in 1905/6 to Phase II design. At the time of construction there had been no decision to have the entire fleet top-covered. The open top seating, railings and panels were thought to have come from cars previously upgraded from Phase I to Phase II. All the route colours were represented in this batch of thirty cars but most were top covered within one year of building.

Numbers:
316-287

(iv) **Phase I/Experimental**

Car 770 only
As per Phase I/1 but with full length canopies and reversed stairs. Became the first illuminated car in 1900 'Orange River State'.

The longer surviving Phase I cars (and 316-287 when new) were given top deck railings of increased height for safety reasons commencing c1905. The route aspect bullseye glasses were soon transferred from above the destination indicators to the saloon bulkheads. The service information painted directly on to upper side panels gradually gave way to detachable slip-boards, listing three 'via' place-names.

312 was one of the 'late construction' open toppers placed in service some five years after the first top covered cars. Note the side lifeguard gates and glass ventilators. 312 did not receive a top cover until 1924 but most of the remainder of the batch did so within a year of entering service. ***STMS Collection***

The second type of 'Unobtrusive' Top Cover featured hopper-pattern opening fan lights and fixed main glazing. This is displayed on louvre ventilator Car No. 472 in Albert Drive. Like the other seventeen cars with this type of top cover, 472 was later repainted with red route colour panels. *G.C.T.*

The Phase II Precursors

The 'Unobtrusive Top Cover' or 'Sinclair Drive' Cars

These cars were taken—apparently at random — from cars of Phases I/1 and I/2 and fitted with totally enclosed top covers which did not extend beyond the original short canopies over the platforms. There were detailed differences among the top covers. Some had hopper pattern ventilators with glazed fanlights while eleven were fitted with drop-light windows which could be let into the car sides with leather straps for height adjustment. Some had high decency boards and others had narrow ones. 472 and at least one other had an opening roof. 450 had no roof overhang above the entrances to the upper saloon. Each tram — at first — retained its original route colour but all gradually gravitated to the Sinclair Drive 'red' service. Due to the lack of strengthening bulkheads, the upper saloons latterly became very loose and all were rebuilt direct to Phase III specification in 1923/24.

Sliding windows were stopped up commencing with car 470 in 1911, and such cars had hopper vents installed later. The first car was inspected in March 1904 and all had been completed by May of that year.

Numbers:

445, 450, 463-465, 469, 470, 472, 473, 486, 487, 529, 582, 636, 742, 873, 964 and 993, total 18 cars

The Phase II Prototypes

Built at Coplawhill in 1904.

Numbers 439 and 438.

These were the first two trams constructed complete with top covers and they contained a number of innovations.

The first car to enter service new with a top cover was 439 complete with reversed stairs and full-drop upper deck windows. Both features had been tried on earlier trams and discarded. The lower saloon ventilators were unique to this car. The top cover was replaced with a standard pattern in 1908. ***G.C.T.***

439 had reversed staircases and full length top deck balconies with completely rounded ends and full length canopy roofs to the same profile. The top deck side windows comprised drop-lights without over-ventilation. Each lower saloon window had two individually opening hopper pattern fanlight ventilators with etched glass quarterlights.

438 had normal staircases of 180° turn pattern. The half length top deck canopy roofs incorporated rounded ends. The upper saloon windows were fixed but with glass ventilators of hopper pattern and an opening roof was provided similar to that on 472. The lower saloon window treatment was similar to 439's but only the end windows had two separate quarterlights. The middle three had one each.

On both cars the lower saloon was of lower than normal height and both cars introduced the henceforward standard 6'-0" long platforms. This permitted the positioning of the controllers centred at the front of the car. 438 and 439 were mounted on the standard Brill 21E 6'-0" wheelbase trucks with standard electrical equipment and were the last cars built with lath-and-space seating in the lower saloon. They were also the last to have the interior lighting switches mounted above the lower deck windows. Henceforward they were placed on the bulkheads.

The Phase II Standard Car

The first one was actually a rebuild from Phase I, car 818 in November 1904.

Building period: 1904-1910, Coplawhill Carworks.

Numbers: 437-338, 337, 336-317 (121 cars built to this specification).

Specification: Top covered, double deck unvestibuled trams with 6'-0" platforms, 180° turn staircases and 'wrap-around' round dashes. The balcony roofs were short as on 438 but with squared ends. Electrical and mechanical equipment remained virtually unchanged from the Phase I standard except where noted.

The first true Phase II car was a rebuild - 818. This car introduced the cadmium orange dashes but had more ornate lining on the upper dashes and lower deck bulkheads. Note the gap between the upper dash panel and corner pillars. ***G.C.T.***

Rebuilding to Phase II:

Most of the Phase I/1 and I/2 cars were upgraded to Phase II specification. The very first example was a rebuild and 818's balcony dashes did not quite meet the upper deck bulkheads. The car also incorporated special livery lining treatment to the upper front panels which was not perpetuated. The introduction

438 was the second of the Phase II Prototypes featuring extended platforms, 180° turn stairs, opening roof panels and reduced height lower saloon. It was the last car built with brown dash panels. The top cover was later transferred to 337. ***G.C.T.***

of cadmium dashes replacing the previous brown dashes became a feature except where stated. 818 became standard very soon. Over 500 trams were built or rebuilt to Phase II standard but the last rebuilds from Phase I went direct to Phase III.

The top covers are subdivided into 1st and 2nd pattern in the fleet tables. The first type appeared in 1904 and construction continued until 1906. No perforated zinc shield was fitted over the swept radius of the ventilators. A 'hit-and-miss' louvred ventilator was provided on the right hand side of the bulkhead and the upper deck ceilings were painted white inside without extraction perforations for vitiated air. Car 956 had its 1st pattern top cover removed in 1907 being replaced later with the 2nd pattern. The 2nd-improved-pattern began to appear around October 1909, commencing with car 989 and continued until the begining of 1911 when Phase III conversions and new cars took over production. The 2nd pattern and earlier versions were altered progressively, mainly in the provision of better interior lighting and balcony lighting. Until the late 1920s modernisation to Phase IV, the top deck ceilings on the 2nd pattern top covers were polished wood with laths of light and dark wood, three of each alternating with the other colour. Draughts were minimised with the introduction of the perforated ceiling laths and zinc shields. The bulkhead vents were dispensed with and the brass operating tube which operated the ventilators over the side windows was concealed.

The five subdivisions within the Phase II specifications are:

(i) **Phase II/1** One car only, built 1906
Narrow body, perforated strip ventilators and internal monitor roof to the lower saloon, built years out of phase with other cars. 337 received a top cover with opening roof thought to have come from 438 which had become standard in 1905. 337 carried this top cover until the end although stopped up for many years. 337 was almost certainly the 'pattern car' constructed very early on as a worked example for craftsmen to inspect and copy. The body incorporated detail features to be found on the early Phase I cars. When the need for this lapsed the car was completed and put into service. It is quite possible that it was numbered 1001 as a Phase I car as one reliable source maintains he saw a car of this number—not one which could be misread easily. If so the most likely outcome is that 1001 acquired 438's cast-off top cover and was renumbered 337, only appearing in existing records from the date of renumbering in this tidying up operation.

(ii) **Phase II/2**
Numbers: 437-338, 316, 315, 310-307, 302-297, 295, 293-288 (119 cars). All except 437-338 were originally Phase I. Brill 21E or Mountain & Gibson 21EM trucks were fitted except where noted in the fleet tables. The cars

had narrow bodies but with glass ventilators and crown roofs in the lower saloon. 437-338 were to have been fitted with top covers of the style fitted to 438 but 818's became standard instead.

The 21EM trucks were supplied with ¾ elliptical springs but these were later replaced with conventional springing. (During some later interchange of trucks, cars 287, 290 and 293 acquired 21EM trucks.)

This is the only known photograph of a Glasgow tram with a radial truck. 438 by 1905 had lost the original top cover with opening roof. A standard top cover was substituted and by 1909 a Mountain & Gibson Radial truck installed. 438 was 'captured' outside John Brown's in Clydebank. ***STMS Collection***

(iii) **Phase II/3**

Numbers: 336-317 (20 cars).

These were generally as per Phase II/2 but had broad lower saloon bodywork 4" wider than hitherto. This became standard on future Phase III new construction. These twenty cars were involved in experiments with trucks and vestibules. Details can be found under the heading 'Phase III Experimentals'.

(iv) **Phase II/4**

These comprised rebuilds from Phase I/1 and I/2 and included perforated and louvred ventilator cars (approx. 500 cars involved).

(v) **Phase II/5**

These were built from the Prototype cars 439 and 438.

They had narrow bodies and the glazed ventilators remained unaltered. 439 was rebuilt in 1908 and 438 in 1905.

Before leaving Phase II, it should be pointed out that side lifeguard gates began to be fitted during 1905 starting with twelve cars and gradually spread to the whole fleet from 1910 onwards. To counteract the effects of pitching, the lifeguards were later fitted with an automatic device to regulate the height of the front and side gates whatever the height of the platforms from the road surface. This had been invented by Mr. A. Dougan at Coplawhill. He later became Works Superintendent.

Two cars (numbers unknown) were fitted with Raworth regenerative control in 1906-07.

A primitive weather shield was fitted to one car in May 1905 which brings us to

432 was one of the first of the production cars built new with top covers. Note the Mountain & Gibson 21EM 6'-0" wheelbase truck with three-quarter elliptical springs. In later years, these were replaced with conventional springs on most cars. ***G.C.T.***

914 was one of the Gloucester-built Standard cars with a first pattern top cover. Standing on the Botanic Gardens siding c1915 it features experimental deep slip-boards with nine places of interest. The lady driver must have been particularly hardy to survive such spartan conditions. *G.C.T.*

Phase III Precursor

Car number 397 (only).

Alteration date: May 1910.

This Phase II car was equipped with vestibules on the driver's platforms and roll-top stair covers over the stairwells to prevent downdraughts. 397 retained the Mountain & Gibson 21EM 6'-0" wheelbase truck through until 1930 when the car was further modernised to Phase IV specification. All other Phase III cars were given 7'-0" wheelbase trucks unless noted otherwise.

Phase III Experimentals Trials with vestibules and radial trucks.
Car numbers 336-317, 856 and 438.
Alteration date 1908-11.

438 was fitted with a Brush radial truck and then one by Mountain & Gibson, later equipped with Warner gear.

Green cars 336-317 were fitted with Mountain & Gibson 8'-6" wheelbase radial trucks. 325 acquired a Brush (Peckham) flexible truck. This car and 317/8 remained green, having lost their radial trucks while the other seventeen were transferred to the London Road red services. Their tendency to climb out of the track when negotiating points and sharp curves or even to oppose the curvature had necessitated their radial trucks being 'rigidified' from 1910 onwards. Other truck experiments implemented during this programme included 6'-0" wheelbase trucks extended to 7'-0", together with a Hurst Nelson 8'-0" wheelbase truck employed on car 336 in November 1911. All the remaining radial trucks were replaced during May 1921. The twenty cars in the batch 336-317 were fitted with vestibules very shortly after entering service and the decision was taken to have these fitted to all top covered cars in February 1911.

336-317 had wider lower saloon bodies than previous cars and heralded the way for new construction to Phase III Specification.

The Phase III Standard Car

The vestibuling from 397 with roll-top stair covers was married to the wider lower saloon glass ventilator style of cars 336-317 and combined with new 7'-0" wheelbase J. G. Brill or equivalent by Brush 21E trucks. New trams to Phase III Specification utilised hexagonal dashes designed to mate easily with the angled vestibule framing. Older rounded dash trams being upgraded retained these dashes; hence the now familiar differentiating terms 'Round Dash' and 'Hex. Dash' Standard trams.

Building period: 1910-24.

Numbers of Cars:

286-137, 136-125, 124-107, 987(II), 106-93, 91-1, 1039, 1040, 1050, 1051, 665(III), 666-685 and 1088 (312 cars built new to this Specification —'Hex. Dash').

Specification:

Double deck, top covered, open balcony, vestibuled with staircase roll-top covers, hexagonal dashes and 7'-0" wheelbase trucks. Electrical and mechanical equipment was initially as per Phases I and II.

Rebuilding to Phase III

Commenced with 336-317, 856 and 438. All Standard cars eventually reached Phase III except 665(II) and 987(I) which were wrecked and dismantled for scrap while still Phase II. 397 was

Newly fitted with vestibules and a Brush Peckham truck, 325 poses for the photographer in Great Western Road. This car was one of twenty with wide lower saloon bodies. Seventeen others with radial trucks were repainted with red route colour panels. G.C.T.

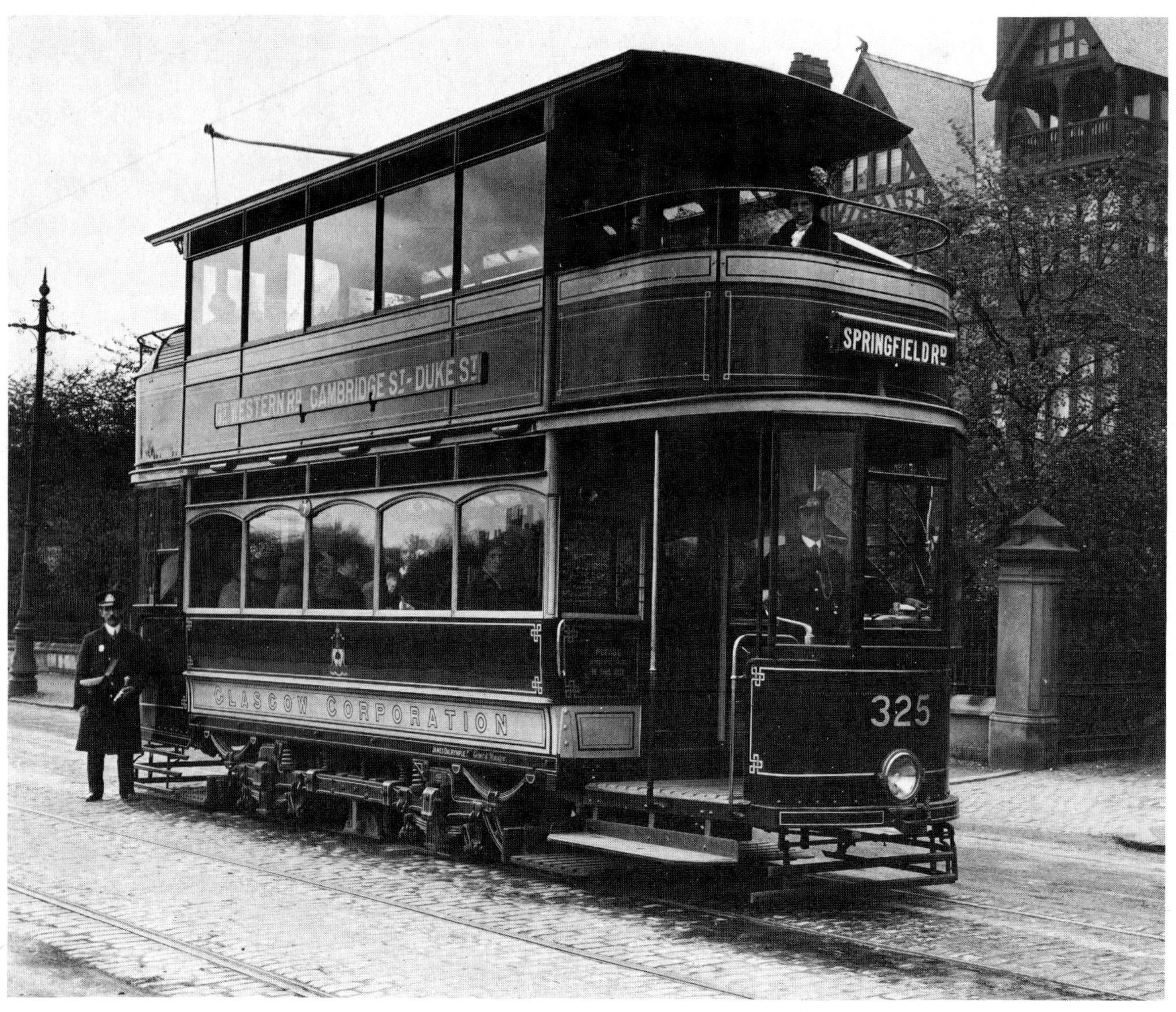

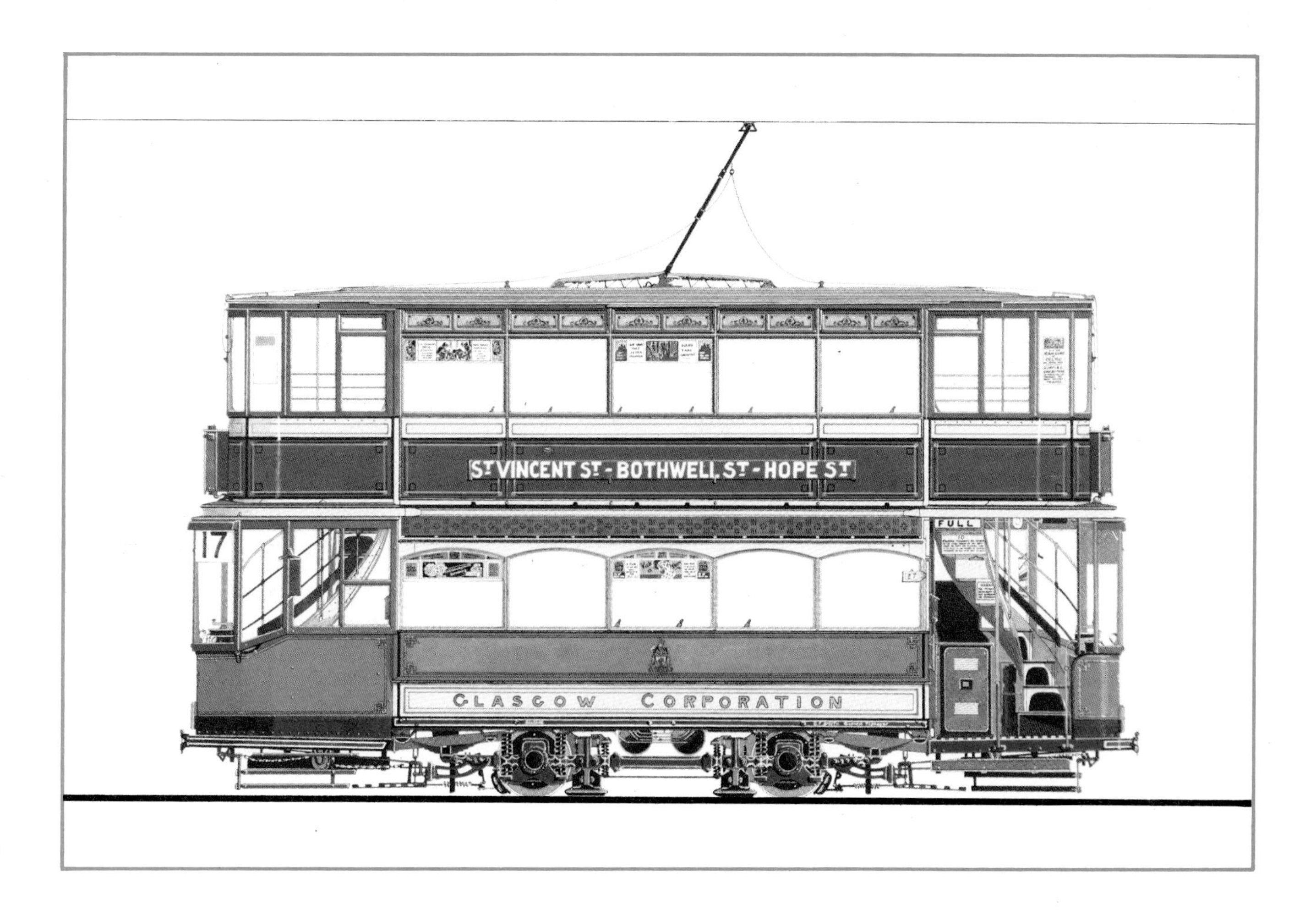

The full lining out applied to Standard trams was still applied until 1938. The decorative treatment to the yellow and white cars used red and black lining while other colours used black and white. Car 500, above, was a late survivor eventually succumbing to the Dalmarnock fire in 1961. 925, on the other hand, was scrapped before the Second World War. Like the other Semi-High Speed Cars, she was not destined to last long and retained the full lining-out after the remainder of the fleet. *Drawings: Author.*

812 was withdrawn in 1960 and despatched to what is now known as the National Tramway Museum in Derbyshire. Five years later it was repainted to portray the pre-war yellow route colour livery. Seeing a lot of use in public service at the Museum the car has since undergone complete rebuilding at a cost exceeding £50,000. 812 is probably the best known of the many preserved Glasgow trams.
J. Henderson

156 passes through an area entirely changed by the still changing Townhead interchange and redevelop Glasgow Royal Infirmary. This was one of several spots, despite every effort to avoid it, where bow collector trams shared the span wires with Corporation Trolley-buses.
W.D. McMillan

never fitted with a 7'-0" wheelbase truck. At first the 30 hp motors continued to be used on new and rebuilt cars. The converted horse cars 1-120 gave up their equipment to new or rebuilt cars. The 45 hp motor of the Westinghouse 323V pattern was adopted as standard after trials with two Brown Boveri 45 hp units on car 132 and BT-H GE200 equivalents on car 144. About forty cars with numbers between 80 and 150 had Westinghouse 220 motors. After the 1927-35 modernisation it was the 323V motor which was retained for Semi-High Speed Standard cars. The second batch of Hexagonal Dash Standard cars was constructed specifically to supersede the remaining electrified horse cars. The last to be built used the T1G controller—a special version made to be compatible with the older controllers then still in use.

The rebuilding period from Phase II to Phase III was not completed until late 1925 to the extent that by

1913—252 cars conformed to Phase III Standards
1914—350 ,, ,, ,, ,, ,, ,,
1915—385 ,, ,, ,, ,, ,, ,,
1916—386 ,, ,, ,, ,, ,, ,,
1917—386 ,, ,, ,, ,, ,, ,,
1918—386 ,, ,, ,, ,, ,, ,,
1919—391 ,, ,, ,, ,, ,, ,,
1920—429 ,, ,, ,, ,, ,, ,,
1921—499 ,, ,, ,, ,, ,, ,,
1922—622 ,, ,, ,, ,, ,, ,,
1923—738 ,, ,, ,, ,, ,, ,,
1924—872 ,, ,, ,, ,, ,, ,,
1925—991 ,, ,, ,, ,, ,, ,,
1926-1025 ,, ,, ,, ,, ,, ,,
(including Car 92 and ex-Paisley 1053-1072)

These figures are taken from the Annual Reports for each of these years as at the Financial Years' end, 31st May.

The Phase III class can be subdivided thus:

Phase III/1

Hexagonal dash cars actually built to Phase III (312 cars) with the following oddities:—

No. 137, experimental, with long platforms to accommodate front exit/rear entrance facilities although the front exit served only the lower saloon. The upper deck had staggered, twin swivelling seats. An Ackley adjustable handbrake gave additional clearance on the platforms by having a vertical wheel.

Nos. 144 & 148, fitted with 40 hp motors in 1915-16 (GE200 and W/H 220 respectively). This enabled top covered cars to be provided to negotiate the Shields Road gradient for the first time.

No. 665 (III) was fitted with a Peckham cantilever 7'-0" wheelbase truck when built.

Phase III/2 (Rebuilds)

Round dash cars with narrow bodies (except 336-317) glass, perforated strip and louvred ventilators in the lower saloon. This covered Round dash cars of both Phases I and II and all subdivisions except those noted above. (692 cars.)

Rebuilding period: 1910-26.

Numbers of cars: 686-1000, 664-398, 396-287.

Due to the reduced height of the lower saloon on cars 438 and 439 the vestibule framing overlapped the top of the round dashes by about 3". All other cars had the framework butting on top of the dash plates.

It was following inspection of a sample in January 1913 that it was decided to arrange for all cars to carry a lifting jack.

The first Hexagonal Dash Phase III cars had small bulkhead-mounted ticket boxes and the detailing of the vestibules' panelling was repeated over the centre window prior to the introduction of the digital headcode above the drop-light.
G.C.T.

888 was photographed outside Langside Depot, a typical example of an original Phase I car having come through Phase II to Phase III. On orthochromatic film, the yellow route colour panels reproduced darker than on cars with Prussian blue.
S. M. Little Collection

Phase III cars constructed new to this specification employed Hexagonal Dashes. One oddity was 137, placed in service with extended platforms incorporating front exit facilities for the lower saloon. Note the vertical hand brake handle. The experiment was unsuccessful. *G.C.T.*

This view of red car 75, photographed when new in Phase III condition, was used as a prototype for the reconstruction of the National Tramway Museum's similar car 22 which now operates at Crich. Note the incorporation into the vestibules of an aperture to display the three track digital headcode. *G.C.T.*

Summary of Experiments and Alterations during Phases I-III

Experiments: (Cars noted are coded 'E' in Fleet Tables)
Speed indicator c1902
Shelter for motorman c1905
Collapsible gates c1905
(Dundee) Side deflection lifeguard c1905 (car 562?)
Wet sandboxes c1906 (car 377)
Side lifeguard c1905 (five cars)
Philipson side lifeguard c1907
Maley brake c1909 (car 782)
Mullins sand gear c1909 (one top covered car)
4-Hurst Nelson sandboxes c1909 (one car)
McNair's sand gear c1909 (one set)
Rev. indicator on axle c1909
Windshields c1909 (two cars, 397 & 438?)
Route Number indicators c1910
Division rail on seats inside c1910 (cars 591 & 705)
Destination lamp for side windows c1911
Teakoid floors & steps c1911 (five cars)
Time meter c1911 (one car)
McClintocks axle boxes c1912
Arthur power saving recorder c1920

Alterations:

New pattern seats	1902
Lifeguard superseded	1902 (440 cars)
Screens on destination lamps	1903
Truck plates	1903
Notices on ends of cars	1903
Inside destination screens	1903
Waterproof bell pushes	1903
Westinghouse-Newall brake	1903
New route head lights	1904
Stair rails & staunchions raised	1904
Wood frames for notices	1906
Re-arrange upper deck seats on 120 top covered cars	1907
Frames for Spitting & Smoking Notices	1907 (300 top covered cars)
Alter doors	1907 (200 top covered cars)
Cummings sanding apparatus	1907
Point shifter holders	1907
Dougan lifeguards	1907
Peacock brakes	1907
Board of Trade tail lamps	1908
'USED TICKET' boxes	1908
Ivorine labels on 'USED TICKET' boxes	1909
Side lifeguards, all cars	1909
Fare Table notices, 337-438	1909
USED TICKET boxes, upper decks	1909
USED TICKET boxes, on dashes	1909
Pedal motion for sand gear	1909
Time card cases	1911
Side screens (12 cars)	1911
Meters (30 cars)	1911
Mirrors on vestibuled cars	1912
Bye-Law frames	1912
Large ticket boxes on bulkheads	(350 cars) 1913
Extra lighting circuit (400 cars)	1913
Holders for 'Points of Interest' leaflets	1914
Replacing glass with mahogany in lower saloon doors of vestibuled cars	1914
Notice boards for dash mounting on hex-dash cars	1914
Mirrors on unvestibuled top covered cars	1915
Money collecting boxes (later used for uncollected fares)	1915
Ends fitted to short canopy seats on vestibuled cars	1915
Obscuring lamps and blinding windows	1916
Platform seats for lady conductors	1916
Closing up old vents on top covered cars (311 cars)	1920
Focussing device on dash lamps	1926

The Experimental Phase

Whereas the evolution of the Phase I ultimate specification and the progression through Phase II to Phase III could be described as unhurried, the monopoly which the tramcar had enjoyed had ended by the mid 1920s when bus competition began to be felt. A series of experiments was put in hand to see how best to equip the tram fleet to cope as it had been found by experience that a speeding up of schedules only aggravated the fore and aft pitching motion imposed by 7'-0" wheelbase trucks. It will be seen that much of the effort of the Department was concerned with truck improvements although not solely in this respect.

The 'test bed' experiments on service trams were applied to 'green' cars coming in for routine overhaul. the need was particularly acute on the Paisley to Uddingston or Airdrie services hence this choice of route colour. By the end of the experimental period when production of Phase IV tramcars commenced, the Department had opted to incorporate more technical developments and improvements to passenger comfort in that two year period than had been put in to practice during the previous twenty.

The following details refer purely to the Standard cars. The high speed single decker or 'pullman' car, No. 1089 was a very important constituent of this programme but details can be found in Chapter 6.

Information below is listed by car number and in chronological order.

15 August 1925

Car 439 was fitted with 7'-0" wheelbase Brill 79E1 truck with Westinghouse 323V motors and wooden cross seats in the lower saloon. (This truck is also quoted in 'Tramway & Light Railway World' as 79EX, large wheel). The springing was found to be too weak on this truck and poor riding qualities were reported.

January 1926

Car 48 was fitted with a single pole bow collector for use on the Shields Road route which was completely outwith the city centre. This route had been equipped for use with bow type collectors with Fischer sliding plates. 48 was thus a 'yellow' car.

1 May 1926

Car 16 was fitted with an EMB Pivotal truck with 10'-0" wheelbase, BT-H 502cs 40 hp motors. Air cushions were fitted into the frames of the old wooden seating in the upper saloon which was also reduced in height by 3" to accommodate the extra height of the truck and equipment. The air cushions were found to be unsatisfactory but the truck, while occupying the attention of the EMB engineers from time to time, gave a considerable reduction on tail-wag. Acquiring air brakes by 1927, 16 was the only known Pivotal car to be so equipped.

10 July 1926

Car 15 became a pilot experiment with maximum traction bogies when the 17'-0" long underframes were extended into the platform areas to a length of 20'-6" to accommodate Brill 39E1 reversed maximum traction bogies with MV101BR motors. The platforms were lengthened but the car retained open balconies. Mosley air cushion seat bases were installed in the lower saloon and fully upholstered seating with full-depth backs was fitted upstairs. The top deck was reduced in height by 3" to compensate for the increased lower saloon floor height. The air cushions were found to be unsatisfactory once again and while these in the top deck were popular, it was decided that henceforward the depth of the backs could be restricted to approximately 7". The General Manager reported that the acceleration was not quite as good as in No. 1089 but that 15's alterations made an excellent car to which he recommended the complete enclosure of the top deck.

11 September 1926

Car 17 was fitted with a Brill 79E2 'Safety' small wheel 8'-0" wheelbase truck with MV101BR motors. G. D. Peters upholstered seating was installed in both decks and found to be satisfactory but the truck springing was reported as being too weak giving poor riding qualities.

8 March 1927

Car 448. On this car the Brill 21E truck was fitted with tail-wag and anti-gallop devices. The Westinghouse 49B motors were retained.

15 March 1927

Car 103 became the Prototype for Phase IV in having the balconies vestibuled and 8'-0" wheelbase truck fitted of 21E style but manufactured by Brush. 60 hp high speed motors were fitted. The canopy bends were not re-profiled. The top deck had new roof boards from end to end. The car achieved a speed of 32 mph on the Mosspark Boulevard reserved track with little evidence of oscillation.

21 April 1927

Car 159 initially was fitted with Peckham P35 pendulum truck of 8'-0" wheelbase and roller bearings of Hoffman manufacture. The motors were 60 hp MV101BR. 159 acquired this new equipment and new G. D. Peters seat cushions inserted into the old frames while retaining the open balconies. The bodywork was upgraded on this date as per 103 except that the areas of new roofing were restricted to the balcony areas only. The profile of the canopy bend over the platforms was not altered and the new balcony vestibule windows did not incorporate any swivelling quarterlights adjacent to the bulkheads. 159's truck was reported to have given the best results of any tested and twenty more were to have been ordered until further work with 103 led to the claim that the 21E pattern could be adapted to give results at least as good.

Car 17 was fitted with the Brill 79E2 'Safety' truck originally destined for 1089. (See also Chapter 6). ***G.C.T.***
Courtesy G.E. Langmuir

26 January 1927

Car 18 was fitted with Brill 21E truck fitted with new axle boxes with swing link attachments and MV104A motors. This was the cheapest alteration of the series of experiments.

26 January 1927

Car 13 was fitted with Brill 21E truck fitted with a sample set of 'Skefko' roller bearing axle boxes and Westinghouse 323V motors.

5 February 1927

Car 19 was fitted with a Kilmarnock Engineering Company Radial axle 10'-0" wheelbase truck and Dick Kerr T84BP motors. Cushions were fitted into the old seat frames with the wooden spars removed. The truck springs were reported as being too heavy and rigid but the truck otherwise pleased the Coplawhill engineering staff.

It was at this time that the General Manager presented a report to the Committee on Tramways outlining the measures listed above and commenting on the adequacy of each in the long term to combat the competition being felt from the independent buses. Orders were placed for 50 new cars—the Standard Double Bogie cars or 'Kilmarnock Bogies', details of which appear in Chapter 7. Regarding the existing rolling stock it was suggested that 332 of the trams were suitable for reconstruction or reconditioning. (The Hexagonal Dash Standards plus 336-317). Second thoughts affirmed that Round Dash Standard trams with narrow bodies and crown roofs (287-316, 338-439) were also worthy of consideration. The monitor roof trams were —at least until September 1928—not believed to be suitable for upgrading. Authority was given to have 150 of the cars reconditioned to similar specification to that of new double bogie cars. The underframes would be extended to 20'-6" in length as in Car 15 but with the body length increased as well. The upper deck would be enclosed, new bogies, motors and air brakes fitted and the cars provided with improved lighting and with heaters and upholstered seating. The estimated cost per car was worked out at £1,500 and car 142 was rebuilt to this specification on 1st June 1927: however £1,200 per car was the cost limit quoted if a Peckham truck similar to 159's was employed. In the end, purchase of 21E pattern equipment from Brush and fitting out Car 103 with a Glasgow Corporation Tramways version of the 21E truck proved to be more acceptable and was adopted as the future Standard. 142 remained an oddity. Further such conversions would have been very time consuming in the body shops at Coplawhill. The Paisley to Uddingston and Airdrie services were selected for the first production run of modernised trams and so the earliest examples carried green route bands. The programme was then carried through progressively on a route by route basis.

The last pre-production experiments concerned Car 21 which was fitted with sample Hoffman roller bearing axle boxes in the existing trucks on 3rd October 1927, thus closely resembling 22 in its present form at Crich. Car 105 was rebuilt as per 103 but on this tram and on further highspeed examples, the canopy bend over the platforms was altered in profile above the step to smooth the appearance of the tram. This final conversion was completed on 28th September 1927. Only cars 15, 16, 103 and 159 together with the last of the semi-high speed conversions were not altered in this way.

In February 1928 the modernisation programme commenced at a rate of about three cars per week to produce:

The Phase IV Standard Car

This involved the Phase III Standard cars including 397 (which had retained the 21EM 6'-0" wheelbase truck) but excluded 665(II) and 987(I) which had been scrapped at Phase II stage and replaced by new Phase III trams carrying the same numbers. Notice that it also embraced the 'unsuitable' monitor roof standard trams.

Car 48 was fitted with a single-arm bow collector for experiments on the Shields Road service. Note the zinc panelling over the trolley plank. This is the extract ventilation feature in the second pattern top covers. The rubbing strip over the centre window is to prevent chafing by the crane cables when the body was lifted from the trucks in the Coplawhill Erecting Shop. G.C.T.

At the end of the modernisation experimental period, 159 was fitted with a Peckham P35 truck immediately before the open balconies were enclosed. This truck was the most successful of all those tested. G.C.T. Courtesy G. E. Langmuir

Rebuilding period: 1928-35
Car Numbers:
1-14, 16-91, 93-141, 143-1000, 1039, 1040, 1050, 1051 and 1088 (= 1002 cars)

Specification:
Double deck totally enclosed cars with 21E pattern 8'-0" wheelbase trucks and roller bearings, high speed 60 hp motors, air brakes, upholstered seating, heaters and, later, bow collector current collection. The transitional or semi-high speed cars retained older Brill 21E trucks with plain bearings, 7'-0" wheelbase, and with 45 hp motors transferred from the newest modernised cars after a considerable exchange of mechanical and electrical equipment occurred to achieve a situation whereby the trams thought to be least

worthy of modernising acquired the semi-high speed equipment.

At this stage it is important to see just how the Tramways Department achieved the complete reconditioning of the vast majority of its tramcar fleet. Although the programme was not entirely complete until 1935, most of the rebuilding of car bodies was finished before 1932, only the cars in poorest condition retaining open balconies and Phase III features until the mid 1930s. How was this done?

It has been said that for the first time since 1900, outside suppliers were used for the 50 new Standard Double Bogie cars. Although much work in fabrication was certainly carried out at Coplawhill and in the former Paisley District Tramways workshops at Elderslie, outside suppliers were used to speed work-flow and three modernised cars were outshopped per week on a route allocation basis rather than necessarily by car type, age or number.

Top deck canopy roof ends were supplied by bus body builders Messrs. Cowieson Ltd. New vestibule framing came from R. Y. Pickering Ltd. and Hurst Nelson, with the latter supplying all the drop-light frames. A decision to retain wooden seating was implemented on Car 7 but soon rescinded in favour of providing upholstered seats. These were supplied by Bennett Furnishing, Siddell & Hilton, G. D. Peters and later by Cowieson Ltd. Trucks tended to be purchased in component parts and assembled at Coplawhill although some were purchased complete and some were eventually made at the Carworks. Although quoted as being 'lengthened', all 8'-0" wheelbase trucks had new truck frames. They were all to the Department's own specification which retained the 21E features but none were supplied by Brill, despite being given this name in official records.

Forgings came from Brush Ltd., and axle boxes from Hoffman, Skefko, British Bock Bearings Ltd., and Ramsome & Marles. Electro magnets were supplied by Metropolitan Vickers Electrical Company Ltd., and EMB Ltd., and air brake equipment by EMB, G. D. Peters Ltd., Maley & Taunton and Westinghouse. Compressors came from Reavel, EMB, and Maley & Taunton. Motors were obtained from Metropolitan Vickers, English Electric, GEC and British Thomson-Houston. Coplawhill undertook the assembly work to provide complete trucks for marriage to completely modernised bodies and only later when the pace had slowed down did the 'Transport Department' (as it had become) involve itself in manufacture rather than assembly. Elderslie's role was mainly confined to vestibuling 300 of the older cars which at first retained older mechanical and electrical equipment and wooden seating. Their involvement ended with the completion of these in October 1930. The subdivisions within Phase IV can now be examined:—

The earliest modernised trams in 1928 had new Brush-manufactured trucks with single magnetic brake units. Note the retention of the long point iron secured to the staircase stringer. Bow collectors were fitted, replacing the fixed head trolleys during 1931-32.
G.C.T.

Car 2 was one of a number used to experiment with pantograph current collectors both before and after the decision had been taken to standardise on the Fischer Bow Collector. Car 2 was a Metropolitan Vickers example and was photographed at Auchenshuggle in February 1933. ***A.E.I. Ltd.***

Phase IV/1

Covered one stage modernisation direct to high speed specification as described. The 21E pattern trucks had 8'-0" wheelbase, 27" diameter wheels and 4½" axles. Air wheel brakes and magnetic track brakes were provided. One magnetic brake unit was installed in each of the earlier modernised cars (noted in the fleet tables) and two in the later conversions. Modern controllers were also installed either English Electric CDB2 or Metropolitan Vickers OK20B, OK23B or OK26B.

The upholstered seating was leather in the upper saloon, navy blue at first but later mostly brown. That in the lower saloon was 'grey lozenge' moquette-covered in the majority of trams, but leather was used in the last to be so upgraded. The layout comprised two-and-one seating in three rows transversely with longitudinal seats for three in each corner. This was a reduction of two from the layout employed in the 1925 experiments but gave greater circulation space. It was adopted following inspection of the LCC Pullman E1 cars by Glasgow officials.

The number of cars modernised direct can be found in the Fleet Tables and totalled 547 cars, among which were some further experimental cars:

Car 91 Full length upper saloon (1 car only)

The top deck bulkheads were removed and replaced by glazed partitions over the stairwells and jack-knife doors similar to the new bogie cars. This was reputed to have followed a suggestion by Baillie P. J. Dollan and 91 was sometimes known as 'Baillie Dollan's Car'.

Cars 532 & 536 Worm drive motors (2 cars only)

These were fitted with MV107 motors with direct worm drive at modernisation. They reverted to Standard Phase IV/1—532 in August 1934 and 536 in January of that year. 532 acquired MV101DR and 536 EEC T105/2HP motors as replacements.

Car 305 MV Remote Control Regenerative Braking Tramcar.

Following a conference of the International Union of Tramways, it was agreed that the Municipal Tramways and Transport Association should arrange to have Regenerative equipment further demonstrated. The General Manager was asked to obtain a set of equipment from Metropolitan Vickers if the MTTA did *not* opt to carry out tests in Glasgow. This materialised in the form of Car 305 which was placed in service on 4th November 1933 with MetroVick line voltage remote control equipment. The MV101CR motors had special fields. The equipment was not a success due to its inability to compensate for fluctuating line voltages and was removed, 305 reverting to standard but retaining outward opening doors on one dash side fitted for access to maintain the original equipment.

Although comparative tests with cars 94 and 108 showed a saving in current exceeding 34%, standard equipment was re-installed on 30th May 1936.

Car 384 Half-drop opening windows (1 car only)

Half-drop windows were inserted into the central window on each side of the lower saloon on 19th September 1934 and two per side of the upper saloon on 12th October 1934. These were removed without trace around 1950 due, presumably, to the effects of body movement.

Car 413 Experimental EMB Flexible Axle truck (1 car only)

This tram was fitted with a sample truck in October 1934. The wheelbase was 8'-6". It was removed on 26th December 1938 and returned to the manufacturers for refurbishing for use under experimental car 1003. (For details, see Chapter 11). oldest cars previously rejected as being unworthy of modernisation thus received the most modern equipment—a situation which obtained right into the 1950s when there was a trend to redistribute the best bodies to the best trucks. Such was the demand for modernised trams that the Department had to continue its programme to embrace all the Standard cars. In so doing it created a rod for its own back in a few years from that time.

Phase IV/2 Two stage modernisation to High Speed.

Details are as described in Phase IV/1 but with the following exceptions:

Phase IV/2A EMB Swing Axle trucks.

Nine cars were fitted with 8'-6" wheelbase trucks (as per Car 413) during April and May 1935.

Car Numbers: 702, 713, 750, 751, 779, 790, 797, 881 and 889.

An idea of the degree of standardisation achieved during the 1930s can be judged by this photograph of football specials at Ibrox. In fact there were many detailed differences among the trams electrically and mechanically. 897 is a Phase IV 'transitional' car with old equipment.
STMS Collection

Phase IV (Transitional) (455 cars)

The 300 or so cars dealt with at Elderslie and the remainder of this class assumed the appearance of Phase IV in being enclosed and having the lighting circuits rewired. They retained their wooden seats but acquired heaters and air brakes. The old 21E trucks were retained with old motors and these cars represented a transition between Phases III and IV. Most eventually achieved full modernisation except where noted below. In the intermediate phase the cars looked very like the later Semi-high Speed Phase IV Standard cars. The latter, however, standardised almost completely on the Westinghouse 323V motors. The transitional cars retained what they had (or in some cases what was displaced from other cars) be it British Westinghouse 49B or 323V or Witting Brothers motors and equipment including the Westinghouse-Newell electromagnetic track-cum-wheel brakes. As listed in the Fleet Tables, all of the transitional Phase IV cars were of the Round Dash variety except for one Hex-Dash car, 1088. The 49B or Witting motors then in stock were modified to allow semi-high speed running.

As this process involved displacement of equipment sometimes in more than one stage before these cars acquired their ultimate trucks and motors as well as new seating, it can be appreciated that the

713's truck was removed in 1941 for lack of essential spares and never re-fitted. 750 overturned on 10th January 1940 and was so extensively damaged that the body was scrapped. The truck was transferred to the body of Car 16 which had been mounted on the Pivotal truck since 1926. This car had been restricted to short workings and then latterly hardly used. The underframe was not in need of substantial alteration to accommodate the truck change and the opportunity was therefore taken to marry the modern truck to a little used body. 16 and the remaining EMB truck cars were converted to GCT Standard 21E in 1956.

Phase IV/2B The Regenerative Braking Cars. Date 1935.

Forty regenerative braking equipments were purchased from British Thomson-Houston Ltd., Rugby, in 1935. They comprised BT-H type OK45B controllers and 60 hp 101J high speed motors. The forty trams, whose numbers are in the Fleet Table, were Phase IV Transitional cars and thus achieved full high speed status in two stages. They were all 'blue' cars. After trials on the Milngavie-Renfrew Ferry service, they were all transferred to the Govan-Springburn routes after it was found that the substation serving the Barrhead area could not take

The acquisition of E.M.B. Swing Axle 8'-6" wheelbase trucks in 1935 resulted in the paradoxical situation whereby some of the oldest trams in the 7xx and 8xx series were fitted with the most modern equipment, ensuring their late survival. 751 is shown here. **R. R. Clark/STMS Collection**

The Regenerative braking or 'Regen' cars (with the accent on the 'gen') rarely figured in photographs. They were confined to the '4' group of services (formerly blue) operated from Govan & Possilpark Depots. 809 was photographed in Albert Drive during one of the car's visits to Coplawhill. **G.C.T.**

the surges of current sent back into the grid by these cars. The driving technique was quite contrary to conventional controllers. Running on resistance notches and coasting on the 'off' position defeated the purposes of the regenerative properties and led to serious damage.

The Regenerative braking properties were not supposed to be used after 1940 and those cars still remaining were altered to normal fields around 1949/50. Many retained a small brass plate on the controller tops inscribed 'REGEN'. One car, 698, was further converted in August 1939 to Maley & Taunton field control equipment. This was unsuccessful electrically and was removed in August 1942. Like 305, 698 retained large outward opening access doors on one dash side for maintenance of the control equipment.

Despite having older bodywork and being the first High Speed cars to be scrapped, the 'Regen' cars retained a higher 'book value' than the others.

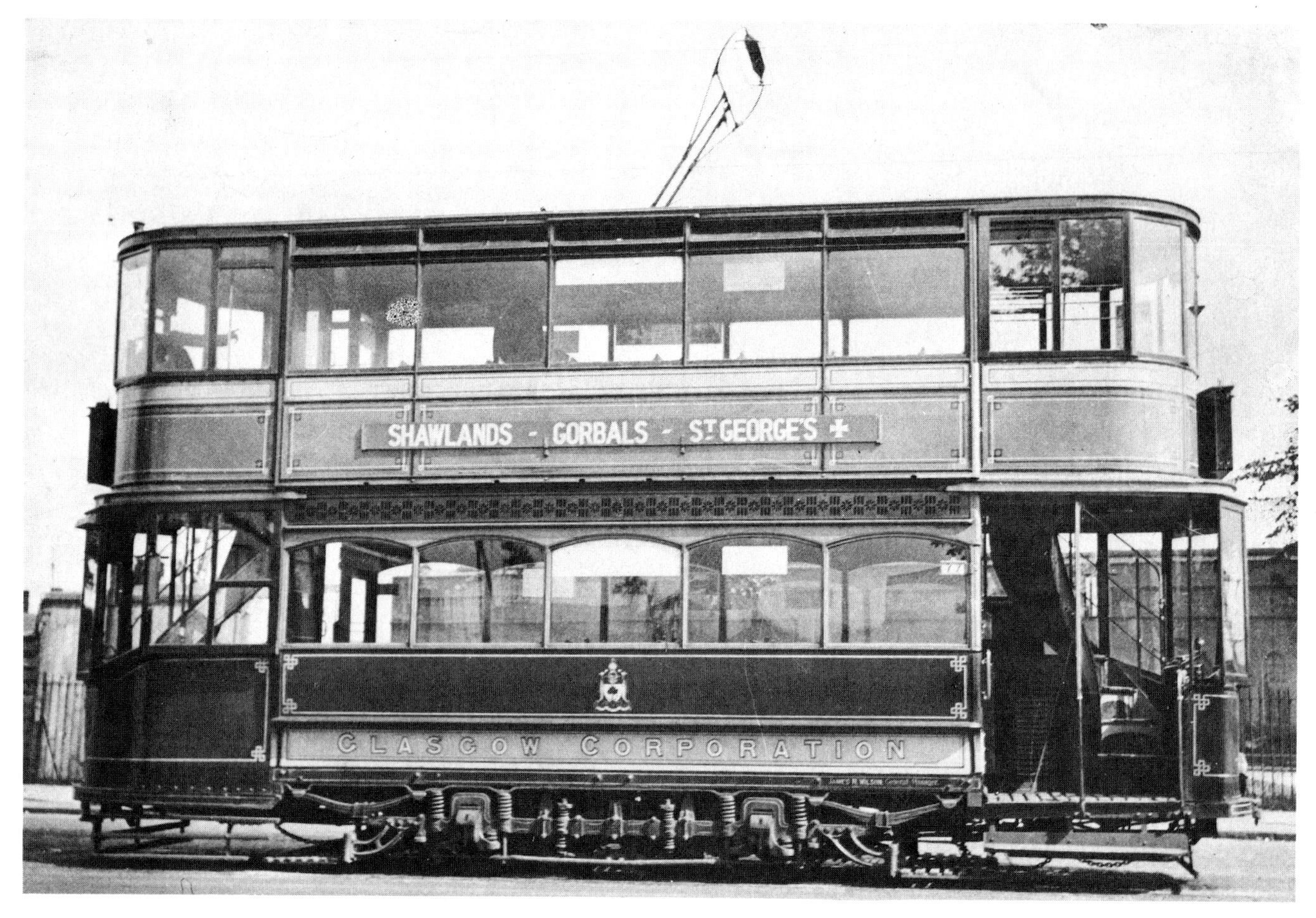

In 1931, 778 was listed as 'Dangerous - withdraw immediately'. The car was still extant and looked healthy enough in 1937 when photographed at Renfrew Ferry. It actually survived until 1949. *W. Fisher, Courtesy D. W. Fisher*

Phase IV Semi-High Speed

A report had been prepared for the General Manager in June 1931 following the examination of 133 cars which remained at the time without enclosed balconies. They were not considered to be value for further modernisation and were subdivided into five classes as follows:—

Class 1

Probable life five years if necessary measures taken to stiffen up body framing.
Car Nos:
699, 712, 718, 719, 731, 763, 774, 783, 788, 807, 821, 826, 844, 925 and 968.

Total 15

Class 2

Probable life three years if necessary measures taken to stiffen up body framing.
Car Nos:
710, 720, 730, 737, 738, 744, 745, 746, 749, 753, 754, 756, 771, 785, 792, 793, 795, 802, 805, 815, 819, 828, 835, 836, 865, 867, 879, 887, 902, 905, 907, 908, 909, 910, 911, 912, 913, 914, 915, 916, 917, 918, 919, 920, 922, 923, 924, 928, 929, 930, 931, 932, 933, 935, 937, 938, 940, 942, 943, 945, 950, 953, 962, 963, 965, 970, and 973.

Total 67

Class 3

Withdraw when due for yearly overhaul.
Car Nos:
716, 765, 906, 926, 936, 944, 946, 954, 955, 957, 961, 967, 971, 972, 974, 976, 977, 979 and 980.

Total 19

Class 4

Withdraw as soon as possible.
Car Nos:
736, 776, 781, 878, 891, 894, 896, 903, 904, 927, 934, 939, 941, 947, 951, 952, 956, 960, 964, 966, 969 and 978.

Total 22

Class 5

Dangerous. Withdraw immediately.
Car Nos:
687, 704, 762, 778, 921, 948, 949, 957, 958 and 975.

Total 10

It should be noted from the tabular information that some of these trams lasted well into the 1950s. 927 survived in service until January 1960.

When the reconditioning programme was embarked upon, the motors which were removed were salved and 125 pairs of Westinghouse ventilated motors of type 323V were made available. These could develop a speed of approximately 23 mph on level track. They were of recent origin — coming from the newest Hexagonal Dash cars—and were felt to have many years of useful life. In addition to the 125 pairs of 323V motors were 98 pairs of Witting Bros. motors in which the field coils had been altered to increase their speed potential to just over 20 mph. Also in stock were quantities of Westinghouse 49B motors which had been rebored and could reach similar speeds.

The 323V motors were initially used to equip cars 'in doubtful condition' which required examination to determine whether it was worth fitting with enclosed tops. In 1930, when these plans were first

965 was photographed at Hillfoot in June 1940. The only all-day duty for Semi-High Speed Standard trams by then was the blue 14 service - longest in Glasgow and in Great Britain at over 22 miles. 965 had Brown Boveri motors at this time.
Struan J. T. Robertson

A surprising move in 1946 was the fitting of flush panels to the lower saloon of Gloucester-built Semi-High Speed Standard cars 960 and 973. The latter car is seen at Renfrew Ferry terminus.
R. R. Clark/STMS Collection

formulated, there were, in addition 129 cars 'on which it was not worthwhile to spend any money'. These were to be equipped with the Witting and re-bored Westinghouse motors for use as rush-hour cars.

By 1934 the situation had changed. There were 817 High Speed cars, (including ex-Paisley cars 1053-1072 and the Maximum Traction cars) 126 'Semi-High Speed' cars with enclosed balconies, 77 'Slow Speed' cars with enclosed balconies, 48 'Slow Speed' cars and 8 'Semi-High Speed' cars remaining with open balconies. The peak hour requirement was far in excess of 900 cars and rising. Even by adding the High Speed and Semi-High Speed totals to provide 943 cars, this—taking into account repairs and overhauls—resulted in slow speed cars being utilised in normal service and they could not maintain a proper service headway. The Semi-High Speed Cars had recently had their bodywork strengthened and were reckoned to have a life expectancy of ten years. Authorisation was given to equip a further 125 additional cars for high speed and the semi-high speed equipment thus displaced was transferred to the slow speed cars, both those with enclosed balconies and those retaining open balconies. The latter, by this time, 53 in all, were upgraded with enclosed balconies and new destination indicators and seats, the last passing through the Coplawhill Workshops in 1935. The standard specification for the Phase IV Semi-High Speed car which evolved from all this was:

Westinghouse 323V motors, Brill 21E 7'-0" wheelbase truck with plain bearings, 31¾" wheels and 4⅛" axles with British Thomson-Houston B18 controllers. The Westinghouse-Newell combined electromagnetic track-cum-wheel brake was retained initially and Westinghouse air brake controls were mounted on a separate pedestal. Four cars were fitted with the experimental semi-high speed motors then in stock:

922 BT-H GE200 (ex-Car 144)
954 Metro-Vick. Type MV104A (ex-Car 18)
965 Brown Boveri, Baden, Switzerland (ex-Car 132)
973 Special Dick, Kerr, Preston, Motors (ex-Car 19?)

Two Semi-High Speed Phase IV cars were fitted in 1946 with flush side panels. Car 960 was fitted with 'Jablo' and 973 with 'silver steel'. 960 had a cream band below the lower saloon windows. All Semi-High Speed cars were scheduled for early withdrawal commencing in 1939 until halted by World events. Post World War II, they were gradually whittled down to about 30 and concentrated at Elderslie Depot until their final demise in 1950-51.

All the ex-Paisley Duntocher cars were scheduled for scrapping in 1939 but only five were then replaced by Semi-High Speed Standard cars cut down to single deck. The roof boards were painted bus green.
Struan J. T. Robertson

One of the deliberate features of all GCT tram design from the alpha to the omega was the ability for the impact damage to be localised. This is thought to be either 792 or 793. The platform resembles matchwood and scrap iron but the saloons are hardly affected.
B. M. Longworth Collection

Phase IV/3 Three Stage Modernisation to Phase IV.

These cars went from Phase III to Phase IV Transitional to Phase IV Semi-High Speed and finally to Phase IV High Speed. Seven cars were dealt with in 1936-37 and fourteen in 1949-53. Some of the last acquired trucks from scrapped ex-Paisley cars 1053-72. For fleet numbers, refer to the Fleet Tables.

95 was once a 'red' car shedded in Partick Depot. The inflexibility of the old colour system for services would never have allowed this car to operate on the 'yellow' service 5 but Glasgow Corporation was wedded to it for over forty years.
R. J. S. Wiseman

826 was modernised from Phase III to Phase IV in three stages, not becoming a High Speed car until the 1950s. On these cars, the overhang above the platform was not shaved off to smooth the appearance as can be seen in this photograph.
Parr-STMS Collection

The Standard cars in the batch 440-509 with louvred ventilators gradually lost these during the 1930s. However 444 retained these until around 1947 when this photograph was taken.
R. R. Clark/STMS Collection

390, photographed in September 1939, carries a transitional livery with simplified lower deck lining married to the full treatment on the upper deck. The black paper has been applied hastily over window adverts to maintain black-out conditions.
Struan J. T. Robertson

G.C.T. policy regarding serious accident victims was somewhat unpredictable. Before the 1930's, these were usually replaced but during the 'thirties and early Second World War years they were not. 869 has overturned at the corner of Kenmure Street and is having its wheel flange profiles examined by officials. This car was subsequently scrapped and its equipment salvaged.
George Outram & Co. Ltd.
Courtesy Dr. R. B. Napier

Conversely, nearly all serious accident casualties during the 1940's were rebuilt to a greater or lesser degree. 643 was not the first car to leave the tracks at Bilsland Drive's downhill curve beneath the aqueduct. Substantial rebuilding was undertaken and the car repainted from bus green to red route colour.
'The Glasgow Herald'

Phase IV/4 Rebuilds

Six cars were extensively damaged in street accidents and 'rebuilt' in the period between 1943 and 1949. In most cases the 'rebuilding' was in name only for the cars were virtually new. Two former Round Dash cars became Hex-dash (334 and 409) while 643 continued as a Round Dash Standard. Some cars retained the original underframes (334) while 27 re-used the lower saloon window posting. 143 and 679 had anemostat roof extract ventilators. Trucks, motors and equipment were ex-stock or from other trams. The rebuilds all incorporated a cream band below the lower saloon windows on the flush panels except on 643 which retained the concave panels and rubbing strake. 643 remained a monitor roof car. The flush panelling was later removed from 27 and 679 to reveal the concave panels with body strengthening which was applied at the time. 679 had been panelled in aluminium for a time and as such had no cream band below the lower saloon windows as part of the livery treatment. All these cars were wired with four lamps in series instead of six. They had improved lighting and featured dash tail lamps. Interior woodwork was light varnished teak. 143 had, for a while, the only Macfarlane Engineering Co. Ltd. motors in the fleet. Car 263 was re-wired in this way but was not a rebuild while cars 78 and 383 received new top-decks, the latter with anemostat ventilators.

Both these trams have had the body strengthening applied to prolong their active lives. The selection of those trams to receive this treatment was not based on age but condition hence cars like 702, built in 1899, were upgraded in this way. ***R. F. Mack***

Developments from Phase IV

From the initial specification of the original Phase IV trams many developments occurred and those which were experimental are listed in ascending car number order at the end of this chapter.

Among the improvements carried out, the following are highlighted as applying to all, or the major portion of the class. Usually one, or a small number of cars would be selected for a trial followed by what was termed a 'campaign change'. It was quite normal with so many cars to be tackled, that one or two would miss out on improvements or alterations.

(a) Fitting of Bow Collectors: the decision was taken in November 1930 to have all cars thus fitted. This followed the equipping of the Shields Road route for bow operation followed by the Uddingston route. Experiments were carried out with pantographs from time to time. GCT purchased the patent rights to manufacture the bow collector gear. The counterbalance plate was extremely shallow due to restricted clearances.

(b) Fitting of EMB interlocks to controllers: commenced around 1935 for application to all high speed cars and prevented operation of the controller without releasing the air brakes.

(c) Alteration to seat handle specification: latter modernised cars employed solid seat handles instead of the open grip pattern.

(d) Installation of 'Kelvin Hall' Illuminated Advert Boards: All cars had these inserted into the cabin vestibules and were wired in special circuitry independent of car lighting. They were later used when service numbers were introduced but became redundant on the introduction of roller blind number boxes in the upper vestibules and went out of use during the 1939-45 war. They were removed shortly afterwards.

(e) Installation of Draught Dodgers on Platforms: Following Trade Union representation, all the Hexagonal dash cars had small folding pull-out partitions fitted on to the platform side of bulkheads in order to eliminate eddying of draughts. This had been prevalent on the wider bodied cars at speed but the policy was not extended to 317-336.

(f) Roller Blind Number Boxes: These began to be fitted to the Hex-dash cars pre-1939 and to the Round dash cars around 1943-44. Balcony lighting was moved to illuminate the service number screen from behind.

(g) Body Strengthening: All cars were stiffened between 1930 and 1940 and this involved strapping of the lower saloon window pillars and diagonal bracing to bulkheads on the inside. Iron coping bar was also applied round the entry to the lower saloon on the platform side, extending along and coach-bolted to the waist rail. More substantial external bracing was applied to certain cars of all types surviving during the 1950s right up until 1958 when the last of the Standard cars received major overhauls. Their numbers are recorded in the Fleet Tables.

(h) Removal of Rubbing Strake and Replacement with Rounded Mouldings: This was applied to most cars of all classes but excluded preserved examples, 488, 779 and 1088.

(i) Alteration to Ventilators in Upper Deck of Cars with 1st Pattern Top Deck: Due to complaints of draughts these cars were modified whereby the ventilators operated on a centre pivot. They were clad internally with perforated zinc obscuring the glazing of the top lights in an ogee shape.

(j) Alteration to Permit Individual Opening of Ventilators: This facility was provided in certain cars of both top deck patterns during the 1950s. The woodwork was in most cases painted cream from the top deck window sills to ceiling level. Fluting of window posts was at first picked out with orange lining.

(k) Installation of Windscreen Wipers: These took various forms and the experiments are noted at the end of the chapter. Most cars had chain-pull operated 'Dickie' wipers which raised and lowered a horizontal blade on the vestibule drop-light which was fixed at this time. This was a retired employee's invention which was patented and taken over. Some cars acquired power-operated units but most eventually had hand-operated radius sweep pattern blades installed in the 1950s.

(l) A problem which was never overcome and which delayed post-war construction of new trams was that of broken truck side frames. The deterioriation of the track did nothing to assist in prolonging their lives. Various steps were taken, as well as purchasing new frames, including 'normalising' broken frames by heat treatment to approximately 870°F. The temperature was critical. Despite much trial and error, there were occasions when a tram with a normalised frame would fail due to the frame having fractured after as little as an hour back in service. It was problems such as these which prompted the Tramways Engineer to press for the purchase of new trucks post 1946 (see also Chapter 11). Originally supplied by Brush, forgings were also obtained from English Electric, R. Y. Pickering and P. & W. McLellan Ltd.

(m) Installation of longitudinal upholstered seating in the lower saloon: this was carried out during 1943-44 to increase the ability of the trams to carry standing passengers under wartime overloading conditions.

If the architecture of the Glasgow Standard Tramcar was in sympathy with the many fine buildings in the city this was doubtless because a creator of the latter was employed by Glasgow Corporation to design what became the Phase II standard tram. Sir John James Burnet (1859-1938) is probably best known in Glasgow for Charing Cross Mansions and the late lamented Alhambra Theatre, to name only two.
Parr/STMS Collection

CODES DESIGNATING TYPES & SUBDIVISIONS OF STANDARD CARS

- 'A' Air Operated Windscreen Wipers
- 'B' Cut Down to Single Deck for Duntocher Service
- 'C' Crown Roof to Lower Saloon (this differentiation applied only to Round Dash Cars)
- 'D' Rebuilt basically to Original Design
- 'E' Used for Experimentation (listed in separate Schedule at end of Tables)
- 'F' Major rebuild to other design
- 'G' Regenerative Car
- 'H' Hex-Dash Car (all with Crown Roofs to Lower Saloon)
- 'I' Body strengthening (1950s Programme)
- 'K' Field Shunt Controllers, OK20B Pattern, at Phase IV
- 'L' Aluminium Lifeguard Spars
- 'M' Monitor Roof to Lower Saloon (this differentiation applied to Round Dash Cars)
- 'O' Longitudinal Seating in Lower Saloon (1943-44 Wartime Conversion)
- 'R' Round Dash Car
- 'S' Semi-High Speed Car (not further upgraded to High Speed at Phase IV)
- 'T' Phase IV Truck with Single Magnetic Brake Unit
- 'U' Unobtrusive Top Cover 1904-23
- 'W' Wide Body to Lower Saloon (this differentiation applied only to Round Dash Cars)
- 'X' Two Stage Modernisation at Phase IV
- 'Z' Three Stage Modernisation at Phase IV

Dates indicated for 'X' and 'Z' are those when upper deck vestibules were fitted.

Note:

Phase I, II, III or IV dates are those of completion of construction.

Many Phase I cars built earlier were stored until 1901.

Similarly some cars were stored for varying periods prior to disposal.

Controllers and motors statistics for Phase IV represent 'stable' period prior to early 1950s.

For example, car 247 is coded 'HETIA'

- H Hex-Dash Body
- E Used for experiments (with step-side Lifeguard Gates 28/1/25)
- T Single Magnetic Brake Truck from Phase IV
- I Body strengthened during 1950s
- A Air operated Windscreen Wipers

Seating Capacities of Trams

Phase I	24 below and 30 above
Phase II (Unobtrusive)	24 below and 40 above
Phase II (early examples)	24 below and 42 above (altered to 24 + 38 from 1906)
Phase II (later cars)	24 below and 38 above.
Phase III (all)	24 below and 38 above
Phase IV/III experimentals	23 below and 38 above.
Phase IV	21 below and 38 above
Phase IV (wartime conversion)	24 below and 38 above.
Car 137 (Phase III)	24 below and 40 above.

Car Number	Code	Phase I Date/ Colour	Phase II Date/ Colour	Phase III Date/ Colour	Phase IV Date/ Colour	Pre-Modernised Motors	Modernised Motor/ Controller	Top Cover	Depots 1920s	1935	1943	Scrap
1	H	—	—	4/23-W	12/28-G	323V	EE/EE	2	b	k	k	10/57
2	HE	—	—	4/23-W	11/28-G	323V	EE/EE	2	b	k	k	2/59
3	HTI	—	—	3/23-B	4/29-G	323V	MV/MV	2	n	k	k	2/59
4	HIA	—	—	3/23-B	11/29-BR	323V	MV/MV	2	n	n	n	2/60
5	H	—	—	3/23-B	8/28-G	323V	MV/MV	2	n	k	k	3/60
6	HT	—	—	2/23-G	6/28-G	323V	MV/MV	2	l	l	—	5/41
7	HT	—	—	2/23-G	5/28-G	323V	MV/MV	2	l	c	m	11/56
8	H	—	—	6/23-G	7/28-G	323V	MV/MV	2	l	l	l	8/56
9	HI	—	—	7/23-R	7/29-R	323V	MV/MV	2	n	n	n	9/60
10	H	—	—	8/23-R	8/29-RS	323V	MV/MV	2	n	n	n	9/58
11	HEI	—	—	7/23-R	6/29-R	323V	EE/EE	2	n	n	n	2/59
12	HET	—	—	8/23-W	10/28-G	323V	EE/EE	2	d	t	d	11/60
13	HEI	—	—	8/23-W	9/28-G	323V	MV/MV	2	n	l	l	4/60
14	HI	—	—	2/23-W	11/28-G	323V	EE/EE	2	n	k	k	1/59
15	HE	—	—	9/22-G	4/33-G	323V	MV/MV	2	l	l	—	4/39
16	HE	—	—	9/22-G	3/31-G	323V	GEC/MV	2	l	l	b	4/59
17	HETI	—	—	9/22-G	9/28-G	323V	MV/MV	2	l	l	d	2/61
18	HETI	—	—	7/23-G	8/28-G	323V	MV/MV	2	l	d	d	5/59
19	HE	—	—	8/22-G	11/28-W	323V	EE/EE	2	l	m	m	7/57
20	HA	—	—	7/22-G	4/28-G	323V	MV/MV	2	lc	c	c	3/58
21	HE	—	—	6/22-B	5/29-R	323V	MV/MV	2	n	b	l	9/59
22	H	—	—	6/22-B	4/30-G	323V	MV/MV	2	n	l	x	*
23	H	—	—	5/22-B	5/29-R	323V	MV/MV	2	n	b	b	3/59
24	HEI	—	—	5/22-B	3/30-W	323V	MV/MV	2	n	n	n	10/59
25	H	—	—	4/22-W	4/29-G	323V	MV/MV	2	n	k	k	12/58
26	HI	—	—	4/22-W	4/29-G	323V	EE/EE	2	n	t	t	4/59
27	HF	—	—	4/22-R	8/29-R	323V	MV/MV	2	n	n	n	2/49
28	HI	—	—	3/22-R	11/29-R	323V	MV/MV	2	n	n	n	10/58
29	HT	—	—	3/22-R	8/29-R	323V	EE/MV	2	n	b	b	6/58
30	H	—	—	3/22-R	7/29-R	323V	MV/MV	2	n	b	b	3/55
31	HE	—	—	2/22-R	6/29-R	323V	MV/MV	2	n	b	b	7/58
32	HI	—	—	2/22-R	6/28-R	323V	MV/MV	2	n	b	b	9/58
33	HT	—	—	2/22-G	8/28-G	323V	MV/MV	2	lc	l	l	5/58
34	H	—	—	2/22-G	8/28-G	323V	MV/MV	2	l	l	l	4/59
35	HTKI	—	—	2/22-G	6/28-G	323V	MV/MV	2	lc	l	l	1/61
36	HI	—	—	2/22-G	6/28-G	323V	MV/MV	2	lc	k	k	6/59
37	HT	—	—	1/22-G	6/28-G	323V	MV/MV	2	l	k	l	4/59
38	HTI	—	—	12/21-G	6/28-G	323V	MV/MV	2	lc	k	k	12/58
39	H	—	—	12/21-B	1/29-G	323V	EE/EE	2	l	d	d	3/59
40	HET	—	—	12/21-B	12/28-G	323V	EE/EE	2	l	k	k	11/59
41	H	—	—	12/21-B	1/29-G	323V	EE/EE	2	n	c	d	7/60
42	HI	—	—	11/21-B	1/30-G	323V	MV/MV	2	n	l	l	5/59
43	HTO	—	—	11/21-B	11/28-G	323V	EE/EE	2	n	k	k	5/58
44	HK	—	—	10/21-B	9/28-G	323V	GEC/MV	2	n	d	p	1/59
45	HEI	—	—	10/21-Y	5/30-Y	323V	MV/EE	2	b	b	b	4/60
46	HE	—	—	(9/21)-Y	7/30-Y	323V	MV/MV	2	b	b	b	5/59
47	HI	—	—	9/21-Y	1/29-G	323V	EE/EE	2	bl	d	d	6/60
48	HEI	—	—	9/21-Y	6/30-Y	323V	MV/MV	2	bl	l	l	7/60
49	HTD	—	—	8/21-W	9/28-G	323V	GEC/MV	2	n	k	k	4/59
50	HT	—	—	8/21-W	10/28-G	323V	EE/EE	2	n	d	d	6/59
51	H	—	—	8/21-W	10/29-W	323V	MV/MV	2	n	b	x	6/60
52	HI	—	—	7/21-W	11/28-G	323V	EE/EE	2	b	k	k	3/59
53	HB	—	—	6/21-W	10/28-G	323V	EE/EE	2	b	d	d	1/59
54	HA	—	—	6/21-W	5/30-Y	323V	MV/MV	2	b	b	b	3/59
55	H	—	—	5/21-Y	5/30-Y	323V	MV/MV	2	bl	l	l	1/49
56	H	—	—	4/21-Y	5/30-Y	323V	MV/MV	2	bl	b	b	5/59
57	HA	—	—	4/21-Y	5/30-Y	323V	MV/MV	2	lb	d	d	10/58
58	HTK	—	—	3/21-G	7/28-G	323V	GEC/MV	2	lc	t	t	8/58
59	H	—	—	4/21-R	8/29-R	323V	MV/MV	2	n	n	n	11/59
60	HB	—	—	(4/21)-R	6/29-R	(323V)	MV/MV	2	t	t	t	4/59
61	HIE	—	—	3/21-G	6/29-G	323V	MV/MV	2	l	l	l	11/60
62	HE	—	—	5/21-R	10/29-R	323V	MV/MV	2	n	n	n	11/59
63	HE	—	—	5/21-R	11/29-R	323V	MV/MV	2	n	n	n	12/59
64	H	—	—	11/20-R	7/29-R	323V	MV/MV	2	n	x	x	11/60
65	HTA	—	—	10/20-R	6/29-R	323V	MV/MV	2	n	x	x	2/60

*Car 22 withdrawn 6/61, now preserved in Phase III condition in the National Tramway Museum

Three Hexagonal Dash Standard cars help to shift the lunchtime crowds from Trongate in 1955.
Parr-STMS Collection

No. 23 had originally been numbered No. 23B when converted from ex-Regen car 814 in 1952. When scrapped in August 1962 the car's maroon paintwork had faded almost to dull grey.
W. D. L. Kerr

Car Number	Code	Phase I Date/ Colour	Phase II Date/ Colour	Phase III Date/ Colour	Phase IV Date/ Colour	Pre-Modernised Motors	Modernised Motor/ Controller	Top Cover	Depots 1920s	1935	1943	Scrap
66	H	—	—	10/20-R	3/29-R	323V	MV/EE	2	n	n	n	12/59
67	H	—	—	10/20-B	2/29-G	323V	MV/EE	2	ln	d	d	2/59
68	H	—	—	10/20-B	11/28-G	323V	EE/EE	2	ln	k	k	4/59
69	HT	—	—	9/20-B	12/28-G	323V	EE/EE	2	ln	k	k	9/59
70	H	—	—	9/20-B	5/30-G	323V	MV/MV	2	ln	l	l	1/59
71	HE	—	—	9/20-B	12/28-G	323V	EE/EE	2	ln	d	d	6/59
72	HI	—	—	8/20-B	4/29-G	323V	MV/MV	2	ln	t	d	10/60
73	H	—	—	8/20-R	2/29-R	323V	MV/EE	2	n	n	n	7/60
74	HI	—	—	8/20-R	3/29-R	323V	MV/EE	2	t	t	t	3/59
75	HI	—	—	8/20-R	3/29-R	323V	EE/EE	2	t	t	t	1/61
76	HTI	—	—	3/21-B	4/29-G	323V	MV/MV	2	ln	t	t	12/62
77	HI	—	—	3/21-B	4/30-G	323V	MV/MV	2	ln	l	l	11/60
78	HD	—	—	3/21-B	4/30-G	323V	MV/MV	2	l	l	l	6/58
79	H	—	—	3/20-R	2/29-R	(323V)	EE/EE	2	b	d	d	11/59
80	HI	—	—	4/20-R	12/29-R	220	MV/MV	2	b	n	n	3/59
81	HTK	—	—	4/20-W	9/28-G	49B	GEC/MV	2	m	d	d	3/59
82	HI	—	—	4/20-R	3/29-R	220	EE/EE	2	t	t	t	6/60
83	H	—	—	2/20-R	7/29-R	323V	MV/MV	2	n	n	t	11/60
84	H	—	—	7/20-R	6/29-R	49B	MV/MV	2	t	n	n	2/59
85	HT	—	—	5/20-R	6/29R	?	MV/MV	2	t	t	t	4/59
86	HT	—	—	10/20-R	3/29-R	323V	MV/MV	2	n	x	x	8/60
87	HT	—	—	9/20-W	9/28-G	323V	EE/EE	2	n	l	l	6/59
88	HT	—	—	10/20-W	10/28-G	323V	EE/EE	2	n	k	n	1/59
89	HI	—	—	1/20-W	4/29-G	323V	MV/MV	2	b	t	t	9/59
90	H	—	—	1/20-R	6/29-R	323V	MV/MV	2	n	n	n	2/59
91	HEO	—	—	1/20-R	10/29-R	220	MV/MV	2	t	t	t	5/59
93	H	—	—	12/19-R	2/29-R	220	MV/EE	2	t	t	t	5/59
94	HI	—	—	12/19-R	11/29-R	?	MV/MV	2	t	n	n	4/59
95	H	—	—	12/19-R	8/29-R	220	MV/MV	2	t	t	t	9/59
96	HTI	—	—	12/19-R	7/29-R	220	MV/MV	2	t	t	x	11/59
97	HEA	—	—	12/19-Y	4/30-Y	220	MV/MV	2	l	l	l	11/60
98	HT	—	—	3/20-W	10/28-GB	?	MV/EE	2	m	d	d	3/59
99	H	—	—	11/19-Y	4/30-Y	220	MV/MV	2	l	l	l	1/59
100	H	—	—	11/19-Y	4/30-Y	220	MV/MV	2	l	b	b	4/59
101	HEIA	—	—	12/19-G	3/28-G	220	MV/MV	2	l	l	l	9/58
102	HTI	—	—	11/19-G	6/28-G	220	MV/MV	2	l	l	l	4/59
103	HET	—	—	10/19-G	3/27-G	220	MV/MV	2	l	l	t	11/60
104	HIE	—	—	10/19-G	3/28-G	220	MV/MV	2	l	k	k	10/58
105	H	—	—	10/19-G	9/27-G	220	MV/MV	2	l	c	m	8/58
106	H	—	—	10/19-G	4/28-G	220	MV/MV	2	l	c	k	4/60
107	HT	—	—	4/20-B	10/28-G	(220)	EE/EE	2	p	k	k	12/58
108	H	—	—	10/19-R	11/29-R	220	MV/MV	2	t	n	n	3/61
109	HIA	—	—	10/19-R	2/29-R	220	EE/EE	2	t	t	t	8/59
110	HI	—	—	10/19-R	7/29-R	220	MV/MV	2	t	t	t	10/59
111	HOL	—	—	8/19-R	8/29-R	?	MV/MV	2	t	t	t	4/59
112	HE	—	—	8/19-R	8/29-R	220/104A	MV/MV	2	t	t	t	3/59
113	HEI	—	—	7/19-B	3/29-G	220	MV/MV	2	lm	t	t	6/60
114	HT	—	—	7/19-B	10/28-GR	?	EE/EE	2	lm	k	p	8/53
115	HI	—	—	7/19-B	3/29-G	220	MV/MV	2	lm	t	t	4/59
116	HT	—	—	7/19-B	11/28-G	?	EE/EE	2	lm	k	n	11/59
117	H	—	—	6/19-B	3/30-B	220	MV/MV	2	ln	t	t	5/59
118	H	—	—	7/19-R	3/29-RS	220	EE/EE	2	t	t	t	2/59
119	H	—	—	6/19-B	12/28-G	?	EE/EE	2	lm	k	k	6/59
120	H	—	—	5/19-R	7/29-R	220	MV/MV	2	t	t	t	9/57
121	HL	—	—	5/19-B	2/29-G	220	MV/EE	2	lm	d	d	6/60
122	H	—	—	5/19-R	8/28-G	220	MV/MV	2	t	k	k	8/58
123	HEI	—	—	5/19-B	11/29-G	220	EE/EE	2	lm	k	p	2/59
124	H	—	—	4/19-R	6/29-R	220	MV/MV	2	t	m	m	9/59
125	HK	—	—	12/17-B	9/28-G	220	GEC/MV	2	lm	d	p	1/59
126	HEI	—	—	1/17-B	8/28-G	?	MV/MV	2	lm	k	d	7/60
127	HI	—	—	1/17-R	6/29-R	?	MV/MV	2	t	m	m	11/58
128	HTI	—	—	12/16-R	6/29-R	220	MV/MV	2	t	m	m	9/59
129	HTI	—	—	5/16-Y	10/28-G	220	EE/EE	2	b	d	d	10/58
130	HTI	—	—	6/15-Y	4/29-G	220	MV/MV	2	b	t	d	2/59
131	HETIA	—	—	5/15-Y	1/29-G	220	EE/EE	2	b	d	d	4/59

116 used as school car during 1946

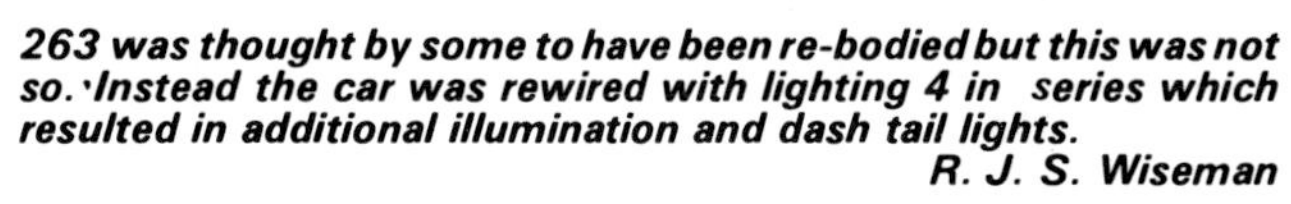
263 was thought by some to have been re-bodied but this was not so. Instead the car was rewired with lighting 4 in series which resulted in additional illumination and dash tail lights.
R. J. S. Wiseman

334 was originally one of the wide bodied Round Dash Standards. After a serious street accident substantial rebuilding was undertaken and the car emerged as shown with Hexagonal Dashes. The original underframing was retained, however, displaying in the spacing of the cross-members evidence of the Mountain & Gibson Radial truck which had been removed in the early 1920s.
R. J. S. Wiseman

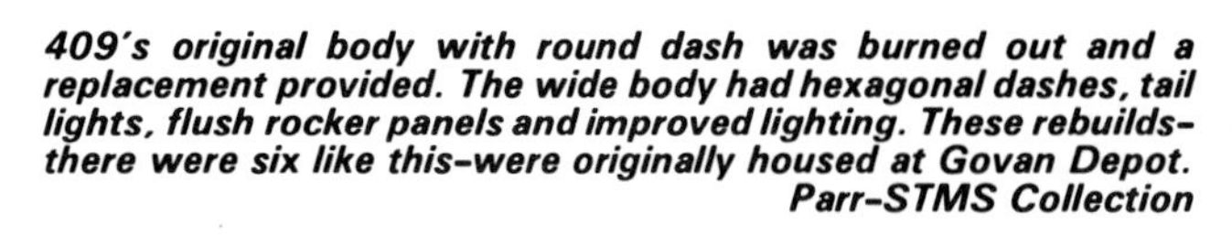
409's original body with round dash was burned out and a replacement provided. The wide body had hexagonal dashes, tail lights, flush rocker panels and improved lighting. These rebuilds-there were six like this-were originally housed at Govan Depot.
Parr-STMS Collection

Car Number	Code	Phase I Date/ Colour	Phase II Date/ Colour	Phase III Date/ Colour	Phase IV Date/ Colour	Pre-Modernised Motors	Modernised Motor/ Controller	Top Cover	Depots 1920s	1935	1943	Scrap
132	HT	—	—	4/15-Y	12/28-G	220/B-B	EE/EE	2	b	d	d	1/60
133	H	—	—	4/15-Y	2/29-G	220	EE/EE	2	b	d	d	6/59
134	H	—	—	3/15-Y	12/28-G	220/323V	MV/EE	2	b	k	k	4/60
135	HTE	—	—	3/15-Y	10/28-G	220	EE/EE	2	b	k	d	1/59
136	H	—	—	2/15-Y	11/28-G	220	MV/EE	2	b	k	k	4/59
137	HEI	—	—	12/14-R	7/30-Y	49B	EE/MV	2	n	b	b	1/59
138	H	—	—	12/13-B	2/30-B	49B	MV/MV	2	ml	t	t	5/59
139	HET	—	—	12/13-B	9/28-GR	49B	EE/EE	2	ml	t	n	2/60
140	HI	—	—	12/13-B	2/30-B	49B	MV/MV	2	ml	d	d	11/59
141	H	—	—	12/13-B	6/30-Y	?	MV/EE	2	ml	d	d	9/59
142	HEF	—	—	12/13-G	(12/27-G)	49B	See under standard double bogie cars					
143	HD	—	—	12/13-Y	3/30-Y	WIT	MV/EE	2	b	l	b	2/44
144	H	—	—	12/13-Y	3/30-Y	200	MV/MV	2	b	l	d	8/60
145	HI	—	—	11/13-Y	6/30-Y	?	MV/MV	2	b	l	l	2/60
146	HEA	—	—	11/13-Y	5/30-Y	220/323V	MV/MV	2	b	b	b	3/59
147	HI	—	—	11/13-Y	5/30-Y	?	MV/MV	2	b	l	d	6/59
148	HK	—	—	11/13-Y	9/28-G	220	GEC/MV	2	b	k	k	1/60
149	H	—	—	10/13-Y	11/29-R	49B	MV/MV	2	b	n	n	4/58
150	HO	—	—	10/13-Y	8/29-R	?	MV/EE	2	b	x	x	4/59
151	H	—	—	10/13-Y	6/30-Y	?	MV/?	2	b	b	—	5/40
152	H	—	—	10/13-Y	5/30-Y	49B/323V	MV/MV	2	b	b	b	9/58
153	HT	—	—	10/13-Y	9/28-G	49B	EE/EE	2	b	d	d	6/59
154	HI	—	—	9/13-Y	11/29-R	?	MV/MV	2	t	d	d	10/59
155	H	—	—	9/13-Y	5/30-YW	49B	MV/MV	2	t	n	m	4/59
156	HA	—	—	9/13-Y	1/30-B	49B	MV/MV	2	t	d	d	2/61
157	HALI	—	—	9/13-Y	6/30-Y	49B	MV/EE	2	t	t	t	10/58
158	HEI	—	—	9/13-W	7/30-YS	49B	MV/EE	2	p	l	d	9/59
159	HET	—	—	9/13-WG	4/27-G	49B	GEC/EE	2	p	l	m	4/57
160	HEI	—	—	8/13-W	3/30-G	49B	MV/EE	2	p	l	l	9/59
161	H	—	—	9/13-W	3/30-G	?	MV/EE	2	p	l	l	9/59
162	HIA	—	—	8/13-G	8/28-G	49B	MV/MV	2	k	k	c	5/59
163	HA	—	—	8/13-G	3/28-G	?	MV/MV	2	k	k	k	7/58
164	H	—	—	8/13-G	6/28-G	49B/323V	GEC/MV	2	k	k	k	2/59
165	HI	—	—	8/13-G	8/28-G	?	MV/MV	2	k	k	k	2/60
166	HTI	—	—	8/13-G	6/28-G	49B	MV/MV	2	k	k	k	12/58
167	HI	—	—	8/13-G	5/28-G	49B	MV/MV	2	k	e	e	9/58
168	HE	—	—	7/13-R	8/29-R	?	MV/EE	2	p	x	x	2/60
169	H	—	—	7/13-R	8/29-R	?	MV/MV	2	p	x	x	5/61
170	HA	—	—	7/13-R	8/29-R	49B	MV/MV	2	p	x	x	8/60
171	H	—	—	7/13-R	8/29-R	49B	MV/MV	2	p	x	x	2/60
172	H	—	—	6/13-R	8/29-R	49B	MV/MV	2	p	x	x	6/60
173	H	—	—	6/13-R	12/29-R	220	MV/MV	2	p	p	p	9/58
174	H	—	—	6/13-R	8/29-R	?	MV/MV	2	t	m	m	7/58
175	HI	—	—	6/13-R	12/29-R	49B/220	MV/MV	2	t	p	p	7/57
176	H	—	—	5/13-B	1/30-B	?	MV/EE	2	t	d	d	2/61
177	HI	—	—	5/13-B	1/30-B	49B	MV/EE	2	p	d	d	6/60
178	HI	—	—	5/13-B	7/30-BS	49B	MV/MV	2	tx	p	p	9/59
179	H	—	—	5/13-B	6/30-Y	49B	MV/MV	2	tx	d	d	3/59
180	HOI	—	—	5/13-B	2/30-B	?	MV/MV	2	tx	x	x	8/59
181	HO	—	—	5/13-B	2/30-B	?	MV/EE	2	tx	t	t	9/58
182	HT	—	—	5/13-G	5/28-G	?	MV/MV	2	t	e	e	6/58
183	HTI	—	—	5/13-G	6/28-G	?	MV/MV	2	t	d	d	11/60
184	HIA	—	—	5/13-G	4/28-G	?	MV/MV	2	t	e	e	5/59
185	HI	—	—	4/13-G	5/28-G	49B/220	MV/MV	2	t	c	d	12/58
186	HI	—	—	4/13-W	3/30-G	?	MV/MV	2	n	k	d	12/58
187	H	—	—	4/13-W	3/30-G	49B	MV/MV	2	n	k	k	4/59
188	HI	—	—	4/13-W	3/30-G	?	MV/MV	2	p	l	l	10/59
189	HE	—	—	4/13-W	1/30-G	49B	MV/MV	2	p	k	k	8/56
190	HI	—	—	4/13-W	6/30-Y	49B	MV/MV	2	p	b	b	9/60
191	HE	—	—	3/13-W	8/30-Y	49B	MV/MV	2	p	b	t	4/59
192	H	—	—	3/13-W	3/30-G	?	MV/MV	2	m	k	d	9/56
193	HE	—	—	4/13-W	3/30-G	?	MV/MV	2	m	k	k	6/58
194	H	—	—	3/13-G	5/28-G	WIT/49B	MV/EE	2	tk	k	k	8/56
195	HTA	—	—	3/13-G	5/28-G	49B	MV/MV	2	tk	c	t	9/56
196	HI	—	—	3/13-G	4/28-G	?	MV/EE	2	tk	e	t	1/59

Car 191 fitted with 21EM Mountain & Gibson, Bury, truck at Phase III

228 was a typical Glasgow Standard tram pre World War I while A91 was a typical Glasgow Standard bus post World War II. The average life of these buses was one third of that of the trams like 228. ***Parr/STMS Collection***

Car 50 in 1953 is one of the Standard cars with cream painted upper saloon woodwork. It is typical of the rolling stock which operated services 1 and 30 until withdrawn in 1960. The truck displays a common practice in Glasgow, one axle being fitted with SKF and the other with Hoffman roller bearings. ***Parr-STMS Collection***

Car Number	Code	Phase I Date/ Colour	Phase II Date/ Colour	Phase III Date/ Colour	Phase IV Date/ Colour	Pre-Modernised Motors	Modernised Motor/ Controller	Top Cover	Depots 1920s	Depots 1935	Depots 1943	Scrap
197	H	—	—	3/13-R	12/29-R	WIT	MV/MV	2	p	p	p	8/57
198	HI	—	—	2/13-R	12/29-R	?	MV/MV	2	p	p	p	6/59
199	HI	—	—	2/13-R	8/29-R	?	MV/EE	2	t	m	m	5/58
200	HI	—	—	2/13-R	9/29-R	?	MV/MV	2	t	m	m	4/58
201	HA	—	—	2/13-R	9/29-R	?	MV/EE	2	t	m	m	8/57
202	HI	—	—	2/13-B	7/30-B	49B	MV/EE	2	p	l	l	9/58
203	HI	—	—	2/13-B	11/29-B	49B	MV/MV	2	p	d	d	4/59
204	H	—	—	1/13-B	6/30-B	WIT	MV/MV	2	p	l	p	7/56
205	HI	—	—	1/13-B	6/30-B	49B	MV/MV	2	p	p	p	4/59
206	HI	—	—	1/13-W	3/30-G	WIT	MV/MV	2	p	l	l	3/58
207	HI	—	—	1/13-W	6/30-Y	?	MV/MV	2	p	l	l	1/59
208	HI	—	—	1/13-W	2/30-G	WIT	MV/MV	2	p	t	t	6/58
209	HI	—	—	12/12-W	2/30-G	WIT	MV/MV	2	p	l	l	10/59
210	HI	—	—	12/12-Y	5/30-YS	?	MV/MV	2	t	t	b	6/58
211	HI	—	—	12/12-Y	6/30-Y	?	MV/MV	2	t	t	t	4/59
212	HI	—	—	12/12-Y	4/30-Y	WIT	MV/EE	2	t	t	b	2/59
213	HIA	—	—	12/12-G	5/28-G	WIT	MV/MV	2	p	e	t	10/58
214	HI	—	—	12/12-G	4/28-G	WIT	MV/MV	2	p	c	t	3/58
215	HTE	—	—	11/12-G	7/28-G	WIT	MV/MV	2	t	k	d	10/56
216	HTEI	—	—	11/12-G	6/28-G	WIT	MV/MV	2	t	e	t	2/59
217	HI	—	—	11/12-G	7/28-G	WIT	MV/MV	2	t	k	p	6/59
218	HI	—	—	11/12-G	6/28-G	WIT	MV/MV	2	t	k	p	11/59
219	HI	—	—	11/12-G	5/28-G	?	MV/MV	2	t	e	t	6/59
220	H	—	—	11/12-Y	4/30-Y	?	MV/MV	2	t	t	b	4/59
221	HL	—	—	11/12-Y	1/30-G	?	MV/MV	2	t	l	l	8/56
222	H	—	—	11/12-Y	4/30-Y	49B	MV/MV	2	t	t	t	8/58
223	HEI	—	—	11/12-R	8/29-RC	WIT	GEC/MV	2	t	b	b	9/58
224	HI	—	—	10/12-R	12/29-R	WIT	MV/MV	2	m	n	n	8/60
225	H	—	—	10/12-W	2/30-G	?	MV/MV	2	m	k	p	1/59
226	H	—	—	10/12-W	2/30-G	WIT	MV/MV	2	m	l	l	3/58
227	HIA	—	—	10/12-R	12/29-R	?	MV/MV	2	m	n	t	5/59
228	HT	—	—	10/12-W	9/28-G	WIT	EE/EE	2	m	k	k	6/58
229	HT	—	—	10/12-B	9/28-G	?	EE/EE	2	p	k	k	11/60
230	HT	—	—	10/12-B	11/28-G	WIT	EE/EE	2	p	k	d	10/59
231	HTI	—	—	9/12-Y	12/28-G	?	EE/EE	2	t	k	p	9/59
232	HIA	—	—	9/12-Y	4/30-Y	?	MV/MV	2	t	t	b	1/60
233	HI	—	—	9/12-W	4/29-G	WIT	MV/MV	2	m	t	t	9/59
234	HT	—	—	9/12-W	10/28-G	WIT	EE/EE	2	m	d	d	11/60
235	HTA	—	—	9/12-W	5/29-G	49B	MV/MV	2	m	t	t	3/60
236	HTI	—	—	9/12-W	1/29-G	?	EE/EE	2	m	d	d	4/59
237	H	—	—	9/12-R	6/29-R	49B	MV/MV	2	n	n	n	5/59
238	HI	—	—	9/12-R	11/29-R	?	MV/MV	2	n	n	n	11/58
239	H	—	—	8/12-G	4/28-G	49B/323V	MV/MV	2	lc	c	d	6/56
240	H	—	—	8/12-R	6/29-R	49B	MV/MV	2	n	b	n	1/59
241	HT	—	—	8/12-G	6/28-G	49B	MV/MV	2	l	c	m	7/57
242	H	—	—	8/12-G	4/28-G	?	MV/MV	2	l	c	t	5/58
243	H	—	—	8/12-G	5/28-G	?	MV/MV	2	lc	c	m	4/57
244	HI	—	—	8/12-G	3/28-G	?	MV/MV	2	lt	l	l	3/59
245	HI	—	—	8/12-G	4/28-G	49B	MV/MV	2	lt	c	c	6/60
246	HI	—	—	8/12-G	6/28-G	49B	MV/MV	2	lt	k	p	5/59
247	HETIA	—	—	8/12-RB	1/29-G	?	MV/EE	2	m	d	d	5/59
248	HI	—	—	8/12-R	6/29-R	?	MV/MV	2	m	x	x	6/60
249	H	—	—	7/12-R	6/29-R	49B	MV/MV	2	p	x	x	2/60
250	H	—	—	7/12-R	8/29-R	?	MV/MV	2	m	x	x	4/59
251	H	—	—	7/12-G	6/28-G	WIT	MV/MV	2	p	e	l	8/57
252	H	—	—	7/12-G	3/28-G	?	MV/MV	2	p	k	k	8/57
253	HT	—	—	6/12-R	7/29-R	49B	MV/MV	2	n	b	b	3/58
254	HLAI	—	—	6/12-R	12/29-R	?	MV/MV	2	n	n	x	2/59
255	H	—	—	6/12-R	9/29-RS	49B	EE/MV	2	n	x	x	6/60
256	HE	—	—	6/12-R	8/29-RS	49B	MV/MV	2	n	x	x	6/58
257	HI	—	—	6/12-Y	2/29-G	49B	EE/EE	2	l	d	t	12/59
258	HTIA	—	—	6/12-Y	10/28-G	?	EE/EE	2	l	l	l	6/60
259	H	—	—	6/12-Y	12/28-G	49B	EE/EE	2	l	d	d	8/56
260	H	—	—	6/12-R	8/29-R	49B	MV/MV	2	n	b	b	4/59
261	HT	—	—	6/12-Y	9/28-G	49B	EE/EE	2	l	l	l	1/49

The platforms of the Standard cars were the working environment for the drivers and conductors. The interlock can be seen on top of the controller to prevent simultaneous power and air brake application. The compressor was located under the stairs. Although open to the elements, the platforms were remarkably draught free. *G.C.T.*

Photographs of Car 15 with reversed 39E1 Maximum Traction bogies are extremely rare with the exception of the official view taken while the car retained open balconies. This photo was taken in 1938 at Paisley West. *W. Fisher Courtesy of D. W. Fisher*

Car Number	Code	Phase I Date/Colour	Phase II Date/Colour	Phase III Date/Colour	Phase IV Date/Colour	Pre-Modernised Motors	Modernised Motor/Controller	Top Cover	Depots			Scrap
									1920s	1935	1943	
262	HI	—	—	6/12-B	11/28-G	49B	GEC/EE	2	nl	l	l	6/59
263	HTE	—	—	5/12-B	12/28-G	49B	EE/EE	2	nl	p	p	6/57
264	HI	—	—	5/12-B	4/29-G	?	MV/MV	2	nl	t	t	1/59
265	H	—	—	6/12-B	2/29-G	49B	EE/EE	2	nl	d	t	7/58
266	H	—	—	6/12-B	2/29-G	?	EE/EE	2	nl	d	d	5/58
267	HI	—	—	5/12-B	11/28-W	?	EE/EE	2	nl	p	p	5/59
268	HE	—	—	5/12-B	12/28-G	?	EE/EE	2	nl	d	d	5/60
269	H	—	—	4/12-W	10/29-WY	?	MV/MV	2	n	n	d	2/59
270	H	—	—	4/12-B	11/29-B	DK	MV/MV	2	nl	d	d	11/59
271	HTI	—	—	11/12-B	9/28-GR	?	EE/EE	2	l	l	n	4/60
272	HI	—	—	10/12-B	1/30-B	49B	MV/MV	2	l	d	d	5/58
273	HE	—	—	10/12-R	10/29-R	49B	MV/MV	2	n	n	p	6/58
274	HI	—	—	8/12-R	3/29-R	?	EE/EE	2	n	b	t	1/59
275	HI	—	—	10/12-G	4/28-G	?	MV/MV	2	lt	c	m	6/59
276	H	—	—	8/12-G	8/28-G	49B/323V	MV/MV	2	lc	k	k	2/59
277	HI	—	—	8/12-G	8/28-G	49B/323V	MV/MV	2	lc	k	k	9/58
278	HTI	—	—	9/12-G	5/28-G	49B/323V	MV/MV	2	lc	c	c	12/58
279	HI	—	—	4/12-G	4/28-W	?	MV/MV	2	l	p	p	6/58
280	HTE	—	—	4/12-G	5/28-G	49B	MV/MV	2	l	c	m	12/56
281	HI	—	—	4/12-R	12/29-R	49B	MV/MV	2	n	n	n	2/59
282	H	—	—	4/12-R	7/30-B	?	EE/MV	2	n	l	p	4/57
283	H	—	—	4/12-R	8/29-R	?	MV/MV	2	n	x	x	5/61
284	HL	—	—	4/12-R	3/29-R	?	EE/EE	2	n	x	x	1/60
285	H	—	—	4/12-R	6/29-R	49B	MV/MV	2	n	x	x	6/57
286	HI	—	—	9/11-Y	10/29-RS	49B	MV/MV	2	bt	n	t	9/60
287	RCI	7/09-W		c1924-W	2/30-G	49B	MV/MV	2	p	l	l	2/59
288	RCI	7/09-W	c1910-W	6/23-W	1/30GWD	49B	MV/MV	2	p	l	l	9/60
289	RC	7/09-G	c1910-G	8/25-G	5/30-G	WIT	MV/MV	2	t	k	k	5/49
290	RC	7/09-G	→	c1911-G	2/30-G	?	MV/MV	2	t	l	l	7/56
291	RCI	7/09-B	c1910-B	?-B	6/30-Y	?	MV/EE	2	tx	b	b	9/58
292	RCE	7/09-B	c1910-B	?-B	11/29-B	WIT	MV/MV	2	txl	x	x	4/59
293	RC	6/09-B	→	c1911-B	7/30-B	?	MV/MV	2	txl	l	l	6/59
294	RC	6/09-Y	→	3/24-Y	4/30-Y	49B	MV/MV	2	t	t	t	6/59
295	RCI	6/09-Y	c1910-Y	?-Y	5/30-Y	?	MV/MV	2	t	t	b	4/59
296	RCI	6/09-Y	→	c1924-Y	5/30-Y	?	MV/MV	2	t	t	b	8/60
297	RCI	5/09-Y	→	c1911-Y	5/30-Y	?	MV/MV	2	t	t	t	4/59
298	RCO	5/09-Y	c1910-Y	?-Y	4/30-Y	?	MV/MV	2	t	t	t	6/60
299	RC	5/09-R	→	c1911-R	1/30-G	WIT	MV/MV	2	m	k	p	6/56
300	RCEI	5/09-R	c1910-R	?-R	12/29-R	?	MV/MV	2	d	d	d	9/60
301	RCI	4/09-B	→	c1911-RB	7/30-B	?	MV/MV	2	m	p	p	1/59
302	RC	4/09-R	c1910-R	?-R	1/30-B	?	MV/MV	2	m	l	l	3/60
303	RCI	4/09-R	→	c1924-R	9/29-R	49B	MV/MV	2	t	b	b	7/58
304	RC	4/09-R	→	2/24-R	10/29-R	49B	MV/MV	2	p	m	m	5/58
305	RCE	3/09-R	→	c1924-R	9/29-BS	?	MV/GEC/MV	2	b	x	p	10/54
306	RCI	3/09-R	→	c1924-R	9/29-R	?	MV/MV	2	b	b	b	5/58
307	RCI	3/09-R	→	11/11-R	10/29-R	49B/WIT	MV/MV	2	d	b	b	6/60
308	RCI	3/09-R	c1910-R	?-R	9/29-RS	49B	EE/MV	2	d	d	d	4/60
309	RCI	2/09-W	c1910-W	?-W	2/30-G	?	MV/MV	2	p	k	k	5/59
310	RCI	2/09-W	→	2/12-W	3/30-G	?	MV/MV	2	p	l	l	3/60
311	RCI	2/09-Y	→	c1924-Y	11/29-R	?	MV/MV	2	b	n	n	5/60
312	RC	2/09-Y	→	5/24-YS	3/30-YS	?	MV/MV	2	b	b	p	3/57
313	RC	2/09-Y	→	11/23-Y	5/30-Y	?	MV/MV	2	b	b	b	3/59
314	RC	2/09-YR	→	4/24-R	7/30-Y	49B	MV/MV	2	b	b	b	12/58
315	RCI	1/09-W	→	c1911-W	2/30-G	?	MV/MV	2	p	k	k	12/58
316	RCI	1/09-W	→	11/11-W	3/30-G	49B	MV/MV	2	p	l	l	5/59
317	RCWI	—	7/09-G	c1911-G	8/28-G	49B	MV/MV	2	d	l	l	8/57
318	RCWI	—	7/09-G	c1911-G	7/28-G	49B	MV/MV	2	d	d	d	5/58
319	RCW	—	10/09-GR	c1911-R	6/29-RS	49B	MV/MV	2	x	x	x	10/57
320	RCW	—	10/09-GR	c1911-R	3/29-RS	49B	EE/EE	2	x	x	x	5/56
321	RCW	—	10/09-GR	c1911-R	6/29-R	49B	MV/MV	2	x	x	x	8/57
322	RCW	—	11/09-GR	c1911-R	6/29-RS	?	MV/MV	2	x	x	x	6/58
323	RCWI	—	11/09-GR	c1911-R	8/29-RS	49B	MV/MV	2	x	x	x	11/58
324	RCW	—	12/09-GR	c1911-R	2/29-R	?	MV/MV	2	x	x	x	5/59
325	RCWE	—	3/09-G	c1911-G	8/28-G	49B	MV/MV	2	d	k	k	11/58
326	RCW	—	12/09-GR	c1911-R	6/29-R	49B	MV/MV	2	x	x	x	6/58

As originally constructed with front exit facilities, 137 employed this ingenious splayed seating arrangement with swivelling chairs which certainly increased the width of the gangway. The design was not repeated presumably due to increased effort required to change over the seats at each terminus. Note the polished lath ceiling. *G.C.T.*

745 was one of the transitional modernised cars at Phase IV eventually becoming Semi-High Speed. Enhanced lighting, heaters and vestibules to the balconies have been installed. The upper deck ceiling is white but the car retains the original wooden seating. The alterations were carried out at Elderslie Depot. This is a second pattern top cover. *G.C.T.*

Car Number	Code	Phase I Date/ Colour	Phase II Date/ Colour	Phase III Date/ Colour	Phase IV Date/ Colour	Pre-Modernised Motors	Modernised Motor/ Controller	Top Cover	Depots 1920s	Depots 1935	Depots 1943	Scrap
327	RCW	—	12/09-GR	c1911-R	8/29-R	?	MV/MV	2	x	x	x	12/56
328	RCW	—	2/10-GR	c1911-R	2/29-RS	?	MV/MV	2	x	x	x	10/55
329	RCWI	—	2/10-GR	c1911-R	7/29-R	?	MV/EE	2	x	x	x	3/58
330	RCW	—	12/09-GR	c1911-R	7/29-R	49B	MV/MV	2	x	x	x	6/56
331	RCW	—	2/10-GR	3/11-R	8/29-R	?	MV/MV	2	x	x	x	5/58
332	RCWI	—	10/09-GR	c1911-R	12/29-R	49B	MV/MV	2	x	x	x	8/59
333	RCW	—	12/09-GR	c1911-R	8/29-R	?	MV/MV	2	x	x	x	12/56
334	RCWDK	—	12/09-GR	c1911-R	9/29-R	?	MV/MV	2	x	x	x	5/46
335	RCWI	—	2/10-GR	c1911-R	7/29-RS	49B	MV/MV	2	x	x	x	4/59
336	RCW	—	8/08-GR	c1911-R	12/28-R	49B	EE/EE	2	x	x	x	8/55
337	RME	1899	3/06-G	6/22-G	10/30-Y	?	MV/MV	1	d	l	l	6/56
338	RCI	—	3/06-R	?-R	9/29-R	49B	MV/MV	1	b	x	x	1/59
339	RC	—	2/06-R	8/23-R	10/29-R	49B	MV/MV	1	d	d	d	6/52
340	RCI	—	2/06-R	4/14-R	12/29-R	49B	MV/MV	1	b	n	k	6/58
341	RCI	—	12/05-R	11/23-R	9/29-R	49B	MV/MV	1	p	n	k	12/58
342	RC	—	12/05-R	?-R	10/29-R	49B	MV/MV	1	p	m	m	2/56
343	RCI	—	2/06-R	1/25-R	10/29-R	49B	MV/MV	1	b	n	k	2/59
344	RC	—	4/06-R	?-R	9/29-R	49B	MV/MV	1	b	d	d	9/58
345	RCI	—	3/06-R	3/25-R	11/29-R	49B	MV/MV	1	b	n	d	6/60
346	RC	—	2/06-R	?-R	12/29-R	49B	MV/MV	1	p	—	—	10/33
347	RC	—	2/06-R	?-R	9/29-W	49B	MV/MV	1	p	p	p	6/56
348	RC	—	1/06-G	4/25-G	2/28-G	49B	EE/EE	1	d	d	d	9/57
349	RC	—	12/05-G	12/25-G	6/30-Y	49B	MV/MV	1	dk	b	b	12/56
350	RC	—	1/06-G	?-G	3/30-G	49B	MV/MV	1	d	k	k	3/51
351	RC	—	12/05-G	?-G	5/29-RS	49B	MV/MV	1	d	b	b	10/56
352	RC	—	1/06-G	?-G	5/29-G	49B	MV/MV	1	d	k	k	8/57
353	RCT	—	10/05-G	?-G	5/29-R	49B	MV/MV	1	d	b	b	6/57
354	RCTE	—	12/05-G	?-G	5/30-G	49B	MV/MV	1	d	k	k	9/57
355	RC	—	11/05-G	?-G	2/30-G	49B	MV/MV	1	d	l	l	8/57
356	RC	—	11/05-G	?-G	4/30-B	49B	MV/MV	1	b	d	d	11/56
357	RC	—	11/05-Y	?-Y	4/30-Y	49B	MV/MV	1	b	l	l	9/56
358	RC	—	1/06-Y	?-Y	5/30-Y	49B	MV/MV	1	b	l	l	6/58
359	RC	—	1/06-Y	?-Y	6/30-Y	49B/323V	MV/MV	1	b	b	b	6/58
360	RC	—	11/05-Y	?-Y	1/30-Y	49B	MV/MV	1	b	b	b	11/59
361	RC	—	2/06-Y	?-Y	1/30-G	49B	MV/MV	1	b	l	l	6/56
362	RC	—	12/05-Y	3/22-Y	4/30-G	49B	MV/MV	1	b	l	l	10/54
363	RCI	—	1/06-Y	10/23-Y	11/29-Y	49B	MV/MV	1	b	l	l	10/59
364	RCI	—	11/05-Y	?-Y	5/30-Y	49B	MV/MV	1	b	n	n	10/58
365	RC	—	11/05-Y	?-Y	4/30-YS	49B	MV/MV	1	d	l	l	5/56
366	RCI	—	11/05-Y	12/23-Y	4/30-Y	49B	MV/MV	1	b	d	d	3/60
367	RCI	—	10/05-Y	?-Y	11/29-Y	49B	MV/MV	1	b	d	d	11/58
368	RCI	—	10/05-R	6/21-R	11/29-R	49B	MV/MV	1	x	n	t	10/58
369	RC	—	10/05-R	?-R	11/29-R	49B	MV/MV	1	x	d	n	10/57
370	RCI	—	10/05-R	4/21-R	11/29-R	49B	MV/MV	1	x	n	n	11/60
371	RC	—	10/05-R	?-R	10/29-R	49B	MV/MV	1	x	d	x	5/57
372	RC	—	10/05-R	?-R	11/29-R	49B	MV/MV	1	b	n	n	11/56
373	RC	—	10/05-R	5/22-R	9/29-R	49B	MV/MV	1	x	d	d	6/59
374	RC	—	10/05-R	1/23-R	2/29-R	49B	MV/MV	1	x	n	n	8/57
375	RC	—	10/05-R	?-R	11/29-RS	49B	MV/MV	1	bx	p	p	2/57
376	RCI	—	10/05-B	5/25-B	3/30-B	49B	MV/MV	1	p	d	d	9/60
377	RCIEL	—	10/05-B	6/25-B	3/30-B	49B	MV/MV	1	p	t	t	9/56
378	RCI	—	10/05-B	?-B	6/30-Y	49B	MV/MV	1	p	b	b	5/58
379	RC	—	10/05-B	?-B	4/30-G	49B	MV/MV	1	p	l	l	4/55
380	RC	—	10/05-W	6/24-W	3/30-G	49B	MV/MV	1	x	l	l	6/55
381	RC	—	9/05-W	11/24-W	8/30-YS	49B	MV/MV	1	p	b	b	11/58
382	RC	—	10/05-W	?-W	3/30-G	49B	MV/MV	1	p	l	t	2/55
383	RCD	—	9/05-W	12/23-W	3/30-G	49B	MV/MV	1/2	x	l	l	11/51
384	RCEI	—	9/05-W	?-WG	5/29-G	49B	MV/MV	1	bx	d	d	12/58
385	RC	—	1/06-W	?-W	3/30-W	49B	MV/MV	1	b	n	d	3/60
386	RC	—	10/05-W	?-W	1/30-G	49B	MV/MV	1	p	l	l	4/54
387	RC	—	1/06-W	11/25-W	3/30-G	49B	MV/MV	1	p	k	k	12/56
388	RCI	—	9/05-W	11/25-W	3/30-WY	49B	MV/MV	1	b	m	d	4/59
389	RC	—	11/05-W	2/21-W	2/30-G	49B	MV/MV	1	b	k	k	12/54
390	RCEI	—	8/05-Y	3/25-Y	5/30-Y	49B	MV/MV	1	b	b	b	6/59
391	RCI	—	8/05-Y	4/23-Y	10/29-R	49B	MV/MV	1	d	n	t	8/57

When black-out conditions were imposed, most of the window areas on trams were later covered with anti-blast netting seen here being glued in position. Note the slotted tin boxes over the light bulbs. The moquette is non-standard. *'Daily Record'*

As late as 1956, a newly turned out Standard tram would still cause heads to turn. 122 is in Parkhead Depot followed by an Albion bus with which that depot was so long associated.
Parr-STMS Collection

Car Number	Code	Phase I Date/ Colour	Phase II Date/ Colour	Phase III Date/ Colour	Phase IV Date/ Colour	Pre-Modernised Motors	Modernised Motor/ Controller	Top Cover	Depots 1920s	1935	1943	Scrap
392	RC	—	8/05-Y	10/23-Y	11/29-R	49B	MV/MV	1	d	d	n	8/57
393	RC	—	9/05-Y	8/25-Y	3/30-Y	49B	MV/MV	1	b	b	b	10/57
394	RCL	—	12/05-B	4/24-B	8/30-B	49B	MV/EE	1	p	p	x	7/60
395	RCE	—	12/05-B	2/24-B	5/30-G	49B	MV/MV	1	p	k	k	9/56
396	RC	—	12/05-G	4/25-GB	10/29-B	49B	MV/MV	1	xd	—	—	4/30
397	RCE	—	12/05-B	5/10-B	6/30-Y	49B	MV/MV	1	p	d	d	4/57
398	RCI	—	12/05-B	?-B	2/30-B	49B	MV/MV	1	xd	d	d	1/59
399	RC	—	11/05-B	1/14-B	6/30-B	49B	MV/MV	1	p	p	p	4/56
400	RCI	—	11/05-B	?-B	11/29-BR	49B	MV/MV	1	pdn	nd	t	4/59
401	RCI	—	11/05-B	?-B	2/30-B	49B	MV/MV	1	p	d	d	11/58
402	RCI	—	11/05-R	5/24-R	10/29-R	49B	MV/MV	1	x	n	t	6/58
403	RCE	—	11/05-R	?-R	10/29-R	49B	MV/MV	1	x	p	p	10/55
404	RCI	—	12/05-R	5/24-R	11/29-RS	49B	MV/MV	1	p	p	t	9/59
405	RC	—	1/06-R	?-R	10/29-R	49B	MV/MV	1	p	p	p	12/56
406	RC	—	12/05-R	?-R	9/29-R	49B	MV/MV	1	p	p	p	5/55
407	RC	—	12/05-R	?-R	10/29-R	49B	MV/MV	1	p	p	p	5/56
408	RC	—	11/05-R	?-R	12/29-R	49B	MV/MV	1	d	d	d	3/51
409	RCD	—	11/05-R	1911-R	9/29-R	49B	MV/MV	1	p	p	p	2/46
410	RC	—	12/05-R	6/14-R	1/30-B	49B	MV/MV	1	p	d	d	8/57
411	RCI	—	7/05-R	?-R	11/29-R	49B	MV/MV	1	d	d	x	9/58
412	RC	—	11/05-R	?-R	12/29-RS	49B	MV/MV	1	d	d	d	1/56
413	RCEI	—	1/06-R	?-R	10/29-R	49B	MV/GEC/MV	1	bx	n	d	3/60
414	RC	—	11/05-R	7/25-R	10/29-R	49B	MV/MV	1	b	n	p	1/57
415	RCEL	—	11/05-G	?-G	7/30-G	49B	MV/MV	1	d	k	p	11/53
416	RCI	—	12/05-R	2/24-R	9/29-R	49B	MV/MV	1	p	p	x	3/59
417	RC	—	5/06-R	?-R	12/29-R	49B	McF/MV/MV	1	b	n	n	9/56
418	RCI	—	7/05-G	?-G	5/29-G	49B	MV/EE	1	dk	d	d	10/58
419	RCTE	—	12/05-G	?-G	5/29-G	49B	MV/MV	1	d	k	k	8/56
420	RCIA	—	11/05-G	?-G	5/29-G	49B	MV/MV	1	dk	t	t	4/59
421	RCEL	—	11/05-G	?-G	5/29-G	49B	MV/MV	1	d	p	p	5/56
422	RC	—	12/05-Y	?-Y	4/30-Y	49B	MV/MV	1	b	b	b	8/58
423	RCI	—	12/05-Y	?-Y	5/30-Y	49B	MV/MV	1	d	b	b	2/59
424	RC	—	6/05-Y	1911-Y	11/29-R	49B	?/MV	1	d	d	—	12/39
425	RC	—	12/05-Y	?-Y	5/30-Y	49B	MV/MV	1	d	d	b	11/54
426	RC	—	9/05-R	4/24-R	1/30-G	49B	MV/MV	1	x	l	x	11/54
427	RC	—	9/05-R	?-R	10/29-R	49B	MV/MV	1	x	p	p	5/56
428	RC	—	12/05-G	5/21-G	5/29-R	49B	MV/MV	1	d	p	p	5/56
429	RCE	—	3/06-G	?-G	2/30-G	49B	MV/MV	1	d	k	k	9/55
430	RCI	—	6/05-G	?-G	2/30-G	49B	MV/EE	1	d	l	l	4/58
431	RC	—	11/05-G	?-G	5/29G	49B	MV/MV	1	d	d	d	11/55
432	RC	—	7/05-G	9/24-G	5/29-G	49B	MV/MV	1	d	d	d	5/54
433	RC	—	5/06-R	?-R	8/29-RS	49B	MV/MV	1	b	p	k	6/52
434	RC	—	6/05-R	3/26-R	9/29-R	49B	MV/MV	1	b	p	p	4/58
435	RCI	—	6/05-R	1/26-R	9/29-R	49B	MV/MV	1	b	p	p	4/59
436	RC	—	6/05-R	?-R	10/29-R	49B	MV/MV	1	b	p	p	7/56
437	RC	—	6/05-R	12/24-R	9/29-R	49B	MV/MV	1	b	p	p	6/56
438	RCEI	—	7/04-GR	c1911-R	11/29-RS	49B	MV/MV	1	dx	n	d	2/59
439	RCEX	—	5/04-G	4/25-G	7/35-G	49B/323V	GEC/EE	1	lkd	l	l	4/52
440	RMX	2/04-G	c1910-G	?-G	5/31-W	?	GEC/EE	2	d	p	p	10/54
441	RMX	3/04-R	c1904-R	?-R	8/29-RS	49B	GEC/EE	1	x	m	m	4/52
442	RMXI	4/04-G	c1910-G	?-G	5/30-B	49B	GEC/EE	2	p	d	x	10/60
443	RMX	2/04-G	c1910-B	?-B	8/29-BS	?	GEC/MV	2	pd	d	d	8/57
444	RMX	3/04-R	c1904-R	7/21-R	8/29-R	49B	GEC/EE	1	x	x	x	12/56
445	RMUI	3/04-Y	1904-YR	3/23-R	12/30-R	49B	GEC/EE	2	b	b	b	3/59
446	RMXI	10/03-R	→	c1911-R	1/30-R	49B	MV/EE	2	b	b	b	3/59
447	RMX	3/04-W	c1910-W	9/25-W	10/29-Y	49B	GEC/EE	2	b	b	b	2/60
448	RME	12/03-G	c1910-G	10/24-G	8/30-B	49B	MV/MV	2	d	l	n	8/51
449	RMX	12/03-G	→	c1911-G	11/29-G	?	GEC/EE	2	d	k	n	1/57
450	RMUX	3/04-G	1904-GR	c1924-R	10/29-RS	49B	MV/EE	2	lb	b	b	8/57
451	RMEI	12/03-R	→	9/11-R	10/30-R	49B	MV/MV	2	x	x	x	10/58
452	RMXE	12/03-R	→	9/23-R	9/29-R	49B	GEC/EE	2	x	x	x	2/59
453	RMX	12/03-R	c1910-R	?-R	10/29-R	?	GEC/EE	2	x	x	x	10/57
454	RMX	12/03-RG	→	c1924-G	11/29-G	49B	GEC/EE	2	p	p	p	11/54
455	RMI	12/03-R	c1910-R	?-G	9/30-B	?	MV/MV	2	dk	p	p	10/58
456	RMX	12/03-R	c1910-R	?-R	1/30-Y	49B	GEC/EE	2	x	d	d	6/57

Charing Cross Mansions is the back-drop for this 1914 scene. Yellow car 222 preceeds green 289 as it rounds the Grand Hotel corner. 289 had received a top cover within one year of being placed in service but had to wait another eleven years to acquire platform vestibules. ***T. & R. Annan***

Car Number	Code	Phase I Date/ Colour	Phase II Date/ Colour	Phase III Date/ Colour	Phase IV Date/ Colour	Pre-Modernised Motors	Modernised Motor/ Controller	Top Cover	Depots 1920s	Depots 1935	Depots 1943	Scrap
457	RMXI	2/04-R	c1910-R	?-R	7/29-W	49B	GEC/EE	1	t	p	p	10/59
458	RMXE	2/04-R	4/06-R	12/24-R	3/30-Y	49B	GEC/EE	1	t	d	d	8/59
459	RMXI	12/03-R	c-1910-R	?-R	11/29-W	?	GEC/EE	2	t	b	b	6/59
460	RMX	11/03-R	c1904-R	?-R	3/30-W	49B	GEC/EE	1	t	m	m	11/54
461	RMXO	11/03-R	c1904-R	?-R	11/29-R	49B	GEC/EE	1	t	x	x	6/57
462	RM	11/03-R	→	7/11-R	12/30-B	49B	GEC/EE	2	t	p	p	9/58
463	RMU	11/03-B	c1904-BR	c1924-R	11/30-RS	?	GEC/EE	2	pb	b	b	12/58
464	RMXU	11/03-R	c1904-R	c1924-R	2/30-RS	49B/323V	MV/MV	2	pb	b	b	9/59
465	RMXU	11/03-B	c1904-BR	8/22-R	2/30-Y	49B	GEC/EE	2	xb	d	d	1/59
466	RMX	11/03-R	c1910-RG	?-GB	5/30-W	49B	GEC/EE	2	d	x	x	6/59
467	RMX	11/03-B	→	c1911-B	5/30-G	49B	GEC/EE	2	px	d	d	11/56
468	RMXI	11/03-W	→	c1924-W	8/29-W	49B	GEC/EE	2	b	b	b	9/60
469	RMXU	11/03-W	c1904-WR	c1924-R	10/29-W	?	GEC/EE	2	b	b	b	6/60
470	RMXU	9/03-R	c1904-R	12/22-R	5/30-G	49B	GEC/EE	2	mb	p	p	9/54
471	RMXI	10/03-B	→	?12/22-B	8/29-BS	49B	GEC/EE	2	p	x	x	7/58
472	RMUI	10/03-W	c1904-WR	c1924-R	9/30-R	49B	MV/MV	2	nb	b	b	3/59
473	RMU	9/03-Y	c1904-YR	8/22-R	9/30-R	49B	MV/MV	2	db	b	b	7/54
474	RM	9/03-Y	→	c1911-Y	7/30-Y	49B	MV/MV	2	d	l	l	11/53
475	RMI	9/03-R	c1910-R	?-R	9/30-B	49B	MV/MV	2	x	l	l	2/59
476	RMXI	9/03-R	c1904-R	?-R	5/30-G	49B	GEC/EE	1	x	p	p	5/59
477	RMXI	10/03-R	c1910-R	?-R	3/30-W	WIT	MV/EE	2	m	m	m	6/60
478	RMX	10/03-R	c1904-R	5/21-R	1/30-RS	49B	GEC/EE	1	x	m	m	4/56
479	RM	9/03-Y	→	12/23-Y	10/30-Y	49B	MV/MV	2	b	b	b	4/59
480	RMX	9/03-Y	→	c1924-Y	5/30-B	?	GEC/EE	2	b	x	x	6/55
481	RMX	10/03-R	→	c1911-R	3/30-Y	49B	GEC/EE	2	b	b	b	2/60
482	RMX	11/03-R	→	6/11-R	4/30-R	49B	GEC/EE	2	x	x	x	5/57
483	RMX	11/03-R	→	c1924-R	4/31-B	49B	GEC/EE	2	x	x	x	6/53
484	RMX	11/03-R	c1910-R	?-R	9/29-R	49B	GEC/EE	2	x	p	p	11/53
485	RMX	9/03-Y	c1910-Y	12/25-Y	7/29-W	WIT	GEC/EE	2	t	n	n	9/51
486	RMU	8/03-G	c1904-GR	c1924-R	11/30-R	49B	GEC/EE	2	db	b	b	3/58
487	RMXU	9/03-G	9/04-GR	4/23-R	6/29-RS	?	GEC/EE	2	db	b	b	9/56
488	RMX	9/03-G	c1910-G	7/23-G	12/29-W	49B	GEC/EE	2	d	x	x	*
489	RM	12/03-G	→	c1911-G	8/30-B	?	EE/EE	2	d	l	l	11/53
490	RM	10/03-G	c1910-G	12/24-G	8/30-Y	49B	MV/MV	2	d	l	l	4/58
491	RMXE	8/03-G	→	c1924-G	1/30-G	?	GEC/EE	2	d	p	p	11/56
492	RMX	8/03-G	→	c1911-G	5/30-Y	49B	GEC/EE	2	d	t	b	10/57
493	RMXL	7/03-G	→	c1911-G	2/30-G	49B	GEC/EE	2	lk	l	x	6/52
494	RMX	7/03-G	c1904-G	?-G	12/29-G	49B	GEC/EE	1	lk	p	p	4/56
495	RMXI	7/03-G	→	c1924-G	2/30-G	49B	GEC/EE	2	k	k	k	9/58
496	RMX	7/03-G	c1910-G	?-G	5/30-B	?	GEC/EE	2	lk	t	t	3/59
497	RMI	7/03-G	c1904-G	?-G	12/30-G	49B	MV/MV	1	pd	p	d	1/59
498	RMX	6/03-G	c1910-G	?-G	3/30-G	?	GEC/EE	2	lk	p	p	9/56
499	RM	6/03-G	c1910-G	?-G	9/30-Y	49B	MV/MV	2	lk	l	l	3/56
500	RMI	6/03-R	c1904-R	10/24-R	10/30-R	49B	MV/MV	1	t	x	x	4/61
501	RMX	6/03-R	c1904-R	1/23-R	4/30-Y	49B	GEC/EE	1	x	b	l	7/56
502	RMXI	6/03-R	c1904-R	?-R	11/29-R	49B	GEC/EE	1	t	x	x	6/60
503	RMX	6/03-R	c1904-R	?-R	4/30-G	49B	GEC/EE	1	t	t	t	7/57
504	RMX	6/03-R	→	c1911-R	12/29-R	?	GEC/EE	2	p	p	p	7/54
505	RMXI	6/03-R	c1910-R	?-R	1/30-R	?	GEC/EE	2	x	x	x	7/60
506	RMXI	6/03-R	c1910-R	?-R	4/30-B	?	GEC/EE	2	x	x	x	7/60
507	RMX	6/03-R	9/06-R	6/25-R	4/30-Y	?	GEC/EE	1	m	d	d	10/56
508	RMX	6/03-R	c1904-R	?-R	8/29-R	?	GEC/EE	1	x	m	m	4/52
509	RMXO	6/03-R	c1910-R	?-R	4/30-Y	49B	GEC/EE	2	x	t	t	10/53
510	RMX	11/02-R	c1904-R	5/22-R	9/29-RS	WIT	GEC/EE	1	m	m	m	3/55
511	RM	11/02-R	11/06-RB	?-B	8/30-B	WIT	MV/MV	1	mld	l	l	9/49
512	RMX	10/02-R	c1904-RB	c1920-B	2/30-WY	?	GEC/EE	1	mld	b	b	9/56
513	RME	8/02-Y	c1910-Y	?-Y	10/30-Y	49B	MV/MV	2	t	t	t	1/49
514	RMX	9/02-W	c1904-W	?-W	12/29-W	WIT	GEC/EE	1	m	b	b	3/57
515	RMX	8/02-R	c1910-R	9/21-R	6/29-RS	WIT	GEC/EE	2	m	m	m	11/56
516	RMX	8/02-W	c1910-W	?-W	10/29-W	?	GEC/EE	2	m	m	m	10/56
517	RMXI	8/02-R	c1904-W	9/24-R	8/29-R	WIT	GEC/EE	1	mt	m	m	9/58
518	RMXO	8/02-G	c1910-G	?-G	3/30-G	WIT	GEC/EE	2	t	t	t	1/56
519	RM	9/02-?	c1904-G	?-G	8/30-B	?	MV/MV	1	tk	p	p	8/52
520	RMXI	7/02-G	c1904-G	?-G	11/29-G	?	GEC/EE	1	t	t	t	10/59
521	RM	8/02-?	c1904-G	10/23-G	11/30-YS	WIT	GEC/EE	2	t	b	b	4/57

Car 488 finally withdrawn 6/61. Now preserved by AMTUIR, Paris

The platforms on Standard trams were cantilevered and designed to be capable of adjustment in the event of drooping. The body-shop at Coplawhill has been over-enthusiastic with 363's leading platform which shows every sign of being above horizontal. The year is 1957. *Parr-STMS Collection*

The final body strengthening given to Standard trams of all ages surviving into the 1950s was the iron angles attached to waist rails and intermediate pillars, shown in this photo of 370 which was the last Round Dash Standard car to receive a 'yearly' overhaul. *Parr-STMS Collection*

234 (photographed in 1950) was a late example of a car with a single magnetic brake unit surviving into the era of advertising on car sides. Around this time these trucks were exchanged for the more standard units with twin magnetic brakes. *Struan J. T. Robertson*

Car Number	Code	Phase I Date/ Colour	Phase II Date/ Colour	Phase III Date/ Colour	Phase IV Date/ Colour	Pre-Modernised Motors	Modernised Motor/ Controller	Top Cover	Depots 1920s	1935	1943	Scrap
522	RMI	8/02-R	c1910-R	?-R	11/30-Y	WIT	GEC/EE	2	m	l	l	2/60
523	RMX	7/02-?	c1904-R	5/24-RB	11/29-W	WIT	GEC/EE	1	m	m	m	8/57
524	RMX	8/02-R	c1904-R	?-R	4/30-R	?	GEC/EE	1	m	m	m	8/55
525	RMX	8/02-R	c1904-R	11/21-R	2/30-R	WIT	GEC/EE	1	m	m	m	11/54
526	RMXO	7/02-R	c1904-R	10/24-RB	9/29-B	WIT	GEC/EE	1	ml	x	x	5/61
527	RMX	8/02-R	c1910-R	4/21-R	9/29-R	WIT	GEC/EE	2	m	m	m	11/56
528	RMO	7/02-W	c1910-W	?-W	11/30-W	?	GEC/EE	2	m	m	m	3/58
529	RMU	8/02-YW	c1904-WR	c1924-RB	9/30-B	49B	MV/MV	2	m	p	p	1/57
530	RMX	9/02-Y	c1910-Y	?-Y	5/30-YS	?	GEC/EE	2	t	t	p	11/54
531	RM	9/02-W	11/06-W	?-W	10/30-W	WIT	MV/MV	2	m	m	m	10/56
532	RMXEI	7/02-Y	c1910-W	?-W	4/30-W	?/323V	MV/MV	2	m	n	n	9/60
533	RMX	8/02-Y	c1910-Y	1/24-Y	11/29-Y	WIT	GEC/EE	2	t	d	d	3/50
534	RMX	8/02-Y	c1904-W	9/24-W	10/29-W	WIT	GEC/EE	1	m	m	m	10/53
535	RM	8/02-?	c1904-G	?-G	11/30-G	?	GEC/EE	1	t	p	p	11/51
536	RME	9/02-?	c1904-W	?-W	10/30-W	?	EE/EE	1	m	n	d	7/56
537	RM	9/02-W	→	c1924-WY	10/30-WY	?	MV/MV	2	m	m	d	10/51
538	RMX	8/02-W	c1910-W	?-W	3/30-W	?	GEC/EE	2	m	b	b	6/58
539	RMX	8/02-W	c1904-W	c1910-W	12/29-W	?	GEC/EE	1	m	m	m	4/51
540	RMX	8/01-G	c1910-G	?-GY	1/30-Y	?	GEC/EE	2	td	l	l	9/58
541	RMI	5/01-G	c1910-G	?-GY	5/30-BW	49B	GEC/EE	2	d	x	x	4/59
542	RMX	8/01-G	c1910-G	2/23-G	8/30-B	49B	MV/MV	2	lk	p	p	5/53
543	RM	8/01-G	c1910-G	?-W	5/30-G	49B	GEC/EE	2	lk	d	d	10/53
544	RMX	8/01-G	c1904-G	?-G	9/30-B	?	MV/MV	1	k	p	p	10/51
545	RM	8/01-G	c1910-G	?-G	2/30-G?	49B	GEC/EE	2	k	n	n	3/54
546	RM	8/01-G	c1910-G	8/23-G	9/30-B	49B	MV/MV	2	k	l	p	3/57
547	RM	8/01-G	c1910-G	?-G	8/30-B	?	EE/MV	2	k	l	l	3/56
548	RM	7/01-G	c1910-G	?-G	8/30-B	?	MV/MV	2	k	l	p	7/56
549	RMI	7/01-G	c1910-G	?-GB	8/30-B	?	MV/MV	2	k	l	l	6/58
550	RMXEI	7/01-G	c1910-G	?-GB	3/30-B	?	GEC/EE	2	k	p	p	7/59
551	RMXI	7/01-G	c1910-G	?-G	12/29-G	?	GEC/EE	2	k	p	d	4/59
552	RMX	7/01-G	c1910-G	?-G	5/30-W	49B	GEC/EE	2	k	b	b	12/53
553	RMX	7/01-G	→	8/23-G	3/30-G	49B	MV/EE	2	k	p	p	11/56
554	RMX	7/01-G	c1910-G	?-G	2/30-W	49B	GEC/EE	2	k	b	p	9/56
555	RMXI	7/01-G	2/04-G	1/12-G	11/29-G	49B	GEC/EE	1	k	d	d	7/58
556	RMXI	7/01-G	c1910-G	6/21-G	3/30-G	49B	GEC/EE	2	k	d	d	7/61
557	RMX	7/01-?	→	c1911-G	5/30-G	323V/49B	GEC/EE	2	k	p	p	4/54
558	RMX	6/01-G	c1910-G	?-G	10/31-G	49B/220	GEC/EE	2	k	d	d	7/56
559	RMX	6/01-G	c1910-G	?-G	5/30-BY	49B	GEC/EE	2	k	x	b	9/51
560	RM	6/01-G	→	6/23-GW	9/30-WY	49B	MV/MV	2	k	b	b	5/59
561	RMX	7/01-G	10/09-G	4/22-G	10/29-G	49B	GEC/EE	2	k	l	l	2/56
562	RME	8/01-G	c1910-G	10/21-G	8/30-Y	49B	MV/MV	2	k	l	l	7/57
563	RMX	7/01-G	c1910-G	?-G	2/30-BY	49B	GEC/EE	2	k	x	b	10/50
564	RM	7/01-G	c1910-G	?-G	8/30-B	?	EE/MV	2	k	p	p	10/52
565	RMXA	7/01-G	→	c1911-GW	5/30-W	?	GEC/EE	2	k	n	d	9/59
566	RMX	7/01-G	c1910-G	?-G	3/30-Y	49B	GEC/EE	2	k	d	d	6/57
567	RM	7/01-G	c1910-G	?-G	8/30-B	49B/323V	MV/MV	2	k	l	l	12/54
568	RMX	6/01-R	→	c1911-R	4/30-W	49B	GEC/EE	2	nx	b	b	6/57
569	RMXO	6/01-YG	c1904-G	?-G	4/30-W	49B	GEC/EE	1	k	x	x	2/56
570	RMOI	6/01-G	c1910-G	?-GW	10/30-W	49B	MV/MV	2	tk	x	x	9/58
571	RM	6/01-B	c1904-B	?-B	11/30-B	?	GEC/EE	1	p	l	l	9/54
572	RM	6/01-G	→	4/23-G	8/30-B	49B	MV/MV	2	td	l	l	7/56
573	RMX	6/01-G	c1904-G	?-G	10/20-BS	49B	GEC/EE	1	kl	d	d	7/55
574	RMXI	6/01-G	c1904-G	?-G	3/30-GR	49B	GEC/EE	1	kl	t	x	10/58
575	RMI	6/01-G	c1910-G	8/25-GY	10/30-Y	49B	MV/MV	2	kl	b	b	2/60
576	RMI	6/01-G	c1904-G	?-G	8/30-B	49B	MV/GEC/MV	1	k	d	d	11/58
577	RMX	6/01-G	c1904-G	?-G	3/30-G	49B	GEC/EE	1	kl	p	p	3/55
578	RMXE	6/01-R	→	c1924-R	9/29-RS	49B	GEC/EE	2	pm	m	m	3/55
579	RM	5/01-G	c1910-G	8/22-G	3/30-W	49B	MV/MV	2	k	n	n	7/56
580	RMI	5/01-?	c1904-R	2/26-R	11/30-W	49B	GEC/EE	1	nm	x	x	4/58
581	RMX	5/01-?	c1904-G	?-G	4/30-G	?	GEC/EE	1	tp	t	t	11/52
582	RMUXI	5/01-G	c1904-YR	c1924-R	12/29-W	?	GEC/EE	2	tm	m	m	11/60
583	RML	5/01-?	c1904-G	?-G	9/30-B	49B	MV/MV	1	tp	p	p	11/54
584	RMXE	5/01-G	c1910-G	?-G	1/30-G	?	GEC/EE	2	kl	d	d	9/52
585	RMXEI	5/01-G	c1910-G	?-GB	5/30-G	323V/49B	GEC/EE	2	kl	d	d	*
586	RM	5/01-?	c1904-G	?-G	9/30-W	?	MV/MV	1	k	n	t	6/52

* Car 585 preserved South Kensington Science Museum, London
Phase IV, blue route colour withdrawn 6/61.

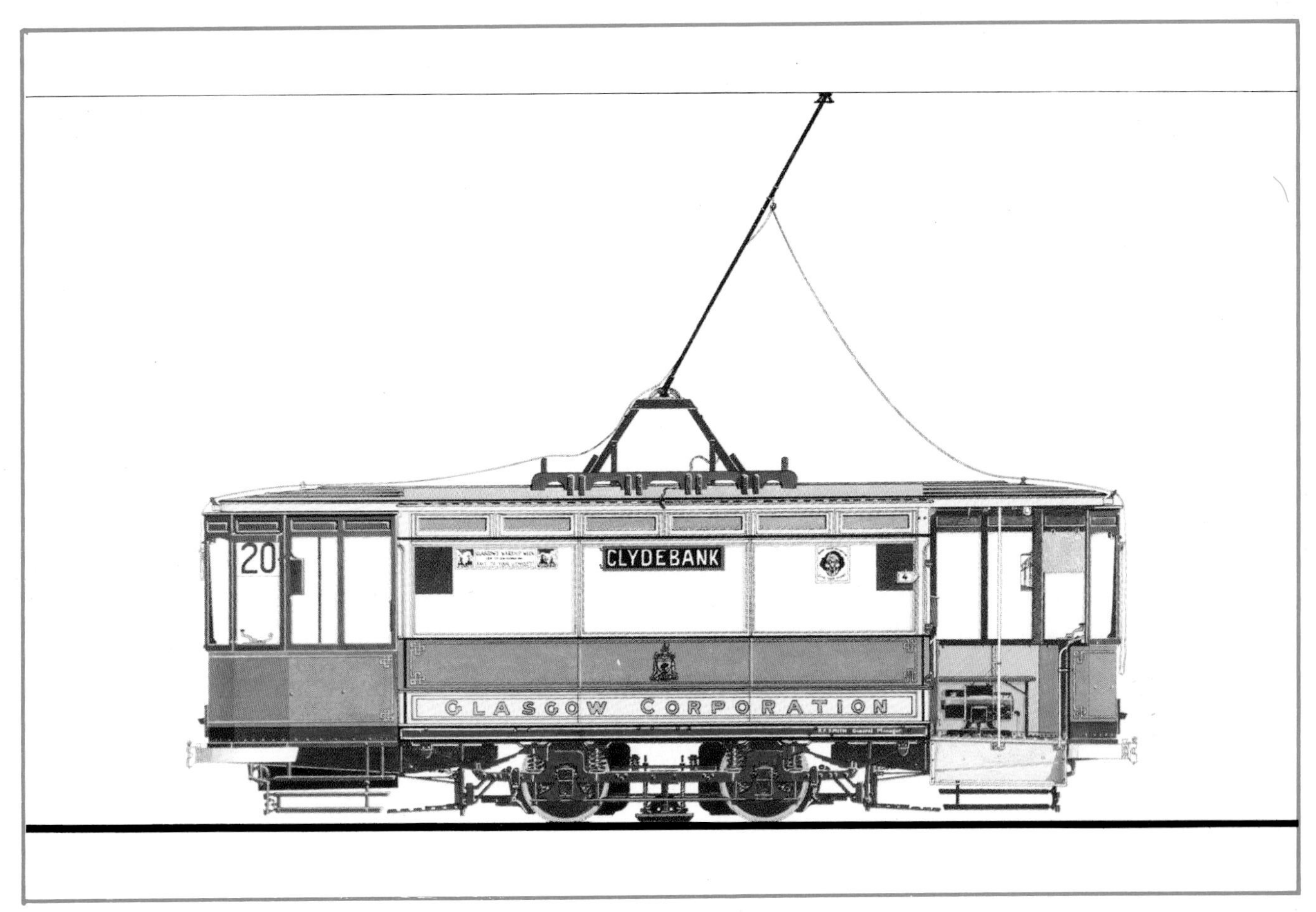

1009 was a typical conversion for the single deck only Duntocher service of an ex-Paisley B.E.C. car. It is portrayed in early Second World War condition with white fenders, head lamp masks and period posters. *Drawing: Author.*

Cars with red, blue and yellow upper panels survived into the era of exterior advertising and 128 is typical of these. At this time the Bisto kids were more Cockney and less 'mid-Atlantic' than they are now. *Drawing: Author*

271 crosses Kelvinbridge on its way to Scotstoun West. Although serving the well-to-do West End of Glasgow it was track restrictions in the East End which dictated the use of four wheelers almost exclusively on this, and companion service 30. *W.D. McMillan*

310 heads east from Bridgton Cross with destination displaying "London Road". Unkind critics once said this curtailment from Auchenshuggle was due to the latter's name on linen blinds having become too illegible due to constant use. *W.D. McMillan*

This side view of a Round-Dash Standard car taken in 1949 shows the final simplification of the livery although slight traces of original lining can be detected through the upper panels. This car has the first pattern of top deck with centre-pivot operated ventilators panelled over on the inside with perforated zinc to create a glorious dirt-trap. **G.C.T.**

For many years 337 was an enigma. It was quite out of phase in design with others with numbers above and below. It now emerges that 337 was the pattern car for tenderers to examine in 1899 before lodging offers for the eighty bodies to be delivered in 1900. The top deck was fitted ex-438 in 1906, suitably modified, and the car numbered sequentially in series. It is quite likely to have been numbered 1001 when first placed in service.
Parr-STMS Collection

Car Number	Code	Phase I Date/ Colour	Phase II Date/ Colour	Phase III Date/ Colour	Phase IV Date/ Colour	Pre-Modernised Motors	Modernised Motor/ Controller	Top Cover	Depots 1920s	1935	1943	Scrap
587	RMX	5/01-R	c1910-R	8/21-G	5/30-W	49B	GEC/EE	2	d	m	m	4/56
588	RMXE	5/01-R	c1910-R	?-R	9/29-RS	?	GEC/EE	2	m	m	m	12/56
589	RMXE	5/01-?	c1904-R	2/24-R	2/30-R	49B	GEC/EE	1	d	x	p	9/54
590	RMX	5/01-R	c1910-R	8/25-R	12/29-W	49B	GEC/EE	2	m	m	m	11/54
591	RMX	5/01-?	c1904-R	?-R	11/29-R	49B	GEC/EE	1	b	b	b	3/55
592	RMX	5/01-?	c1904-R	5/21-R	12/29-W	49B	GEC/EE	1	m	m	m	12/55
593	RMXO	5/01-?	c1904-R	?-R	12/29-R	?	GEC/EE	1	mt	t	t	9/52
594	RMX	4/01-R	c1904-RB	11/24-B	7/29-BS	49B	GEC/EE	1	ml	p	p	2/56
595	RMXE	4/01-R	c1904-R	?-R	1/29-R	49B	GEC/EE	2	m	m	m	8/53
596	RM	4/01-RG	c1904-G	?-G	8/30-BS	?	MV/MV	1	mltk	p	p	10/54
597	RM	4/01-RG	c1904-G	?-G	9/30-B	?	MV/MV	1	mlktp	l	l	9/52
598	RMX	4/01-R	c1910-R	1/14-R	2/30-R	49B	GEC/EE	2	m	m	m	1/56
599	RM	4/01-R	c1904-R	?-R	12/29-RS	49B	GEC/EE	1	m	m	m	2/55
600	RM	4/01-?	c1910-R	?-R	7/29-R	?	GEC/EE	2	x	p	p	5/53
601	RM	4/01-?	c1904-R	?-R	9/29-RS	?	GEC/EE	1	x	p	p	9/53
602	RMI	4/01-?	c1904-R	2/21-R	9/29-R	49B/323V	MV/EE	1	n	n	t	5/58
603	RMI	4/01-R	3/11-R	12/25-R	3/30-R	?	GEC/EE	2	nm	m	m	3/57
604	RMI	4/01-R	c1910-R	11/23-R	1/30-Y	49B	GEC/EE	2	x	d	d	10/58
605	RM	4/01-?	c1904-R	10/24-R	7/29-R	49B	GEC/EE	1	x	d	d	10/55
606	RM	4/01-R	c1910-R	?-R	3/30-W	49B	GEC/EE	2	m	m	m	3/54
607	RM	4/01-R	c1910-R	?-R	11-29-R	?	GEC/EE	2	m	m	m	9/52
608	RM	3/01-B	c1904-B	8/22-B	8/29-B	49B	GEC/EE	1	x	x	x	3/57
609	RM	3/01-R	c1910-R	?-R	4/30-R	?	GEC/EE	2	m	m	m	10/57
610	RMI	3/01-B	→	c1911-B	8/29-B	?	GEC/EE	2	p	x	x	6/58
611	RM	3/01-?	c1904-R	?-R	11/29-R	49B	GEC/EE	1	p	p	p	5/55
612	RMX	3/01-B	c1904-B	4/23-B	8/29-B	49B	GEC/EE	1	x	x	x	6/58
613	RM	3/01-W	c1910-W	?-W	11/30-WY	?	MV/MV	2	n	n	d	2/57
614	RMX	3/01-B	c1904-B	?-B	8/29-B	49B	GEC/EE	1	x	x	x	8/56
615	RMX	3/01-?	c1904-W	9/21-W	4/30-G	49B	GEC/EE	1	n	d	d	8/52
616	RMX	3/01-W	c1910-W	?-W	10/29-W	?	GEC/EE	2	n	m	m	6/54
617	RMX	3/01-W	c1910-W	12/24-W	8/29-W	49B	GEC/EE	2	n	b	b	8/58
618	RMX	3/01-R	c1910-R	11/20-R	9/29-R	49B	GEC/EE	2	b	m	m	3/56
619	RMX	3/01-R	→	c1911-R	2/30-R	49B	GEC/EE	2	n	x	p	6/53
620	RMXI	3/01-?	c1910-R	?-R	3/30-Y	?	GEC/EE	2	d	b	b	10/59
621	RMXI	3/01-?	c1904-R	?-R	3/30-W	?	GEC/EE	1	t	p	p	12/58
622	RMX	3/01-?	c1904-R	8/25-R	11/29-W	49B	GEC/EE	1	x	p	p	5/55
623	RMX	3/01-?	→	c1911-R	1/30-R	49B	GEC/EE	2	b	b	p	12/53
624	RM	3/01-?	c1904-R	?-R	11/30-RS	?	GEC/EE	1	n	n	n	6/56
625	RMX	3/01-B	→	c1911-B	8/29-B	49B	GEC/EE	2	x	x	x	8/58
626	RMXI	3/01-?	c1904-R	?-R	2/30-R	?	GEC/EE	1	mt	t	t	5/58
627	RMX	3/01-Y	c1910-Y	?-Y	7/29-W	?	GEC/EE	2	l	b	b	6/54
628	RMX	3/01-?	c1904-R	2/23-R	8/29-RS	49B	GEC/EE	1	x	m	m	4/51
629	RMX	3/01-?	c1904-R	?-R	1-30-WY	49B	GEC/EE	1	d	m	b	9/57
630	RMX	3/01-R	c1910-R	5/25-R	2/30-W	49B	GEC/EE	2	x	p	p	5/54
631	RMX	3/01-?	c1904-R	?-R	4/30-Y	?	MV/MV	1	x	l	l	9/56
632	RMX	3/01-?	c1904-R	?-R	7/29-R	?/323V	GEC/EE	1	x	b	b	5/55
633	RMX	3/01-?	c1904-R	3/23-R	4/30-G	49B	GEC/EE	1	d	p	p	11/56
634	RMX	3/01-?	c1904-R	?-R	11/29-W	49B	GEC/EE	1	x	p	x	9/55
635	RMX	2/01-?	c1904-R	?-R	3/30-R	?	GEC/EE	1	n	p	p	8/51
636	RMUX	2/01-G	c1904-GR	11/22-R	2/30-W	49B	GEC/EE	2	lm	x	p	9/52
637	RMX	2/01-R	c1910-R	?-R	11/29-W	49B	GEC/EE	2	x	b	b	7/54
638	RMX	2/01-?	c1904-G	?-G	2/30-G	?	GEC/EE	1	d	d	d	10/56
639	RMX	2/01-R	c1910-R	?-R	8/29-RS	WIT	GEC/EE	2	m	m	m	3/58
640	RM	2/01-?	10/05-G	6/21-G	8/30-B	?	MV/MV	1	k	x	x	1/56
641	RMX	2/01-G	c1910-G	?-G	2/30-W	?	MV/MV	2	d	m	m	10/54
642	RMI	2/01-G	c1910-G	?-GB	8/30-B	49B	MV/MV	2	d	x	x	5/59
643	RMXD	2/01-G	c1910-G	1/23-G	10/29-W	49B	GEC/EE	2	dl	p	p	5/47
644	RMX	2/01-G	c1904-G	?-G	5/30-G	?	GEC/EE	1	dk	d	d	10/50
645	RMX	2/01-?	c1904-W	?-W	5/30-G	49B	GEC/EE	1	m	d	d	2/57
646	RM	2/01-G	c1910-G	3/14-G	11/30-YS	49B	GEC/EE	2	dl	b	b	6/54
647	RMXI	2/01-R	c1910-B	2/21-B	3/30-B	49B	GEC/EE	2	ml	x	x	3/59
648	RMXE	2/01-G	c1910-G	?-G	10/29-G	49B	GEC/EE	2	dl	d	d	4/57
649	RM	2/01-?	c1904-Y	9/25-Y	10/30-YS	49B	MV/MV	1	k	b	b	7/52
650	RMX	2/01-?	c1904-R	?-R	1/29-R	?	GEC/EE	1	t	t	x	5/54
651	RMX	2/01-B	→	c1911-B	9/29-B	?	GEC/EE	2	x	x	x	11/55

Until the 1950s Corporation trams were not allowed to be disfigured with external advertising. This rule was waived, however, during the First World War when the full potential of the trams was used to promote war effort, recruiting and patriotic slogans, as can be seen on 339 and 767. **G.C.T.**

The enlarged detail from the side panelling of a converted Mineral Wagon used to promote war effort exploits patriotism of the Glaswegian citizens. Judging by the haunted expressions of the soldiers, the glamour of the War had already worn off. **G.C.T.**

240 was photographed at Rouken Glen beside 768 in 1915. The event appears to have been publicity shots for the first 'lady conductor'. As long as male Tramways Department staff were wooed into the Armed Forces it was necessary to woo female replacements. **G.C.T.**

Car Number	Code	Phase I Date/ Colour	Phase II Date/ Colour	Phase III Date/ Colour	Phase IV Date/ Colour	Pre-Modernised Motors	Modernised Motor/ Controller	Top Cover	Depots 1920s	Depots 1935	Depots 1943	Scrap
652	RMX	2/01-?	c1910-R	?-R	8/29-R	49B	GEC/EE	2	t	t	t	10/60
653	RMX	2/01-G	c1910-G	?-G	5/30-G	?	GEC/EE	2	dk	d	d	7/57
654	RM	2/01-?	c1904-W	4/25-W	10/30-W	49B	MV/MV	1	x	m	m	9/53
655	RMX	2/01-?	c1904-R	?	11/29-YS	49B	MV/EE	1	t	d	d	2/57
656	RM	2/01-?	c1910-W	?-W	11/30-W	?	MV/MV	2	m	m	m	3/56
657	RM	2/01-B	c1910-RG	2/22-G	8/30-B	49B	MV/MV	2	dk	x	x	9/59
658	RMXI	1/01-R	c1910-R	12/24-R	9/29-R	49B	GEC/EE	2	t	t	t	6/59
659	RM	1/01-Y	c1910-Y	9/25-Y	8/30-Y	49B	MV/MV	2	b	b	b	12/55
660	RMXEI	1/01-R	c1910-R	?-R	8/29-RS	?	GEC/EE	2	t	m	m	6/58
661	RMX	1/01-?	c1904-W	1/23-W	10/29-W	49B	GEC/EE	1	x	x	p	7/56
662	RMXI	1/01-Y	c1910-Y	?-Y	11/29-YS	49B	MV/MV	2	b	b	b	3/59
663	RMX	1/01-W	c1904-W	9/22-W	11/29-W	49B	GEC/EE	1	m	m	m	7/54
664	RM	1/01-Y	c1910-Y	2/21-Y	4/29-W	49B	GEC/EE	2	b	p	p	6/53
665(i)	RM	1900-?	c1904-W	—	—	—	—	1	(m)	—	—	c1912
665(ii)	HEI	—	—	5/23-R	3/29-R	323V	MV/MV	2	n	n	n	11/60
666	H	—	—	6/23-Y	3/29-G	323V	MV/MV	2	l	k	k	3/59
667	H	—	—	6/23-Y	12/28-G	323V	EE/EE	2	l	d	d	9/59
668	HI	—	—	6/23-Y	1/29-G	323V	EE/EE	2	l	d	d	2/59
669	HIA	—	—	8/23-Y	8/29-G	323V	MV/MV	2	l	t	t	4/59
670	H	—	—	8/23-Y	6/29-RS	323V	MV/MV	2	l	x	x	6/58
671	HI	—	—	8/23-Y	2/29-G	323V	EE/EE	2	l	d	t	4/59
672	HE	—	—	9/23-W	2/29-G	323V	MV/EE	2	b	d	d	4/59
673	H	—	—	9/23-G	4/28-G	323V	MV/MV	2	lc	c	c	6/58
674	H	—	—	10/23-G	5/28-G	323V	MV/MV	2	lc	c	p	4/59
675	HI	—	—	10/23-G	8/28-G	323V	MV/MV	2	lc	l	l	2/59
676	H	—	—	10/23-Y	3/29-G	323V	MV/MV	2	l	t	t	2/59
677	HI	—	—	11/23-Y	4/29-G	323V	MV/MV	2	l	t	?	3/60
678	HK	—	—	11/23-Y	9/29-G	323V	GEC/MV	2	l	l	l	8/58
679	HED	—	—	12/23-B	4/30-G	323V	MV/MV	2	n	l	l	2/43
680	HI	—	—	12/23-B	6/30-Y	323V	MV/MV	2	n	b	b	10/58
681	H	—	—	1/24-B	7/30-B	323V	MV/MV	2	n	x	x	9/60
682	HI	—	—	2/24-B	6/30-Y	(323V)	MV/MV	2	n	b	b	6/59
683	HET	—	—	2/24-B	9/28-G	(323V)	EE/EE	2	n	k	k	6/57
684	H	—	—	3/24-B	5/30-G	323V	MV/MV	2	n	l	x	8/57
685	HI	—	—	3/24-B	12/28-G	323V	EE/EE	2	n	k	k	5/59
686	RM	10/98WG	c1910-G	?-G	5/35-G	49B/323V	GEC/EE	2	dlk	d	d	11/49
687	RMXS	11/98WB	c1904-B	?-B	6/34-B	49B/323V	323V/BTH	1	nl	r	l	2/48
688	RMXG	1/99WB	c1910-B	?-B	8/30-BS	WIT/323V	BTH/BTH	2	p	l	l	10/50
689	RMXG	1/99WB	c1910-B	2/24-B	8/30-BS	WIT/323V	BTH/BTH	2	p	l	l	6/51
690	RMXG	1/99WB	c1910-B	?-B	8/30-BS	?/323V	BTH/BTH	2	x	p	p	2/52
691	RMX	1/99-W	c1910-R	?-R	11/30-WS	?/323V	GEC/EE	2	nm	b	b	7/52
692	RMXG	3/99WB	c1904-B	?-B	6/30-B	49B/323V	BTH/BTH	1	xd	p	p	11/51
693	RMXG	3/99WB	c1904-B	?-B	8/30-B	49B/323V	BTH/BTH	1	pd	p	p	6/52
694	RMXG	5/99WB	c1910-B	1/22-B	8/30-BS	WIT/323V	BTH/BTH	2	p	l	l	3/51
695	RMX	3/99-W	c1910-W	?-W	9/30-G	49B/323V	GEC/EE	2	m	t	t	3/54
696	RMX	3/99WB	→	5/21-B	9/29-B	WIT/323V	GEC/EE	2	p	x	x	6/57
697	RMXE	5/99-W	c1910-Y	?-Y	1/30-YS	49B	GEC/EE	2	bd	b	b	6/57
698	RMXE	6/99WB	c1910-B	?-B	10/30-B	49B/323V	BTH/MV/BTH	2	ld	p	t	5/52
699	RMXS	7/99-W	c1904-G	?-G	11/32-B	49B/323V	323V/BTH	1	k	n	e	11/49
700	RMX	7/99-W	c1904-R	?-R	10/30-G	49B/323V	GEC/EE	1	n	d	d	5/52
701	RMX	-/99-W	c1904-R	?-R	12/30-R	49B/323V	GEC/EE	1	n	m	m	10/56
702	RMXEI	-/99-WB	c1910-B	?-B	8/30-Y	49B/323V	GEC/EE	2	x	b	b	5/59
703	RMXG	-/99-WR	c1910-R	?-R	?-B	49B/323V	BTH/BTH	2	n	p	p	11/50
704	RMXS	-/99-WG	c1910-G	?-G	?-B	49B/323V	323V/BTH	2	l	m	e	12/49
705	RMXI	-/99-WR	c1910-R	?-R	7/30-R	49B/323V	GEC/EE	2	x	x	x	12/58
706	RMXG	-/99-WR	c1910-R	?-R	9/30-BS	49B/323V	BTH/BTH	2	p	l	p	6/51
707	RMX	-/99WG	c1910-R	12/13-R	1/30-R	49B	GEC/EE	2	p	d	n	10/50
708	RMX	-/99-WR	c1910-R	?-R	10/30-G	49B/323V	GEC/EE	2	n	p	p	2/55
709	RMX	-/99-W	c1904-G	8/25-G	8/30-R	49B/220/323V	GEC/EE	1	l	d	d	8/53
710	RMXS	-/99-WR	c1910-R	11/21-R	11/32-B	49B	323V/BTH	2	d	m	l	5/51
711	RMX	-/99-WG	c1910-R	?-R	1/30-G	49B/WIT	GEC/EE	2	n	p	p	9/56
712	RMXS	1/00WG	c1910-B	?-B	2/35-B	49B	323V/BTH	2	d	n	n	6/50
713	RMXET	1/00WB	2/10-R	5/24-R	6/30-R	49B/WIT/323V	EE/EE	2	d	t	n	3/58
714	RMXG	11/99WB	c1910-B	?-B	9/30-B	49B/323V	BTH/BTH	2	p	l	l	6/52
715	RMXG	11/99-B	c1904-B	?-B	10/30-BS	49B/323V	BTH/BTH	1	p	l	l	9/52

A part of Glasgow never featured by the squalor-seeking media is Botanic Gardens in the West End . Blue 'Gloucester' car 932 leads green 518 citywards while another enters the siding to the right of 644 heading for Anniesland over the hill. ***T. & R. Annan***

Car Number	Code	Phase I Date/ Colour	Phase II Date/ Colour	Phase III Date/ Colour	Phase IV Date/ Colour	Pre-Modernised Motors	Modernised Motor/ Controller	Top Cover	Depots 1920s	1935	1943	Scrap
716	RMXS	11/99-RB	c1910-B	?-B	6/34-B	49B/323V	323V/BTH	2	p	n	l	4/50
717	RMX	11/99?	c1910-R	9/23	8/30-G	49B/323V	GEC/EE	2	b	k	p	7/52
718	RMX	11/99-B	c1904-B	?-B	11/32-BY	49B/323V	GEC/EE	1	d	nb	b	7/56
719	RMXS	11/99-B	c1904-B	?-B	11/32-B	49B	323V/BTH	1	x	r	n	10/49
720	RMXS	11/99-B	c1910-B	c1920-B	11/32-B	49B	323V/BTH	2	d	n	n	12/49
721	RM	11/99-B	c1910-B	?-B	9/30-B	49B	MV/MV	2	p	p	p	10/55
722	RMXG	11/99-B	c1910-WB	8/23-B	9/30-B	49B/323V	BTH/BTH	2	d	p	p	8/54
723	RMXE	11/99-B	c1904-B	?-B	11/30-BR	49B/323V	GEC/EE	1	l	n	b	7/55
724	RMXG	11/99-B	c1910-B	4/22-B	7/30-B	49B/323V	BTH/BTH	2	x	p	p	7/51
725	RM	11/99?	c1910-W	8/24-W	12/30-W	49B	GEC/EE	2	b	m	m	9/56
726	RMX	11/99-B	c1904-B	5/21-B	11/30-BR	49B/323V	GEC/EE	1	x	n	n	9/57
727	RMX	11/99-G	3/11-G	11/25-G	7/30-W	49B/323V	GEC/EE	2	k	b	b	1/57
728	RMX	2/00WB	c1910-B	?-B	9/30-BR	?/323V	GEC/EE	2	t	p	p	7/55
729	RMI	2/00-W	10/24-B	1/25-B	8/30-B	49B	GEC/EE	2	l	d	d	2/59
730	RMXS	2/00-R	c1910-R	9/21-R	11/32-B	49B	323V/BTH	2	x	m	e	5/51
731	RMXS	2/00-B	c1910-B	?-B	11/32-B	49B	323V/BTH	2	t	m	e	2/52
732	RMX	2/00-G	c1910-G	?-G	6/30-B	?/323V	GEC/EE	2	l	l	p	9/53
733	RMX	2/00-G	c1904-B	?-B	9/30-B	49B/323V	GEC/EE	1	l	x	x	3/56
734	RMXG	2/00-?	c1910-W	8/22-W	10/30-B	49B/323V	BTH/BTH	2	b	p	p	11/53
735	RMXG	2/00-B	c1904-B	?-B	9/30-BS	49B/323V	BTH/BTH	1	t	l	p	5/51
736	RMXS	2/00-B	c1904-B	?-B	6/34-B	49B/323V	323V/BTH	1	t	r	n	3/48
737	RMXS	2/00-W	c1904-W	?-W	11/32-B	WIT/49B	323V/BTH	1	p	n	n	3/50
738	RMXS	2/00-W	1911-R	7/24-R	10/32-W	49B	323V/BTH	2	d	n	—	3/39
739	RMX	2/00-W	c1910-W	?-W	11/30-Y	?/323V	GEC/EE	2	n	d	d	3/57
740	RM	2/00-W	c1904-W	?-W	10/30-W	49B	MV/MV	1	n	n	t	12/54
741	RMXG	2/00-W	c1910-Y	?-Y	7/30-BS	49B/323V	BTH/BTH	2	d	p	p	6/51
742	RMUX	2/00-W	c1904-WR	c1924-R	3/30-W	49B/323V	GEC/EE	2	m	m	m	11/55
743	RMX	2/00-W	c1910-W	?-W	8/30-BY	?	GEC/EE	2	b	b	b	6/56
744	RMXS	2/00WB	c1904-B	11/25-B	11/32-B	49B	323V/BTH	1	x	n	n	3/50
745	RMXS	2/00-R	1911-R	9/24-R	10/32-R	49B	323V/BTH	2	p	p	—	1/39
746	RMZ	2/00-?	c1904-R	?-R	11/32-R	49B/323V	GEC/EE	1	d	t	?	2/57
747	RMXG	2/00-W	c1910-W	?-W	6/30-BS	49B/323V	BTH/BTH	2	n	p	p	4/52
748	RMXA	2/00-?	c1904-W	?-W	11/30-W	?/323V	GEC/EE	1	m	b	b	1/55
749	RMXS	2/00-W	→	7/23-W	10/32-W	WIT/49B	323V/BTH	2	n	n	—	2/39
750	RMXE	2/00-W	1906-W	1911-W	1935-W	?/323V	GEC/EE	1?	n	n	—	1/40
751	RMXEI	2/00-?	c1904-R	?-RW	10/32-WS	49B/323V	GEC/EE	1	d	n	b	6/60
752	RMX	2/00-W	c1910-W	1926-W	6/30-R	?/323V	GEC/EE	2	np	x	x	10/57
753	RMZ	2/00-R	c1910-R	6/21-R	11/32-R	49B/323V	MV/EE	2	mt	t	t	12/53
754	RMXS	2/00-?	c1910-R	?-R	11/32-RB	49B/323V	323V/BTH	2	d	n	n	7/49
755	RMX	2/00-W	c1910-W	?-W	9/30-G	49B/323V	GEC/EE	2	nx	e	p	4/54
756	RMZ	2/00-B	c1910-B	c1920-B	11/32-B	49B/323V	MV/EE	2	ld	n	l	7/54
757	RMG	2/00-B	→	c1911-B	11/30-B	?/323V	BTH/BTH	2	lx	p	p	10/51
758	RMX	2/00-?	c1910-G	?-G	8/30-BY	?/323V	GEC/EE	2	lk	rt	k	11/53
759	RMX	2/00-W	c1910-W	?-W	6/30-R	49B/323V	GEC/EE	2	np	x	x	4/55
760	RMX	2/00-B	c1910-B	9/21-B	9/30-BY	49B/323V	GEC/EE	2	l	et	t	4/56
761	RMXO	2/00-R	c1910-R	?-R	9/30-R	?/323V	GEC/EE	2	n	t	t	9/56
762	RMXS	3/00-B	→	1911-B	2/35-B	49B	323V/BTH	2	d	r	—	5/39
763	RMXS	3/00-R	c1910-R	?-R	11/32-R	49B/323V	323V/BTH	2	p	x	l	6/50
764	RMX	3/00-G	c1910-G	1/21-G	10/30-G	49B/323V	GEC/EE	2	dk	k	p	9/53
765	RMXS	4/00-B	c1910-B	?-B	6/34-B	49B/WIT	323V/BTH	2	l	n	n	9/50
766	RMX	3/00-R	c1910-R	7/25-R	8/30-R	49B/323V	GEC/EE	2	p	n	b	2/56
767	RMX	3/00-R	c1910-R	10/21-R	9/30-R	49B/323V	GEC/EE	2	p	n	t	10/56
768	RMX	3/00-R	→	c1911-R	11/30-Y	49B	GEC/EE	2	n	d	d	6/54
769	RM	3/00-B	c1910-B	?-B	9/30-BS	?	MV/MV	2	x	l	l	9/49
770	RME	4/00-W	-/11-W	2/21-W	6/35-G	49B/323V	GEC/EE	2	n	l	l	9/51
771	RMZ	4/00-B	c1910-B	?-B	11/32-B	49B/323V	MV/EE	2	x	n	l	2/55
772	RM	4/00-R	c1910-R	?-R	8/31-Y	?	GEC/EE	2	mt	d	d	2/57
773	RM	4/00-R	c1910-R	10/24-R	10/35-BW	49B/323V	GEC/EE	2	d	b	d	11/55
774	RMXS	4/00-B	→	c1911-B	11/32-B	49B	323V/BTH	2	x	n	n	3/50
775	RMXGO	4/00-?	c1904-R	?-R	6/30-BS	49B/323V	BTH/BTH	1	nm	l	l	10/50
776	RMXZ	4/00-?	4/06-G	12/13-G	6/34-G	49B/323V	GEC/EE	1	p	k	p	5/53
777	RMXG	4/00-G	c1910-G	9/23-G	7/30-GBS	49B	BTH/BTH	2	k	p	p	5/51
778	RMXES	4/00-?	c1904-G	?-G	6/34-B	49B	323V/BTH	1	k	n	n	6/49
779	RMXE	4/00-W	c1910-R	?-R	11/30-RY	49B	GEC/EE	2	d	b	b	•
780	RMX	4/00-B	c1904-B	10/23-B	10/30-BY	49B	GEC/EE	1	x	nb	b	8/57

• 779 Preserved, Museum of Transport, Glasgow Phase II condition
Last ran 11/62. Withdrawn from normal service 12/59.

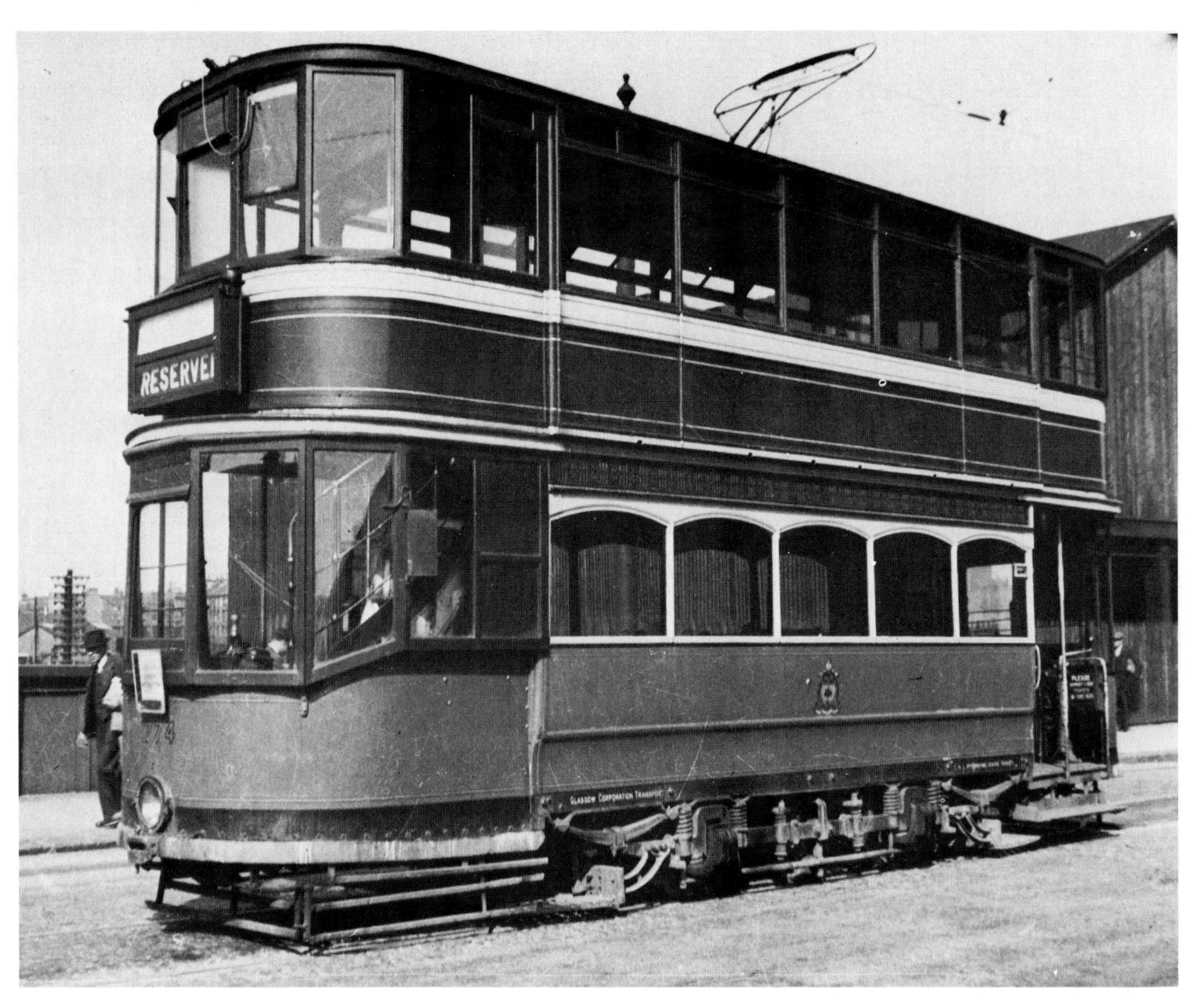

After graduating through the Motor School and Motor School Car 1017, trainee motormen would be allowed to drive through the streets in normal traffic conditions. Their trams were adorned with G.C.T. 'L' plates and Semi-High Speed cars such as 774 were often used in the 1940s. ***R. R. Clark/STMS Collection***

Standing at the extremity of the last street tramway extension in Great Britain at Boydstone Road, Carnwadric is 585, looking a little tired, in August 1950. Soon it would be repainted and acquire advertisements. It now rests in London's South Kensington Science Museum translated into 1930s condition. ***R. R. Clark/STMS Collection***

The early Standard cars withstood remarkably well the stresses and strains of high speed running, rapid acceleration and deceleration as well as the acquisition of the top cover for which they were never designed. 631 shows her age more than most in the Govan Depot Forecourt in August 1956. ***Parr-STMS Collection***

Car Number	Code	Phase I Date/ Colour	Phase II Date/ Colour	Phase III Date/ Colour	Phase IV Date/ Colour	Pre-Modernised Motors	Modernised Motor/ Controller	Top Cover	Depots 1920s	1935	1943	Scrap
781	RMXS	4/00-R	→	c1911-R	6/34-YB	WIT/49B	323V/BTH	2	p	m	l	9/50
782	RMXEO	4/00-?	3/05-R	4/22-R	8/30-R	49B/323V	GEC/EE	1/2	n	p	p	11/52
783	RMXS	4/00-R	1909-R	7/21-R	11/32-R	49B	323V/BTH	2	n	p	—	7/39
784	RMX	4/00-R	→	c1911-R	8/30-RB	49B/323V	GEC/EE	2	n	t	t	7/55
785	RMXS	5/00-R	c1910-R	1914-R	11/32-RB	49B	323V/BTH	2	x	n	—	6/39
786	RMXE	5/00-?	c1904-R	11/23-R	11/30-G	49B/WIT/200	GEC/EE	1	p	k	p	11/50
787	RMXG	5/00-?	c1904-R	?-R	8/30-B	49B/323V	BTH-BTH	1	nm	l	l	6/51
788	RMXS	5/00-R	→	c1911-R	12/32-RB	49B	323V/BTH	2	d	n	e	8/50
789	RMX	5/00-R	c1910-R	?-R	8/30-R	?/323V	GEC/EE	2	x	m	m	4/54
790	RMXE	5/00-G	c1910-G	?-G	9/30-YS	?/323V	GEC/EE	2	pk	b	b	3/60
791	RMZ	5/00-G	c1910-G	?-G	6/34-B	49B/323V	MV/EE	2	dk	n	l	10/51
792	RMXS	5/00-?	c1904-G	?-G	12/32-G	49B	323V/BTH	1	k	t	l	6/50
793	RMXS	5/00-?	c1904-G	11/23-G	12/32-G	49B	323V/BTH	1	k	k	l	9/49
794	RMX	5/00-G	c1910-G	?-G	11/30-G	49B/323V	GEC/EE	2	k	k	p	9/52
795	RMXS	5/00-R	c1910-R	1912-R	5/35-YB	49B	323V/BTH	2	x	lm	—	6/39
796	RMX	5/00-R	c1904-R	?-R	6/30-G	49B/323V	GEC/EE	1	bp	k	p	11/55
797	RMXE	5/00-?	c1904-R	?-R	9/30-R	49B/323V	GEC/EE	1	p	n	b	9/59
798	RMX	6/00-R	9/09-R	?	11/30-Y	?/323V	GEC/EE	2	x	l	l	6/57
799	RMX	6/00-?	c1904-R	?-R	12/30-WS	49B/323V	GEC/EE	1	pk	m	m	2/55
800	RMX	6/00-?	c1904-R	?-R	2/30-Y	?	GEC/EE	I	x	d	d	7/56
801	RMXL	6/00-?	c1904-R	8/21-R	10/30-B	49B/323V	GEC/EE	1	x	d	d	1/57
802	RMXS	6/00-R	c1910-R	?-R	12/32-Y	49B	323V/BTH	2	p	t	l	9/50
803	RMX	6/00-R	c1910-R	1/24-R	11/30-B	49B/323V	GEC/EE	2	t	p	p	10/53
804	RMXG	6/00-B	c1904-B	?-B	8/30-B	?/323V	BTH/BTH	1	d	l	l	6/51
805	RMXS	6/00-R	→	c1911-R	12/32-R	49B	323V/BTH	2	n	t	l	4/50
806	RMX	6/00-?	c1904-R	?-R	4/30-G	49B	GEC/EE	1	m	p	p	9/56
807	RMXGL	6/00-B	c1910-B	c1920-B	12/32-B	49B/323V	BTH/BTH	2	lt	p	p	10/52
808	RMXI	6/00-R	c1904-RB	6/25-R	9/30-RW	49B/323V	GEC/EE	1	ml	m	m	9/58
809	RMXG	6/00-?	c1910-B	c1920-B	8/30-B	?-323V	BTH/BTH	2	ld	l	l	5/51
810	RMXI	7/00-G	→	c1924-G	7/30-G	49B/323V	GEC/EE	2	pl	e	e	3/58
811	RMXG	7/00-B	c1910-B	?-B	8/30-B	?/323V	BTH/BTH	2	l	p	p	5/52
812	RMI	7/00-GB	5/10-B	12/11-B	9/30-BS	49B	MV/MV	2	l	l	n	*
813	RMX	7/00-R	10/09-R	7/25-R	2/30-R	?	EE/EE	2	x	x	x	9/58
814	RMXG	7/00-W	c1904-G	?-G	8/30-B	49B/323V	BTH/BTH	1	lp	p	p	9/52
815	RMXS	7/00-R	c1910-R	?-R	12/32-R	49B	323V/BTH	2	x	b	b	5/50
816	RMXG	7/00-B	c1904-B	?-B	10/30-B	?/323V	BTH/BTH	1	l	l	l	9/51
817	RMXG	7/00-B	c1904-B	?-B	7/30-B	?/323V	BTH/BTH	1	ld	l	l	11/53
818	RMXE	7/00-?	11/04-G	?-G	6/30-G	49B/323V	GEC/EE	1	k	e	e	7/50
819	RMXS	7/00-B	→	9/11-B	12/32-B	49B	323V/BTH	2	l	n	e	6/50
820	RMX	7/00-R	3/05-B	8/23-B	9/30-BG	49B/323V	GEC/EE	1	x	p	n	4/55
821	RMXSEB	7/00-R	5/06-R	?-R	10/32-R	49B	323V/DK	2	x	mn	—	5/39
822	RMX	7/00-R	c1910-R	10/21-R	9/30-G	49B/323V	GEC/EE	2	p	n	e	10/50
823	RMXG	7/00-B	5/10-B	4/14-B	8/30-BS	49B/323V	BTH/BTH	2	lt	p	p	6/51
824	RMX	8/00-?	c1904-W	?-W	10/30-YS	?/323V	GEC/EE	1	p	l	n	4/59
825	RMXI	8/00-B	c1910-B	?-B	10/30-BR	?/323V	GEC/EE	2	x	n	x	5/60
826	RMZO	7/00-R	c1910-R	?-R	12/32-R	49B/323V	GEC/EE	2	p	p	l	9/59
827	RM	8/00-R	c1904-R	?-R	12/30-B	?	MV/MV	1	n	p	p	6/53
828	RMXS	8/00-W	→	c1924-W	12/32-WB	49B	323V/BTH	2	x	m	e	5/49
829	RMXG	8/00-B	c1904-B	10/23-B	8/30-BS	?/323V	BTH/BTH	1	x	l	l	10/51
830	RMXG	8/00-?	c1904-R	6/25-R	11/30-BS	49B/323V	BTH/BTH	1	n	p	p	6/54
831	RM	8/00-B	c1904-B	?-B	8/30-B	49B	MV/MV	1	x	d	d	6/58
832	RMX	8/00-R	c1910-R	2/22-R	10/30-YS	49B/323V	GEC/EE	2	p	l	p	1/59
833	RMX	8/00-?	c1904-R	?-R	12/29-WS	?	GEC/EE	1	k	b	b	7/58
834	RMX	8/00-R	1/10-R	2/14-R	7/30-R	?/323V	GEC/EE	2	x	p	p	8/56
835	RMXS	8/00-B	c1910-B	c1920-B	12/32-B	49B	323/BTH	2	ld	n	n	5/50
836	RMXSB	8/00-B	1910-B	11/22-B	12/32-B	49B/323V	323V/DK	2	l	n	—	8/39
837	RMX	8/00-RB	→	c1924?-B	9/30-B	?/323V	GEC/EE	2	l	r	x	5/52
838	RMX	8/00-R	c1910-R	?-R	11/30-Y	49B	GEC/EE	2	t	d	d	2/57
839	RM	8/00-Y	4/05-Y	3/25-Y	10/30-Y	49B	MV/MV	1	d	l	t	3/58
840	RM	9/00-R	c1910-R	?-R	11/30-B	?	GEC/EE	2	m	x	p	10/53
841	RMXG	9/00-?	c1904-Y	6/24-Y	10/30-BS	49B/323V	BTH/BTH	1	b	p	p	10/51
842	RM	9/00-?	c1904-Y	?-Y	12/30-YS	49B	GEC/EE	1	b	b	b	7/55
843	RMEX	9/00-YG	c1910-G	?-G	10/30-WS	49B/323V	GEC/EE	2	bk	b	b	6/54
844	RMXS	9/00-B	10/13-B	10/22-B	12/32-BS	49B	323V/BTH	2	xp	r	e	10/49
845	RMXGO	9/00-?	c1910-Y	?-Y	6/30-B	49B	BTH/BTH	2	t	p	p	12/53

* 812 withdrawn 3/60 but preserved in the National Tramway Museum. Phase IV condition, yellow route colour.

103, above was the first Standard car to be modernised to Phase IV High Speed status in 1927 and differed in minor detail from the production run. 929 was the last to achieve High Speed status in 1954 when it was re-trucked and re-equipped from being a Semi-High Speed car. 812 is the survivor, however, and is seen perched rather uncomfortably on a trailer, about to enter what is now the National Tramway Museum at Crich.

R. F. Mack (103)
Parr/STMS Collection (929)
R. J. S. Wiseman (812)

Car Number	Code	Phase I Date/ Colour	Phase II Date/ Colour	Phase III Date/ Colour	Phase IV Date/ Colour	Pre-Modernised Motors	Modernised Motor/ Controller	Top Cover	Depots 1920s	Depots 1935	Depots 1943	Scrap
846	RMX	9/00-?	4/06-R	3/23-R	12/30-Y	49B	GEC/EE	1	x	t	t	5/54
847	RMXE	9/00-?	c1904-B	8/21-B	6/30-BR	49B/323V	MV/EE	1	nl	nb	b	5/57
848	RMX	9/00-?	c1904-R	1/26-R	12/29-RS	WIT	GEC/EE	1	m	m	m	12/56
849	RMX	9/00-?	c1904-R	?-R	4/30-G	?	GEC/EE	1	t	t	t	6/52
850	RMXI	9/00-?	c1904-R	?-R	11/30-BY	?/323V	GEC/EE	1	m	rt	t	4/58
851	RM	9/00-G	c1904-G	?-G	9/30-W	?	MV/MV	1	dk	b	b	12/53
852	RMX	9/00-?	9/09-R	1926-RW	11/30-R	49B/323V	GEC/EE	2	x	x	x	2/59
853	RMX	9/00-?	c1904-R	?-R	11/30-G	?/323V	MV/EE	1	x	e	n	11/56
854	RMX	9/00-R	3/05-R	2/12-R	3/30-Y	49B	GEC/EE	1	mt	d	d	5/53
855	RMEL	10/00-Y	c1904-Y	?-Y	11/30-W	?	MV/MV	1	td	m	m	6/53
856	RMX	10/00-R	8/10-R	4/11-RG	8/30-R	WIT/323V	MV/EE	1	dk	d	d	1/57
857	RMX	10/00-R	→	8/11-R	6/30-BR	49B/323V	GEC/EE	2	m	b	m	5/52
858	RMX	10/00-R	c1910-R	?-R	12/29-R	?	GEC/EE	2	t	t	t	5/53
859	RMXG	10/00-W	c1910-W	?-W	10/30-B	49B/323V	BTH/BTH	2	n	l	l	9/50
860	RMXG	10/00-R	→	c1924-R	11/30-B	49B/323V	BTH/BTH	2	t	l	l	10/53
861	RMX	10/00-B	c1910-B	?-B	10/30-BR	?/323V	GEC/EE	2	x	m	m	12/55
862	RMI	10/00-Y	→	c1911-Y	12/30-Y	?	GEC/EE	2	b	b	b	9/59
863	RMXG	10/00-R	c1910-G	?-G	9/30-BS	?/323V	BTH/BTH	2	dk	l	l	11/51
864	RMX	10/00-R	c1910-R	?-R	1/30-R	49B	GEC/EE	2	t	t	t	10/53
865	RMXS	10/00-?	c1904-R	?-R	12/32-R	49B	323V/BTH	1	t	x	l	6/50
866	RMX	10/00-R	c1904-R	3/21-R	8/30-R	49B/323V	GEC/EE	1	x	p	p	4/52
867	RMXSE	10/00-G	c1904-G	?-G	1/33-B	49B/323V	323V/BTH	1	p	n	n	9/50
868	RMX	10/00-Y	→	c1911-Y	6/30-BWY	?/323V	GEC/EE	2	b	b	b	2/55
869	RM	10/00-?	→	1912-W	1931-W	49B	MV/MV	2	b	m	—	6/39
870	RMX	10/00-Y	c1910-Y	5/21-Y	6/30-B	?-323V	GEC/EE	2	b	rp	x	8/57
871	RMXG	10/00-?	c1904-Y	?-Y	9/30B	?-323V	BTH/BTH	1	b	l	p	4/53
872	RMX	10/00-Y	c1910-Y	?-Y	9/30-Y	?-323V	GEC/EE	2	b	b	b	9/57
873	RMXGU	10/00-Y	c1904-YR	9/22-R	9/30-B	49B/323V	BTH/BTH	2	bm	l	l	6/54
874	RMI	11/00-WY	c1904-Y	?-Y	9/30-Y	?	MV/MV	1	td	p	x	11/59
875	RMXG	11/00-Y	c1910-Y	?-Y	6/30-B	49B/323V	BTH/BTH	2	td	p	p	6/51
876	RMX	11/00-?	c1910-G	?-G	11/30-G	49B/323V	GEC/EE	2	p	e	x	3/58
877	RMXGE	11/00-B	c1910-B	8/21-B	11/30-B	49B/323V	BTH/BTH	2	tx	l	l	10/50
878	RMXS	11/00-B	c1904-B	c1924-B	6/34-B	49B	323V/BTH	2	p	n	n	10/49
879	RMXS	11/00-?	c1910-G	?-G	1/33-GB	49B	323V/BTH	2	lk	n	n	6/49
880	RMXI	11/00-?	c1904-W	?-W	12/29-W	49B	GEC/EE	1	b	b	b	3/59
881	RMXE	11/00-YR	→	c1924-R	12/30-R	49B/323V	GEC/EE	2	b	n	b	5/59
882	RMX	11/00-R	c1910-R	?-R	12/29-R	49B	GEC/EE	1	t	b	b	7/56
883	RMX	11/00-R	→	c1911-R	10/30-BR	49B/BB	GEC/EE	2	n	n	t	3/53
884	RMX	11/00-R	c1910-R	c1914-R	12/30-R	?/323V	GEC/EE	2	x	x	x	9/55
885	RMX	11/00-WY	2/11-Y	12/23-Y	1/30-Y	49B	GEC/EE	2	b	b	b	9/54
886	RMX	11/00-?	7/06-G	?-G	10/30-BG	49B	GEC/EE	1	k	re	e	6/56
887	RMXS	11/00-WY	1909-Y	3/26-Y	5/35-Y	49B/323V	323V/BTH	2	b	b	—	2/39
888	RMXI	11/00-WY	c1904-Y	?-Y	6/30-BYS	49B/323V	GEC/EE	1	b	mb	b	5/59
889	RMXEI	11/00-W	c1910-W	11/22-YB	6/30-BY	49B/323V	GEC/EE	2	nl	mb	b	2/59
890	RMX	12/00-WY	c1904-Y	?-Y	6/30-W	?/323V	MV/EE	1	bd	p	x	1/56
891	RMZ	12/00-R	c1910-G	1/23-G	12/30-G	?/323V	MV/MV	2	dk	l	l	8/57
892	RMX	12/00-R	c1910-R	?-R	11/30-R	?/323V	GEC/EE	2	x	b	b	10/55
893	RMX	12/00-R	c1904-R	?-R	7/29-RS	?	MV/MV	1	x	p	p	8/52
894	RMXS	12/00-R	1910-G	1923-G	1934-Y	49B	323V/BTH	2	lk	b	—	3/39
895	RMXI	12/00-R	c1904-B	?-B	8/29-B	?	GEC/EE	1	p	x	x	10/58
896	RMXS	12/00-R	1910-R	4/23-R	7/35-RB	49B	323V/BTH	2	x	r	—	6/39
897	RMX	12/00-?	c1904-Y	?-Y	6/30-W	49B	GEC/EE	1	b	b	b	7/56
898	RMX	12/00-B	c1904-B	8/21-B	8/30-G	49B	GEC/EE	1	l	l	p	11/53
899	RMX	12/00-?	c1910-Y	6/22-Y	10/29-Y	?	MV/MV	2	b	b	b	9/53
900	RMX	12/00-?	c1910-R	?-R	11/29-R	49B	GEC/EE	2	t	t	t	5/54
901	RMZ	5/00-Y	→	c1911-Y	12/29-Y	?	GEC/EE	2	b	d	d	2/56
902	RMXS	5/00-W	c1910-R	1914-R	1935-RB	49B	323V/BTH	2	t	n	—	5/39
903	RMXS	5/00-R	c1910-R	12/22-R	6/34-R	49B/323V	323V/BTH	2	x	b	b	5/50
904	RMZI	5/00-Y	c1904-Y	11/24-YW	6/34-WB	49B/323V	MV/MV	1	bd	m	l	6/58
905	RMXS	5/00-Y	→	c1911-Y	6/34-YB	WIT/49B	323V/BTH	2	b	bn	e	6/50
906	RMZE	5/00-Y	c1904-G	?-G	6/34-B	?/323V	MV/EE	1	dk	r	l	4/54
907	RMXS	5/00-?	c1909-R	R	8/35-R	49B	323V/BTH	2	x	b	—	2/39
908	RMXS	5/00-Y	c1904-Y	?-Y	2/33-YB	49B	323V/BTH	1	tl	bn	e	5/50
909	RMZI	5/00-R	c1904-R	2/12-R	2/33-RB	49B/323V	MV/EE	1	x	bn	e	9/58
910	RMXS	5/00-W	c1910-W	?-W	1/33-WB	49B	323V/BTH	2	x	r	e	12/49

For a short time after the introduction of service numbers in 1938, slip-boards were retained in position along the upper deck sides. 268 displays '1A' in the vestibule corner window as it passes Central SMT open staircase L21 at St. George's Cross.

T. & R. Annan

Car Number	Code	Phase I Date/Colour	Phase II Date/Colour	Phase III Date/Colour	Phase IV Date/Colour	Pre-Modernised Motors	Modernised Motor/Controller	Top Cover	Depots 1920s	1935	1943	Scrap
911	RMXS	5/00-Y	c1910-Y	?-Y	1/33-YB	49B	323V/BTH	2	bd	r	e	3/50
912	RMXS	5/00-W	1909-W	8/21-W	1934-W	49B	323V/BTH	2	n	n	?	7/39
913	RMXS	5/00-Y	1911-Y	8/22-Y	1935-YB	49B	323V/BTH	2	bd	n	—	4/39
914	RMZ	5/00-Y	c1904-B	?-B	1/33-B	49B/323V	MV/MV	1	td	m	l	3/57
915	RMXS	5/00-?	c1904-R	?-RY	1/33-YB	49B	323V/BTH	1	p	n	e	4/49
916	RMXS	5/00-Y	c1910-Y	?-Y	2/33-Y	49B	323V/BTH	2	b	b	b	4/50
917	RMZ	5/00-?	c1904-Y	?-Y	1/33-Y	49B/323V	MV/MV	1	b	t	l	6/58
918	RMXS	6/00-Y	c1910-G	12/25-G	1/33-G	49B	323V/BTH	2	dk	p	l	2/51
919	RMXS	6/00-Y	c1904-Y	9/21-Y	2/33-Y	49B	323V/BTH	1	b	b	b	6/50
920	RMXSE	6/00-Y	c1904-Y	1/13-Y	2/33-Y	49B	323V/BTH	1	b	l	b	4/50
921	RMXS	6/00-?	c1904-Y	7/22-Y	7/34-WB	49B	323V/BTH	1	b	r	e	8/50
922	RMXSE	6/00-R	c1910-R	?-R	1/33-R	49B	200/BTH	2	x	t	l	4/49
923	RMXSB	6/00-Y	c1910-Y	1914-Y	2/33-Y	WIT/49B	323V/DK	2	b	r	—	10/39
924	RMXS	6/00-G	1911-G	11/21-G	1935-G	WIT/49B	323V/BTH	2	lk	e	—	4/39
925	RMXS	6/00-W	c1910-W	5/14-W	1933-W	49B	323V/BTH	2	n	m	—	3/39
926	RMXSB	10/00-Y	→	1911-Y	6/34-YB	49B	323V/DK	2	t	n	—	6/39
927	RMZI	10/00-?	c1904-W	?-W	6/34-W	49B/323V	GEC/EE	1	x	m	l	1/60
928	RMZ	10/00-YG	c1910-G	?-G	2/33-G	49B/323V	GEC/EE	2	p	p	p	3/58
929	RMZ	10/00-Y	→	c1911-Y	2/33-B	49B-323V	GEC/EE	2	b	r	l	4/59
930	RMXS	10/00-Y	c1904-B	?-B	2/33-B	49B	323V/BTH	1	pd	m	l	4/50
931	RMXS	10/00-W	c1910-W	8/24-W	2/33-W	49B	323V/BTH	2	p	p	l	12/49
932	RMXS	10/00-B	→	1909-B	1933-B	49B	323V/BTH	2	x	r	—	8/39
933	RMXS	11/00-Y	c1910-Y	5/14-Y	1933-Y	49B	323V/BTH	2	bl	t	—	2/39
934	RMXS	11/00-W	c1910-W	6/23-W	7/34-WB	49B	323V/BTH	2	x	bn	e	11/51
935	RMXS	11/00-R	c1904-R	?-R	2/33-RB	49B	323V/BTH	1	x	n	e	10/50
936	RMXS	11/00-Y	c1910-G	?-G	7/34-B	49B	323V/BTH	2	lk	r	e	2/48
937	RMXS	11/00-R	→	c1911-R	1934-RB	49B	323V/BTH	2	p	m	—	3/39
938	RMXS	11/00-W	c1910-W	?-W	3/33-W	49B	323V/BTH	2	m	b	e	6/50
939	RMZI	11/00-Y	c1910-Y	?-Y	7/34-Y	49B/323V	GEC/EE	2	kl	d	l	12/58
940	RMXS	12/00-G	c1904-G	?-G	2/33-G	49B	323V/BTH	1	kp	e	e	3/48
941	RMXS	12/00-R	→	c1911-R	7/34-R	49B	323V/BTH	2	n	m	e	4/51
942	RMZI	12/00-Y	→	9/11-Y	3/33-Y	49B/323V	GEC/EE	2	l	t	l	1/59
943	RMXS	12/00-W	c1910-W	11/22-W	3/33-W	49B	323V/BTH	2	b	b	e	6/50
944	RMXS	12/00-W	c1910-W	?-W	7/34-W	49B	323/BTH	2	b	b	e	10/49
945	RMZ	12/00-R	c1910-R	?-R	3/33-B	49B/323V	GEC/EE	2	tb	m	e	4/56
946	RMXS	12/00-Y	c1904-G	?-G	7/34-Y	49B	323V/BTH	1	tb	n	n	8/49
947	RMXS	12/00-?	4/04-RG	?-G	7/34-B	49B	323V/BTH	1	kl	m	l	2/48
948	RMXS	12/00-?	c1904-G	?-G	8/34-G	49B/220	323V/BTH	1	dk	l	l	10/50
949	RMXS	12/00-R	c1910-R	11/22-R	11/34-R	49B/323V	323V/BTH	2	x	t	—	5/39
950	RMX	12/00-W	c1904-G	?-G	3/33-BR	DK	GEC/EE	1	tk	m	m	6/53
951	RMXS	3/01-B	c1910-B	?-B	8/34-B	49B	323V/BTH	2	p	n	n	2/48
952	RMXS	3/01-G	→	c1911-G	1935-B	WIT/49B	323V/BTH	2	dk	r	—	7/39
953	RMXS	3/01-W	c1910-W	10/23-W	1935-W	49B	323V/BTH	2	m	m	—	3/39
954	RMXSE	3/01-W	c1910-W	?-W	8/34-W	49B	104/BTH	2	b	b	e	5/50
955	RMXS	3/01-?	c1904-W	?-W	3/33-W	WIT/49B	323V/BTH	1	n	n	e	12/49
956	RMXS	3/01-W	c1910-W	?-W	8/34-WY	49B	323V/BTH	1&2	n	mb	b	4/50
957	RMXS	4/01-G	1909-G	1925-G	1/35-B	49B/220	323V/BTH	2	tk	r	—	8/39
958	RMXS	4/01-?	c1904-G	?-G	8/34-G	49B	323V/BTH	1	tk	k	e	4/48
959	RMXS	4/01-G	c1904-G	?-G	8/34-GB	49B	323V/BTH	1	dk	r	e	2/48
960	RMXSE	5/01-G	c1910-G	?-G	8/34	49B	323V/BTH	2	dk	e	e	12/49
961	RMXS	4/01-G	c1904-G	?-G	8/34-B	49B	323V/BTH	1	dp	r	e	5/49
962	RMXS	4/01-G	c1910-G	?-G	3/33-G	49B	323V/BTH	2	dk	e	e	7/49
963	RMXS	4/01-G	→	c1911-GY	3/33-YB	49B	323V/BTH	2	dk	n	e	10/49
964	RMXSU	4/01-B	c1904-BR	c1924-R	8/34-RB	49B	323V/BTH	2	pm	m	l	4/50
965	RMXSE	4/01-G	c1910-G	?-G	3/33-GB	WIT/49B	BB/BTH	2	dk	r	e	11/49
966	RMXS	4/01-G	c1910-G	1911-G	1935-G	49B	323V/BTH	2	dk	e	—	6/39
967	RMXS	5/01-Y	c1910-Y	3/25-Y	8/34-Y	49B/323V	323V/BTH	2	tl	l	l	5/50
968	RMXS	5/01-YR	→	8/23-R	3/33-B	49B	323V/BTH	2	bm	n	e	9/50
969	RMXS	5/01-RG	c1904-G	?-G	8/34-B	49B	323V/BTH	1	mk	n	n	6/49
970	RMXS	5/01-?	c1904-R	?-R	3/33-Y	49B	323V/BTH	1	n	l	l	7/50
971	RMXS	12/00-R	1910-R	5/25-R	1934-R	WIT/49B	323V/BTH	2	nm	m	—	3/39
972	RMXS	12/00-R	1911-R	1912-R	1935-RB	49B	323V/BTH	2	tb	n	—	5/39
973	RMXSE	12/00-RG	→	7/23-G	3/33-G	49B	DK/BTH	2	mk	e	e	10/51
974	RMXS	12/00-R	→	c1911-R	8/34-RB	49B	323V/BTH	2	mn	n	n	6/49
975	RMXSB	12/00-R	1905-G	?-G	8/34-B	49B	323V/DK	1	lk	bn	—	8/39

994 was typical of the High Street white cars. This pre-1914 scene shows how busy the Trongate-High Street intersection was at this time when the Corporation trams were the only mechanised transport in any quantity. Only 34 open-top Standard cars then remained.
T. & R. Annan

Car Number	Code	Phase I Date/ Colour	Phase II Date/ Colour	Phase III Date/ Colour	Phase IV Date/ Colour	Pre-Modernised Motors	Modernised Motor/ Controller	Top Cover	Depots 1920s	1935	1943	Scrap
976	RMXS	12/00-R	1905-R	1923-R	?-RB	49B	323V/BTH	2	nm	m	—	5/41
977	RMZL	12/00-R	c1904-R	11/21-R	9/34-B	49B/323V	EE/EE	1	td	rx	x	8/55
978	RMXS	12/00-G	1911-G	1914-G	4/35-B	49B	323V/BTH	2	k	m	—	5/39
979	RMXS	12/00-R	c1910-R	1914-R	1934-RB	49B	323V/BTH	2	mx	n	—	8/39
980	RMXS	12/00-R	c1904-R	6/25-R	9/34-R	49B	323V/BTH	1	nm	d	l	8/50
981	RMX	12/00-W	c1910-W	?-W	3/30-W	49B/220	GEC/EE	2	b	m	m	6/56
982	RME	12/00-W	c1910-W	?-W	11/30-W	?	MV/MV	2	b	m	m	11/53
983	RMX	12/00-W	c1904-Y	?-Y	9/29-W	WIT	GEC/EE	1	tl	b	b	9/54
984	RMX	12/00-W	→	c1911-W	8/30-G	49B/323V	GEC/EE	2	x	t	t	10/52
985	RME	12/00-W	c1910-Y	9/24-Y	11/30-Y	49B	GEC/EE	2	bl	l	l	2/49
986	RMXE	12/00-Y	4/11-Y	?-Y	10/29-Y	?	GEC/EE	2	b	b	b	3/58
987(i)	RM	12/00-?	c1904-W	—	—	?	—	1	—	—	—	1/16
987(ii)	HLI	—	—	8/19-B	2/30-B	?	MV/MV	2	lx	d	d	5/59
988	RMX	12/00-B	5/10-B	12/22-B	9/29-B	49B	GEC/EE	2	lp	x	x	12/59
989	RM	12/00-Y	10/09-Y	?/Y	10/30-YS	?	MV/MV	2	bl	l	t	7/53
990	RMX	12/00-W	c1910-W	?-W	12/29-W	?	GEC/EE	2	m	p	p	4/54
991	RM	12/00-Y	c1904-G	9/24-G	11/30-W	49B	GEC/EE	1	tp	m	m	2/54
992	RMI	1/01WB	→	8/11-B	8/30-B	?	MV/MV	2	x	d	d	11/59
993	RMXU	1/01-Y	c1904-YR	10/22-R	8/29-RS	49B	GEC/EE	2	tp	m	m	3/54
994	RMX	1/01-?	12/04-W	6/21-W	11/29-W	?/220	GEC/EE	1	b	b	b	3/58
995	RMXO	1/01-W	c1910-W	12/22-W	7/30-R	?/323V	GEC/EE	2	b	x	x	6/57
996	RM	1/01-Y	c1910-Y	12/22-Y	12/30-Y	49B	GEC/EE	2	b	b	b	7/56
997	RM	1/01-G	c1910-G	7/24-G	11/30-G	49B	GEC/EE	2	lk	l	l	12/54
998	RMX	1/01-R	c1910-R	6/22-R	11/29-R	49B	GEC/EE	2	x	d	d	11/53
999	RMX	1/01-Y	c1910-Y	?-Y	2/30-W	49B	GEC/EE	2	b	m	m	3/58
1000	RMX	1/01-?	c1904-R	?-R	11/29-R	49B	MV/MV	1	td	m	m	9/53
1001?	See under 337											
1039	HET	—	—	5/24-B	1/29-G	323V	EE/EE	2	n	d	d	6/59
1040	HI	—	—	3/24-B	4/29-G	323V	MV/MV	2	r	t	t	10/59
1050	H	—	—	4/24-B	5/30-Y	323V	MV/MV	2	r	b	b	6/60
1051	HLI	—	—	5/24-B	5/30-Y	323V	MV/MV	2	r	b	b	6/61
1088	HX	—	—	6/24-B	1/33-B	323V	EE/EE	2	r	d	d	*

* 1088 preserved Glasgow Museum of Transport, see below. Finally withdrawn 6/61.

Certain Preserved Standard cars have had trucks, motors and controllers altered to provide equipment in optimum condition for museum purposes. Thus:—

22		W			MV/MV	Truck with Hoffman Bearings
488		—	S		MV/EE	Truck with Bock Bearings
585		—	B		MV/EE	Truck with Hoffman Bearings
812		—	Y		MV/MV	Truck with Skefko Bearings
1088		—	B		EE/EE	Truck with R & M Bearings

Rebuilt Standard Cars

Car Number	Code	Phase I	Phase II	Phase III	Phase IV	Pre-Modernised Motors	Modernised Motor/ Controller	Top Cover	Depots 1920s	1935	1943	Scrap
27	HFI	—	—	—	2/49-R	—	MV/MV	2	—	—	(I)	11/60
143	HF	—	—	—	2/44-S	—	McF/MV	2	—	—	(I)	4/59
334	HF	—	—	—	5/46-S	—	MV/MV	2	—	—	(I)	11/59
409	HF	—	—	—	8/46-S	—	MV/MV	2	—	—	(I)	2/59
643	RMF	—	—	—	11/47-R	—	GEC/EE	2	—	—	(I)	6/59
679	HFI	—	—	—	6/43-S	—	MV/MV	2	—	—	I	4/58

Cars indicated 'I' had flush sides removed when bodywork strengthened
Car 643 not provided with flush side panels when rebuilt
(Car 166 overturned and was returned to service completely unaltered, it is therefore not included)

Single Deck Standard Cars (Cut down from semi-high speed double deckers)

Car Number	Code	Phase I	Phase II	Phase III	Phase IV	Pre-Modernised Motors	Modernised Motor/ Controller	Top Cover	Depots 1920s	1935	1943	Scrap
821	RMSOB	—	—	—	5/39-S	—	323V/DK	nil	—	—	t	1/50
836	RMSOB	—	—	—	8/39-S	—	323V/DK	nil	—	—	t	1/50
923	RMSOB	—	—	—	10/39-S	—	323V/DK	nil	—	—	t	1/50
926	RMSOB	—	—	—	6/39-S	—	323V/DK	nil	—	—	t	1/50
975	RMSOB	—	—	—	8/39-S	—	323V/DK	nil	—	—	t	1/50

By the mid-1930s very few glass ventilator cars remained with white route livery. 725 was typical of the Monitor roof cars which operated the Mosspark-University service from Newlands or Maryhill Depots. Most of their white trams were maintained in immaculate condition. *T. & R. Annan*

Schedule and Summary of Cars used for Experimentation or Deviations from Standard Specification Coded 'E' in Fleet Table

2 MV Sample Pantograph until 16/2/33
7 Retained wooden seating initially after conversion to Phase IV
11 Coronation Mark I pattern headlamps 25/3/39
12 First car with platform draught excluders 1/5/33
13 1925/27 Experiments: Brill truck WH323V motors, 26c magnets, no air brakes, SKF Roller Bearings
15 1925/27 Experiments: To service (Govan) 10/7/26, Brill 39E1 reversed maximum traction bogies, MV101BR motors, 25B magnets, WH air brakes and air cushion seats for 23 + 38.
16 1925/27 Experiments: EMB 10'-0" wb Pivotal truck, to service (Govan) 1/5/26, BT-H 502cs motors, 25B magnets, no air brakes initially but later fitted.
EMB Swing Axle 8'-6" wb truck ex-750, 4/3/40, off 1956. Canopy bend not reprofiled over platform steps.
17 1925/27 Experiments: Brill 79E-2 'Birney' Safety truck, 8'-0" wb. To service (Govan) 13/9/26 with MV101BR motors, 25B magnets. Removed 27/5/29.
18 1925/27 Experiments: Brill 21E truck with MV104A motors and swing link axle boxes, no air brakes. To service (Govan) 26/1/27. Removed 8/4/29.
19 1925/27 Experiments: Kilmarnock Eng. Radial truck 10'-0" wb. To service (Govan) 5/2/27 with Dick, Kerr T.84BP motors, 25B magnets. Peters air brakes and round top seats.
21 1925/27 Experiments: Standard truck and equipment but with sample set of Hoffman roller bearing axle boxes 3/10/27. To car 103 and later 867.
24 Stainless steel seat handles, door handles and handrails 10/12/30.
30 Early experiments with carbon bow collectors.
31 Platform covered with Flintkope 14/5/31.
40 Experiments with Cellotex lining 28/5/36.
45 Experimental operation with bow collector, Shields Road Service 1926/27.
46 Ditto.
48 Ditto, using bow collector with one supporting arm.
61 Experimental operation with bow collector, green car, 24/10/28.
62 Prototype car, 9/51 for upper saloon ventilation improvements and new painting style with cream paint.
63 Sample pantogaph fitted until 16/2/33.
71 Fitted with electroplated commode handles 19/12/38.
78 New top deck fitted following blitz damage 1941.
91 Upper saloon bulkheads removed, staircase partitions fitted 24/10/29 ('Baillie Dollan's Car').
97 Truck used to provide Maley & Taunton 8'-6" equivalent which was described as 'reconditioned' prior to fitting to 1001.
103 Prototype Phase IV car. Canopy bend not reprofiled over platform steps. 3-pass balcony seating fitted with backs.
104 Fitted with Westinghouse self-graduated interlocked air brake until 1950. (pedestal-mounted)
112 New teak roof fitted 27/6/30. MV104A motors 29/3/29.
113 Occupied/vacant seat indicator for upper saloon fitted until 30/1/44.
123 Sample Fischer Pantograph fitted 17/3/30.
126 Sample MV Pantograph fitted 16/2/33.
131 Fitted with run-back brake 20/4/42.
135 Fitted with india-rubber pads instead of axle box springs 1/49.
137 Experimental Passenger Flow Front-Exit car 18/12/14 until 5/7/30.
139 First car with driver's seat 8/1/31.
142 Converted to Maximum Traction Hurst Nelson bogies 4/4/27.
144 Early experiments with 40 hp motors 8/6/16, GE200
148 Early experiments with 40 hp motors 8/6/16, WH220
144 and 148 both for Shields Road Service
158 Fitted with destination box under stairs 3/8/39.
Fitted with glass substitute on all saloon 5/42.
159 Fitted with Peckham P35 8'-0" wb truck with Hoffman Roller Bearing axle boxes 21/4/27 with MV101BR motors until 8/7/31. Top deck vestibules added 30/5/27. Canopy bend not reprofiled over platform step.
160 First car with motorman's overhead rear observation mirror 15/8/33
168 Fitted with bus type head and tail lamps 16/4/43
189 Fitted with Indoroleum flooring 7/5/27
193 Lower saloon handrail brackets nickel plated 7/11/49
215 Streamlined (green) livery and enlarged headcode number box 6/6/36
223 Repainted with cadmium instead of red route colour until 27/6/49
234 Lower saloon handrail brackets nickel plated 7/11/49
247 Lifeguard side-gates to step-side of platforms 23/1/25
256 Fitted with non-slip platform step 1/8/29
262 Mountain & Gibson-Warner non-parallel axle truck at Phase III
263 Re-wired 4 lamps in series, with dash tail lights c1945
268 Fitted with electro-plated commode handles 19/12/28
273 Lower saloon bulkhead window shutters removed, green glass substituted 2/10/32
288 Painted wartime all-over grey 5/3/42
292 Pattern car with roller blind service number in top vestibules 1/9/38
300 Trafficators, semaphore arm pattern 21/10/32
305 Electropneumatic remote control (Regen) 4/11/33 until 8/34. Line voltage
310 Whipple power operated windscreen wipers 28/8/35
325 Brush Flexible (Peckham) truck, Phase III
337 Top deck with opening roof, Phase II
349 Mountain & Gibson 21EM truck replaced with

The whole of Parliamentary Road at Castle Street has been razed and redeveloped. In 1957 the buildings at this spot were already derelict. 621 stops to pick up a passenger on circular service 33 while a Cunarder heads for Millerston. An Alexander's bus waits impatiently having been thwarted in an attempt to overtake on the offside. *W.D. McMillan*

In 1956 the Maximum Traction cars were (officially) not to receive full overhauls. However, cars like 602 nearly three decades older were still being given the full treatment. It is a pity that the lower destination screen was not renewed at the time.! *W.D. McMillan*

The side elevation of the 'Unobtrusive' Standard Cars was not their most attractive. This shows the first pattern with side windows which could be let into the upper side panelling with height adjustment via leather straps. The car is 470. *Drawing: Author*

The intermediate livery style can be seen in this illustration of yellow car 97. It was introduced by General Manager R.F. Smith eliminating the cream rockers or concave panels and all Greek corner pattern detailing. Note the initial retention of the slip board brackets although disused after 1938. *Drawing: Author.*

By 1914, late open-topper 299 had already been modernised to Phase III condition while 343, built as a Phase II car, remains as constructed. World War I was soon to put a stop to any further upgrading work. ***Strathclyde Regional Archives***

Preston Compensating truck 5/09
354 E.E. Pantograph 18/10/33
383 New top deck 22/4/43 with anemostat roof ventilators
384 Droplight windows, lower saloon 19/9/34. Upper deck 12/10/34
390 Special carbon bow collector for Shields Road service 10/10/40
395 Fischer pantograph 2/8/33
397 Prototype Phase III conversion from Phase II
403 Anti-freeze device for air braking system c1930
413 EMB Swing Axle 8'-6" wb truck 4/10/34. Returned to EMB for reconditioning 23/12/38 and returned for fitting to 1003
415 Fischer pantograph 22/11/33
419 Fischer pantograph 1/8/33
421 EMB Trico windscreen wipers 15/1/36
429 EE pantograph 19/10/33
438 Precursor Phase II car, opening roof. Brush radial, then Mountain & Gibson radial truck 3/08
439 Precursor Phase II Car but with reversed stairs
448 Anti-galloping device 2/3/27
451 Streamlined (red) livery 15/8/36 until 3/8/38
452 Cork tiling 16/5/31 until 17/3/34
458 Trafficator 21/3/36
491 Experimental route number box c1936
513 Folding shutter on platforms 12/12/37
532 MV107 worm drive motors 1930-34. Motorman's seat 18/3/32
536 MV107 worm drive motors 1930-34.
550 Bow collector lubricator 14/6/33 until 14/6/34
578 White Lincrusta ceiling in lower saloon at Phase IV
584 Fitted with twin aspect day and night illuminated route colour indicators 17/5/40. Removed due to Police objection. Fitted c1940 with new LPTB headlamp and emergency light fittings working off 6 volt battery circuit
585 Fitted with India rubber pads instead of axle box springs 1/49
588 Air operated windscreen wipers 12/11/33
589 Pattern car 30/11/31 for special slip-board lighting in vestibule
591 Brass stanchions mid-way along lower saloon, Phases I-III
595 Platform cork tiling 25/3/31
660 Fitted with India-rubber pads instead of axle box springs 1/49
665(III) Brush Peckham Pendulum (P22) truck fitted 8/1/24
679 Fitted with Hutchison's Bow Collector c1940
683 Fitted with Sievewright & Bacon Pantograph 14/6/33 until 28/6/33
697 Whipple electric windscreen wipers 24/8/33. Special bow collector 3/41
698 Converted from Regenerative control to Maley & Taunton field control with watt meter 25/8/39 until 25/8/42
702 EMB Swing Axle 8'-6" wb truck 30/5/35. Off 1956

705 Fitted with two brass stanchions from seat bases to lower saloon ceilings at Phases II & III
713 Truck as 702, 13/6/35. Removed 25/10/41 with broken axle bearings. No replacements in stock. Truck cannibalised
719 Experimental louvred ventilators 22/12/27
723 Alhambrinal panels to roof 30/4/34 until 5/8/37
726 Brown dash panels with yellow numbers at Phase II
750 Truck as 702, 16/5/35. To car 16, 4/3/40
751 Truck as 702, 6/6/35. Off 1956
770 Extended canopies and reversed stairs 19/4/00 at Phase I
778 Fitted with anti-tail wagging device 15/1/27
779 Truck as 702, 31/5/35. Off 27/11/56
782 Perforated zinc shields over hopper ventilators in type 1 top deck 23/1/25
786 Hurst Nelson 21E pattern truck transferred to this car ex-Elderslie 4/12/30. Off 23/11/35
790 Truck as 702 6/6/35. Off 17/1/57 on acquiring standard truck ex-44
797 Truck as 702 23/5/35. Off 14/12/56 on acquiring standard truck ex-7
804 Brown dash with aluminium numbers at Phase II after repaint from Standard livery
807 First Regenerative braking car 15/12/34
818 Pattern car from Phase II. Dashes to upper deck and livery styling non-standard.
843 Special sample BT-H type 502 motors until 24/9/25
847 GE KH8 Oerlikon controllers 21/9/36
855 Alhambrinal panelling to lower saloon sides 23/5/34
867 Sample Hoffman roller bearing axle boxes ex-21, fitted to Semi-High Speed car.
877 Fitted with India-rubber pads instead of axle box springs 1/49
881 Truck as 702, fitted 1/6/35. Off 12/11/56
888 Brown dashes with yellow numbers, Phase II
889 Truck as 702, fitted 13/6/35, Off 1956
906 Fitted with India-rubber pads instead of axle box springs 1/49
920 Bow collector fitted for testing bridge under canal at Maryhill 5/5/31
922 Acquired experimental semi-high speed motors, GE200, 23/11/35
954 Acquired experimental semi-high speed motors, MV104, 7/2/31
960 Lower saloon strengthened and flush panelled 20/6/46
965 Acquired experimental semi-high speed motors, Brown-Boveri, 29/11/35 (transferred to car 687, 5/2/48)
973 Flush panelled lower saloon sides 3/46
982 External water rail from top deck roof 28/12/32
985 Pantograph fitted 29/5/44 until 3/6/44. Bow collector re-installed
986 Fitted with India rubber pads instead of axle box springs 1/49
994 Louvre ventilators 9/5/28
1039 Numa air bells 20/8/24

With varnish peeling from its upper panels and the top deck drooping visibly over the rear platform, 471 could only have operated from Dalmarnock Depot-not renowned for the pristine condition of its fleet, even in 1956. ***Parr/STMS Collection***

CHAPTER 4

The Ex~Paisley District Tramcars 1001~1072

THE EX-PAISLEY TRAMCARS: 1001-1072

The acquisition of the Paisley District Tramways Company on 1st August 1923 by GCT increased the Glasgow fleet by 73 trams. The Glasgow stock was numbered neatly between 1 and 1000; the few remaining gaps were being filled by the last of the Standard trams then under construction. The ex-Paisley fleet was conveniently renumbered from 1001 upwards by adding 1000 to the original number of each car.

The Paisley fleet comprised BEC-(cars 1-40) or Brush-(41-49) built trams. There is some doubt as to the extent of the Brush involvement in the last nine cars as the order had originally been placed with BEC for the entire batch. These were the original stock, followed by two works cars 50 and 51. Then there was 52, constructed as, was 51, by Hurst Nelson Ltd. These were the two trams driven in the course of delivery in that famous continuous run from Motherwell to Elderslie Depot. 53-72 were larger, though still open top, vehicles known as the LCC type—logically, for they had LCC 'M' class saloons, even to having certain brass castings stamped 'LCCT'. 53-62 were built by Brush and 63-72 by Hurst Nelson. 53-58 were the second bearers of these numbers. The first had been open balcony low height cars with Hurst Nelson swing bolster trucks apparently unsuited to the Paisley track. They had been sold to Dundee Corporation Tramways. Only car 52 was top covered on acquisition by GCT and this feature had been added in 1910. The top cover, like those sold, was of the LCC pattern but for the open balconies and the Glasgow style of short balcony roof. All cars had three windowed saloons and none were vestibuled. 68-72 were very late examples of such basic construction. The last car to be acquired was ex-Sheffield Corporation single decker No. 202, built in 1903 and sold to the Paisley Company in 1920. The car sat 28 passengers and was mounted on a Peckham truck regauged by Sheffield Corporation Tramways for the Paisley system and fitted with GE 52 motors.

It is thought that this car had been purchased with a view to its operation on the Abbotsinch service but it does not seem to have been numbered nor used in Paisley. It was certainly not given a fleet number nor used by Glasgow. The only reference to it is the disposal of the Peckham truck in 1926 and the body in 1928.

1002 was one of the original BEC cars to be rebuilt by the Paisley District Tramways prior to acquisition by G.C.T. This photograph was taken at Kilbarchan terminus in 1932 on the last day of the service. The car has green upper deck decency panels.
STMS Collection

At the time of acquisition, cars 1-50 had Brush trucks with British Thomson-Houston GE 58 motors. 51 and 52 also had these motors but with Hurst Nelson 21E-style trucks. The Paisley Company had rebuilt cars 1-8 and they were evidently in very good condition but the same could not be said about the remainder of the original cars, some of which were reported as being in very bad shape and in need of extensive imminent repair.

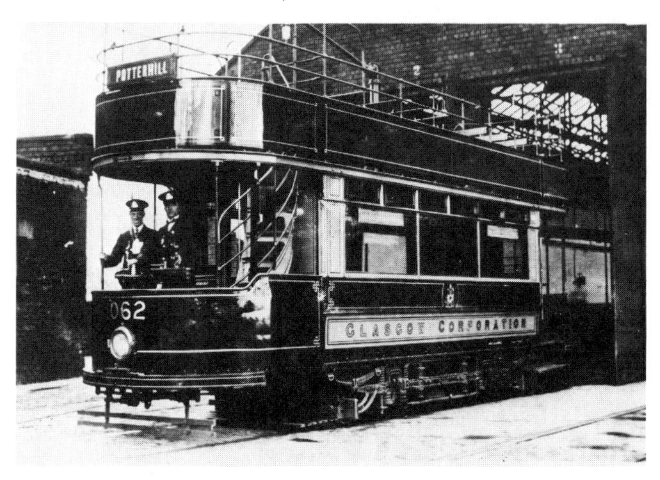

The first alterations carried out to ex-Paisley District 'LCC' class trams were to fit driver's mirrors and paint them in G.C.T. livery. The route colour on 1062 is blue. The lining out on these cars departed from normal practice in a number of details.
STMS Collection

Brush cars 53-62 were in very good order and condition and their substantial steel underframes drew favourable comment in the GCT General Manager's report on the Paisley Rolling Stock. These cars also employed GE 58 motors. The Hurst Nelson cars were to a very similar specification differing in the height and profile of the top deck sides and railings and also in the use of GE 200 motors. These cars were virtually new when inspected by Glasgow staff and due credit for this was given. The Sheffield car, however, was only rated 'in fair order'.

The small open top cars 1-49 were not really suitable for city use although applicable to Paisley services. If fitted with Glasgow Standard top covers they would not have passed beneath bridges in Barrhead and Elderslie. Some were extensively rebuilt to single deck with hexagonal dashes designed to accept Standard car vestibules. Their place was taken by ex-Airdrie & Coatbridge cars whose system had, by this time, been connected to Glasgow metals. The single-deckers were provided with air brakes for use on the Kilbowie Road service from Clydebank to Duntocher, the first section of which opened with these cars in 1924. No cars from the batch 1-8 were selected as these did not by this time need any rebuilding.

Originally there were to have been eight conversions to single deck. By December 1923 four were ready and had been tested. The only problem soon encountered in service apparently related to the continual pumping of the compressor as the air brakes checked speed on the continual descents into Clydebank. This was cured by installing larger reservoirs. On 20th December, Mr. Dalrymple had caused some consternation by decreeing that the eight Duntocher cars—designed for crew operation—should be converted for one man working. This meant altering the nearly completed four by reversing the dashes, providing nearside front entrance/exits with doors and folding platform steps and re-siting

1013 (ex-Paisley 13) was converted to One-Man Operation for the Clydebank-Duntocher service in 1924, one of four proposed for such treatment. It only ran for a short time in this guise, having had its rebuilding as a crew operated car altered midstream only to be changed back again. The continental bow collector is of interest. A close-up of the platform is shown below.
STMS Collection

the compressors and reservoirs to the offside. It is not known how many of the existing conversions were further altered (possibly, three) or indeed if any were rebuilt direct to one man operation. At least 1013 was completed to be featured in trade advertising with continental-style bow collector. A cryptic note in Drawing Office records states: 'These cars were changed back to two-man operation after running for a period'. A further batch of eight two man cars followed shortly afterwards. All were fitted with 'run-back' brakes.

The single deckers retained the Brush 'A-A' trucks of 6'-6" wheelbase and the GE 58 motors. However the controllers became English Electric DK type. In this form they made useful driver training cars and 1014 was thus used in this way to release Standard car 729 for passenger duties. Then 1017 was specially converted to single deck with narrow platform doors and most of the bulkheads removed to provide visibility for onlookers assessing and learning driving techniques. Wooden transverse seats for 18 were fitted in this conversion which was completed in January 1925. In this role the car was fitted out with a variety of controllers including the 90 and B18. Motors varied from GE 58 to MV 104A and 1017 was stabled at Langside until later years when Coplawhill became its home. The Duntocher single deckers were shedded at Partick and these, with 1017, were

The Duntocher single deckers rarely strayed from their Clydebank home except to travel to Partick Depot or the Carworks. It took the efforts of the Luftwaffe to put them to use in city service when Kilbowie Road was severed by bomb craters in 1941. 1022 is seen at Duntocher in 1936. W. Fisher, Courtesy D. W. Fisher

The standardised platform arrangement for the crew-operated Duntocher car can be seen on this view of 1037. Note the rheostat situated adjacent to the compressor over which a seat for two passengers is located. The air brake controls are situated to the right of the controller. These cars all acquired a central grab-rail at the platform edge. G.C.T.

equipped with standard bow collectors in 1933. Those on the passenger cars had specially long arms to enable them to negotiate the low bridge in Kilbowie Road.

Another conversion centred around 1008 in December 1934 when it went from open top condition to become the 'Kelvin Hall' decorated car. A large box-like structure looking like an overpanelled saloon was applied to the top deck and the staircases removed. In this way 1008 could carry purpose-made hoardings and will be best remembered with its World War II slogans if not as previously disguised. The car was scrapped in 1949 after it sustained extensive damage in the Newlands Depot fire.

Seven other BEC cars were converted to become Tool Cars Nos. 26-33 in the Works fleet. These conversions were undertaken during 1933-34 and the cars ran initially without vestibules. Paisley cars 39 and 40 were never given Glasgow stock numbers but were set aside for conversion to Works fleet use. 39 became Tool Van No. 20 for the Mains Department in February 1925. 40—actually listed as 'scrapped' in March 1924—was used to construct No. 25, a mineral wagon, although little more than the truck, underframe and running gear could have survived from the original tram. Of the remaining 'small' cars, some had been given top deck railings of increased height at the ends to afford protection to passengers in the event of broken trolley springs. Most cars treated in this way were in the batch 1-8 built by the Paisley Company before acquisition. All were given 'green' route colour bands and operated in the Paisley territory. When buses took over their normal services on the Kilbarchan route in 1932, some cars ended their days conveying Permanent Way Engineering staff while others became 'Sleeping Cars' for the PW Staff. The last to be scrapped was 1029 in May 1938, quite definitely the last open topper in Glasgow.

1052 was also painted with a green route colour band. In 1927 it had been equipped with a Brush 21E pattern truck displacing its latter day Hurst Nelson 6'-6" wheelbase equivalent. At the same time the GE 58 motors were removed and substituted with Westinghouse 49B units. 1052 was scrapped in 1933.

1053-1072 were dimensionally compatible with the Glasgow Standard car. In fact they were slightly longer despite having three window saloons for they had the double corner pillar feature found in the LCC E1 and M class trams. Their very strong steel under-framing and recent vintage made them obvious candidates for adaptation to City use. But first they were repainted in Glasgow style with 'blue' route bands before being taken to Coplawhill for upgrading to Phase III Standard car specification. The original trucks were replaced with Brill 21E equipment with 7'-0" wheelbase and 45 hp motors by the same manufacturers as were standard at the time. Standard top covers of the second pattern were married to the LCC design of lower saloon. Cabin vestibules were also fitted together with roll-top storm shutters over the staircases. The blue route colours were retained and the batch transferred to Renfrew Depot except 1066—the first conversion— which became a 'green' car and was soon transferred to Partick.

The 'Standardising' process was evidently deemed successful for these cars also became involved in the modernising to Phase IV like the true Standard cars.

Their relative lateness in being further upgraded was due to their being blue cars: the greens and then the reds were generally dealt with first. Each car received the full treatment—8'-0" wheelbase Brush-GCT truck of 21E pattern with roller bearing axle boxes, high speed 60 hp motors, heaters, air brakes, improved lighting, upholstered seating and enclosure of the balconies. One retained blue and all the other route colours were represented in the class. Eleven were further modified at the time by having 6" sliced off the foot of the upper deck pillars, panelling and dash-plates to produce extra low height cars which retained Standard car glass sizes for the window frames. These cars were intended to operate on the open-topped tram services to Kilbarchan and were indeed tried on this single track with passing loop section beyond Johnstone. (The low bridge was located just beyond the depot). The eleven cars were given distinguishing 'red' route colours. Unfortunately the longer wheelbase trucks could not negotiate the passing loops and the open top cars continued to operate the service through to Kilbarchan until replaced by Corporation buses in May 1932. Three of the low height cars became green and were transferred to Parkhead Depot while the others remained at Elderslie where they operated Paisley local services, still 'red'.

The normal height cars were dispersed around the system and the style of lining on all the cars differed in detail treatment in the lower panels from the Glasgow Standard car. Much was left to the paintshop manager's judgement and Elderslie Depot—with its own paintshop—turned out its own variations from time to time.

All of the 'LCC' class of ex-Paisley cars except 1066 were painted with blue upper deck panelling for the Paisley-Barrhead services. 1060 later had the top deck height reduced by 6" when modernised from Phase III to Phase IV. ***STMS Collection***

Service number roller blinds were not fitted to the ex-Paisleys until some time after the 1939-45 War and, even then, many of the cars operated in Paisley did so without blinds, but with boards inserted into the number box apertures. There was a gradual dispersal from city depots back to Elderslie by 1949-50 which was not completed for the first—1066 was scrapped in 1949, giving up its truck to car 904 which then completed its three-stage modernisation. By this time these ex-Paisley Standards were scheduled for early withdrawal and by 1953 only 1062, 1068 and 1069 remained. 1068 was set aside and used for shunting duties at Elderslie pending a preservation bid by the Scottish Tramway Museum Society. When Elderslie closed in 1957, 1068 was noted by the author being towed to Dalmarnock for storage and, when presented to the STMS, arrangements were made for its transfer to the Tramway Museum at Crich, Derbyshire where it arrived in September 1960. There 1068 has become 68 once more as a Paisley open-top car and has been rebuilt for passenger service under a Manpower Services Commission Job Creation Scheme.

Ex-Paisley car No. 17 was converted from open top Glasgow 1017 to become a purpose-made School Car for training motormen in 1925. Stabled at Langside Depot for many years, it was generally to be seen plying up and down Coplaw Street alongside the Samaritan Hospital. This single track section was unused by normal services. ***R. J. S. Wiseman***

An ex-Paisley car at Paisley Cross, 1054, although originally with red route colour, was one of those painted bus green pre-1940. The low-height top cover was provided on eleven of these cars. ***Dr. Hugh Nicol***

Paisley No.	GCT No.	Built	Rebuilding (GCT) Phase 3	Phase 4	Duntocher	Colours 1927	1934	Code	Depots 1927	1943	Ultimate Truck/Motors/CTR	Withdrawn /Scrap
1	1001	1904	—	—	—	G	G	O/T PWE	e	—	Brush/GE58/B18	9/35
2	1002	1904	—	—	—	G	G	PW32(T)	e	—	Brush/GE58/B18	9/34*
3	1003	1904	—	—	—	G	—	PW28(T)	e	—	Brush/GE58/B18	11/33*
4	1004	1904	—	—	—	G	G	PW31(T)	e	—	21E/WH49B/B18	9/34*
5	1005	1904	—	—	—	G	—	PW27(T)	e	—	21E/WH49B/B18	2/33*
6	1006	1904	—	—	—	G	G	O/T	e	—	Brush/GE58/B18	9/34
7	1007	1904	—	—	—	G	—	PW29(T)	e	—	Brush/GE58/B18	4/34*
8	1008	1904	—	—	—	G	G	Illum	t	n	Brush/GE58/B18	12/34*
9	1009	1904	—	—	c1924				t	t	Brush/GE58/B18	5/49
10	1010	1904	—	—	c1924				t		Brush/GE58/B18	9/39
11	1011	1904	—	—	1/25				t	t	Brush/GE58/B18	1/50
12	1012	1904	—	—	2/25				t	t	Brush/GE58/B18	2/50
13	1013	1904	—	—	c1924			OMO	t	t	Brush/GE58/B18	5/49
14	1014	1904	—	—	c1924			Sch (1)	t	—	Brush/GE58/B18	6/39
15	1015	1904	—	—	1/25				t	t	Brush/GE58/B18	5/49
16	1016	1904	—	—	c1924				t	t	Brush/GE58/B18	2/50
17	1017	1904	—	—	1/25			Sch (2)	b	Works	Brush/GE58/B18	8/60
18	1018	1904	—	—	12/24				t	t	Brush/GE58/B18	1/50
19	1019	1904	—	—	9/24				t	t	Brush/GE58/B18	3/50
20	1020	1904	—	—	—	G	—	O/T	e	—	21E/WH49B/B18	1/31
21	1021	1904	—	—	—	G	—	PW26(T)	e	—	Brush/GE58/B18	3/33*
22	1022	1904	—	—	c1924				t	t	Brush/GE58/B18	1/50
23	1023	1904	—	—	2/24				t	t	Brush/GE58/B18	1/50
24	1024	1904	—	—	c1924				t	t	Brush/GE58/B18	1/50
25	1025	1904	—	—	—	G	—	O/T	e	—	Brush/GE58/B18	1/32
26	1026	1904	—	—	—	G	G	PW30(T)	e	—	Brush/GE58/B18	8/34*
27	1027	1904	—	—	c1924				t	—	Brush/GE58/B18	8/39
28	1028	1904	—	—	—	G	G	O/T	e	—	Brush/GE58/B18	5/35
29	1029	1904	—	—	—	G	G	O/T/PWE	e	—	Brush/GE58/B18	5/38
30	1030	1904	—	—	—	G	—	O/T	e	—	Brush/GE58/B18	5/33
31	1031	1904	—	—	—	G	—	O/T	e	—	Brush/GE58/B18	2/32
32	1032	1904	—	—	—	G	—	O/T	e	—	Brush/GE58/B18	3/32
33	1033	1904	—	—	—	G	—	O/T	e	—	Brush/GE58/B18	3/32
34	1034	1904	—	—	—	G	—	O/T/PWE	e	—	Brush/GE58/B18	3/35
35	1035	1904	—	—	—	G	G	O/T	e	—	Brush/GE58/B18	8/32
36	1036	1904	—	—	—	G	—	O/T	e	—	Brush/GE58/B18	5/33
37	1037	1904	—	—	c1924				t	—	Brush/GE58/B18	7/39
38	1038	1904	—	—	c1924				t	—	Brush/GE58/B18	8/39
39	—	1904	—	—	—	—	—	Mains 20(T)	—	—	Brush/GE58/B18	c1924
40	—	1904	—	—	—	—	—	PWD 25?	—	—	Brush/GE58/B18	c1924
41	1041	1905	—	—	—	G	G	O/T	e	—	Brush/GE58/B18	12/34
42	1042	1905	—	—	—	G	—	SL O/T	e	—	Brush/GE58/B18	5/33
43	1043	1905	—	—	—	G	G	O/T	e	—	Brush/GE58/B18	11/32
44	1044	1905	—	—	—	G	G	O/T/PWE	e	—	Brush/GE58/B18	8/34
45	1045	1905	—	—	—	G	—	O/T	e	—	Brush/GE58/B18	8/34
46	1046	1905	—	—	—	G	—	O/T	e	—	Brush/GE58/B18	11/33
47	1047	1905	—	—	—	G	G	O/T/PWE	e	—	Brush/GE58/B18	10/35
48	1048	1905	—	—	—	G	—	O/T	e	—	Brush/GE58/B18	11/32
49	1049	1905	—	—	—	G	—	O/T	e	—	Brush/GE58/B18	11/31
50	—	See under Permanent Way Vehicles										
51	—	See under Permanent Way Vehicles										
52	1052	1908	HNTC	—	—	G	—		e	—	Brush/WH49B/B18	8/33
53	1053	1915	1924	10/30	—	B	G	LH	r	e	2IE/MV/MV	3/52
54	1054	1915	1924	10/30	—	B	RS	LH	r	e	21E/MV/MV	9/51
55	1055	1915	1924	10/30	—	B	G	LH	r	e	21E/MV/MV	10/52
56	1056	1915	1924	10/30	—	B	RG	LH	r	k	21E/MV/MV	1/52
57	1057	1915	1924	10/30	—	B	G	LH	r	k	21E/MV/MV	11/52
58	1058	1915	1924	4/31	—	B	W		r	m	21E/GEC/EE	3/52
59	1059	1912	1924	4/31	—	B	W		r	m	21E/GEC/EE	5/52
60	1060	1912	1924	10/30	—	B	R	LH	r	e	21E/GEC/EE	9/51

N.B. Paisley Nos. 39 & 40 not allocated GCT numbers

Cars 1-49 had seating for 55 passengers and were too tall accommodate top covers of the Glasgow Standard pattern.

* Refers to conversion dates

The Duntocher conversions were all scheduled for substitution by cut-down Standard cars c1939 but only five were scrapped at this time.

No enthusiasts' tour which included the Paisley services was complete without a visit to Elderslie Depot. The Depot visit was incomplete if 1068 was not driven out for photographers. This was the last surviving ex-Paisley District tram and had been set aside for the Scottish Tramway Museum Society. The tram is now operating at the National Tramway Museum minus its full-height Glasgow Standard top cover. It has reverted to open top as Paisley 68. This is c1956: note 1142, the tour car, on the left.

K. MacKay

Paisley No.	GCT No.	Built	Rebuilding (GCT) Phase 3	Phase 4	Duntocher	Colours 1927	1934	Code	Depots 1927	1943	Ultimate Truck/Motors/CTR	Withdrawn /Scrap
61	1061	1912	1924	4/31	—	B	W		r	p	21E/GEC/EE	5/51
62	1062	1912	1924	4/31	—	B	W		r	p	21E/GEC/EE	8/53
63	1063	1916	1924	10/30	—	B	R	LH	r	e	21E/GEC/EE	6/52
64	1064	1916	4/24	4/31	—	B	W		r	p	21E/GEC/EE	2/52
65	1065	1916	1924	11/30	—	B	R	LH	r	e	21E/GEC/EE	6/51
66	1066	1916	1924	10/30	—	G	R	LH	t	e	21E/MV/MV	5/49
67	1067	1916	1924	10/30	—	B	R	LH	r	e	21E/GEC/EE	9/51
68	1068	1919	6/24	5/31	—	B	BYS		r	l	21E/GEC/EE*	8/60
69	1069	1919	1924	5/31	—	B	W		r	p	21E/GEC/EE	5/53
70	1070	1919	1924	5/31	—	B	W		r	p	21E/GEC/EE	11/51
71	1071	1919	1924	5/31	—	B	W		r	p	21E/GEC/EE	11/51
72	1072	1919	1924	10/30	—	B	G	LH	r	k	21E/GEC/EE	5/51
—	—	1899 Ex-Sheffield s/d not numbered by P & D or GCT Peckham Truck sold by GCT and body scrapped										5/28

* 1068 despatched to Crich with MV101DR motors (truck ex-751)

Codes:

O/T =	Remained open top
PWE	used for permanent way employees transport (1933)
PW—(T) =	To works use, for details see under that section (T) = Tool Car
Illum =	Converted to Illuminated Car
OMO =	One Man Operated Car, 1924, to Standard Duntocher
Sch (1) =	First School Car for Driver Training
Sch (2) =	Second School Car for Driver Training Stabled at 'b'
LH =	Low Height Top Deck (Reduced by 6" in height at Phase IV)
SL =	Used as Sleeping Car for PW employees
HNTC =	Hurst Nelson Balcony Top Cover (1910)
21E =	21E pattern GCT/Brush Truck (Cars 1053-1072 only)

A marriage of giants: take a London County Council Tramways lower saloon, surmount this with a Glasgow Corporation Tramways top cover and you have an ex-Paisley District 'Standard' car. Both 1060 and 1066 are of the low height pattern. This class was selected for low bridge use as the lower saloon was also lower than standard in Glasgow. *R. R. Clark/STMS Collection*

CHAPTER 5

The Ex-Airdrie & Coatbridge Tramcars 1073-1087

THE EX-AIRDRIE & COATBRIDGE TRAMCARS: 1073-1087

The Airdrie & Coatbridge fleet had comprised fifteen Brush built tramcars. Twelve were open topped seating 56 passengers and had four window saloons. The other three had balcony top covers and seating for 58. They also had four window saloons and matching top covers. The original cars entered service in 1902, while the top covered examples followed three years later. When the system was acquired by GCT, it was physically isolated. After connection to the Glasgow metals, it was closed for upgrading before being interworked by Glasgow Standard cars.

The original Airdrie vehicles were put into GCT colours immediately and logically should have been renumbered from 1001. Being smaller than the Glasgow Standard, they were despatched to Elderslie Depot. Some stopped briefly at Parkhead. Paisley was the only user of small capacity double deckers. The Airdrie fleet conveniently filled the gap caused by the despatch of these ex-Paisley trams to Coplawhill required for fitting with top covers or conversion to single deck for the Duntocher service. Their use of swivel-head trolleys matched the practice adopted in Paisley.

This view of what became 1086 shows the detail which would not be expected in a commercial postcard. STMS Collection

The Airdrie trams were painted with green route bands and used on the service from Renfrew Ferry to Kilbarchan which, at the time, was the only route unsuitable for any of the then Phase III double deckers. The livery applied to the trams was standard except in the use of smaller fleet numbers. This was due to the lack of space for the application of normal transfers above the headlamp on the dash panels. It seems possible that they were not renumbered until transfer to Glasgow depots. It would have been more convenient to undertake renumbering completely of these fifteen cars than the 72 ex-Paisley vehicles acquired later.

Particular details of these trams can be found in the Fleet Tables. It will be seen that most were scrapped upon cessation of tramway services to Kilbarchan and their replacement by Corporation buses in 1932. 1073 became a decorated car in 1927 while 1076 had become an overhead inspection tower bearing the stock number 'No. 24' in the Works fleet numbering series. Very few alterations were carried out on the others except for some truck changes to the top covered cars only, in 1927. All fifteen were listed for changes in the longitudinal seating from open to closed laths but it is doubtful if any were in fact thus treated.

For years it seemed that the ex-Airdrie & Coatbridge fleet had totally escaped the attention of the camera. At last the N.B. Traction group discovered this old commercial postcard view of Renfrew Town Hall with none other than 1085 passing by. N.B. Traction

Even the ex-Airdrie & Coatbridge open - toppers eluded the cameras although the one conversion to become a Decorated Car - 1073 - was snapped by the official photographer. Note the number of the 'house' - 1073 - above the door. G.C.T.

The paintshop at Coplawhill in June 1926 held two ex-Airdrie & Coatbridge trams including 1081 on the left as well as a Duntocher single decker. By this time the ex-Airdrie vehicles were operating in Paisley from Elderslie Depot. While no one would deny their right to be proud of the fruits of their labours, one can't help wishing the painters could have stepped to one side . . . STMS Collection

Airdrie No.	GCT No.	Built	Builder	Depot c1927	Colour c1927	Code	Withdrawn /Scrap	Remarks
1	1073	1902	Brush	e	G	O/T	12/1927	Converted to Decorated Car
2	1074	1902	Brush	e	G	O/T	3/1930	
3	1075	1902	Brush	e	G	O/T	3/1930	
4	1076	1902	Brush	e	G	O/T	2/1925	Became No. 24 in Works Fleet
5	1077	1902	Brush	e	G	O/T	1/1932	
6	1078	1902	Brush	e	G	O/T	12/1931	Brill 21E 7'-0" wb truck 1927 ex-142
7	1079	1902	Brush	e	G	O/T	12/1931	
8	1080	1902	Brush	e	G	O/T	1/1931	
9	1081	1902	Brush	e	G	O/T	8/1931	
10	1082	1902	Brush	e	G	O/T	1/1932	
11	1083	1902	Brush	e	G	O/T	4/1931	Rec'd GE58 motors ex-1087
12	1084	1902	Brush	e	G	O/T	4/1931	Rec'd Brill 21E truck and GE58 motors
13	1085	1905	Brush	e	G	T/C	8/1934	Rec'd Brill 21E truck and WH49B motors
14	1086	1905	Brush	e	G	T/C	8/1933	Rec'd Brill 21E truck and WH49B motors
15	1087	1905	Brush	e	G	T/C	5/1933	Rec'd Brill 21E truck and WH49B motors

O/T = Remained Open Top
T/C = Open Balcony Top Cover (when acquired)
Truck changes were in 1927
10 Brush motors displaced by WH 323V (5 cars involved)
Original motors were Brush 30 hp Type 1002
1073 scrapped as Decorated Car, 1/1935, replaced by 'No. 50', Works Fleet numbering series
The Brush motors were generally withdrawn in favour of GE58 or WH49B equivalent from 1925

150 entered service in October 1913 but still looked newly outshopped in Jamaica Street six months later. At that time standard cars had yet to acquire large ticket boxes. Bare feet were still the order of the day. *T. & R. Annan*

CHAPTER 6

The Experimental Single Decker 1089

EXPERIMENTAL SINGLE-DECKER No. 1089. 'BAILLIE BURT'S CAR'

'Object:

To provide a light swift vehicle and one with a higher standard of comfort than has been the practice in the past in Tramway Car Design in order to find out if such a vehicle would be able to win back the Department's traffic which has been lost to private bus concerns on the interurban runs.'

Such was the brief issued to the Tramway Department's drawing office designers for the High Speed Car on which design work commenced on 25th June 1925. This high speed car was to be 1089 which was despatched for service on 15th August 1926 and many were the alternatives which were considered before the design was complete. 1089 was the only brand new product during the experimental period dealt with in Chapter 3.

Original thoughts had centred round a four wheeled single decker mounted on a Brill 79Ex 2 truck. The tram would have had seating for 32 passengers and be 6'-10" wide. Motors would have been of MV104 pattern, chosen because of their small diameter. In the event 1089 emerged as a bogie car and a concession was wrought from the Ministry of Transport whereby the width was increased to 7'-2". The Brill 79Ex 2 truck was acquired but fitted to the body of car 17 and the MV104 motors installed in car 18. (*q.v.*)

Although 1089 is said to have been designed following a suggestion by Baillie Peter Burt, Transport Convener, he receives no credit for this in the official minutes. However, to this day, 1089 bears the Baillie's name and this may have been due to his frequent visits to the drawing office where he postulated various ideas—some adopted, like fully upholstered seating; others not, like a seated motorman and foot brake. The final specification for 1089 called for a high speed pullman style single decker bogie car with a steel framed body incorporating passenger flow via front exit and rear entrance.

J. G. Brill & Co. supplied two 77E1 bogies of 5'-4" wheelbase placed at 13'-0" centres and with 26" diameter wheels. Motors were by British Thomson-Houston, type BT-H 264A, there being four rated at 25 hp each. Controllers were Metropolitan Vickers Type T4A and the air brakes were operated from a Westinghouse DH16 compressor mounted between the bogies. The air cylinders and resistance were accommodated on the platforms adjacent to the controllers to leave clear access for passengers. The hexagonal dash body was straight sided with domed roof. Transverse and longitudinal seating for 36 passengers was supplied by G. D. Peters Ltd., and originally covered in green leather.

The car was despatched new to Newlands Depot and in August 1928 it was operated from Langside on the Sinclair Drive service. It was employed on this

The substantial construction of pullman single decker 1089 can be seen in this view of the car while being built at Coplawhill in 1926. The destination box aperature was designed to accommodate a standard screen box as then used on all open balcony cars.

G.C.T.

In its original form 1089 operated on the passenger flow principle but was unsuccessful–like all three such experiments by G.C.T. - because it was a single car in a standardised fleet. The body styling represents a transition from traditional to semi-modern appearance. This photograph was taken at Scotstounhill during the Tramways Committee Inspection. ***'Daily Record'***

service and around several other depots to train motormen on air brakes in advance of the general equipping of the Standard Cars with this modification. June 1929 saw 'temporary' transfer to Partick Depot until September 1929 when Parkhead played host. In April 1930 a further transfer was made to Elderslie Depot from which 1089 was operated usually between Johnstone Centre and Paisley Cross. This service was closed on 1st May, 1932. By August 1932 1089 was back at Partick where she was to remain for use on the single decker operated Clydebank-Duntocher service. This was hardly suitable for 1089's potential, so what went wrong? The answer lies in the General Manager's Rolling Stock Report prepared in March 1927.

The efficiency in acceleration received the highest praise and the equipment was considered to be excellent. The cross-seats were reported to be very comfortable for those fortunate enough to get on them. Their lack of numbers forced too many passengers to stand. Standing passengers were not comfortable passengers and hindered the collecting of fares. The separate exit was felt to be unnecessary as Glasgow passengers did not waste time joining and leaving cars but the short platforms did nothing to assist this. Lengthening these would be at the expense of more seats and it was affirmed that 32'-6" of street space would be better used by providing a tramcar with two decks.

When 1089 was confined to Kilbowie Road the opportunity was taken to alter the bodywork. The original wire plough lifeguards had been replaced with conventional units in 1929. In 1932 the front exits were removed, probably following transfer from Elderslie. Baillie Burt's car remained on the Clydebank-Duntocher shuttle until it closed in December 1949. It succumbed to enemy action in March 1941 when it became isolated from the rest of the system due to the severance of the track by bomb craters. Transport to Coplawhill for examination was effected by lorry. In March 1943 the seating was rearranged longitudinally when the controllers were altered to GEC KH8 pattern. A speedometer was fitted for test purposes in October 1945. About this time there were thoughts of converting 1089 into a four door double decker (see Chapter 12).

Following the closure of the Duntocher service in 1949, 1089 was transferred to Langside Depot for storage in March 1950. After some agitation about this unused depreciating asset, the tram was returned to Coplawhill in December 1951 and re-entered service with half of the longitudinal seating removed for 'crush-load' operation on shipyard services. 20 seats remained but 38 standing passengers could be accommodated. New lighting was installed using Subway car pattern globes and more standard MV OK26B controllers were fitted.

1089 remained at Partick and performed reliably,

The interior of 1089 shows off its clean, functional appearance. Lighting was improved, together with ventilation in 1951. Note the lincrusta ceiling panels later used in 1090-1140. 1089 was the first car with upholstered double transverse seating. ***G.C.T.***

setting off from the Depot each day for the evening (and,sometimes, morning) trip to John Brown's yard in Clydebank, helping to shift the crowds. This duty was carried out until August 1960 when the number of standing passengers on trams was reduced to five. Spasmodic appearances followed until the loss of fifty cars in the Dalmarnock Depot fire dictated the return to the former regular evening special duty until mid June 1961. Thereafter the car was stored at Partick for nearly a year to be repainted (somewhat hastily) to participate in the closing procession on 4th September 1962. At the last minute the tram was set aside and is now displayed in the Museum of Transport in Glasgow.

Even in its final days 1089 looked quite presentable. On shipyard runs, the cramped platform access presented fewer problems as nearly all passengers boarded at one point, decanting as the tram headed back to Partick. This photograph was taken in August 1954 ***R. J. S. Wiseman***

Dimensions:

Overall length	32'-6"
Saloon length	22'-6"
External width	7'-2"

CHAPTER 7

The Standard Double Bogie Tramcars 1090~1140

THE STANDARD DOUBLE BOGIE CARS: 142, 1090-1140

In summing up the results of the 1925-27 experiments the General Manager, Lachlan Mackinnon, confessed that he had not yet found a four wheel truck which eliminated the unpleasant 'tail wagging' motion although it had been much improved in the apparatus tested. No single or four-wheeled truck was found to get rid completely of the kick and hammer at rail joints and (he said) 'for smooth riding the double bogie is supreme.' It was in this context that he suggested authorisation of the purchase of 50 new cars of the latest double bogie pattern but to GCT specification. Contemporary London County Council and Metropolitan Electric Tramways Company practice had been examined but, while their influence was acknowledged as regards seating and upholstery, any thoughts of copying the London Maximum Traction bogie went unsaid.

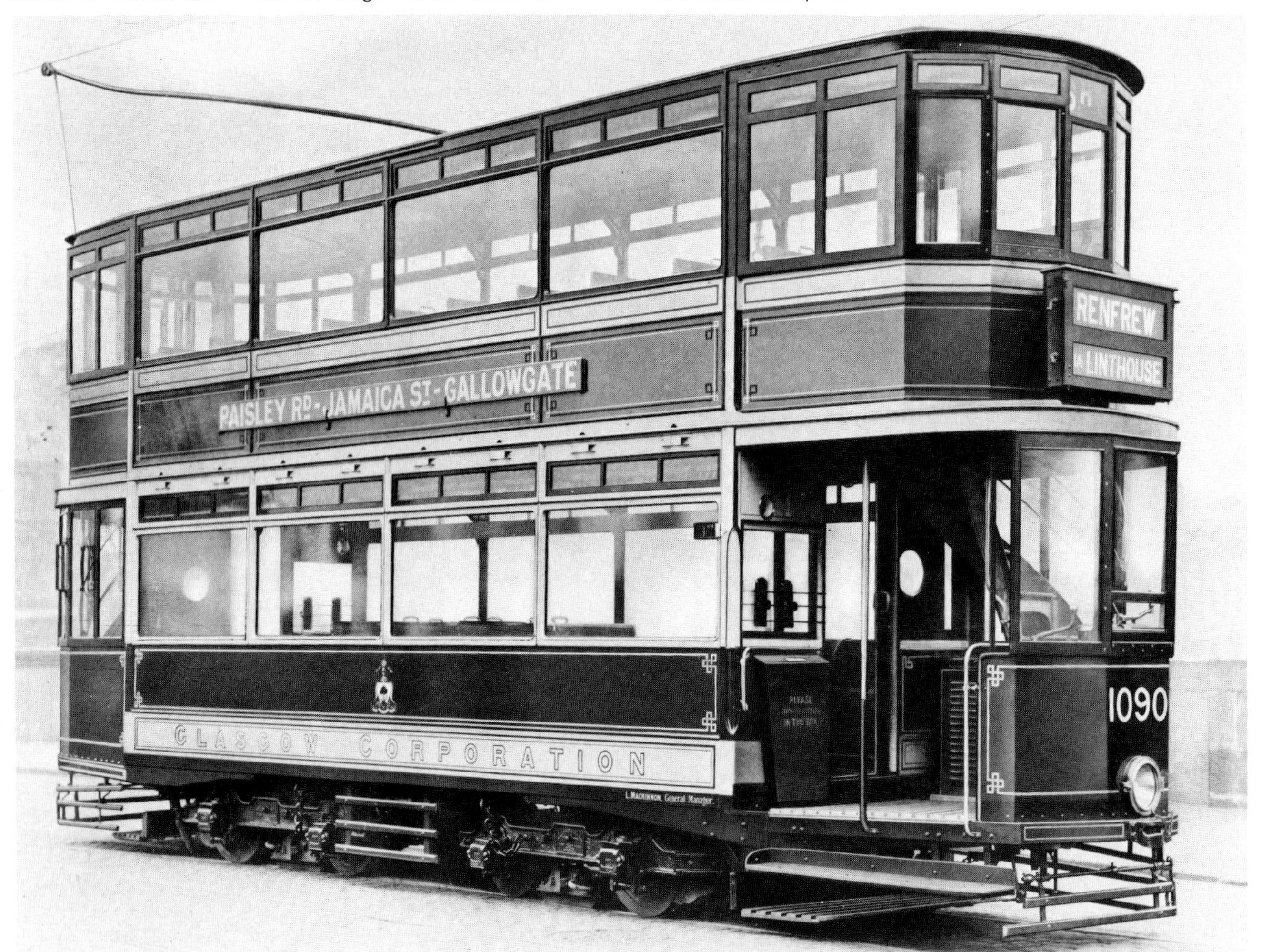

1090 was the prototype Standard Double Bogie car built by G.C.T. This car, with 142, had Hurst Nelson LCC pattern maximum traction bogies. Note the 4'-2" wheelbase with offset magnetic brakes. 1090 was scheduled to receive ex-Liverpool E.M.B. Lightweight bogies in 1951 but this never took place. ***G.C.T.***

The new bogie trams were to be augmented by rebuilding 150 of the newest Standard trams to a similar specification and the Tramways Department set about constructing two prototypes: 1090 as a pattern car for the 50 new vehicles and 142 as the pattern car for the intended rebuilds. Both were given Hurst Nelson maximum traction bogies of 4'-2" wheelbase. These were of LCC pattern.

142's rebuild was much more extensive than that given to sister car 15 whose saloon length remained as before. On 142, the saloon was lengthened to 20'-6" by the insertion of a half-length window (with bow top) at each end and the platform bulkheads taken to the new extremities. Contrarily, the upper saloon, while matching externally the lower deck window spacing, retained the original bulkheads and introduced additional half-height bulkheads above those at platform level. The space thus created between the two left just enough room for one single longitudinal seat in each of the four corner positions.

The upper balconies were enclosed and their end-sweep panels angled to fit the vestibule framing. Upholstered seating was installed, blue leather upstairs and grey lozenge moquette below. 142 was strengthened with external strapping just below the rubbing strake but the body became none the less bowed in later years. The estimated cost for this conversion was £1,500 but it was evidently felt that it was more prudent to spend £1,200 per car and retain the four wheel truck in more modern form with less work load on the body shop at Coplawhill. 142 remained unique.

The other prototype was 1090—a new car on similar Hurst Nelson bogies. It has been said that 142 was the prototype for the design of 1090 but this was not so. 1090 was available for service before 142 and was the pattern car for outside contractors. The estimated cost of each of the production cars was £2,400 and the actual cost came to £2,399 16s 9d. What excellent estimating and cost control!

An order was placed with Hurst Nelson Ltd., Motherwell for 30 car bodies, R. Y. Pickering Ltd., of Wishaw and Brush Ltd., Loughborough each securing orders for 10 car bodies. Certain parts were supplied from Coplawhill to each builder as patterns.

A side view of 1090 confirms that the air brakes compressor was originally mounted between the bogies. ***G.C.T.***

Most of the fitting out was undertaken by GCT at Coplawhill, eg bogies, controllers, etc. The electrical equipment and other specific details are listed in the following tables as they applied to each car. It will be seen that they were completely compatible with the contemporary Phase IV Standard cars. The order for the maximum traction bogies went to the Kilmarnock Engineering Company whose tender for the 4'-6" wheelbase bogies was cheaper than that lodged by Hurst Nelson. The cars were therefore nicknamed 'Kilmarnock Bogies' by the enthusiasts but not by GCT. They were officially 'Standard Double Bogie Cars' until the end. Each builder's product was virtually identical although very detailed differences could be detected in roof treatment above the upper vestibuling and also in the lower saloon side panelling. Many body parts were common to the Standard cars to ease the stocking of spares.

The bodies were of composite construction with four window saloons. Steel strengthening was incorporated in the pillars. This permitted slender posting and maximum lengths of glazing with minimum thickness of body sides. The platform dashes and upper deck equivalents were of hexagonal pattern. The upper saloon was open internally except for the partitions around the stairwells which incorporated jack-knife doors. Handrails were brass but other bright treatment was electroplated to resemble antique copper. The ceilings were lincrusta in the lower saloon and plain enamelled white in the upper deck. Woodwork was light polished teak with dark mahogany inserts in the casement panels. The overall appearance of these trams was impressive but for the upper deck front where the windows were many and narrow giving a cluttered effect not nearly so neat as on the enclosed Standard cars whose vestibules had not formed a part of the original design.

The need for new cars had been most acute on the two 'green' services from Airdrie or Uddingston to Paisley or the north west of Glasgow. Nearly 100 Standard trams had already been upgraded for these services resulting in increased patronage and it was logical that the bogie trams should acquire green route bands also. The early depot allocations for the class reflect their use.

Car 1100 was completely standard initially but departs the scene early when the Kilmarnock Engineering Company bogies were removed to be substituted by J. G. Brill equivalents c1929. 1100 deserves Chapter 10 all to herself.

The early promise of these cars was short lived as their maximum traction bogies found little compatibility with the Glasgow pattern of pointwork at the time.

Embarrassing derailments occurred at the City's busiest junctions where right angle turns had to be negotiated and chaos reigned. After some perseverance and much frustration the entire batch of trams except the then unique 1100 was reallocated to Partick and Dalmarnock Depots for use on the 'red' group of services along London Road, Argyle Street and Dumbarton Road. The straight terrain suited them well and they were virtually confined to these services until withdrawn. Their robust construction necessitated few alterations and excellent suspension almost nullified the hammer-blow effect at rail joints. EMB interlock was added to the controllers in the 1930s concurrently with the Standard cars. Skefko or Maley & Taunton roller bearing axle boxes were fitted first to the motor driven axles and then the pony axles between 1936 and 1944.

142 was to have been the prototype for 150 such conversions from Phase III Hex-dash Standard cars. Thankfully this was the only ungainly product of the drawing office's imagination. ***Struan J. T. Robertson***

In 1943/44 the seating in the lower saloons was rearranged longitudinally in all but 142, 1090 and 1131 to increase their ability to handle crush loads on the heavily trafficked shipyard services. The transverse seating was never reinstated as in the modern Coronation trams. Roller blind number boxes

142, again, with drooping bodywork, near her end. Note the non-standard location of the service number box.
M. H. Waller, Courtesy N.B. Traction

were fitted at the end of the war and platform draught excluders between then and 1954. A more ornate form of upper deck lining was retained until the late 1940s incorporating much of the pre-war style of Greek corner patterns.

Plans to derive better availability from these cars can be seen crystallised in 1100's modifications around 1941 which could also be examined in the context of the construction of 1001-1004 and car 6. Then there were proposals which went little further than the drawing board for the adaptation of the underframes to accept EMB Lightweight bogies which could have been acquired from Liverpool. 1128 is thought to have been involved in some practical experiments to this end. Certainly, quite a considerable sum was expended on 1128 under this heading. The modifications which were necessary were quite extensive but by this time an equivalent number of complete modern trams was in the process of purchase from Liverpool Corporation. 1090, with the non-standard Hurst Nelson bogies, was particularly listed for such a conversion but nothing further came of any thoughts regarding modernising the maximum traction fleet. Indeed the official policy after 1949 was not to repair any extensively damaged car of this type, not that official policy was always followed in Glasgow!

Although painted with bus green upper panels, 1098 and the red counterparts within the ranks of Maximum Traction cars retained more ornate lining on the upper panelling than on Standard cars until the mid-1940s. This is Burnside terminus.
R. R. Clark/STMS Collection

And so after 1954 few were even repainted and the scant attention devoted to them often amounted to little more than a revarnish. It is to their credit that scant attention was all that they seemed to need. Among those given full repaints, however, was 1115 now preserved in the Crich Tramway Museum collection. The withdrawal dates for the others are given in the fleet table which follows.

Here are some statistics for 142 and comparative dimensions:

Reconstruction commenced April 1927, completed December 1927.

SKF Roller bearings 1942 on motored axles, 1944 on pony axles.

Seating 27 below and 42 above. Allocated to Dalmarnock Depot.

Heaters by Young, Osmonds and Young, 2-piece.

Hurst Nelson maximum traction bogies, LCC pattern. 4'-2" wheelbase.

Height of 142 .... 16'-2½"
Height of 1090 .... 16'-2½"
Height of 1131 .... 16'-1½"

The Maximum Traction cars were characterised by their pronounced lean, evidently due to weak springing. One can't help detecting that the photographer had his tongue in his cheek as he tilted the camera to accentuate this feature. This is 1122 in August 1954. ***Parr/STMS Collection***

Seating capacity of the standard double bogie cars 1091-1099 and 1101-1140 was 30 below and 38 above. Grey lozenge moquette was used in the lower saloon with navy blue leather above.

In 1950 the London Transport Executive made approaches to Glasgow Corporation Transport regarding the purchase of surplus HR/2 equal wheel trams with Metro-Vick 109 pattern 35 horsepower motors and OK29B controllers. The extensive reconditioning and fitting with air brakes to bring these trams—which dated from c1930—into line with Glasgow requirements dictated refusal of the offer. They were offered at £250 plus £150 transport charges but a further outlay of £750 was estimated, notwithstanding their being offered in serviceable condition. They were from a batch constructed by the English Electric Company.

A later letter was received from the Secretary of the Light Railway Transport League concerning possible operation in Glasgow of London's E3 Maximum Traction cars. Emitting a polite response, previous experience with such bogies in Glasgow promoted even less enthusiasm than was accorded to the offer of equal wheel cars.

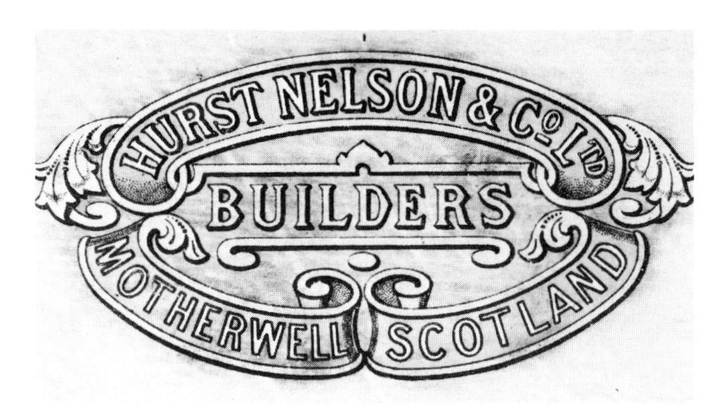

The outside contractors who built the bodywork for the Maximum Traction cars mounted builders' transfers on the lower saloon casement panels. These were latterly obliterated by dark stained varnish. This is Hurst Nelson's. ***Struan J. T. Robertson***

The upper saloon of the Standard Double Bogie cars was bright and spacious with the abandonment of bulkheads and introduction of glossy white ceilings. Due to abuse the jack-knife doors at the stairheads were to prove a maintenance headache. The maximising of width of the lower saloon in the Standard Double Bogie cars was achieved by enabling the pillars to be made slender by incorporating steel strengthening and abandoning the waisted sides. 1090 (illustrated) differed in detail from the production cars. G.C.T.

Car Number	To Service	Builder	Motors/ Controllers	Depots 1930/31	1935	Scrap	Remarks
142	12/27	GCT	MV/MV	?	x	3/1954	HN Bogies, transverse seats in lower saloon
1090	11/27	GCT	MV/MV	l	x	12/1960	HN Bogies, transverse seats in lower saloon
1091	10/28	HN	MV/MV	l	x	11/1960	
1092	10/28	HN	MV/MV	l	x	2/1961	
1093	10/28	HN	MV/MV	l	x	6/1961	Painted Standard Green 1939
1094	10/28	HN	EE/EE	l	x	1/1961	
1095	10/28	HN	MV/MV	l	x	11/1960	Painted Standard Green 1939
1096	11/28	HN	MV/MV	l	x	5/1960	
1097	11/28	HN	MV/MV	l	x	1/1961	
1098	11/28	HN	MV/MV	l	x	9/1960	
1099	11/28	HN	EE/EE	l	x	2/1961	
1100	11/28	HN	EE/EE?	k	k	(9/1962)	Rebuilt & Non-Standard. Preserved, see Chapter 10
1101	11/28	HN	EE/EE	k	t	8/1960	
1102	11/28	HN	EE/EE	l	t	5/1960	
1103	11/28	HN	EE/EE	l	x	2/1961	
1104	12/28	HN	EE/EE	k	x	11/1959	
1105	12/28	HN	EE/EE	k	x	10/1960	
1106	12/28	HN	EE/EE	k	t	6/1961	
1107	12/28	HN	EE/EE	k	t	11/1960	Painted Standard Green 1939
1108	12/28	HN	EE/EE	l	t	11/1960	
1109	12/28	HN	EE/EE?	l	x	3/1954	
1110	12/28	HN	MV/MV	l	x	2/1961	
1111	1/29	HN	MV/MV	l	t	12/1960	
1112	1/29	HN	EE/EE	l	t	12/1960	
1113	1/29	HN	EE/EE	t	t	5/1961	Retained Air Bells until withdrawn
1114	1/29	HN	MV/MV	t	t	8/1960	
1115	1/29	HN	MV/MV	t	t	6/1961	Converted to EE controllers, preserved
1116	1/29	HN	MV/MV	t	t	10/1960	
1117	1/29	HN	EE/EE	t	t	9/1960	
1118	2/29	HN	EE/EE	t	t	10/1960	
1119	2/29	HN	EE/EE	t	t	10/1960	
1120	2/29	HN	EE/EE	t	t	5/1960	
1121	10/28	RYP	MV/MV	l	x	5/1960	
1122	10/28	RYP	MV/MV	l	t	3/1961	
1123	11/28	RYP	MV/MV	l	x	5/1960	Overturned at Whiteinch 1931; weak field controllers
1124	11/28	RYP	GEC/MV	l	x	9/1960	Weak field controllers: converted to MV motors 1955
1125	11/28	RYP	MV/MV	l	x	12/1960	Painted Standard Green 1939
1126	12/28	RYP	GEC/MV	k	t	12/1960	Weak field controllers
1127	12/28	RYP	MV/MV	l	x	12/1960	
1128	12/28	RYP	GEC/MV?	l	x	9/1952	Burned & scrapped at Elderslie. See footnote
1129	1/29	RYP	EE/EE	l	x	12/1960	
1130	1/29	RYP	EE/EE	t	t	1/1961	
1131	10/28	BH	GEC/MV	?	x	10/1960	Weak field controllers: converted to MV motors. Retained transverse seating.
1132	10/28	BH	GEC/MV	l	t	3/1959	Weak field controllers: converted to MV motors
1133	11/28	BH	GEC/MV	l	t	8/1961	Weak field controllers: converted to MV motors
1134	11/28	BH	GEC/MV	l	t	7/1960	Weak field controllers: converted to MV motors
1135	11/28	BH	EE/MV	k	x	10/1960	Painted Standard Green 1939
1136	11/28	BH	MV/MV	l	x	6/1960	
1137	12/28	BH	MV/MV	?	x	1/1961	
1138	12/28	BH	MV/EE	l	x	11/1960	
1139	12/28	BH	MV/MV	l	x	3/1959	
1140	3/29	BH	GEC/MV	t	t	2/1961	Weak field controllers: converted to MV motors

Builders:
- HN = Hurst Nelson Ltd., Motherwell
- RYP = R. Y. Pickering Ltd., Wishaw
- BH = Brush Ltd., Loughborough
- GCT = Glasgow Corporation Tramways

Motors (All 60 hp)
- MV = Metropolitan Vickers MV101DR Motors
- EE = English Electric Co. DK105 Motors
- GEC = General Electric Co. WT 28 Motors

Controllers
- MV Controllers, Type OK23B or OK26B (OK20B for weak field pattern)
- EE Controllers, Type CDB2 Form 'F'

All cars converted to lower saloon longitudinal seating (except where noted) commencing with 1113, 1943-44

Roller Bearing Axle Boxes: SKF on motored axles c1935/6
SKF or Maley & Taunton on pony axles 1936-44

EMB Interlock fitted to all types of controllers c1938/39

Car 1090 Scheduled to receive first set of ex-Liverpool EMB lightweight bogies following scrapping of 142 to eliminate the two sets of Hurst Nelson bogies from the fleet. (Not pursued)
This car had a different style of seating with deeper cushions and backs. A luggage rack (railway carriage pattern) was originally fitted in the lower saloon.

Car 1128 Has been listed in records as 'gutted by fire, 3/6/49' and 'scrapped 10/2/53'.
All cars were probably fitted with air bells when placed in service.

The Maximum Traction cars were tried on several services such as Rouken Glen and Sinclair Drive before settling on the 'Red' services along Argyle Street and Dumbarton Road. Last of the Hurst Nelson batch, 1120, was photographed at Dalmuir West in 1938. W. Fisher, Courtesy D. W. Fisher

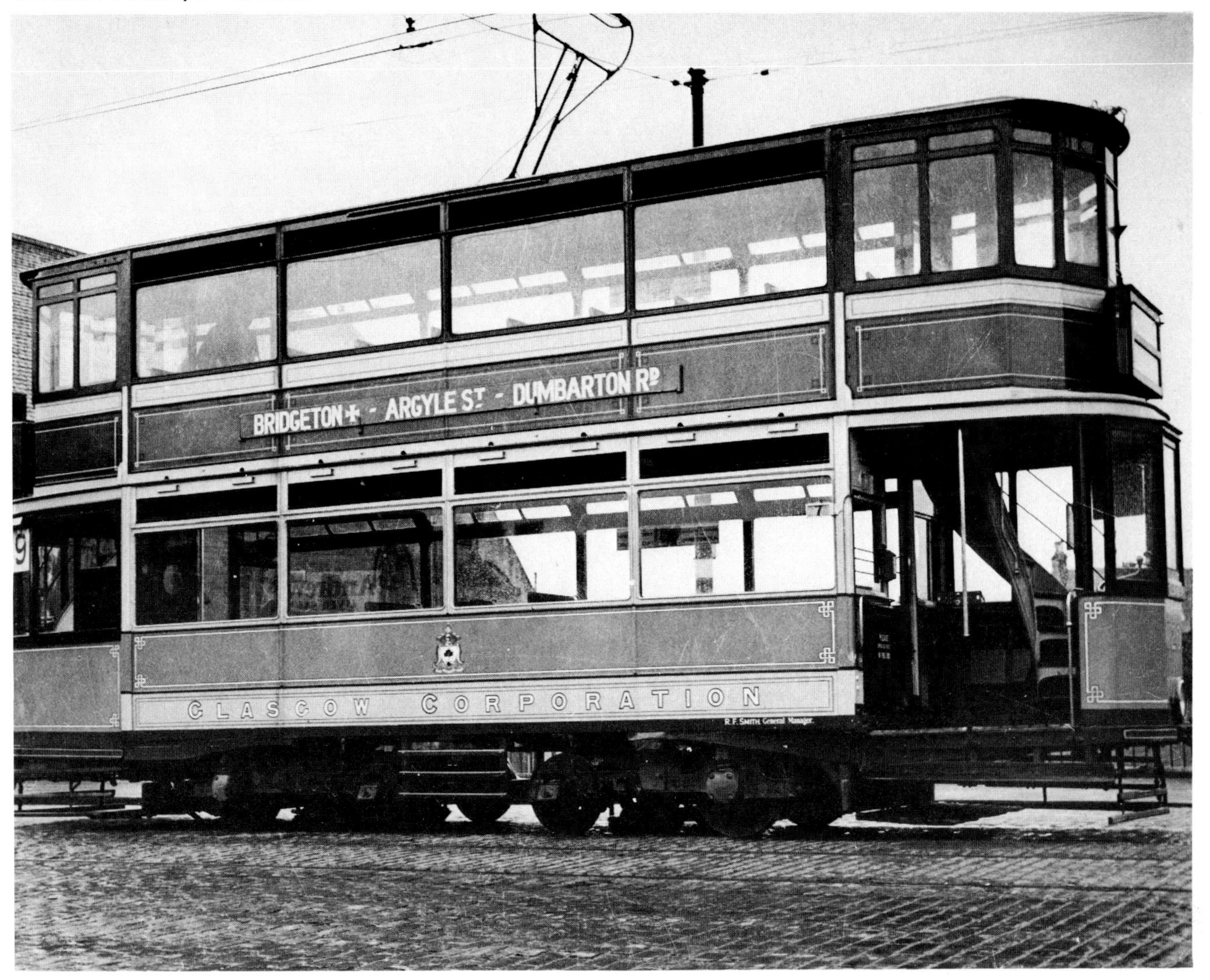

Mixed bow collector and trolley operation can be seen in this T. & R. Annan view of 'red' cars 1125 and 95 passing each other at the Argyle Street-Union Street crossing in 1930.

CHAPTER 8

The Experimental Saloon Cars 1141~1142

EXPERIMENTAL SALOON CARS 1141 and 1142

During the period from 1932 until 1936 the Transport Department found itself having to deal with ever increasing numbers of trams for daily use. The typical requirement was for between 859 and 869 cars in December 1932 but this had risen to between 925 and 974 cars four years later. It was the popularity of the reconstructed and modernised cars from the existing fleet which had created the demand for further rebuilding to trams which had not been candidates for such treatment as originally planned. Even so, although no open balcony trams had remained in service after 1935, the advanced age of the bodywork on some—particularly the Gloucester-built cars in the series 901-980—dictated that they should not be subjected to the rigours of high speed equipment. Yet they were having to be pressed into regular service and could not maintain the timetable headways. How often the various General Managers were heard to confirm that the speed of the service was as fast as the slowest car!

The last tram to enter service new was 1140 on 9th March 1929 but the Transport Department did not let matters rest there. Experiments were always being carried out. Some were adopted. Some were not. Some can clearly be seen, with the benefit of hindsight, as consolidating plans for new construction. Examples of these were the contactor equipment on Car 305, use of Alhambrinal decorative panels for side linings on 855 and for the upper deck ceiling on 723. Trafficator arms, composition floors, power operated windscreen wipers, cork tiling, controller interlocks, and various alternative moquette seat coverings were tried and tested. So it is not too surprising that the Glasgow Corporation's Tramways Engineer, A. B. Findlay, got it 'right first time' when his prototype experimental saloon cars entered service.

Glasgow Corporation approved in council in March 1936 the purchase of one set of EMB and one set of Maley & Taunton bogies for test purposes along with

This view of 1141 when newly built shows the original air intake, above the cabin, for the ventilation system. This was found not to be rainproof. Note the rubber guttering above the upper deck windows. *G.C.T.*

The first Prototype Saloon Car, 1141, at Millerston in 1937 with the original heavyweight body. Note the visor fitted over the air intake above the driving cabin. The destination apertures on this car and 1142 were slightly smaller than on production cars.
W. Fisher, Courtesy D. W. Fisher

Metropolitan-Vickers electrical equipment. This was used in the two prototypes soon under construction. Equal wheel bogies were selected following the success of 1089 and unfavourable results with Maximum Traction bogies. 1141 employed Electro-Mechanical Brake Co. Lightweight equal wheel bogies with a 4'-9" wheelbase while 1142 was mounted on Maley & Taunton Ltd. Swing Link bogies with a 4'-2" wheelbase. GCT had some experience with EMB trucks and component parts but until that time Maley & Taunton had supplied little in the way of major equipment for the Tramways Department. The electrical equipment was common to both trams. The motors, of type MV109AW were manufactured by Metropolitan-Vickers who also provided the remote control equipment, electro-pneumatically operated and housed in a cabinet in one corner of the lower saloon with easy access for maintenance. Compressed air was employed to operate the power and brake contactors (15 and 7 respectively) and the hissing and clicking noises emitted during acceleration and braking were to become a familiar feature in these and other cars which followed. Other controls were effected via battery fed 36 volt circuitry and this also ensured that the contactor equipment would operate rheostatic braking under main power failure conditions. The compressor was mounted centrally between the bogies, provided charging of the batteries and eventually took on the operation of the windscreen wipers. Air wheel braking was used for normal service stops. A separate bogie-mounted air cylinder operated its own brake shoe while separate cylinders were used to apply the track shoes to the rail. This was dictated by the application of the braking notches on the controller which, with further application, energised the electromagnets on the track shoes for an emergency stop. At this time EMB interlocks were being fitted to all High Speed Standard trams and this feature was also incorporated in the controllers of the new saloon cars. This ensured release of air from the air wheel braking system in the event of power being applied. A conductor's emergency brake was fitted under each staircase. This was capable of operation from either end to apply the air track brake if the driver took ill or, for any reason, became unable to control his tram while it was in motion. A small hand brake was also incorporated. This was intended to hold the tram at rest once the other braking systems had been applied as it was quite unsuitable for stopping a moving tram. Although drivers were instructed to use this brake in the event of air braking faults, passengers were supposed to be transferred to another car.

The EMB bogies were mounted at 11'-0" centres. Their design had evolved from the equal wheel bogies of the LCC HR/2 cars to those produced in 'Heavyweight' form for Johannesburg and Liverpool. Riding performance on the latter's sleeper tracks had dictated development of lighter construction, hence the 'Lightweight' bogie. 50% of the car body weight was carried on the centre on three rubber pads on each bogie. The track brake cylinders were vertical and without mechanical leverage. Motors were slung inside the axles; the axle boxes themselves were unrestrained by hornways.

The Maley & Taunton bogies were also fitted at 11'-0" centres but differed in several respects from EMB practice. Their design carried the whole weight of the body on the bogie as far out to the extreme width of the car as possible. The weight of the body was carried on half elliptical springs in series with rubber pads. Both features were reported as providing a more stable and better sprung vehicle when justifying the acceptance of Maley & Taunton tenders for trucks post war (see Chapter 13) but were not substantiated by actual fact. The EMB cars could be hard riding with tail-wag at speeds but the Maley & Taunton bogies were even harder to the track and the passenger. The latter bogies incorporated horizontal track brake cylinders with levers and the motors were slung outside the axles. The Maley & Taunton bogies were, however, 15 cwt lighter per car than the EMB 'Lightweight' equivalents. Both designs used 27" diameter wheels and, with four motors per car each of 35 hp, performance was brisk and lively.

1141 received a new body more in line with the normal pre-war production specification following the Newlands Depot fire in 1948. The windscreen was slightly smaller than the later standard one-piece pattern. This is 1952.
R. R. Clark/STMS Collection

Construction of 1141 commenced on 17th September 1936 to be completed by December 28th. EMB delivered the bogies on October 6th. The body was a complete departure from anything previously seen in Glasgow (or anywhere else for that matter). The design avoided the ultra-light flimsy construction that was later to prove difficult to strengthen in Liverpool or Belfast without going to the other extreme. Substantial bulkheads were provided together with welded steel underframing (supplied by Brush Ltd.) and composite pillars. The result was that dropped platforms were almost unknown on Glasgow's modern trams. The Coplawhill Carworks knew only too well that the vestibule framing on their Standard trams called for a disproportionate amount of accident repair and so curved glass was avoided except for the eaves glasses which helped to produce a light and airy upper saloon. Only the 20'-6" x 7'-3" wide saloon dimension owed anything to previous practice, being the same as on the Standard Double Bogie Cars 1090-1140. However, extra total length was gained by tapering the car ends so that separate cabins could be provided and still maintain clearance on nearly all the tightest curves in the City. The separate cabins had a tip-up seat, doorway direct to the street (off-side) and two-way hinged door to the car interior. The car had four panoramic safety glass windows per saloon side, set in pans for easy removal and replacement. These employed large radii for easy cleaning.

The cabin windscreen employed a geared half-drop window and a horizontal blade chain-driven electrically operated windscreen wiper. Above the windscreen was a bar-framed intake grille and similar slots were situated above the lower saloon windows at each end of the illuminated etched glass

If the change from Standard Car to Maximum Traction Car interior was a contrast, what can be said about the further improvements built into the first experimental saloon 1141. Note the Sundeala panelling and vaulted roof concealing ventilation ducting in the lower saloon. 1141's upper saloon was even brighter than that on the Standard Double Bogie cars due to the eaves glasses and less cluttered vestibule windows. Note the loudspeaker grille on the partition. The circular extract diffusers are called 'Anemostats'. *G.C.T.*

1142 was the second prototype Saloon Car and incorporated five main side windows. Despite this a substantial saving in weight was achieved compared with 1141's. The lighting diffusers also served as ventilation ducting, saving weight and increasing natural light. The jazzy moquette was typical of the period. The upper saloon in 1142 utilised detailing which became standard in the future production Coronation trams. Alhambrinal decorative panelling was introduced together with cork floor tiling. G.C.T.

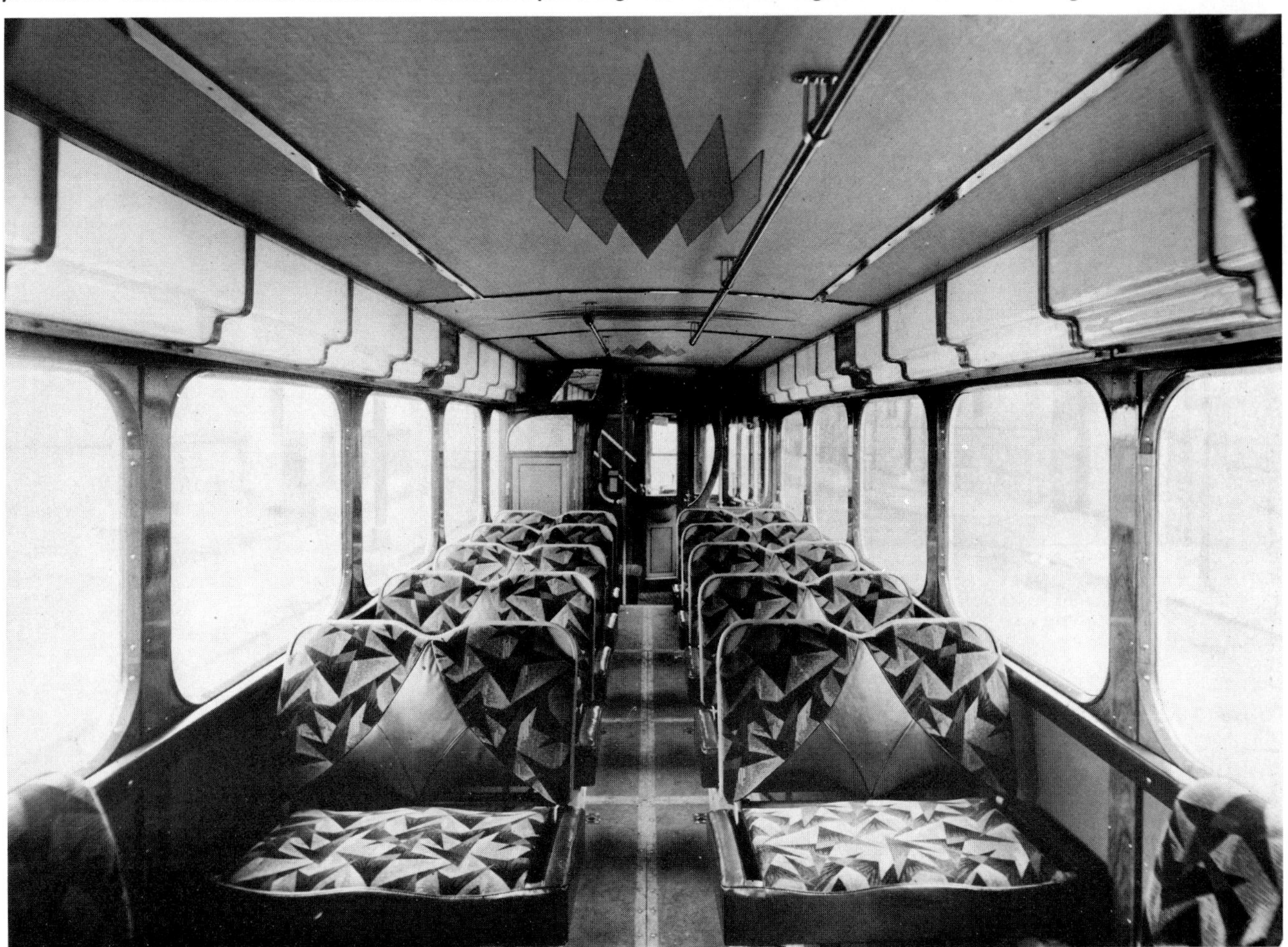

clerestory panels displaying 'CORPORATION TRANSPORT'. There were, however, no side windows with passenger operated ventilators. 1141 was the first tram in Great Britain to have forced air ventilation providing a more than adequate 45 air changes per hour. This was mostly achieved at speed by the ram effect of the car but at slow running or when stationary the deficiency was made up by propeller fans located above the cabins, platform doors and contactor cabinets. These discharged air through anemostat ventilation diffusers strategically placed on bulkheads and at intervals along the lower saloon roof which was vaulted to accommodate ducting and recessed luminaires.

Decorative panelling was supplied by Sundeala and the seating by G. D. Peters to a very high specification, similar to contemporary practice on the Blackpool Corporation Railcoaches. Another new feature was the incorporation of a public address system with loudspeakers mounted on the upper and lower saloon bulkheads. The upper saloon was finished to an equally high standard with seats in hide as opposed to moquette but the atmosphere was typical of the lush cinema architecture of the 1930s. Seating was provided for 27 in the lower deck and 38 above. Many undertakings would accommodate that number, or more, on a single truck car so it can be seen how roomy the new tram was. The body was constructed as a whole unit instead of normal practice whereby the two decks were built separately and then assembled together. Flooring was slatted in the saloons and covered with green studded rubber on the platforms and stair-treads. Folding platform doors ensured draught-free conditions and a central grab-rail was mounted external to these. Exterior panelling was smooth and featured armoured

Although Glasgow Corporation Tramways took full advantage of the spectacle which illuminated trams could achieve, a brand new Coronation tram at night was like a beacon; witness 1142 when newly placed in service. 'Glasgow Herald' Collection

plywood covered with zinc in one complete saloon side length. Dash and cabin panelling was sheet steel. A central headlamp incorporating the tail light with focusing device was surmounted by stop-lights and trafficators and chromium plated decorative fenders were supplied by the English Electric Co. Immediately below the front window to the upper saloon was the destination display. This comprised a non-digital number/letter code aperture left of destination and via displays, for the first time accessible from within the car. Access to the bow rope was gained by opening the geared half-drop windows at the ends of the upper saloon. The bow rope was kept in alignment by piping shaped to the profile of the roof dome but if anything required attention, access to the roof could be gained via a trap door which could be slid open and provided additional ventilation on the hottest summer days (although this was not officially permitted!).

Livery treatment had just a hint of previous streamlining attempts on Standard cars 215 and 451 but introduced 'bus' green to the trams. The green used on Corporation buses was lighter, with more yellow pigment than the darker green used for service differentiation. The orange lower panels and upper panels both featured a downswept band of colour which more than made up for the otherwise angular appearance of the car. For there were no three dimensional panel-beaten curves anywhere. The fleet number was displayed immediately below the destination box in gold, double shaded blue numerals which the Transport Department used on their underground trains. Such was 1141, necessarily described at some length. It was driven on to Albert Drive for Transport Committee inspection late in December 1936 and was ready for service on 1st January, 1937 when it was despatched to Newlands Depot. Costing £4,406 its impact was without precedent and the car proved very popular indeed with all who were fortunate enough to travel on it, often quoted as being 'undoubtedly the finest short-stage vehicle in Europe' (which it probably was).

At the next meeting of the Finance and Works Subcommittee, it was proposed that one hundred more cars should be put in hand right away, suggesting that 75 should be built by outside firms and 25 at Coplawhill. On 3rd February, 1937 the Transport Committee endorsed this but accepted Councillor P. J. Dollan's amendment that the whole batch should be constructed at Coplawhill and this was confirmed at a meeting of the Corporation on 18th February.

Meanwhile, 1142's construction was underway. One of the few criticisms about 1141 related to its weight of 18 tons 11 cwts 2 qrs., and every effort was made to reduce this. It has been seen that 15 cwt could have been saved by using the Maley & Taunton bogies but further measures were taken with the bodywork to produce a tram with a weight of 16 tons 19 cwt 1 qr.

Although electrically identical to 1141, the body had little in common other than the basic dimensions. The seating capacity was the same, albeit to different trim, and the forced air ventilation and loudspeakers were retained. The saloon, however, had five windows per side and the cabins were constructed with divided windscreens in protruding vee-formation. The interior trim was simplified in some respects with much of the moulding detail later used in production cars. Flooring was covered with cork tiles within the main saloon areas. Lining and ceiling panels were Alhambrinal and further weight saving was achieved by utilising the continuous lighting diffusers for ventilation ducts as well. This also had the effect of making the lower saloon interior lighter via the illuminated clerestory glazed panels above the main side windows. The dash panels retained the chromium plated bumpers and incorporated a separate tail lamp immediately adjacent to the main headlamp in addition to the stop lamp and fog lamp.

35 has just past the short-lived terminal stop at Colston off Kirkintilloch Road. Some trams (like 35) were given body strengthening in 1957/58 and only treated to repainting of the lower orange and maroon panels. *W.D. McMillan*

101 is shown in a typical Glasgow setting with a background of tenements and a fore ground of cobbled setts at Keppochhill Road in 1957. This was just before curtailment of service 4 to Hillington Road. *W.D. McMillan*

By 1930, 137 was rebuilt from its experimental form with front exit to become a normal Phase IV Standard Car. It is seen in 1957 at Parliamentary Road on service 32. *W.D. McMillan*

260 was an ex-Elderslie Depot car seen in Cambridge Street after withdrawal of the Paisley services. The poster for the Empire, Odeon and Alhambra are evocative of the period. Their site is occupied by a modern hotel. *W.D. McMillan*

The front view of 1142 shows the original divided cabin windscreen in outward vee formation. Presumably this obstructed the driver's vision. It was altered to standard following fire damage in 1940. *G.C.T.*

But it was the livery applied to 1142 which was to make it memorable to the Glasgow public. Authorised late in 1936, 1142's construction was commenced on 21st December of that year to emerge on 11th March, 1937. It was chosen to carry a special livery to mark the Coronation of King George VI in May 1937 comprising red lower panels, a blue band along the upper deck sides, downswept at the ends and silver grey elsewhere. Not surprisingly, the name applied by the travelling public was 'The Coronation Car' and this name remained not only with 1142 but with all the modern cars built both pre-war and post-war. They were also described as 'new' cars right until the end; a tribute, surely, to Mr. Findlay's design and vision.

1142 remained very much a 'one-off'. After spells at Possilpark and Partick Depots, the car settled down to a quiet existence at Newlands Depot. Normal livery was applied on 29th January, 1938 and fire damage on 4th April, 1940 resulted in some rebuilding which eliminated the vee-formed cabin front panels and windscreen together with the rubber rain guttering along the top of the upper deck windows which had been a feature of 1141 and 1142 when new. Remaining 'odd', however, it had an entry in its history card at Coplawhill dated 4th December, 1943 to the effect that 'this car is better done as a special job in place of general overhaul. Too many complications to be tackled for yearly routine work. When the car is being overhauled put two extra fitters on from beginning of week'.

The lower deck seating was altered to provide enhanced standing lobbies by rearranging the longitudinal and transverse seating in what was termed 'composite' layout. This was completed on 17th February, 1945 and resulted in a reduction in capacity to 26 seats. As if to concentrate the complications on one vehicle, a set of resilient wheels was acquired and fitted to 1142 on 6th May, 1945. They might have been fitted to the post-war experimental car as many enthusiasts believe they should but what was to become '1005' had still to be approved, let alone constructed. Two years later these wheels were still proving satisfactory in service but no conclusions were drawn until they wore out. By May 1948, the General Manager's Annual Report indicated that they would be run to destruction but that a new replacement set was available to keep 1142 on the road; these were fitted on Christmas Day 1948. A new set of tyres was fitted in March 1950, manufactured from harder steel and of larger thickness to extend life. They were removed on 15th November, 1952 and normal wheels substituted. Glasgow had gained a much longer life from its resilient wheels than Blackpool Corporation but employed a much harder rubber. The only other alterations carried out to 1142 were to remove the droplights in October 1956 and substitute perspex diffusers for the hinged lamp shades in the lower saloon in November 1958. Scrapping took place at Coplawhill in February 1960, earlier than most modern cars but dictated by its non-standard specification and a reluctance thus to spend money on the car. Although the major design features were not perpetuated, much of the interior detail was incorporated in series production cars.

Concerning its driving techniques and response to controls, the Driving Instructor reported that notching had to be a little slower than on the other Coronation trams although there was no lack of speed once achieved. It had a tendency to 'jazz' at all speeds after its first rewheeling but this was later cured. The automatic exhausting of the air wheel brake was sluggish when the power handle was moved from the 'OFF' location at both ends and a periodic leak in the air wheel brake had been evident from its earlier days. Air track braking and magnetic braking effect were good but motormen did not like 1142's air wheel brake. The controls were very sensitive to over-switching the 'OFF' position whereby the air track brake could be unconsciously applied and no air wheel brake was available. With the EMB cars, the action of the air wheel brake was more rapid than on 1142. Automatic Emergency Braking (AEB) was installed around 1948.

Reverting to 1141, this car seemed to subside into anonymity quite soon. It was given its first repaint in February 1938 but had very soon been provided with a visor over the air intake grille no doubt due to its shipping water. No photographs have come to light showing the car in post war condition before it was seriously damaged at the Newlands Depot fire on 11th April, 1948 sufficient to warrant rebodying. The car re-entered service after rebuilding in August 1951. By this time the car was virtually standard to the specification of the series production cars and further details of the car from then on are given in Chapter 9.

1142 in 1954 at Newlands Depot resembled the production cars more closely following rebuilding of the cabins. Coachpainters rarely applied the city coat of arms in the right position, being used to centering it below a window pillar in cars with four main windows instead of five. ***Parr/STMS Collection***

(opposite page, upper)
Photographed at Renfrew, 1142 shows the original red, silver and blue livery which gave rise to the designation 'Coronation Tram'. It was also a foretaste of the many silver painted buses placed in service for Queen Elizabeth's Silver Jubilee, forty years later.

(opposite page, lower)
A rare view of 1142 with the original design translated into green, cream and orange shows the concave panel below the destination box. The photograph was taken at Dalmuir West in 1938.
both W. Fisher, Courtesy D. W. Fisher

Dimensional information:

Height 15'-5¼" Length-34' 0"
Overall width 7'-3½"
Minimum rail radius 32'-6"

Resilient wheels treads mileage 49,000 (normal wheels exceeded 70,000).

Blackpool trams thus equipped achieved 13,000 miles.

6C
VIA
TRANSPORT
CORPORATION
23
STOP

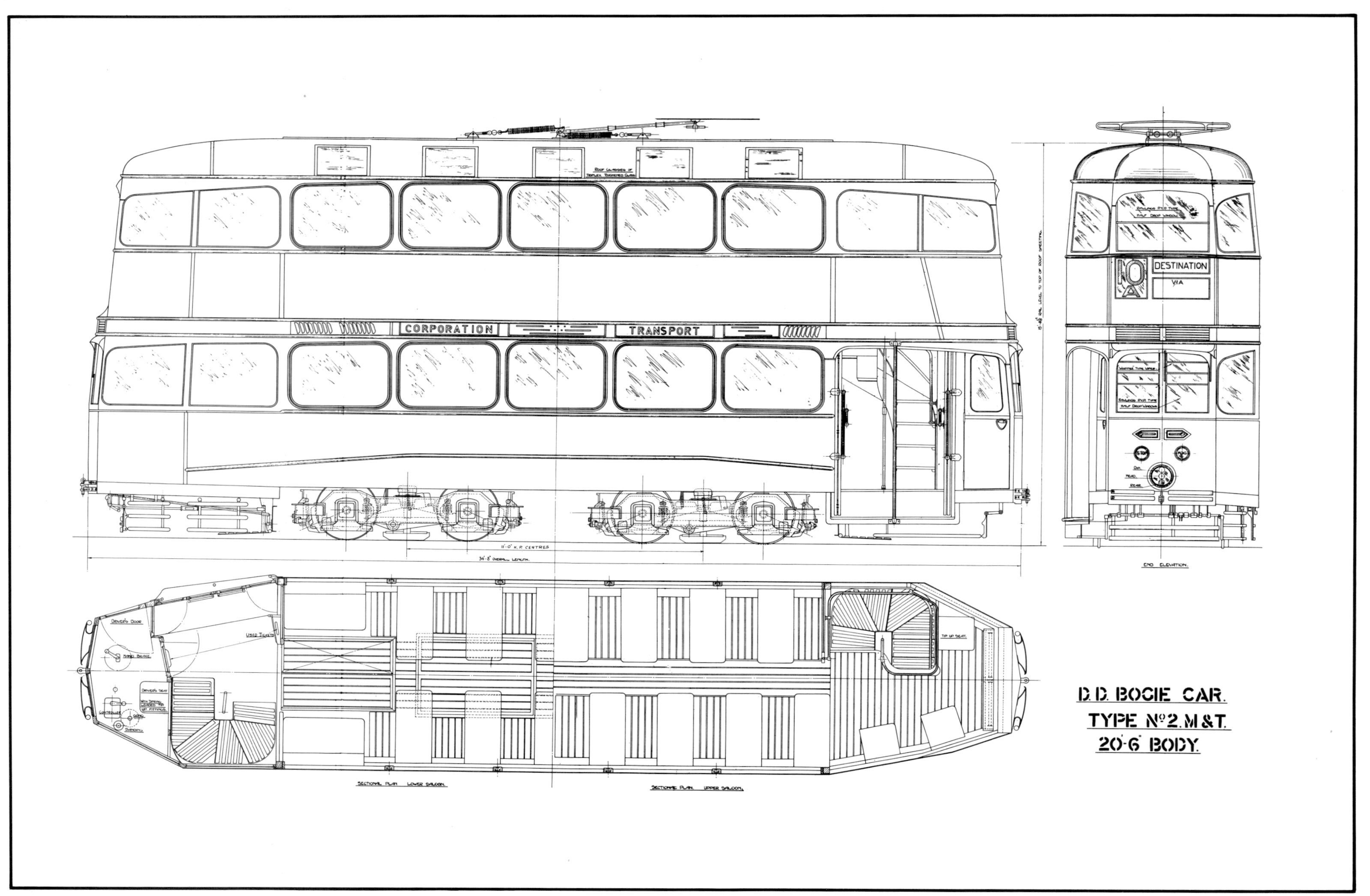
CORPORATION
TRANSPORT
DESTINATION
VIA
11'-0" B.P. CENTRES
34'-8" OVERALL LENGTH
END ELEVATION
SECTIONAL PLAN LOWER SALOON
SECTIONAL PLAN UPPER SALOON
D.D. BOGIE CAR.
TYPE Nº2 M&T.
20'-6" BODY.

CHAPTER 9

The Coronation Cars Production Batch 1143~1292

The livery styling of the production Coronation cars settled down to this appearance for the first 100 cars and 1146 was typical. Close examination of this official view shows that the car was not quite finished, with certain handrails still to be fitted. ***G.C.T.***

Even while the two prototypes were under construction the rise in the demand for trams continued unabated. Drastic short-term measures had to be taken to keep sufficient trams continually available to meet the peak needs. The body strengthening programme then under way with the Standard trams was delayed and the ever increasing shortage was partly filled by despatching trams overhauled and repainted at Coplawhill without their finishing coats of varnish. In this context it is not surprising that the response to the Corporation's approval to proceed with the construction of 100 new cars on 18th February 1937 was swift. The first of these, 1143, was started on 30th April. What was surprising under the circumstances was the decision, prompted by Baillie Dollan, that the whole batch should be built in Coplawhill Carworks. There was no doubt as to the quality of any article finished by the Corporation Transport Department's own craftsmen, but they were hard-pressed at the time, and resorting to outside contractors in 1928 had produced 50 new trams in under four months. However, this was neither the first nor the last display of a decided preference under all circumstances to undertake all construction 'in house'.

Tenders were invited for the supply of bogies and electrical equipment. EMB were successful with the result that 1142's Maley & Taunton bogies remained unique in Glasgow until the arrival of the first ex-Liverpool cars in 1953. While Metropolitan-Vickers had supplied the electrical equipment and motors for 1141 and 1142 together with experimental equipment for 305, they lost the series production order to British Thomson-Houston Ltd., of Rugby. The equipment was virtually identical except in name, but Metropolitan-Vickers were to have long memories about this when tenders were being accepted for post war construction (see Chapter 13). The BT-H motors were their type BT-H 109AW rated at 35 hp, and underframes were supplied by the English Electric Company Ltd.

Glasgow was to host the 1938 Empire Exhibition at Bellahouston Park and the Transport Department was anxious to have as many as possible of the new trams available to provide the basic service for routes to that venue. As is usual with the first car of a new production batch, 1143 took rather longer to build than when a routine had been established. Completion was not achieved until November 20th 1937 and the finished product was once more the subject of the Transport Department's official photographer.

1143 was closer to 1141 than 1142 in concept, but efforts to reduce weight resulted in much of 1142's interior specification being retained. Thus 1143 was more a four-windowed version of the 1142 body than a repeat of 1141's. It was noticeably neater in detail and built as two quite separate decks to be married together later. The rubber rain guttering around the top deck cant rails was omitted. The number, destination and 'via' aperatures were slightly larger. Seating trim was less 'jazzy' and painted aluminium panelling was used for the bulkheads dividing the driving cabins from the car interiors. Elsewhere, decorative trim was in Alhambrinal. The interior lighting was supplied by Thomas Scott & Co., comprising top hinged aluminium-framed etched glass shades forming air ducts to discharge air supplied via the ventilation fans and anemostat diffusers to the lower saloon. The lower saloon lighting was also used to illuminate the etched glass 'CORPORATION TRANSPORT' clerestory panels which were supplied by the City Glass Company and located above the main side windows.

Upper deck ventilation was provided via the front half-drop windows which had been altered from the prototype design to be of the pinch-grip instant opening pattern since the winding gear had been too slow in action when the conductor had been required to assist in the flipping over of the bow collector. Lighting levels of 100 lux were achieved.

Exterior panelling was supplied by the Tucker Armoured Plywood Company Ltd., providing a smooth unjointed appearance along the entire saloon length, a feature now common on luxury coaches. Maley & Taunton Ltd., secured the order for platform brake gear and switches. Other specification items conformed to 1142's. The chromium plated bumpers and trafficators were omitted, however, and the whole dash panel tidied up. The headlamp was mounted above the tail lamp which was flanked on the left by a 'STOP' lamp and on the right by a fog lamp.

As to livery, this was similar to 1141's although executed with more style. The green band around the upper deck was downswept in such a way that the visor over the cabin windscreen was also green, while the orange was swept down on each side of the dash

A front view of 1158 in Renfield Street illustrates the original appearance of the Coronation Mark I car. Note the absence of step iron and grab rail for adjustment of the driver's mirror. Until 1943 the Via aperture display always included the word 'VIA' on the screens. ***'The Glasgow Herald'***

panel which was overall cream. The rail-shield over the upper deck front opening window was also featured in green. The 'bus green' shade remained described in this way until the end by which time there was no other green colour used!

1143 was despatched new (like most of the early Coronations), to Newlands Depot which later shared the increasing numbers of new trams with Maryhill Depot to provide services of luxury cars advertised in publicity leaflets for the Empire Exhibition visitors. 1144, and subsequent cars, were altered only in that the orange band around the lower deck sides was carried straight round the front of the trams and that the fare-table holders were altered in shape to accord with the interior trim of the trams and not retain the original shape inherited from the monitor roof standard trams.

The Exhibition opened on 3rd May, 1938. A new service numbering system had been introduced to supersede the digital headcodes previously used. The 'number' apertures on the Coronation cars had originally been designed to accommodate a service number with suffix letter below, but the suffixes were from then the exception rather than the rule. The University-Mosspark service which could be either 8 or 8A or 8B depending on the terminus used became, simply, '3'. The Exhibition closed on 31st October, and after this, redistribution of the new cars then in service took place and the depot allocations stabilised as shown on the Fleet Tables, until further regrouping occurred in 1943.

In the late 1930's there was a strong 'Pro-trolleybus' lobby in Glasgow Corporation. Faced with this, the General Manager prepared a Report on Trolleybuses for the Members of the Transport Committee on 8th August, 1938. He did not recommend introduction of this then fashionable mode of transport but instead recommended that the tramway system should be continued and maintained in the best condition, extended where advisable. He also recommended that the 125 semi-high speed trams should be replaced at a cost of £2,500 each and that half the tramcar fleet (say 500 cars) be fitted with new bodies and trucks at an estimated expenditure of £1,500 each. At the meeting on 7th September, the Subcommittee on Finance and Works rejected the advice on trolleybuses and agreed to experimenting with them although it did agree to continue consideration on rebuilding or replacement of the tramway fleet. The Transport Committee overturned the decision to experiment with trolleybuses and endorsed the General Manager's advice in this respect. This was further endorsed at the full Corporation meeting on 13th October, 1938.

Pursuing further his proposals regarding upgrading of the tramway fleet, the General Manager sought authorisation to construct two new four wheel cars and modernise two high speed cars for evaluation. This was placed before the Subcommittee on 11th November, rejected, and countered with a suggestion to replace 600 cars with Coronations. The Transport Committee tried unsuccessfully to reject this but the Corporation did reject the Subcommittee's ambitious proposals on 18th December. Instead, they agreed to the four experimental cars and a second batch of 25 new Coronations in addition to 25 agreed a fortnight before.

On 11th April, 1939 the Finance & Works Committee recommended construction of a further 50 cars to continue to provide employment after the two batches of 25 had been completed and while awaiting the outcome of the four wheeled car experiments. The Transport Committee delayed approval of these proposals pending receipt of a further report from the General Manager stressing that such proposals envisaging large-scale production of expensive to build and operate Coronation trams would render invalid the financial conclusions in his Trolleybuses Report. These had been based exclusively on four-wheeled trams. Trolleybuses would be cheaper to operate than a fleet comprised entirely of Coronations by up to £100,000 per annum.

A final request for 25 was remitted back for further consideration in May 1939, and continued in Committee until Britain was at war with Nazi Germany when there was no question of such expenditure being approved by central Government even if the Corporation had wanted it. Certain materials were already becoming difficult to obtain and were to keep some of the final, otherwise completed cars in storage for several months. The prewar Coronation trams thus totalled 150, plus the two prototypes.

The last car of the 100 batch was 1242, completed in February 1939. There was a gap of just over two months while manufacturers tooled up before 1243 appeared. The opportunity was taken to include some improvements to the original specification. The handrails along the ceilings were extended to run the full length of each saloon. The centre grab rail was resited behind each of the folding platform doorsets and ventilation slots were introduced to the cabin visors in order to render saloon ventilation less reliant on the fans. This followed experiments with earlier cars. As a result, there was no room for the fleet number which was displaced to the dash panel immediately below the windscreen. Its place on the visors was taken by the City Coat of Arms. The roof

The immediate reaction to the declaration of war in September 1939 was the pasting of black paper over most of the extent of glazing and painting white fenders and grab rails. These features are exemplified on Coronation car 1196 outside the Men's Union at Glasgow University. ***Struan J. T. Robertson***

extract cowls were improved in design to prevent water ingress and the lining treatment on the lower panels simplified by eliminating the white lining on the orange panels. These amendments were included in the original cars on the occasion of their first routine overhauls.

By September 1939 black-out conditions were imposed and all Coronation cars—like the remainder of the fleet—had lamps painted with blue lacquer, black paper applied to most of the window area, all exposed edges painted white and masks fitted over the headlamps. The Coronations probably suffered more than most, however. In addition to these measures, the triplex eaves glasses were painted black, the illuminated clerestory panels were over-painted black and in many cars, not only were the transverse seats in the lower saloon replaced with longitudinal seats during 1943/44, but the attractive etched glass diffusers over the light fittings were either partially obscured with black-out paint or removed entirely to be replaced with slotted tin boxes set into brown-painted cove panelling. The shades were carefully stored until after the war was over but some suffered as a result.

Once hostilities were over, matters reverted to something approaching normal and further alterations were carried out to all cars, some were improvements—others were retrograde. These can be summarised as follows.

(1) The pre-war standard of lighting was restored and those fittings whose glass was broken while in storage had this substituted with perspex. There was, however, a tendency for the hinged fittings to swing out when the catches worked loose. Despite several attempts, this was never cured.

(2) The longitudinal seating was restored to a combination of transverse and corner longitudinal seats reducing capacity in the lower saloon from the pre-war 27 to 26. The standing lobbies were increased in size and these displaced the former single corner seats to storage, only to re-emerge later in the last of the Cunarders. Coronation trams which had never received longitudinal seats went direct to 'composite' seating.

(3) Ventilation fans were removed and reliance was placed entirely on the motion of the cars. This saved considerably on maintenance.

(4) Exterior panelling had lost its appearance due to skellowing and was replaced with aluminium panelling from 1948 onwards as replacement became necessary.

This photograph of 1175 was actually taken so that a commercial artist could hand paint an advertisement on the upper side panelling to illustrate the impact this would achieve. The view shows some of the alterations carried out to these cars since original construction. ***G.C.T.***

(5) All cars, including 1141 and 1142, were fitted with Automatic Emergency Braking (AEB) which brought the cars to a halt when air pressure was lost, and operation of contactors for normal control could not be guaranteed. Cars with this alteration could be distinguished by a hand-inscribed notice comprising red letters 'AEB' on a small white diamond on the light switch door above the Contactor cabinet. The equipment was fitted in 1947 and 1948.

(6) The half-drop driver's windows were not wanted by the traffic staff. They were draughty and were stuffed up with paper. This became unsightly and restrictive to vision. They were initially stopped up permanently but replaced from 1954 onwards with a single fixed pane of glass.

(7) The end windows on the upper saloons had the half-drop units removed to be replaced with solid glazing in timber astragals with a small port for access to the bow rope. The first car to be altered in this way was 1189 in 1949 but not all were completed until 1958.

(8) The ventilation duct above the cabins discharging air to the bulkhead from the intake behind the visor was, in some cars, removed but in all, rendered inoperative when the visors were removed and replaced with plain panelling.

(9) The swinging lamp shades in the lower saloons were removed from most trams and replaced with a perspex valance—inscribed with green lining on some. At this time the ventilation to the lower saloon was direct from outside as the air ducts were eliminated in the removal of the lamp diffusers.

(10) Modifications were carried out to the air piping cooling system to cut out winter freezing.

(11) Although the Standard trams had 'open' platforms, the cabins on Coronation trams were notoriously draughty and all were fitted with heaters at the request of the traffic staff.

(12) The commode rails attached to the folding platform doors were extended from around 1946 to increase safety for passengers boarding and leaving.

(13) Following a request from the Claims Department the internal cabin doors were removed after an accident from which a motorman's escape had been impeded by his internal door. These were taken out from 1952 onwards.

(14) The studded green rubber flooring from platforms and steps had begun to billow with foot-wear, becoming hazardous and was substituted with 3" strips of larchwood—on the platforms and iron treads on the stairs where necessary.

(15) The semaphore pattern trafficators were over-panelled and eventually removed.

(16) A grab-rail and step were provided to facilitate adjustment of external mirrors.

(17) To eliminate fire hazards, the contactor cabinet linings were replaced with glass silk and fibreglass instead of Cellotex sound-proofing.

(18) Ventilation to rheostats was improved by ducting direct to atmosphere below the stairs. The sliding windows in this location had become corroded and inoperable, and the glazing was remounted in fixed frames.

(19) All cabling was replaced with PVC insulation when repairs were due.

(20) Following a fire in car 1145 on 28th January, 1959, all Coronation trams had an additional automatic circuit-breaker installed above the staircase on the ceiling at one end to ensure that the 'live' supply cables could not be cut in any accident. A campaign change was pursued with some vigour to ensure that all metal-panelled cars were altered as soon as possible.

A close-up of the platform of 1220 shows the extended commode rails fitted to the doors after 1946, the larch slatting which has replaced the studded rubber from the flooring, the composite seating and the air-operated windscreen wiper. G.C.T.

Several Coronation trams sustained serious damage sufficient to warrant rebodying. 1169 was burned-out at Bellahouston Park on 1st November, 1938. 1275 was badly damaged in the Clydebank Blitz and was virtually rebodied, emerging with only white handrails instead of the normal cherry red as a clue to its attention in Coplawhill. 1163 received a new top deck in 1942 following severe damage by fire at Coatbridge on 7th January, 1941. 1220 was also rebodied in 1942 after destruction by fire at Clarkston on 1st February of that year. On 9th October, 1944, 1178 collided with 805 at Nelson Street and required substantial rebuilding while 1195 ran downhill to crash through a wall and hoarding at Rouken Glen on 8th November, 1941, also requiring much attention from the bodymakers at Coplawhill. On 11th April, 1948 the Newlands Depot fire claimed 1141, 1148 and 1239 while serously damaging 1241 and 1272. 1279 was burned out at Giffnock on 26th November, 1948. The repairs to1241 were hardly noticeable and it is thought that most damage was confined to exterior scorching. The others, however required new bodies.

This work was undertaken following completion of the last Cunarders through the bodyshops at Coplawhill. All cars re-entered service in May 1951 and were near-replicas of the original construction except that the forced air ventilation was omitted and the bulkhead mirror decorations were not reinstated. Several experimental features were included such as one piece cabin windscreens on 1141, 1148, 1239 and 1279 together with flush mounted glazing on 1148. The latter car had the staircase stringers externally painted in ivory with black and orange lining, as on the Standard cars, while on 1239 the green band was carried straight round the front, as on the Lightweight cars, and the cabin visors painted gold. This was altered to standard prior to entry to service.

The first clamourings for a uniform colour to supersede the route colour differentiation system had originally first been heard from the operational staff in 1936 in order to make the rostering of trams much easier. They eventually got their way, but the colour system was resurrected from time to time post war. One scheme envisaged most of the Coronation cars being painted red, with a few retained in green and some in neutral white. This idea was put forward in 1949 and, despite official denials, it is too much of a coincidence that three Coronation Cars, 1238, 1244 and 1278 appeared with red upper deck sides. Two more, 1234 and 1264, were also treated in this way but were repainted green before entry to service. The modelling of the red bands on the panels with the downsweeping treatment was different, employing a 'flatter' curve than on the normal trams, and 1234 and 1264 retained this after repainting back into green.

Further major rebuilding treatment was given to 1188 and 1249 which received plain aluminium top deck ceiling panels, painted white. It should be noted that, while the embossed Alhambrinal panels had been found difficult to clean, it was not until 1951/2 that any received overpainting so they did save on maintenance costs until that time.

Several Coronation cars were used for experimental work which did not come into widespread use and these are noted in the fleet tables. Two cars, 1156 and 1275 were re-trimmed internally conforming to the specification for the 1954 examples 1393-98.

1279 was burned out again on 26th April, 1954, while 1255 caught fire in Coplawhill on 25th February, 1955. Both cars were rebodied to the 1954 design and specification and details can be found regarding them in Chapter 14.

1255 was the last Coronation car to be rebodied or receive substantial expenditure and any later candidates for this were dismantled for spares pending implementation of the scrapping programme to encompass the modern cars.

That the 1937 design was basically used for the new construction undertaken after the Cunarders is a tribute to the conception by the designer of these excellent cars, A. B. Findlay. They were popular with the operating and maintenance staff as well as the travelling public. They would have outlasted the Cunarders had the 22nd March, 1961 fire at Dalmarnock Depot not created shortages which could be filled only with retention of their post-war sisters.

One further tram remains to be mentioned. On 27th October, 1948 Car 1256 was fitted with Metropolitan-Vickers Electrical Co. Ltd., automatic acceleration series-parallel equipment. The motors had already returned to Trafford Park, Manchester for alteration the previous January, being sent back to Glasgow in August. 1256 was Metro-Vick's answer to the VAMBAC control fitted to experimental car 1005. They claimed that it used their proved and simple design of electro-pneumatic gear to provide automatic multi-notch control. Normal current consumption was maintained using series-parallel control to give two combinations of motors, and

1170 at University terminus displays the first advertisement ever carried by Glasgow trams, first appearing in 1950 on car 130. The use of the 'via' aperture for the ultimate destination is unusual. ***R. F. Mack***

1279's second body was of the pattern awarded to all the Newlands Depot fire victims. This body was later destroyed by fire and replaced by one of the 1954 designs. ***Parr/STMS Collection***

A handful of pre-war Coronation trams was given a full interior re-trim following deterioration of the original finish. This is 1275 in 1959. The effect is still pleasing despite some simplification in standard. ***Struan J. T. Robertson***

smooth acceleration achieved by bridge transition with careful attention to notch spacing.

The automatic acceleration was of the sequence-interlock type controlled by an accelerating relay which had four settings dependent on the position of the controller handle. It was possible to use the controller conventionally, notch by notch, if the driver preferred.

The resistance was at first a British Thomson-Houston grid type with mica tube insulators, but this was later replaced by a Metro-Vick RP type ceramic rheostat. Normal motors were installed in April 1951 and the car was inspected by Brigadier Langley of the Ministry of Transport on 17th August, 1951.

Although 1256 was much less troublesome in performance than 1005 when fitted with VAMBAC equipment. The acceleration rate, compared with conventional cars, performed less favourably in the low speed ranges, despite being better in top speed potential. Accordingly, no further such equipment was ordered although 1256 retained the experimental equipment until victim to a stolen Central SMT bus on 16th December, 1961. The car was scrapped twelve days later, but the automatic acceleration contactor equipment was set aside, cleaned, and is now on display in the Glasgow Museum of Transport.

The weight of the production cars had been successfully reduced following criticism of 1141's.

1143-1255 and 1257-1292 weighed
16 tons 17 cwts 1 qr.
1256 weighed 17 tons 4 cwts 3 qr.

Car Number	Date to Service	Depots 1939	Depots 1954	Withdrawn/ Scrapped	Remarks
1141	29/12/36	n	n	26/10/61	Prototype Car Rebodied 16/8/51 after Newlands Fire
1142	16/3/37	t	n	8/2/60	Prototype car See text
1143	19/11/37	n	d	27/2/62	Fare table holder as on Standard cars. Wartime seating alteration
1144	27/11/37	n	c	24/8/62	Wartime seating alteration
1145	3/12/37	n	k	29/10/59	Wartime seating alteration Burned to frames 21/1/59
1146	10/12/37	n	t	8/11/61	
1147	27/12/37	n	k	4/9/62	Wartime seating alteration Last car to be scrapped 9/2/63
1148	24/12/37	n	n	1/9/62	Rebodied 25/5/51 after Newlands fire. Claytonright glazing
1149	30/12/37	n	t	1/9/62	Wartime seating alteration
1150	19/1/38	n	t	1/9/62	Wartime seating alteration
1151	11/1/38	n	t	1/9/62	
1152	25/1/38	n	t	19/1/59	Wartime seating alteration
1153	1/2/38	l	c	7/4/61	Wartime seating alteration Flush mounted glazing, top deck. Destroyed Dalmarnock fire 22/3/61
1154	8/2/38	m	m	1/9/62	
1155	14/2/38	m	m	1/9/62	Wartime seating alteration
1156	21/2/38	m	m	14/4/61	Wartime seating alteration Cunarder Lighting in both saloons Dalmarnock fire 22/3/61
1157	28/2/38	m	m	30/3/61	Handgrips in lower saloon Destroyed Dalmarnock fire 22/3/61
1158	7/3/38	m	m	6/4/62	
1159	14/3/38	m	m	4/4/61	Dalmarnock fire 22/3/61
1160	21/3/38	m	m	12/3/62	Retained original lighting difussers in lower saloon
1161	21/3/38	n	k	24/8/61	Whistles fitted 4/5/39 Wartime seating alteration
1162	28/3/38	l	c	21/3/62	Wartime seating alteration
1163	28/3/38	l	c	14/6/62	Wartime seating alteration New top deck 13/5/42
1164	4/4/38	l	c	29/5/62	Wartime seating alteration
1165	4/4/38	l	k	1/9/62	Wartime seating alteration
1166	11/4/38	k	k	1/9/62	Wartime seating alteration
1167	11/4/38	k	k	17/3/61	Klaxon horns 4/5/39 Wartime seating alteration
1168	18/4/38	k	t	3/8/61	
1169	18/4/38	n	k	8/3/61	Burned out 2/11/38 Rebuilt 24/11/38 Trucks to 1228 Wartime seating alteration
1170	25/4/38	k	k	31/8/62	Wartime seating alteration
1171	25/4/38	k	k	22/6/62	Wartime seating alteration
1172	2/5/38	n	k	4/9/62	Wartime seating alteration Damaged Newlands fire 11/4/48
1173	2/5/38	n	t	4/9/62	Wartime seating alteration Damaged Newlands fire 11/4/48 Preserved Glasgow
1174	9/5/38	n	t	4/9/62	Wartime seating alteration
1175	9/5/38	n	t	18/10/61	Wartime seating alteration
1176	16/5/38	n	t	1/9/62	
1177	16/5/38	n	t	19/4/62	
1178	23/5/38	n	t	14/7/61	Wartime seating alteration Four lamps in series
1179	23/5/38	n	t	29/5/62	Received Liverpool bogies & motors 8/9/51. To 1393 in 1954
1180	30/5/38	l	c	5/9/38	Wartime seating alteration
1181	30/5/38	l	c	1/9/62	Wartime seating alteration Hand grips in lower saloon
1182	7/6/38	l	c	1/9/62	Wartime seating alteration
1183	7/6/38	l	c	21/11/61	Wartime seating alteration
1184	14/6/38	l	c	14/6/62	Wartime seating alteration
1185	14/6/38	l	c	24/11/61	Wartime seating alteration Retained original lighting diffusers
1186	20/6/38	l	c	1/12/62	Wartime seating alteration
1187	20/6/38	l	m	28/6/62	Wartime seating alteration
1188	27/6/38	l	t	4/9/62	Fire damage 11/53—Top deck repaired with plain ceiling panels
1189	27/6/38	l	t	1/9/62	Wartime seating alteration First car with revised bow-rope access
1190	4/7/38	l	t	1/9/62	Wartime seating alteration
1191	4/7/38	l	m	4/7/61	Wartime seating alteration
1192	11/7/38	l	m	29/3/61	Wartime seating alteration
1193	11/7/38	l	c	8/2/62	Wartime seating alteration Flush mounted glazing, top deck
1194	2/8/38	n	m	5/7/62	
1195	15/7/38	l	m	1/9/62	Wartime seating alteration Flush mounted glazing, top deck
1196	8/8/38	n	b	10/8/62	
1197	8/8/38	n	n	27/3/62	Wartime seating alteration
1198	15/8/38	n	b	1/9/62	
1199	15/8/38	n	m	1/9/62	
1200	22/8/38	k	k	4/9/62	Wartime seating alteration Experimental Maley & Taunton control 11/45
1201	22/8/38	k	k	21/2/62	Wartime seating alteration
1202	29/8/38	k	k	2/10/61	Wartime seating alteration Scorched, Dalmarnock fire 22/3/61, repaired

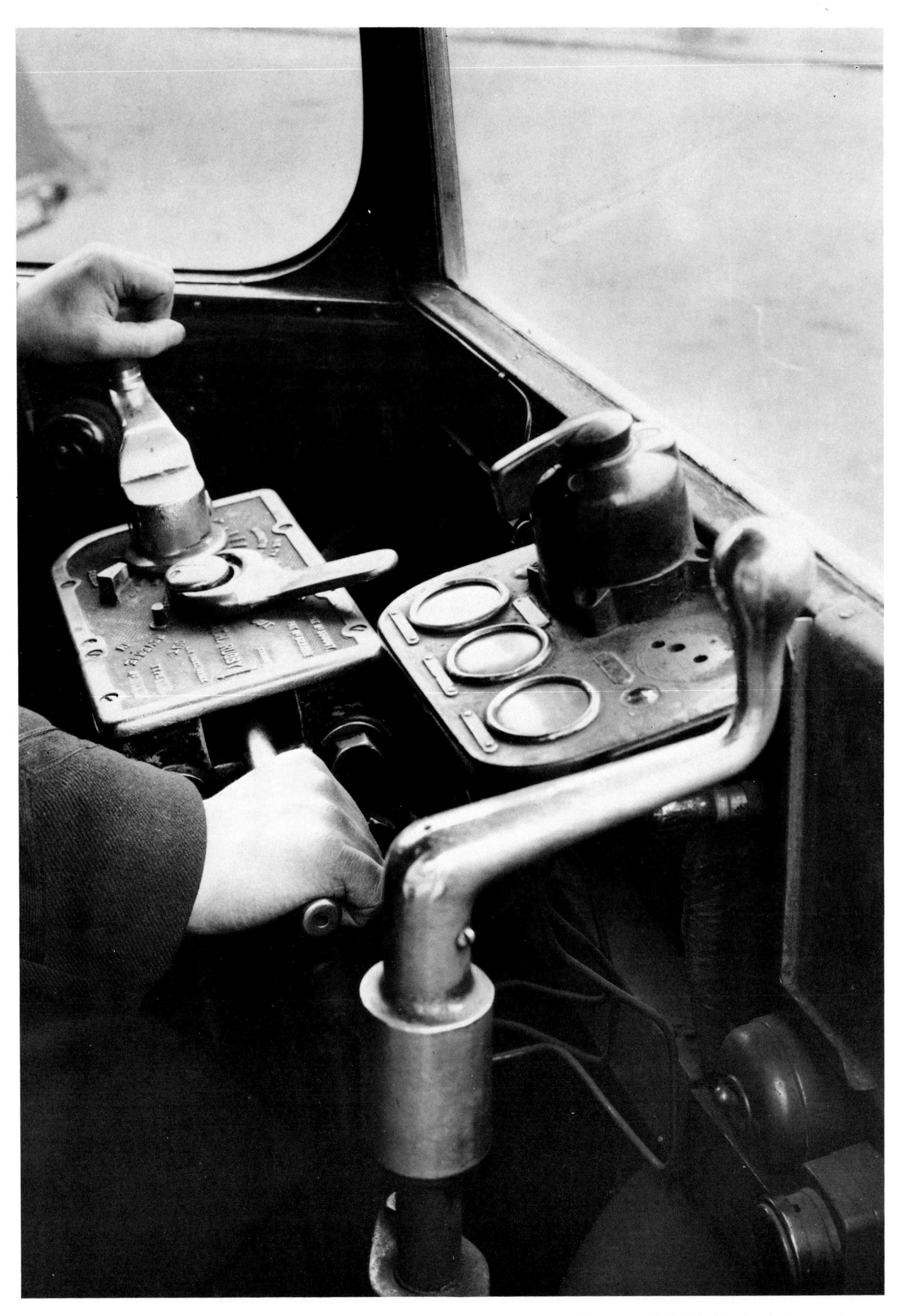

The cabin of the Mark I Coronation was rather cramped and – although functional – rather spartan in finish. Despite the luxury of a seat and a heater, many drivers preferred to stand at the controls on the exposed platforms of the Standard Cars. Note the original large pattern of trafficator switch. *G.C.T.*

Car Number	Date to Service	Depots 1939	1954	Withdrawn/ Scrapped	Remarks
1203	29/8/38	k	k	7/12/61	Wartime seating alteration
1204	5/9/38	k	k	6/4/61	Wartime seating alteration Burned out, Dalmarnock fire 22/3/61
1205	5/9/38	k	k	22/9/61	Wartime seating alteration
1206	12/9/38	k	k	13/6/61	Hand grips in lower saloon
1207	12/9/38	k	d	5/4/61	Wartime seating alteration Burned out, Dalmarnock fire 22/3/61
1208	19/9/38	k	k	11/4/61	Wartime seating alteration Burned out, Dalmarnock fire 22/3/61
1209	19/9/38	k	k	29/6/62	Wartime seating alteration Additional vents latterly above platform doors. Flush mounted glazing, top deck
1210	27/9/38	b	b	5/5/61	Burned out, Dalmarnock fire 22/3/61
1211	27/9/38	b	b	29/6/62	
1212	3/10/38	b	b	5/10/61	
1213	3/10/38	b	b	1/9/62	
1214	10/10/38	b	b	13/4/61	Burned out, Dalmarnock fire, 22/3/61
1215	10/10/38	b	b	3/11/61	Wartime seating alteration
1216	17/10/38	b	b	27/4/61	Burned out, Dalmarnock fire, 22/3/61
1217	17/10/38	b	b	8/6/62	
1218	24/10/38	b	d	12/1/61	
1219	24/10/38	b	n	1/9/62	First car with composite seating 2/45. Last with cabin half-drop windows, 6/58
1220	1/11/38	b	b	2/4/62	Rebodied 1942 with trucks ex-1256
1221	1/11/38	b	b	12/4/62	
1222	7/11/38	b	b	4/9/62	Last car to be re-wheeled
1223	7/11/38	b	b	22/6/62	Severely damaged, enemy action 13/3/41
1224	14/11/38	p	k	12/12/61	Wartime seating alteration
1225	14/11/38	p	k	11/8/61	Hand grips in lower saloon
1226	21/11/38	p	k	31/8/61	Wartime seating alteration
1227	21/11/38	p	k	7/4/61	Wartime seating alteration Perspex lamp diffusers. Burned out, Dalmarnock fire 22/3/61
1228	28/11/38	p	n	8/9/61	Trucks ex-1169 1938. Wartime seating alteration. Back to back seating. L/S 1945. Fluorescent lighting 1947/48
1229	28/11/38	p	k	20/4/61	Wartime seating alteration Burned out, Dalmarnock fire 22/3/61
1230	5/12/38	p	k	1/9/62	Wartime seating alteration
1231	5/12/38	p	k	28/9/61	Experimental Maley & Taunton control 11/45
1232	12/12/38	p	d	1/9/62	Wartime seating alteration
1233	12/12/38	p	k	25/4/61	Wartime seating alteration Burned out, Dalmarnock fire 22/3/61
1234	19/12/38	p	d	18/5/62	Wartime seating alteration Painted red 1949 but not in service thus
1235	19/12/38	p	k	4/12/61	Wartime seating alteration
1236	26/12/38	t	d	5/3/62	
1237	26/12/38	t	d	26/1/62	
1238	5/1/39	t	n	13/6/62	Wartime seating alteration Painted red 1949, placed in service
1239	17/1/39	t	n	11/6/62	Burned out Newlands fire, returned to service 24/5/51
1240	18/1/39	t	d	1/9/62	
1241	13/2/39	t	b	6/6/62	First car with entrance grab-rail re-sited. Severely damaged, Newlands fire 1948
1242	28/2/39	t	b	7/6/62	Wartime seating alteration
1243	16/5/39	k	k	1/9/62	Wartime seating alteration First of second batch of series production
1244	22/5/39	k	d	1/5/61	Wartime seating alteration Painted red 1949, placed in service Burned out Dalmarnock fire 22-3-61
1245	29/5/39	k	k	19/6/62	Preserved, East Anglia Transport Museum, Lowestoft
1246	5/6/39	k	k	16/1/62	
1247	12/6/39	k	k	5/7/62	Wartime seating alteration
1248	19/6/39	l	d	1/9/62	Wartime seating alteration
1249	26/6/39	l	d	18/6/62	Wartime seating alteration New top deck 7/53 after fire damaged—plain ceilings, aluminium lifeguard spars
1250	3/7/39	l	c	23/1/62	Wartime seating alteration Bench seating at ends of top deck, 1941. Retained original lighting diffusers in lower saloon
1251	10/7/39	l	c	4/5/61	Wartime seating alteration Burned out, Dalmarnock fire 22-3-61
1252	14/8/39	d	d	16/11/61	Wartime seating alteration
1253	31/7/39	d	b	1/9/62	Wartime seating alteration
1254	22/8/39	d	d	1/9/62	
1255	7/8/39	d	d	1/9/62	Wartime seating alteration Hand grips in lower saloon Burned out at Coplawhill 25/2/55. Rebodied
1256	15/8/39	d	n	28/12/61	Automatic acceleration equipment (Met-Vick) 10/48-end
1257	21/8/39	d	n	20/12/61	
1258	28/8/39	d	b	15/3/62	

1256 looked like any other Mark I Coronation tram unless its controller was examined closely. This was the car fitted with automatic acceleration equipment–Metropolitan Vickers' answer to the VAMBAC equivalent installed in 1005. *Parr/STMS Collection*

1145, photographed in 1954 on the Baillieston reserved track, anticipates the later appearance of cars 1393-1398. This car was burned to the frames in January 1959 when a lorry backed into the car in fog severing the main cable on the live side.
R. R. Clark/STMS Collection

Car Number	Date to Service	Depots 1939	Depots 1954	Withdrawn/ Scrapped	Remarks
1259	5/9/39	d	n	16/2/62	Wartime seating alteration Extended commode handles 1946 Flush mounted glazing, lower saloon
1260	12/9/39	l	k	1/9/62	Wartime seating alteration Aluminium lifeguard spars
1261	19/9/39	l	k	4/7/62	
1262	9/10/39	l	k	4/9/62	Wartime seating alteration One bogie to USA, 1963 as spare for 1274 at Seashore Museum
1263	9/10/39	l	k	20/6/62	
1264	20/10/39	l	k	13/11/61	Wartime seating alteration Painted red, 1949 but not placed in service thus
1265	20/10/39	l	k	20/6/62	Wartime seating alteration
1266	2/11/39	e	e	25/12/61	Wartime seating alteration
1267	14/11/39	e	e	15/12/61	Wartime seating alteration
1268	22/11/39	e	e	10/10/61	Wartime seating alteration First car of second 25 batch
1269	29/11/39	e	e	4/6/62	Wartime seating alteration Retained original diffusers for lower saloon lighting Bogies ex-1177 to 1282 for preservation
1270	13/12/39	e	e	15/6/62	Wartime seating alteration
1271	13/12/39	e	e	13/9/61	Wartime seating alteration
1272	23/12/39	n	e	26/6/62	Wartime seating alteration Cabin heaters 12/39 Severely damaged, Newlands fire 11/4/48 rebuilt
1273	27/12/39	n	e	18/5/62	Rebuilt after blast damage, 1941
1274	6/1/40	t	e	/4/62	Preserved, Seashore Trolley Museum, USA, despatched 11/9/63
1275	17/1/40	t	e	6/6/62	Rebodied after damage in blitz 1941. Fire damage 1957. Complete interior re-trim & flush-mounted glazing
1276	23/1/40	t	e	1/9/62	Wartime seating alteration
1277	30/1/40	t	e	22/9/61	Last tram to operate in Paisley, 5/57
1278	20/2/40	t	e	9/8/62	Wartime seating alteration Blitzed 13/3/41. Red livery 1949, placed in service thus
1279	20/2/40	t	e	1/9/62	Blitzed 1941 Burned Giffnock 26/11/48, rebodied 2/7/51. Burned Renfrew Ferry 26/4/54, rebodied 5/54
1280	21/2/40	t	e	13/10/61	Wartime seating alteration First car with step/handrail for mirror, 2/46
1281	28/2/40	t	e	3/7/62	Wartime seating alteration First car with Mark II L/S lighting 11/53
1282	5/3/40	t	e	6/9/62	Last tram to run in Scotland. To National Tramway Museum, Crich, 1963
1283	12/3/40	t	e	4/6/62	
1284	5/4/40	m	m	23/8/62	Experimental windscreen wipers 16/4/40
1285	11/4/40	m	m	1/9/62	
1286	25/6/40	m	m	24/5/62	To storage, Newlands Depot 25/4/40 Wartime seating alteration Handgrips in lower saloon
1287	3/7/40	m	m	1/9/62	To storage, Newlands Depot 25/4/40
1288	9/7/40	m	m	31/10/61	To storage, Newlands Depot 1/5/40 Wartime seating alteration
1289	13/7/40	m	m	21/1/59	To storage, Newlands Depot 1/5/40 Wartime seating alteration. Overturned & scrapped
1290	3/8/40	m	m	1/9/62	To storage, Newlands Depot 1/5/40
1291	4/12/40	m	m	30/5/61	To storage, Newlands Depot 8/6/40
1292	5/7/41	m	m	27/6/62	To storage, Newlands Depot 8/6/40

Preserved Cars

1173 At Glasgow Museum of Transport. Restored as nearly as possible to 1938 condition

1245 At East Anglia Transport Museum. Restored to post 1957 condition

1274 At Seashore Trolley Museum, USA. Restored to post 1957 condition

1282 At National Tramway Museum, Crich. Operating following complete rebuild to c1952/3 condition

Note:

1269 Was set aside for the Scottish Tramway Museum Society who were donating a Mark I Coronation Car to the Crich Tramway Museum. 1269 retained the original light fittings in the lower saloon. On close examination the body was found to be in poor condition compared with other trams then available and 1282 was substituted at the end of August 1962. Coincidently, 1282 was selected to operate special commemorative runs in Clydebank two days after the final procession in Glasgow and therefore became the last tram to operate in Scotland. Happily the original light fittings from 1269 were able to be removed and refitted in 1282.

1173 Was withdrawn from passenger service for restoration 2/62.

By April 1957, 697 was easily the oldest tram in the fleet and is seen at High Street Renfrew alongside rebodied car 643 on the left. For those with broader minds the Western SMT AEC Regent Mark II will also be of interest. *W.D. McMillan*

994 should be compared with the view of the same tram 43 years earlier on page 77. By this time the car had heavy bracing fitted internally to the lower saloon pillars. Service 12 never entered the City Centre but was no rest cure for trams. Its track latterly was in a parlous state. *W.D. McMillan*

Having played its part as the last illuminated tram for the 1959 Scottish Industries Exhibition No. 27 was the last Works Car to be repainted and is the best representative to display their livery. *W.D. McMillan*

154 swings round the north west corner of George Square past the now-concealed arch of Queen Street Station. The '1' and '30' services were the last to be entirely served by Standard trams until closure in 1960. *W.D. McMillan*

CHAPTER 10

The Experimental Bogie Tramcar 1100

EXPERIMENTAL DOUBLE BOGIE CAR — 1100

1100 leads 402 on special workings from Partick Depot to Dalmuir West. The new tapered ends grafted on to the original Hurst Nelson body can be seen together with the twin aspect route colour lights retained on this car. A Standard Double Bogie car brings up the rear in this February 1954 view.
R.J.S. Wiseman

As can be seen under the heading of 'Standard Double Bogie Cars', 1100 did start off as a completely standard car in its class, being one of thirty constructed by Hurst Nelson Ltd., entering service in November 1928. In October 1929, however, the car was called to Coplawhill Carworks to have the Kilmarnock Engineering Co. maximum traction bogies removed and substituted with an equivalent pair by J. G. Brill & Co., their model 61 E1. These resembled externally the 39 E1 variants by the same manufacturers then in use with Car 15 but are thought to be the only ones used in Great Britain. From then on, 1100's history becomes confusing and complex, not completely recorded and difficult to explain. Much of what follows is a reconstruction based on scant evidence available here and there. If facts are not known for sure these are highlighted.

1100 was originally a Parkhead Depot car and remained there after acquiring the Brill maximum traction bogies. When the other members of the class had to be re-allocated from Govan and Parkhead to Partick and Dalmarnock Depots, 1100 remained in Parkhead — the only bogie tramcar there. When the others were repainted with red route colour bands 1100 remained green. It sat higher on its bogies than the other maximum traction cars and apparently was not permitted to pass beneath the railway bridge in Coatbridge immediately adjacent to the hump-backed bridge over the canal. This restriction apart, 1100 had freedom over all the green services operated from Parkhead whereas the other maximum traction cars were limited to the Argyle Street and Dumbarton Road services from Clydebank/Dalmuir West to Auchenshuggle or Burnside.

Some time in the 1930s, 1100 is believed to have run with the maximum traction bogies reversed—that is, with the pony axles leading. A pantograph is also thought to have been fitted for a short time.

Between September and November of 1940, the Brill, or 'Yankee' bogies as they were termed, were dismantled and scrapped being replaced by two Kilmarnock Engineering Co. maximum traction bogies, differing from standard only in their having individual bogie-mounted air cylinders. Presumably it was not desired to hold spares for the Brill bogies and those from Car 15 scrapped during the previous year. The Kilmarnock bogies came from stock and at least one of the MV 101DR motors came from Hexagonal dash Standard Car 151 which had overturned at Clarence Drive, sustaining such damage as to warrant scrapping of the body.

The experiments with four wheeled modern cars (see Chapter 11) envisaged the possibility of experiments with other trucks. Between November 1940 and May 1941, 1100 remained at Coplawhill. The controllers and rheostat were removed and the ends rebuilt completely to assimilate the Coronation cars of the period with symmetrical taper to provide separate cabins. Platform doors were provided and new reversed stairs ascending clockwise over the driving cabins. The sliding bulkhead doors were removed and the cabins were not provided with any doors. Dash-mounted service number screens were located on the near side to the right of the entrance in similar fashion to those on 1001-1004. (*q.v.*) The front panels were narrower than on Coronation cars and there was insufficient width to place the service number screen immediately to the side of the 'destination' and 'via' apertures. Instead, the number was placed above, reverting to the style displayed by 1938/39 buses supplied by Weymann and Cowieson to GCT. Interestingly and uniquely, 1100 (and Standard Car 584) were fitted with twin aspect service colour light indicators capable of day and night illumination mounted on the nearside next to the front upstairs half-drop window. It would appear that this was a proposed development of the route colour system, similar to Edinburgh's. These provided five colours on rotating turrets, red, green, blue, white and yellow but trouble was experienced with the Police. The indicator was taken off 584 while 1100's remained *in situ* out of use. It is thought that there were objections to the display of red aspects at the front of the car and this is substantiated by 1100's red lenses being painted black until restoration at the Crich Tramway Museum in 1965/66.

Between what was left of the bulkheads, the car remained structurally a 'Kilmarnock Bogie' although acquiring brown leather seats on both decks from scrapped Semi-High Speed Standard trams. The ends incorporated recessed lighting of the same pattern as that installed in Car 1003 (Edinburgh Shrubhill Standard tram pattern). The cabins were provided with one-piece windscreens and ventilation was effected by an outward-opening hinged glazed flap operated from within by a gearwheel and protected from collision damage by an external visor. The transformation was aided by painting the car in Coronation livery with cream upper deck window frames and vestibules but would have been complete had the rebuild been taken to its logical conclusion in the provision of a domed roof. The flat roof with tapered, semi-streamlined ends resulted in an unfortunate clash of styles. Seating was repositioned to accommodate 70 passengers (40 + 30). The original drawings indicate luggage racks located in the positions later provided with single seats over the sand hoppers.

Maley & Taunton field control equipment was installed. This worked on line voltage but it was sensitive to fluctuations and this caused the tram to stall on heavily loaded sections of route. As it became disabled, cars queued up behind, ceased to draw current, the voltage rose, 1100 became live again

1100 heading east with helpful destination display shows the final modification to the vestibuling and upper saloon front window. Note the dash service number box. These had also been incorporated in the experimental cars 1001-1004 and 6, but on these cars this feature was removed post 1947.
Parr/STMS Collection

and continued on its way until those behind did likewise, the voltage dropped and 1100 stalled. This was to occupy Maley & Taunton's most patient engineer for many weeks but he did not have the benefit of hindsight.

The ascending staircase treads were found to come into contact with the driver's head on too many occasions to be coincidental and the opportunity was taken to amend the design to incorporate conventional Coronation pattern anti-clockwise stairs and a new set of platform doors. At this time — August 1942 — 1100 acquired Skefko pony axle roller bearing axleboxes and the field control equipment was removed to be replaced by conventional British Thomson-Houston remote electropneumatic control equipment. This was altered at Coplawhill from a standard four motor unit and its siting within the lower saloon resulted in a loss of one corner seat to give a total of 29. During and after these metarmorphoses, 1100 remained a Partick car, seldom appearing east of Partick — although until 1946 there are records of minor repairs being undertaken at Dalmarnock Depot and the car did perform some special duties which took it along Great Western Road until this line closed.

Latterly, the car had regular duties and regular crews on shipyard morning and evening specials. It was also in demand — particularly towards the end — for enthusiasts' tours of the system. 1100 was not repainted after 1947 and never had advertisement blank panels. The original pattern Partick red service screens with 'via' display were retained until very late on. The Glasgow Coat of Arms remained on the upper panels but when paper bills were applied to the sides, the crest was applied to the lower sides, hence at times there were two per side. In August 1949 and again in October 1950, 1100 was scheduled for scrapping with the other oddity, 142. 142 went but 1100 survived. Few subsequent alterations were carried out except the removal of the half-drop upper deck front windows and substitution with hinged glazed flaps. At this time, the cabins were altered to reduce the height of glazing by providing a small rectangular panel on which the windscreen wiper and motor were mounted. Automatic emergency braking equipment was not fitted, nor was the emergency cut-out switch. The fleet number was transferred from the dash to this panel which also acted as a sun-visor. The No. 2 end vestibule was dented during careless shunting in Partick Depot, hence that end repaired in 1957 was noticeably cleaner than the other still displaying its 1947 paint. 1100 was last recorded as allocated to Partick at November 2nd, 1961 but may not have been used after that in a passenger service.

1100 left Coplawhill for the Crich Tramway Museum in 1964, the last tram to leave. How it got there is another story . . .

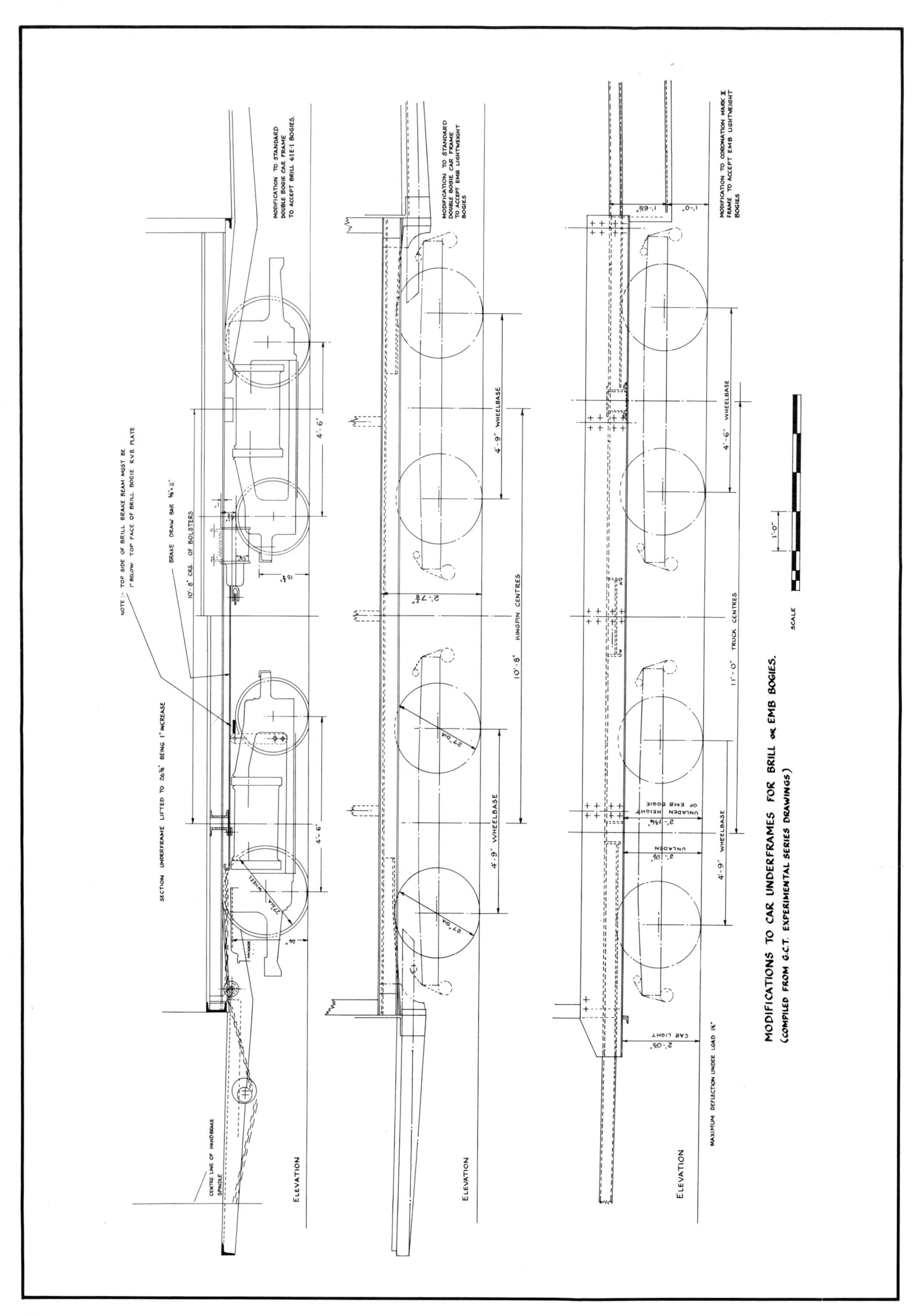

The need to achieve greater versatility from the robust Maximum Traction cars can be seen in the drawings prepared by G.C.T. to have these cars mounted on Brill and then EMB bogies. 1100 ran with Brill 61E-1 bogies throughout the 1930s, while 1128 had a not inconsiderable sum spent in modifications for EMB Lightweight bogies. The car did not enter service thus equipped. The modification of the Coronation Mark II underframe is even more intriguing. It would seem to be the embryo of an idea to construct new bodies for ex-Liverpool bogies which might have been purchased rather than a substitution for the Maley & Taunton equipment.

CHAPTER 11

The Experimental Lightweight Tramcars 1001–4 and 6

THE EXPERIMENTAL 'LIGHTWEIGHT' CARS 1001-1004 AND 6

In Chapter 9 we saw that caution won the day and rather than proceed with the construction of six hundred Coronation Cars on 8th December, 1938 it was decided to build four experimental four wheel tramcars. There have been many examples of industries where the product was too good and the company failed. The Transport Department was not failing — far from it — but their Coronation Cars were so luxurious and so popular that GCT had created a rod for their own backs. The travelling public would expect this standard to be maintained. The new cars, however, were expensive to build, expensive to operate and expensive to maintain. This was the obvious background to the instruction given to the General Manager 'to construct two new four-wheeled cars and to modernise two high speed cars'. They can also be seen as the justification in not proceeding with trolleybuses, in maintaining the tramway system and replacing the semi-high speed cars.

That this instruction was interpreted somewhat liberally will be seen because the General Manager reported on 21st December, 1938 that he had obtained offers for the supply of two 'hornless' trucks and also for the reconditioning and conversion of two existing four wheeled trucks into the hornless type. It was agreed that contracts should be placed with Maley & Taunton Ltd. for one new truck costing £512 and one reconditioned truck at £355, together with the EMB Co. Ltd. for one new and one reconditioned truck costing £480 and £300 respectively. The Transport Committee gave the General Manager the remit to submit a report on the possibility of experiments being carried out with other types of trucks. (Car 1100, perhaps?) The fact of the matter was that one of the existing four wheeled trucks which was to be converted into hornless trucks was already hornless pattern. The EMB reconditioned truck was from car 413 — the first to be thus equipped in 1934 — and of their Swing Axle pattern with 8'-6" wheelbase.

The other truck came from Car 97 and was of 1930 vintage. It is listed in official records variously as having been transferred to Car 1001 as a Maley & Taunton unit, complete, or having been reconditioned. On looking into the matter and examining drawings and photographs referring to this car, it would seem most likely that material was salvaged from the original Brush/GCT 21E pattern truck to be incorporated in the Maley & Taunton truck which was to all intents and purposes 'new'. In January 1940, 97's motors (MV 101DR) were taken into stock while 413's GEC motors were actually transferred to another experimental car 1003. The other two new cars constructed at the time were all new: 1002 was mounted on a Maley & Taunton truck with 1004 on an EMB Co. equivalent, each being visually identical to the same suppliers' equipment on sister cars 1001 and 1003 respectively.

Whether or not this interpretation of the Transport Committee remit satisfied them will never be known. No doubt they would have had in mind the situation whereby the very oldest trams in the fleet (one dating from 1898) on which no money had intended to be spent only eight years previously, were operated with the newest trucks and electrical equipment.

Mr. R. F. Smith was able to confirm that machining of the timber for the four new cars had commenced by June 1939 and these would utilise underframes

An experimental car under construction (probably 1001). The top and bottom decks had just been assembled together after separate construction. ***G.C.T.***

supplied by R. Y. Pickering Ltd., of Wishaw, builders of Maximum Traction cars 1121-1130. 1001 was completed in October 1939 and 1002 in November with the remaining two in January 1940. Completion had been held up by the delays in obtaining certain materials due to the hostilities which commenced in September 1939.

Each new car was individually different in specification to the other. The specifications were listed as follows:—

Weight	*Tons*	*Cwts*	*Qrs*	
1001	11	11	1	Overall length 31'-0"
1002	11	15	2	Overall breadth 7'-3½"
1003	12	10	—	with 10" rake from
1004	12	16	—	waist rail to roof

The height to the roof boards was 14'-10" on 1001 and 1002 and 15'-2" on 1003 and 1004.

Improvements introduced on these cars over and above the high standards obtained on the Coronations included side service number screens adjacent to the loading points, step lights illuminating the lower steps which were only 9¼" from the ground on a loaded car and lower saloon floors ramped at each end to permit as low a step as possible. The front number screens were relocated to the nearside of the destination information so that they could be more easily read when in a line of trams.

Car 1001 was mounted on the 'reconditioned' Maley & Taunton truck similar to their type 588. This was later to appear on Sheffield's post war cars and was probably derived from the Glasgow version. The

The front view of 1001 as built shows a family resemblance to the Coronation Mark I car with some features later to appear on the Mark II. Note the dash service number box and the Whipple horizontal bladed windscreen wipers. The destination layout later became standard for postwar Corporation buses until 1956. G.C.T.

The upper saloon of 1001 incorporates much of the comfort and detail found in the contemporary Coronation trams but illustrates a transition between the Coronation Mark I and Mark II cars in such features as lighting, plain ceilings and ventilation. G.C.T.

underframe was electrically welded and weighed under one ton. Two 60 hp MV 101DR motors were fitted ex-Coplawhill stock and the controllers were Metropolitan Vickers OK 26B pattern near to standard but with a circular interlock box similar to those on the Leeds 'Horsfield' tramcars. A separate air brake valve and handle were provided together with visual 'pop-up' low air pressure warning. Seating was provided for 62 passengers — only three less than on the Coronations at the time — 24 below and 38 above.

Car 1002 had the all-new Maley & Taunton truck, also of 8'-6" wheelbase. The two Crompton Parkinson 70 hp C162B8 motors were carried on roller bearing sleeves to reduce noise over crossings. Truck suspension was on rubber springs, like those on 1001. A patent device was incorporated to eliminate brake block chatter. Crompton-West remote control was installed with separate Maley & Taunton air braking facilities on the master controllers. The contactor equipment was tucked under the staircase at one end and incorporated radio interference suppressors. The battery circuit operated at 36 volts. For the first time in Glasgow, automatic acceleration was provided to ensure that however carelessly the controller handle was carried over the power notches, the control drum for the contactor magnet valves followed the handle at a controlled correct speed. Seating on 1002 and on 1003/4 was provided for 60 passengers — two less being accommodated within the upper saloon than on 1001.

Car 1003 incorporated the reconditioned EMB Swing Axle 8'-6" truck from car 413 complete with the latter's 60 hp GEC WT28 motors. The manual controllers were, like 1001's, of the OK26B pattern but with an extra-deep interlock box and 'nine o' clock "off" ' position.

Car 1004 had the new EMB truck virtually identical to that on 1003 but with two 60 hp GEC WT283 motors operated by GEC remote control similar to 1002's and master controllers with EMB interlock. Part of the weight of the tram was carried through the air cushion in the cylinders to prevent jarring of the car body. Armatures were roller bearing.

Current consumption under tests was shown to be:—

1001 2.2 units per car mile
1002 2.0 units per car mile
1003 2.26 units per car mile
1004 2.0 units per car mile

The reduction on the cars with remote control can be seen in spite of their carrying additional weight. These figures should be compared with consumption for Coronation Cars of 3.19 units per car mile (average) and 2.13 for Standard Cars.

The comparative costs were:—

1001 — £2,359 1003 — £2,078
1002 — £3,140 1004 — £2,946

This compared with production Coronation cars, each £3,354.

The bodywork was virtually identical on all four cars with 1003/4 being noticeably higher off the ground than on 1001/2 with the result that more of the trucks could be seen from the pavement. On all except 1003, the interior decor was very similar. If 1005 was to become the precursor of the 100 post war Coronation Mark II cars, the experimental cars were the precursors of 1005 although some features went direct from them to the Mark II cars without being applied to 1005. Concealed lighting was fitted behind flat etched glass panels which incorporated mirror glass reflectors. The upper deck interior was lightened with curved eaves glasses. The saloons were of the four window pattern incorporating sliding vents as installed on the contemporary Corporation buses. Alhambrinal panelling was extensively used as on the Coronation Cars but the upper saloon ceilings — prone to discolouring — were enamelled white.

This could be repainted as required whereas the Alhambrinal had been found difficult to keep clean due to nicotine staining. On 1003, the bodywork did not have eaves glasses and the interior was much more basic in treatment of finish and decor. Both saloons had plain white ceilings with inset lamp fittings similar to those on Edinburgh Corporation's Shrubhill standard trams of the time. Seating was brown leather in both decks, ex-scrapped semi-high speed Standard trams and thus 1003 was the nearest interpretation to the brief given by the Transport Committee that existing equipment should be used. (1001 was intended to utilise such seating but was equipped with new seats.) All four cars had sliding pullman doors instead of the hitherto normal jack-knife pattern used on the Coronation cars. No separate cabin doors were fitted either direct to the street or to the interior of the trams.

1001 was despatched new to Partick Depot. The other three were allocated to Newlands where they were later joined by 1001. In livery treatment they were similar to the Coronation Cars but the green band was not downswept at the ends. GLASGOW CORPORATION was applied by transfers to the panels above the lower saloon windows similar to the contemporary Corporation buses. No illuminated clerestory panels were fitted.

Recalling the suggestion that experiments with other trucks should be put in hand, there was little chance that any progress could be made with this during the Second World War due to severe restrictions on delivery of materials. However, an opportunity arose when Standard Car No. 6 sustained a direct hit on 13th March, 1941, the night of the Clydebank Blitz. It was decided to provide a replacement for this car and — probably for insurance or due to government restrictions — the number '6' was re-used rather than utilise the next number in the experimental series — '1005' — which was vacant. Construction was put in hand during 1941/2 as material and labour became available. The bodywork was similar to 1003's, that is, without eaves glasses but finish and seating was nearer to that of the other three experimental cars. Meantime the bomb-damaged 6's truck was transferred to Car 178 and a new truck made up to the GCT/Brush specification, 21E inspired, as fitted on the Standard cars but of 8'-6" wheelbase. Let the myth be exploded once and for all that not one nut or bolt from Hex-dash Standard Car No. 6 went into the construction of Lightweight experimental car No. 6 which instead was the true assessment of the feasibility of using existing equipment with new bodies.

Car 6 was fitted with the field control equipment which had been unsuccessfully installed in rebuilt car 1100 until August 1942. It was equally unsuccessful in Car 6 although altered to be operated by a belt-driven motor generator set. This proved impractical due to belt slip and a 12 volt battery set superseded it very soon. The motors were MV 101DR 60 hp latterly operated through MV OK26B controllers with

Experimental 'Lightweight' Car 1001 was originally allocated to Partick Depot and was photographed at Auchenshuggle in 1940 showing wartime adaptations such as headlamp masking and over-painted eaves glasses. ***W. Fisher, Courtesy D. W. Fisher***

Standard Car 6 was demolished by a Luftwaffe direct hit in 1941 but was replaced with a completely new car. This was rebodied following the Newlands Depot fire seven years later. The rebodied car is seen at Paisley Cross. Utility low bridge buses were no competition for Paisley's modern trams.

W. A. C. Smith

standard EMB interlocks. 6 was despatched to Newlands Depot and remained there until severely damaged in the fire on 11th April, 1948. By October 1949 it had been scheduled to receive a new body and it was duly rebuilt in 1951. This was slightly more utilitarian in that it incorporated fewer sliding ventilators but it did include Coronation Mk I pattern seating.

The experimental cars were less popular in service due to their being non-standard and less familiar to operating and maintenance staff. Newlands Depot used them quite extensively nonetheless with the only complaints noted being lack of handrails fitted to facilitate adjustment externally to the cabin mirrors. These were fitted as requested. Motorman fatigue was reported on 1001/3 due to the cramped conditions in the cabins with full sized controllers. The installation of remote control as in 1002/4 was requested. This was not pursued.

Few alterations were undertaken except the removal of the dash-mounted number screens, substitution of radius-sweep windscreen wipers for the horizontal chain driven units and simplification of livery eliminating GLASGOW CORPORATION and transferring the fleet numbers from below to above the windscreens. Only 1003 acquired untenanted blank advertisement panels. The half-drop upper saloon front windows were replaced with hinged bow rope access flaps during the 1950s except on 1003.

It was decided in May 1951 to transfer the five members of the class to Elderslie Depot to operate the Glenfield-Renfrew Ferry service. Clearance checks were made showing that there were possible difficulties at entry to and exit from the single track section at Weir Street but subject to caution being exercised that no other trams were in the way this was not considered to pose any problem. The cars settled down there until the service ended in May 1957, only occasionally journeying into Glasgow for some attention that Elderslie Depot's own workshop facilities could not fulfil.

When the Paisley services were withdrawn, 6 was transferred to Possilpark Depot for a few days and the others to Govan, later joined by 6 which was obviously too much for Possilpark. No doubt some clerk in 46 Bath Street had thought that 6 was a Standard car like all the others in Possilpark!

Govan Depot used the experimental cars on special workings from the shipyards at rush hours only. They operated without number screens, displaying only naked light bulbs although Standard car number screens could be accommodated.

After almost a year at Govan Depot these cars were transferred to Newlands where they were never used, returning to Govan after that depot closed. When the power was cut off in February 1959 they were sold to Connell's of Coatbridge for scrap, being non-standard.

Although of an experimental nature and not repeated as such, the impact of the 'Lightweights' should not be underestimated. Many of their features were incorporated in later construction and in modifications to the existing fleet. Due to the advanced age of existing trucks after the War it was not considered feasible to re-use any trucks. Indeed major problems were encountered from then on with broken side frames which were never really cured. After completion of the 100 post war cars, Mr. Findlay, Tramways Engineer, wanted to salvage 20 of the best trucks from the converted Regenerative cars and ex-Paisley cars, purchase 40 new trucks and build 60 new bodies of the 1001-4 and 6 design. Like so many other proposals, this was not approved.

CHAPTER 12

The Experimental One Way Car 1005

EXPERIMENTAL 'ONE-WAY' CAR: No. 1005

The idea of tramcars having separate entrance and exit facilities is not new to Glasgow; it can be seen in the experiments which took place in Standard car No. 137 in 1914 and Single Decker 1089 in 1926. The Glasgow public was incapable of being educated to use the separate doorways due, for the most part, to the 'one off' nature of the experiments. A single car on any route which is different from all the others in this respect is doomed to failure and it was pointed out with justification that in any case passengers in Glasgow do not waste time in boarding or leaving. The benefits did not outweigh the disadvantages. By 1932 both trams concerned had reverted to normal.

During the Second World War there emerged via Corporation elected members further agitation to pursue a policy of building trams with separate entrance and exit provision. Whether this emanated from visits to Newcastle or Bournemouth will probably now never be known. With difficulties in obtaining materials, spare parts and labour, the Transport Department was in no position to undertake any actual construction other than to keep its fleet of trams going. However, the drawing office at 46 Bath Street prepared some plans used either as feasibility study documents or for discussion. These drawings included general arrangements of the Single Decker Car 1089 converted to double deck with tapered ends (Coronation style) and four doors. With its extra long saloon it would have been better placed than others to accommodate staircases outwith the platform areas. Other drawings prepared comprised 'Lightweight' experimental bodywork (1001-4, etc.) amended to accommodate four sliding doors, with staircases (straight) transferred to the saloons. This resulted in a reduction in seating capacity to 50 and a considerable loss in revenue per car mile compared with the maximum of 62 which could otherwise be carried.

On 6th August, 1945 the Transport Committee authorised the General Manager to proceed with the construction of an experimental double-deck tramcar with a separate entrance and exit. It is no longer a matter of speculation why the tram was made unidirectional with a cabin at one end only. The following are the facts which enabled the decision to be taken in this respect:—

(a) Providing two sets of entrances and exits caused too many revenue seats to be lost as can be seen previously.
(b) The modern control equipment proposed could not be accommodated in a tram with cabins and lifeguard gear at both ends.
(c) There was insufficient space beneath the floor to site ancillary equipment due to the space occupied by the bogies which were of 6'-0" wheelbase.

With authorisation given, the GCT Drawing Office commenced preliminary work on the proposed tram and wrestled with the problems posed above. There were many letters exchanged between it and Crompton Parkinson Ltd., of Chelmsford whose quotation of 15th September was to provide the starting point as it also included a suggested layout of equipment. This indicated that the accelerator would be located under the rear platform but the suppliers would have preferred this under the front of the car. The designers in Glasgow were reluctant to commit themselves without sight of a detailed drawing for the equipment concerned but foresaw difficulties in having this approved by the then Ministry of War Transport due to limited clearances in the event of someone falling in front of the car. Crompton Parkinson also indicated that the Contactor Box would be located under the rear staircase but would have preferred to see this housed beneath the car. This was also ruled out due to lack of space.

It was hoped to place the Master Controller below the driver's seat but Crompton Parkinson wanted this, too, to be located below the floor. This posed insurmountable problems with the platform bearers which could not be spread. Originally, a foot-operated controller had been proposed, incorporating one or two notches for reversing. It was agreed to provide a separate rear-mounted shunting controller electro-pneumatically operated, since air would be incorporated for braking in any case.

Crompton Parkinson Ltd. went to Glasgow on 23rd November, 1945 to carry out tests with a typical Coronation tramcar on a typical route. The car chosen was 1289 on service 8 between Rouken Glen and Millerston. Rates of acceleration and deceleration were recorded under city and suburban conditions, together with the associated current consumptions. On the outskirts with longer runs of up to 915 ft., the running time recorded was 43.5 seconds with a rate of acceleration of 1.2 mphps. Cut-off speed was 24 mph and the rate of braking 1.7 mphps. The starting current was 110 amps series for 7 seconds and 140 amps at the point of cut-off, which was 25 seconds from the start. The energy consumption was 3.65 units per car mile. Comment was made that the driver held his car on 7th series notch for too long before moving over to the first parallel notch, resulting in a current peak with lower performance than if the transitional period had been less than the 4 seconds taken. In the inner city, the average run equated to 560 ft. covered in 42 seconds. Initial acceleration was 1.2 mphps. The rate of braking was as before but it was noted that the driver never went beyond the series notches on the controller, reaching a speed of 13 mph. The starting current of 110 amps was maintained for approximately 9 seconds after which it fell to 50 amps at 16 seconds. Typically, the driver would notch up again on to full series for 5 seconds with a current consumption of approximately 50 amps. For these runs, the consumption was evaluated at approximately 1.55 units per car mile.

Crompton Parkinson proposed to arrange the motors and control gear for the new car to provide a starting current of 200 amps or 100 amps per motor on a notch to reproduce Coronation Car service. With identical performance, they calculated the energy consumption at 3.14 units per car mile. To do this, they proposed to have a notch on the controller corresponding to a starting current of 200 amps per car up to full field only. For shorter city runs they proposed to provide a notch for full field running with a starting current of 80 amps per motor or 160 amps per car to achieve an energy consumption of 2.88 units per car mile. This would be reduced if increased coasting was possible.

From these tests and calculations it was claimed that it would be possible on the new car to achieve the same performance as on the existing Coronation cars with less energy consumption and without exceeding the peak starting currents which they obtained. Drivers, though, would have to amend their techniques to eliminate the pause on the full series notch.

1005 was one of the most handsome trams ever built by G.C.T. The striking livery in three shades of blue complemented the clean lines of the bodywork. Its unidirectional features were dictated by lack of space to accommodate two sets of entrances and exits.
G.C.T.

Crompton Parkinson's traction engineers also commented generally that the Coronation cars were cabable of operating at substantially higher speeds than demanded of them and that Car 1002 consumed substantially less energy for the same performance. (It should be recalled that 1002 incorporated the only Crompton Parkinson motors in the fleet at that time.) The proposal was to flatten the motor characteristic in the new tram to reduce the speed of the car free running on the full field characteristic. Increased acceleration rates would promote earlier cut-offs.

In the General Manager's report for the year ending 31st May, 1946, he was able to report that the experimental tram was being built. By the time Mr. Fitzpayne issued his report for the following financial year the tram was still awaiting electrical equipment. Reference to Chapter 13 shows recommendations for improving the existing Coronation trams put forward by Mr. A. B. Findlay, Tramways Engineer. It was resolved to put some of these into practice within the new experimental car before finalising details for batch construction. Hence the new car was in many ways the precursor of the Mark II Coronation. Construction commenced on 15th January, 1946. What emerged was, without exaggeration, sensational! Seating 72 passengers — the most ever achieved by GCT in their own designs —the car had a graceful symmetrical taper at the front while the rear was more blunt. The lower saloon accommodated 34 passengers on Coronation Mk I car patterned moquette seating while the upper held 38 on hide seats. With low window sills and relatively high seats, passengers on the upper deck commanded excellent views. With no need for reversing, the seats were fixed, bus fashion, and exceptionally comfortable. The saloon was 20'-6" long and provided with four panoramic windows per side. Each had sliding top ventilators. Alhambrinal panelling was used for interior side linings and also for the lower deck ceiling. The upper saloon ceiling was enamelled white and made lighter by perspex eaves glasses set into the roof curvature. Lighting comprised exposed fluorescent tubes set immediately above the windows to give very high levels of illumination. The platforms were both on the nearside. Those at the front, under the direct eye of the driver from his offside cabin, had air operated folding doors but the rear platform was without doors. These acted, respectively, as entrance and exit. The height of the tram was 16'-0¼".

The bogies were 6'-0" wheelbase, type HS44 manufactured by Maley & Taunton Ltd., and had spoked wheels fully exposed to view since the PCC-derived design incorporated inside frames. The motors were Crompton Parkinson 45 hp type 90-A-10 mounted opposed to the axles and driving through David Brown worm gear. The front end controller was by Crompton-West and comprised their type CT/MM1 located beneath the motorman's seat operated by 'joystick' type levers on each side of the seat. VAMBAC (Variable Automatic Multi-notch Braking and Acceleration Control) equipment was located beneath the rear platform. Its vulnerability to flooding was to pose problems to be resolved during the first few months in service.

The upper saloon in 1005 looking towards the rear shows the two offside staircases and fixed leather seating. Note the non nicotine staining ceiling panelling totally devoid of wooden trim - a feature not to appear again until 1957 in Corporation buses. **G.C.T.**

Having produced a modern tramcar bristling with innovation and features unfamiliar to the Glasgow travelling public, the Transport Department was determined to create the immediate impression with its customers that here was something 'completely different'. They achieved this impact via the special livery chosen. '1005' — numbered in the 'experimental' series — emerged in a stylish livery of three shades of blue: Prussian blue below the lower saloon windoes, sky blue for the upper deck side panels with roof and window frames in pale Wedgewood, the whole being tastefully lined out in gold, black and white. Various alternatives had been tried on paper, using red or green. The destination and via apertures, only, appeared in the screen box at the front with the service number displaced to the nearside where it was intended to be read easily from the pavement. When ready, 1005 was despatched for service on 22nd December, 1947 to Possilpark Depot for service 33 (circular). The tram was restricted to certain motormen only.

The General Manager's Annual Report for the year ending 31st May, 1948 confirmed 1005's entry to service while admitting that the tram was not free from teething troubles. Electrical faults frequently took 1005 out of service. After a few months the car had settled into fairly regular and routine service. It was too early, thought Mr. Fitzpayne, to draw definite conclusions other than to advise that the fluorescent lighting being experimented with on 1005 (and 1228) needed further development by the manufacturers because of unduly high capital and revenue costs. Complaints were received that this lighting had dazzled passengers when passing from the bright interior into the darkened streets. Blackpool Corporation had found this, too, and taken steps to reduce the level of illumination from 360 lux to 150 with their fluorescent lighting. Glasgow achieved 100 lux with tungsten fittings on Coronation trams.

Before long, 1005 was transferred to Maryhill Depot and operated on a schedule all its own, being a combination of services 3 and 40, sometimes clockwise, sometimes anti-clockwise. To turn round in the suburbs it used the track along Paisley Road West and Mosspark Boulevard joining in Corkerhill Road, and the St. Vincent Street loop in the City. Later still, remaining in the blue livery, 1005 operated another special schedule on service 18 from Maryhill Depot forecourt to the Moir Street loop at Glasgow Cross. These duties were set at a maximum of 7 hours per day in order to make a crew duty of a day's work.

By February 1949 the experimental car came under the penetrating scrutiny of Mr. Findlay once again. He reported to the General Manager that the separate entrance and exit had been arranged deliberately to enable entering passengers to pass the driver at the front because statistics had shown that boarding accidents were more prevalent than leaving

The lower saloon of 1005 was very close to the Cunarders 1293-1392 in detail. Only the moquette and handrail brackets were as per the pre-war cars. Lighting was fluorescent with exposed tubes and the seating was non-reversible. The shunting controller can be seen on the rear window ledge. ***G.C.T.***

accidents. In addition, since the folding doors with which 1005 was equipped moved inwards, passengers using them as an exit could have the doors open against them as they were about to leave. He felt that the experiment had not been a success due to the Glasgow public's familiarity with boarding vehicles at the rear resulting in wasted time arising in diverting intending passengers to the correct point of entry. The traffic department wanted the locations exchanged and although Mr. Findlay was against this, they had their way. He commented on the performance of the car's electrical equipment which was modelled on PCC lines. 1005 had a very smooth start. It was tested on Mosspark Boulevard against an ordinary Coronation car taken at random from service to give the following results:—

At 100 ft Car 1265 led by 34 ft.
At 200 ft Car 1265 led by 45 ft.
At 870 ft both cars were level
Thereafter 1005 'forged ahead' of 1265.

This proved — to Mr. Findlay — that in a congested city like Glasgow with eight stops per mile a tram had little opportunity to reach a top speed and that the importance of achieving a better acceleration outweighed the potential to achieve higher speeds. The 15% extra cost over that for Coronation equipment was not justified by results. He felt that there might be a better application for use with single deck cars if it was ever decided to operate any.

In October 1949, 1005 reverted to standard livery of green, cream and orange. The entrance and exit positions had been exchanged not long before this time. In February 1949 the automatic accelerator had required to be stripped down completely and it was removed again in February 1950. On the occasion of major overhaul in August 1951 it was again removed not to be replaced. Instead, more conventional electropneumatic control by British Thomson-Houston was installed in a Coronation pattern contactor cabinet with EMB master controller and BT-H interlock. The fluorescent lighting was taken out and replaced by tungsten fittings concealed behind Cunarder-style perspex diffusers. It is interesting to note that the tram was listed for re-modelling to standard doors and seating with cabins at each end as early as October 1949.

Comparative tests with loading times were undertaken in June 1948 between 1005 and other cars on the 3/40 services at various times with various loads:—

Wednesday 16/4/48

1.44 pm	Car 1005 M	Average seconds per stop	5.71
	Car 242 H	,,	8.48
2.10 pm	Car 1005 M	,,	7.00
	Car 1236 H	,,	11.23
5.01 pm	Car 1005 H	,,	9.21
	Car 1252 H	,,	7.77
5.37 pm	Car 1005 L	,,	3.11
	Car 572 L	,,	2.93

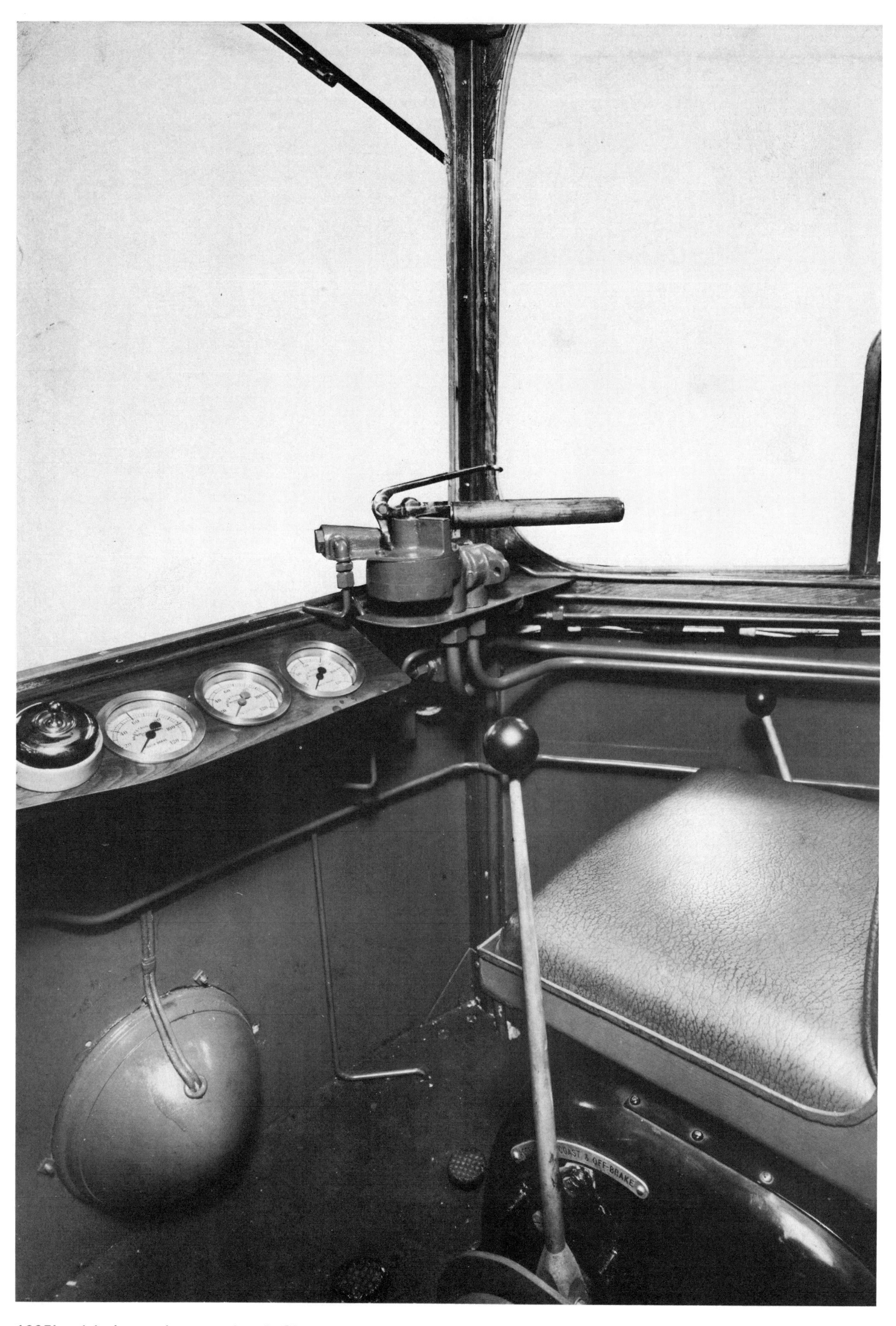

1005's original controls were unique in Glasgow and only selected staff were permitted to drive the car after familiarisation. The 'joystick' handles took over the function of the more familiar drum controller. *G.C.T.*

The rear aspect of 1005 was less pleasing than the front, with a somewhat 'blunted' look. Note the open platform without doors. The acceleration unit can just be seen beneath the rear skirting. *G.C.T.*

By 1950, 1005 was operating its own special duty on service 18 and can be seen here at Charing Cross, still looking striking in appearance after three years in fairly constant use.
T. & R. Annan

Friday 18/6/48

Time	Car		Figure
1.44pm	Car 1005 L	,,	4.05
	Car 242 L	,,	2.75
2.10pm	Car 1005 L	,,	7.08
	Car 1236 H	,,	9.40
5.01pm	Car 1005 H	,,	9.63
	Car 38 H	,,	7.25
5.37pm	Car 1005 L	,,	3.75
	Car 571 M	,,	6.83

M = Moderate traffic, L = Light and H = Heavy traffic.

The results were described as 'inconclusive' but do indicate that under heavy traffic conditions 1005 was no better than any other cars then in use.

From then on until 1955, 1005 settled into an uneventful life running on its special service 18 duty and, later, on service 29. The terminii of the 29 duty were the same as the 18's but the route taken was different, utilising New City Road, Cowcaddens and Hope Street instead of St. Georges Road, Charing Cross and Bothwell Street into the City Centre at Argyle Street. By October 1955, new schedules were prepared and 1005's 'special' duty was restricted to only 11 hours per week on some occasions. Staff shortages were preventing the availability of spare, or overtime crews to operate this duty. This brought matters to a head and the Transport Committee was asked in November to authorise conversion to normal operation at a cost of £500 to gain better use from a modern vehicle when there was a shortage of these. This was duly authorised.

The offside of 1005 did not quite possess the style of the nearside. Shown here when translated into green and orange this car was destined for conversion to double-end operation by 1951. The more conventional electro-pneumatic control cabinet can be seen at the rear of the lower saloon.
Struan J. T. Robertson

This conversion process was completed on 9th May, 1956. The finished result gave a tram which was still different at each end. Face on, the former 'rear' end looked very like a Mark II Coronation slightly squashed so as to avoid extension of the platform bearers. The staircase was therefore pushed further into the lower saloon than was normal on the Mark II Cars. Brown leather seating for both decks came from scrapped Standard Cars. The original 'front' retained much of its former appearance but lost its chromium-plated sliding vents from the front upstairs window in favour of a hinged flap. Although by then almost a conventional car, it was still confined to rush hour special duties, mostly on services 18 and 29 but with frequent trips to the Clydebank area to serve the shipyards. The emergency switch was fitted in December 1959.

In mid-August 1961, 1005 was transferred from Maryhill to Partick Depot from which it continued to be used on special duties, appearing at rush hours with 1089 and 1100 to serve the Clydebank shipyard traffic until despatched to Coplawhill for storage in May 1962. One bogie was retained for the Glasgow Museum of Transport. Lighting diffusers were salvaged and sent to Crich for use in their Cunarder 1297.

When rebuilt for normal operation the former 'rear' end of 1005 closely resembled a Coronation Mark II car somewhat compressed. This was the last major conversion or rebuilding undertaken at Coplawhill for normal service and was completed in 1956.
R. F. Mack

It has often been said that the Glasgow public would not adapt to the separate entrance/exit feature on a one-off basis. This was proved to be so with 137, 1089 and 1005. In the years 1970-72 Glasgow Corporation Transport placed in service nearly 300 buses with this feature. These were all converted to single doorway after proving to be unworkable in Glasgow . . .

CHAPTER 13

The Mark II Coronations or 'Cunarders' 1293~1392

THE MARK II CORONATIONS OR 'CUNARDERS' 1293-1392

In 1939, the necessity to replace the Semi-High Speed Standard tramcars had been recognised. Doubtless they would have been scrapped earlier than this with the arrival of the Coronation trams in increasing numbers, but the number of trams required for service had temporarily risen during the period of the 1938 Empire Exhibition. The Transport Committee had been undecided as to future requirements.

1001-1004 had been built for experimental use to test the most modern four-wheeled trucks then available. 1001 and 1003 had utilised the best equipment already in stock. The replacement car 6 employed the standard GCT / Brush truck albeit of 8'- 6' wheelbase.

To compensate, there was a saving in permanent way maintenance costs which could not be quantified. It was felt that the travelling public would not be impressed with the inferior riding quality of single truck cars, having sampled the delights of the Coronation, although it was admitted that no complaints had been received concerning 1001-1004.

Mr. A. B. Findlay, the Tramways Engineer, staked his claim early and, almost as soon as the suggestion was first put to the Transport Committee, set out his ideas on how to improve the Coronation design. These comprised:—

1. Three steps at the entrance to the vehicle to provide a straight-through compartment and slightly raise the height of the driver's position.
2. Ventilation via sliding windows instead of fans.

Photographed in 1948 at Thornliebank are the first Cunarder, 1293, in original form together with a Daimler single decker with bodywork also by G.C.T. showing traces of Coronation tram ancestry. 1189 is bringing up the rear. ***G.C.T.***

With World War II over, all existing equipment was older by six years and its re-use was by then a less attractive proposition, taking into account the severe stress imposed during the years of hostilities.

By October 1945, there was in prospect the return from war service of increasing numbers of Transport Department staff and consideration was given once again to a construction programme of new tramcars to supersede the Semi-High Speed Standard trams then remaining in service. Estimated comparative costs showed bogie trams to cost £1,000 each more than the equivalent single truck examples. Conversely 100 bogie trams would fulfil the role of 125 single truck cars with respect to carrying capacity, hence the total expenditure for each option was roughly equal. On the other hand, the Coronation trams had been found to be much more expensive to operate than the remainder of the fleet:—

Overall costs were	+12%
Depot maintenance	+24%
Cleaning Costs	+100% (this was 'subject to review')
and Power Costs	+50%

3. Full length hand poles carried through each saloon.
4. Elimination of the driver's door to the street.
5. Substitution of a blind for internal driver's door to the platform.
6. Increase the seating capacity to a minimum of 69.
7. Simplify the interior decoration, particularly in the upper saloon.
8. Employ safety glass throughout the vehicle instead of sheet or plate glass.
9. Increase acceleration in series notches.

The traffic superintendant was consulted on these points and only agreed with items 2, 3, 7 and 8 but subsequent events show that Mr. Findlay generally got his way.

In November 1945 the Transport Committee asked the General Manager to comment on the inclusion of a separate entrance and exit in the specification for the new tramcars. He pointed out that he had already been authorised to build such a car but that the length of cars in Glasgow was limited by certain curves such as that from Renfield Street into Sauchiehall Street.

The interior of the production Cunarders is exemplified by 1293. The lower saloon appeared warmer than on the experimental predecessor, 1005-helped, doubtless, by the concealed lighting and redesigned moquette. 1293's upper saloon was a blend of the design of 1001 and 1005. The seating was red leather trimmed with green. (Mark I cars used green trimmed red.) Some later cars had lower backs. Note the half-drop window, mis-shapen even before the car had entered service. G.C.T.

Length governed seating capacity and seating capacity was related to revenue per mile. Fares were bound to rise but would rise further due to enhanced costs associated with the construction, operation and maintenance of Coronation-type trams and the wisdom of reducing income by limiting the number of seats due to the inclusion of a separate entrance and exit was questioned. He recommended that 100 new tramcars should be constructed, with alternative tenders invited for four-wheeled car equipment and Coronation type equipment. Only on receipt of this information should the Committee decide upon which option to pursue. The tenders were duly received and reported on in March 1946 showing that an eight wheeled car would cost £5,400 against £4,400 for a four wheeled car.

The General Manager set out all the pros and cons in an extremely balanced fashion for each alternative and concluded that 'the Committee may think that only the best is good enough for Glasgow, and the public too, having seen the best, may not take kindly to second best'. He indicated that he would submit the tenders once the Committee had made this decision. These tenders were considered in April 1946. By then the bogie tram had won the day and approval to proceed was given on 2nd May.

The tenders for the electrical equipment presented some problems requiring careful consideration. The two lowest offers were equal — those lodged by British Thomson-Houston and Metropolitan-Vickers. As both were members of the Associated Electrical Industries combine, it had been thought fair to divide the order 50/50. Unfortunately the unit costs would not be the same on reduced numbers and, after representation from an aggrieved Metropolitan-Vickers regarding previous bulk orders lost to them after their initial research and also about servicing arrangements, it was agreed that they would receive the order for 100 sets.

The tenders for bogies were submitted (in financial order) by Maley & Taunton and by EMB. By this time EMB was more interested in concentrating on diecasting work and any truck construction or reconstruction orders were subcontracted via M. Wild. The double profit margins and handling charges were no doubt reflected in the price. Glasgow's only pair of Maley & Taunton bogies were fitted to Car 1142 against which comparisons of similarly-aged EMB bogies were made over a five year period to examine reasons for and numbers of withdrawals directly attributable to bogies. 1142 did not fair very well in comparison having been withdrawn 31 times in the period 1941-44 compared with 8 times for 1141, 13 for 1143, 26 for 1144 and 12 for 1145. During this period the mileages run by those trams and the rewheeling mileages were:—

	1141	1142	1143	1144	1145
1941-46 Mileage	133,000	107,000	168,000	184,000	144,000
Rewheeling Mileage	93,000 30,000	61,000	74,000 46,000	75,000 56,000 47,000	89,000 60,000

The average number of track shoes per year was 5½ on the EMB cars as against 3½ on the Maley & Taunton-equipped 1142. This was considered to be very important as it was easier to renew wheels than to renew track, not forgetting the cost advantage.

Both designs emerged with credit and it was readily admitted that most of the causes of withdrawals were of a minor nature.

The features of design were critically compared with respect to body bearing, body springing, track brake cylinders, position of driving motors and weight. The EMB bogie weighed 15 cwt more per car than the Maley & Taunton version. The views of the Traffic Superintendent and the Chief Driving Instructor were sought on 1142 respectively on performance and ease of driving. Three other undertakings were also approached — Leeds, Liverpool and Lisbon—and none of the views expressed on the Maley & Taunton bogies was at all critical. In the end, while that Company received the order from Glasgow Corporation Transport for 100 sets of bogies, the only equipment on offer was their HS44 type 596 inside frame version which was just about as far removed as could be from the swing link bogies used in 1142. Of course the weight of the HS44 would be further reduced but it would seem that the General Manager was selling the Company as much as the product in these otherwise irrelevant comparative tests and examinations. Maley & Taunton's tender was accepted in May 1946.

By February 1947 the Superintendent at Coplawhill was beginning to find himself under pressure to start construction of a sample car. The first underframe was not due from the suppliers P. & W. McLellan until the following April but in any case wood utilised would have had to come from maintenance stock — and much of that was still drying out. He was in no hurry to start construction of a number of trams simultaneously which, in their partially completed state, would occupy workshop space awaiting materials and labour. It was preferred to build up stocks of parts to enable the start of a production programme to be put in hand during the early part of 1948. By and large that was what happened.

The first 'Cunarder' was 1293, sent for service in December 1948 with up to 1297 ready by the end of the year. This nickname was quickly applied and — this time — accepted by the Transport Department. Basically the design was a smoothed of version of the pre-war Coronation, slightly lengthened by 6".

Some design aspects from the Experimental cars influenced the specification for the Cunarders in detail features. The unidirectional 1005 gave much of its architecture to the Cunarders. It bore an obvious family resemblance and could be regarded as a precursor, although 1293 had little in common with 1005, technically.

Many of the features later applied to the Mark I, pre-war Coronation first appeared on the Mark II: one piece windscreen, perspex panelled lighting diffusers, slatted platform floors. In addition to Mr. Findlay's recommendations mentioned previously the illuminated 'CORPORATION TRANSPORT' clerestory panels were dispensed with. A strange omission was the roof hatch. Its absence caused delays in dealing with minor problems.

Seating for 70 was provided, 40 upstairs on hide covered seats and 30 below on moquette of similar appearance but slightly different pattern to Mark I cars. The minimum of 69 stipulated by Mr. Findlay was exceeded only at the expense of limiting severely the space between seats. The bases were higher off the floor than on the pre-war cars and on some Cunarders the backs were quite high giving an added impression of restriction. The three steps to the platform, in spite of maintaining a flat floor throughout the lower deck, drew adverse criticism from less agile passengers. The platform doors were of jack-knife pattern with the two middle leaves folding together to form a divided entrance. These were fitted with handrails which further cramped the entrance passage.

The curved end panels were aluminium with sheet steel on the dash plates but the main side panels of both decks as originally constructed were of resin bonded Canadian Birch plywood in one continuous 20'-0" length. The lower saloon ceilings retained decorative Alhambrinal panelling which was also used throughout for interior side linings but ceilings upstairs were of non-nocotine staining traffolite which did not require painting. The three dimensional roof domes were painted sheet metal, and stained brown until overhaul when they emerged white with the traffolite remaining cream.

The most obvious differences within the class were originally related to livery. 1293-1300 had the upper deck green carried straight round the front as on the Lightweight cars. 1301-1339 were similar but the green band was downswept to run between the upper and lower apertures of the destination boxes. From 1340 onwards the band was further downswept to pass beneath the lower aperture and these later examples incorporated blank advertisement panels which displaced the City Coat of Arms to the lower deck sides. 1303 originally carried standard treatment of the second style but translated into red instead of green. One side of the red panels was lined in silver with the other in gold.

The topmost channel iron protective rail beneath the side panelling on the Cunarders was found to interfere with jacking and crane lifting. These official photographs were taken to show how it should be done. The car is 1304. ***G.C.T.***

As production progressed — most cars were completed during 1950 — detail differences emerged. The signalling flap window to the cabin near side was omitted. These had been prone to much damage and abuse. The seating was reduced in the lower saloon to 26 creating larger standing lobbies. A louvred vent was introduced to the cab sides at high level. 1385 and 1387-1392 were placed in service without perspex eaves glasses although all except 1385 later acquired these.

During preliminary tests with 1293, problems arose with the inside framed bogies. Although they gave what was quite the most resilient ride of any Glasgow trams, while performing well on street track, they rode badly on sleeper track. The riding qualities of 1005 had been found quite satisfactory, and it had been decided to make the springing on 1293 similar. Maley & Taunton's engineers visited Glasgow on 15th September, 1948 and comparative tests were carried out with 1005, 1293 and 1200 on both street and sleeper track. Under normal service conditions, all performed well enough but when driven flat out the Cunarder oscillated on the sleeper track at Mosspark Boulevard. The Mark I car was reported as 'hard' on solid track, setting up a tail-wagging motion at speed. Maley & Taunton were informed that the springing would have to be improved on the new cars and, although reluctant to do so (all the springs had been delivered by this time) eventually discussed the matter with their suppliers Messrs. Jones Woodhead & Sons. Experiments were then implemented very much on a trial and error basis to achieve the correct balance of rubber and laminated steel and ultimately dampers were fitted on each side of the truck frames to give satisfactory results. 1293's wheel brake beam was found to be in need of reinforcement but this modification was undertaken for the other cars prior to delivery. Brake cylinders on the first sixteen cars were found to be porous. They had been constructed from Malleable Iron in order to save weight. These, and subsequent deliveries, had to be impregnated to obviate the problem.

The original prices quoted by Maley & Taunton and EMB Co. Ltd. were, respectively, £1,300 and £1,495 per car set. Since the date of tender, wages and materials costs had risen to make the final cost £1,462 10s which was still cheaper than the original EMB offer. Aberdeen Corporation ultimately paid £2,106 for the bogies supplied for their 20 post war centre entrance cars. In this context, Glasgow Corporation could hardly avoid accepting Maley & Taunton's tender. Not many experiments were undertaken with the production cars but an interesting one was pursued on 1306. This car entered service with air operated doors in September 1949. The car's performance in use was unsatisfactory and was the subject of reports and internal memos within Head Office. It was readily agreed that platform accidents related to boarding and leaving were considerably reduced but the car repeatedly lost time on the 8/25 services between Jamaica Street and Castle Street, notwithstanding its operation on these services still time-tabled to suit Standard cars. It had been thought that the superior acceleration of the Cunarder would compensate for any delay in boarding passengers. The problem was not technical but one of the driver not being able to observe the rear platform when the Conductor was elsewhere, either due to the interior mirror view being obstructed by standing passengers or the external mirror not providing adequate coverage due to the rear taper of the car. Motormen erred on the ultra-cautious rather than close the doors against passengers and it was resolved that such doors could only be feasible where they were located adjacent to the operator.

Cunarder 1303 caused a mild sensation by being placed in service with red supplanting green for the upper deck sides. Lining on one side was gold (normally used for green cars) and on the other, silver. *G. E. Langmuir*

Examination of the fleet tables will show that production of the Cunarders was at times painfully slow and thus gave much cause for concern on the part of both the Transport Department and the Corporation's Transport Committee during 1949. At that time, there was an acute shortage of space in the Car Works due to stock-piling of equipment for the new trams, the necessity to maintain ever more frequently the aged trams which could not be scrapped because the new trams could not be built to replace them and a shortage of labour to do both. A way out of this vicious circle was sought in obtaining a tender from R. Y. Pickering Ltd., of Wishaw, to construct 50/60 Cunarders. Glasgow Corporation Transport were to arrange for the supply of materials, including underframes, to Wishaw and to collect the completed bodies at Pickering's works. The vehicles would be supplied with the top decks secured to the bottom decks, complete with all paintwork down to the underframe but were to exclude seating, lifeguard equipment and running gear which would be fitted at Coplawhill. The Transport Department would supply one set of fully machined timber parts and a set of ironwork as patterns for production together with a complete issue for all bodies for furnishings, fittings, electrical fittings and power cables, paints and oils, bolts, screws etc., as per the detailed schedules prepared for cars constructed 'in house'. The cost—taking into account work still to be undertaken by GCT—was approximately £300 more than on a complete GCT vehicle but the advantage in completing the 100 cars by the end of 1950 was considered to outweigh this. Messrs. Hurst Nelson Ltd. had also been approached in connection with this order but had declined stating that they were fully committed at the time with wagon repairs. R. Y. Pickering & Co. Ltd. were the only contractors in Scotland with any recent experience in building modern tramcars, having just completed an order for

One of G.C.T.'s motorised tower wagons on duty at Newlands Depot junction impedes the Cunarder's progress. The tram livery is the second style applied to these cars. The coat of arms has been covered up by the biscuit advert and not reinstated on the lower panels. G.C.T.

twenty centre entrance trams for Aberdeen Corporation Transport.

By November 1949 a special meeting of the Municipal Transport Committee heard a Deputation from the Carworks. A concession on the employment of dilutee labour in the form of a further twenty men was wrought and it was noted that, with these and the elimination of some restrictive practices, production could be increased to 4/5 cars per working month. On that basis, the need for subcontracting was much less obvious. Furthermore it was predicted that there could be labour difficulties if outside sources were used for car construction. It was not doubted that it would be a condition, so far as the dilution of labour concession was concerned, that no part of the work should be given out. So nothing further came of the proposal to contract out the construction of Cunarder trams.

On 1st April, 1949 the General Manager submitted proposals for constructing ten of the 100 new cars as single deckers for evaluation on one route. There would be no financial penalty as construction costs would be roughly the same as for a double decker. Provision would be included in each for 44 seats with 26 standing. A recommendation to this effect was to be put to the Transport Committee on 18th April pointing out that the restrictions in length which the Ministry of Transport imposed on buses and trolleybuses did not apply to trams. Excepting the routes using Renfield Street, Hope Street and West Nile Street, Mr. Fitzpayne claimed that trams up to 45 ft long could be operated successfully in Glasgow. This should be contrasted with his opinions expressed in November 1945. He supported his proposals for single deckers by quoting opinions related to the greater safety, better current consumption, comfort and acceleration from Mr. A. A. Shoebridge, Assistant Commissioner for Rapid Transport and Tramways, Sydney, Major Hayter, OBE, General Manager for Northern General Transport and — significantly — Mr. Luff of Blackpool Corporation Transport, who sang the praises of his railcoaches and mentioned in particular the imminent re-equipping of the Marton route. This was significant because Mr. Fitzpayne was modelling his proposals very much on the design of the Blackpool railcoach body. The later operation of single deck trolleybuses in Glasgow with seated conductor was unrelated to this and emanated from a visit made by the General Manager to Stockholm. Unfortunately the Transport Committee did not share his vision and rejected the idea on 12th April, 1949.

Two for the price of one: neatly captured in a single photograph are two Cunarders from early and late production. 1386, on the left, is substantially as built while 1298 has had its upper deck half-drop window replaced with a hinged flap for access to the bow rope. This is Riddrie terminus, Smithycroft Road in 1955. R. J. S. Wiseman

In 1954, 1392's first yearly overhaul was due. The upper saloon side panels are showing clear signs of delamination and the car did not acquire perspex eaves glasses until 1957. If the General Manager's proposals had been approved 1392 would have been one of ten single deckers. The drawing reproduced below is one of several prepared. Its resemblance to the Leeds single deckers of 1953 will be noted. By that time G.C.T.'s Tramways Engineer was General Manager in Leeds. *Parr/STMS Collection*

After production of the 100 cars was complete further alterations were made. The length of the bow collector arms was increased. The half-drop bow change windows were replaced from around 1955 by fixed glazing with a hinged flap for access to the bow-rope. Rheostat ventilation was improved by increasing the free area of the grille. 1315 sustained fire damage in Thornliebank and was substantially rebuilt with a completely new top deck. The

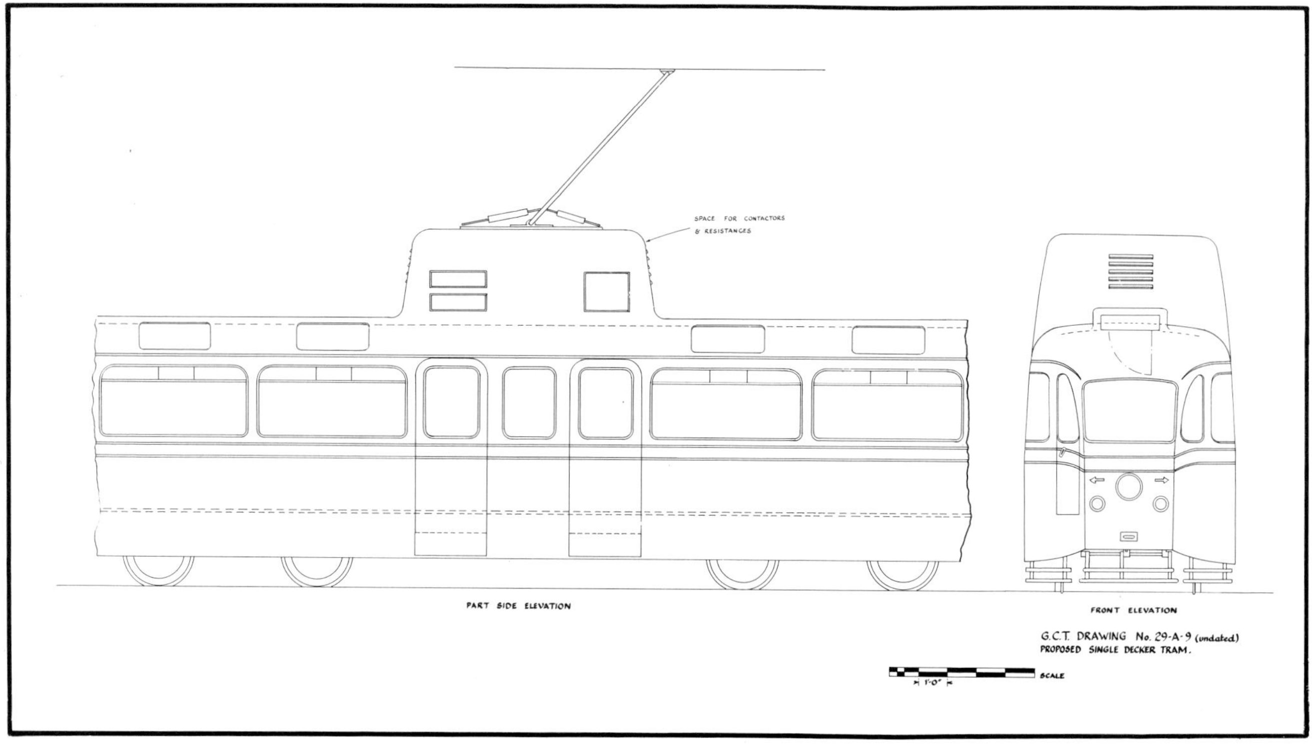

1386 seems to effervesce with its own light and positively dims her surroundings–particularly the standard tram in front. The car has been newly outshopped after her first major overhaul and repaint in 1954. ***R. R. Clark/STMS Collection***

Alhambrinal ceiling panels in the lower saloon were damaged by heat and replaced with sheet steel enamelled in cream. On all cars, difficulties were encountered in jacking or lifting and in order to simplify procedures, the top bar of the protective iron rails below the lower saloon skirt panels was removed. The 1340 livery treatment became standard throughout the class. Aluminium panels replaced the timber from the upper sides of all cars and from the lower sides on some, too, following accidental damage.

Electrically and mechanically, the Cunarders underwent few obvious alterations. The fitting of dampers to the trucks was not completed until late spring 1950 retrospectively and to new construction from then on. Until then the Cunarders were kept off the 3 and 14 services which incorporated sleeper track. Having had much available space postwar and being near Coplawhill, Newlands Depot was the initial home for the entire class until some dispersal occurred to spread modern cars throughout Glasgow.

The motors were Metropolitan-Vickers MV109AR, each of 36 hp. Remote control equipment was also by Metropolitan-Vickers and Maley & Taunton interlock was fitted to the controllers. This was less popular with motormen since the air wheel brake could not be applied concurrent with rheostatic/magnetic. Emergency isolating switches were fitted into all cars in 1959 following the fire on 1145. No heaters were installed although estimates were obtained in 1951. The handrails were soon removed from the door leaves and re-sited on the body panels to ease clearance.

1293 had commenced production in June 1947 but it took until December of 1948 to place the car in revenue-earning service. There was a three month delay after completion of 1300 before the next cars followed on due to a back-log of repairs to the existing fleet. Only sixteen cars could be completed that year, but once the dilutee labour was employed, five cars per month were despatched for service at the height of production — one per week for three weeks and two on the fourth.

Two Cunarders are preserved, 1297 is substantially in its original form at the Crich Tramway Museum and 1392 — the last to be constructed — is at the Glasgow Museum of Transport having been exhibited for some years at the Clapham Museum of British Transport in London. 1392 entered service in February 1952 but had been completed for some months previously except for non-delivery of some bought-in items. One bogie, ex-1377, is also displayed in the Glasgow Museum of Transport.

A summary of the man hours devoted to constructing a Mark II Coronation Car is given below:—

Bodymakers	2600	Blacksmith	90
Painters	710	Fitters	890
Trimmers	119	Plumbers	262
Tinsmith	940	Electricians	300

Car Number	Date to Service	Date Withdrawn	Code
1293	1/12/48	9/11/62	
1294	20/12/48	12/10/62	
1295	23/12/48	7/4/60	
1296	27/12/48	20/8/60	
1297	30/12/48	4/9/62*	
1298	21/1/49	13/4/61	
1299	3/2/49	30/8/62	
1300	18/2/49	27/4/62	
1301	17/5/49	29/3/61	
1302	30/5/49	11/5/62	
1303	29/6/49	7/5/62	R
1304	13/7/49	17/8/62	
1305	12/8/49	30/8/62	
1306	8/9/49	23/10/62	E
1307	7/9/49	7/9/62	
1308	/10/49	22/8/62	
1309	5/10/49	6/11/62	
1310	24/10/49	7/8/62	
1311	4/11/49	26/10/62	
1312	18/11/49	17/9/62	
1313	1/12/49	15/10/62	A
1314	14/12/49	9/11/62	
1315	30/12/49	13/7/62	T
1316	28/12/49	10/5/61	F
1317	18/1/50	16/10/62	
1318	2/2/50	30/10/62	
1319	2/2/50	12/11/62	
1320	15/2/50	14/11/62	
1321	16/2/50	21/9/62	
1322	22/2/50	13/8/62	
1323	1/3/50	11/4/61	F
1324	13/3/50	7/4/61	F
1325	15/3/50	11/4/61	F
1326	22/3/50	10/4/61	F
1327	31/3/50	3/8/62	
1328	5/4/50	2/8/62	
1329	12/4/50	2/2/62	
1330	19/4/50	24/10/62	
1331	26/4/50	10/4/61	
1332	3/5/50	7/9/62	
1333	10/5/50	12/4/61	F
1334	18/5/50	12/4/61	F
1335	24/5/50	27/4/61	F
1336	31/5/50	15/8/62	

Car Number	Date to Service	Date Withdrawn	Code
1337	7/6/50	17/4/61	F
1338	14/6/50	27/8/62	
1339	21/6/50	1/11/62	
1340	30/6/50	10/7/62	
1341	2/8/50	1/8/62	
1342	5/7/50	28/11/61	
1343	12/7/50	22/12/60	
1344	3/8/50	12/4/61	F
1345	9/8/50	8/5/61	F
1346	23/8/50	7/4/61	F
1347	16/8/50	1/5/61	F
1348	24/8/50	5/9/62	
1349	5/9/50	10/9/62	
1350	6/9/50	20/4/60	
1351	28/9/50	16/11/62	
1352	13/9/50	19/11/62	
1353	21/9/50	19/4/61	F
1354	28/9/50	15/5/61	F
1355	2/10/50	11/7/62	
1356	18/10/50	19/9/62	
1357	12/10/50	19/4/61	F
1358	25/10/50	19/9/62	
1359	26/10/50	21/8/62	
1360	1/11/50	17/9/62	
1361	15/11/50	20/9/62	
1362	8/10/50	22/10/62	
1363	16/11/50	18/10/62	
1364	22/11/50	13/2/62	
1365	30/11/50	3/5/61	F
1366	14/12/50	10/1/62	
1367	7/12/50	20/11/62	
1368	15/12/50	20/4/61	AF
1369	20/12/50	1/5/61	F
1370	19/1/51	1/5/61	F
1371	18/1/51	23/10/61	
1372	20/2/51	17/10/62	
1373	18/1/51	14/8/62	
1374	16/2/51	5/9/62	
1375	23/2/51	6/8/62	
1376	15/2/51	24/4/61	F
1377	8/2/51	16/8/62	
1378	15/2/51	8/8/62	
1379	21/2/51	13/11/62	
1380	28/2/51	28/9/62	

Car Number	Date to Service	Date Withdrawn	Code
1381	23/3/51	22/3/61	
1382	7/3/51	19/10/62	
1383	29/3/51	31/10/62	
1384	22/3/51	5/1/62	
1385	29/3/51	8/11/62	G
1386	11/4/51	2/5/61	F
1387	5/4/51	11/5/61	GF
1388	17/8/51	1/5/61	GF
1389	24/8/51	25/10/62	G
1390	20/9/51	21/1/60	G
1391	30/11/51	3/5/61	GF
1392	12/2/52	4/9/62*	G

Notes

Class intended to seat 30 below and 40 above.

However, 1349-1392 entered service seating 26 below and 40 above. Some earlier cars altered similarly, eg 1326, 1343.

Code:

- * = Preserved
- R = Red band instead of green 1949-52
- A = Aluminium life guard spars
- T = New top deck following fire damage, 1951
- F = Totally destroyed Dalmarnock Depot fire 22/3/61
- G = Not fitted with eaves glasses on entry to service. All except 1385 subsequently equipped
- E = Experimental air operated doors

1392 Has non-standard trim on upper deck seating (ie green, edged red insted of red, edged green)

1388-1392 entry to service delayed due to non-delivery of components

Depot allocation for all cars on entry to service was Newlands. From 1954-57, 1293-1336 remained at Newlands while the rest were transferred to Govan.

Car 1392 – the last Cunarder – was also the last completely new double decker to be constructed in Great Britain. For this reason it was selected for exhibition in the Museum of British Transport at Clapham, London. It was not a one-way journey, however. 1392 returned to Glasgow's own museum when Clapham closed in 1972. *Struan J. T. Robertson*

CHAPTER 14

The Replacement Mark I Coronations 1393~1398

'REPLACEMENT' CORONATION TRAMS 1393-1398 AND 1255, 1279

The fire in Newlands Depot on 11th April, 1948 had seriously damaged Mark I Coronation trams 1141, 1148, 1239, 1241 and 1272 while 1279 had also been burned out in a street accident. 1148 and 1239 were officially categorised as 'destroyed'. The immediate replacement needs for these were met from the construction of Cunarders and, later, replacement by rebuilding with equivalent Mark I cars bearing the same fleet numbers; this was completed in 1951. For many years it had been believed that the batch of six new bodies constructed in 1954 for bogies purchased from Liverpool Corporation were in some way tied up with the six damaged Coronations which it was later possible to rebuild. They were not.

Insurance money had been obtained for the damaged Standard cars in Newlands. These were55, 261 and 513 (officially listed as 'destroyed'), 211, 656 and 985 ('destroyed') — of which 211 and 656 were returned to service — and No. 50 and 1008 — the Decorated cars. In addition, 289 had been burned out while in service. The General Manager recommended to the Transport Committee that this insurance payment should be used to construct replacement Mark I Coronation bodies on ex-Liverpool EMB Lightweight bogies. In his report dated 29th January, 1951, several economies in construction were tabled to bring the costs within the amount of the insurance settlement.

Firstly, the detailing of the glazing was to be simplified by utilising the Clayton-Wright flush-mounted system for the main side windows instead of window pans used on the pre-war cars.

Secondly it was decided to re-employ double seat frames and re-trimmed cushions ex-stock. These had been rendered redundant from the original Coronation cars when the lower saloon seating was re-arranged after the war to composite pattern. Only the single seats had to be purchased new.

Coplawhill's erecting shop is the setting for the construction of the 1954-batch of Coronation cars reverting to the basic Mark I shell but built and specified down to a price.
Parr/STMS Collection

Thirdly, the bodywork design was simplified by eliminating some of the more flamboyant features more reminiscent of the 1930s, etched glass lighting diffusers, Alhambrinal panelling, studded rubber matting and decorative mirrors. Handrails were omitted from ceilings and replaced in the lower saloon only by hand-grips.

Glasgow Corporation had purchased six sets of EMB bogies from Liverpool in 1948. These were no doubt salvaged by Liverpool after the extensive fire in their Green Lane Depot in 1947. Mark I Coronation tram 1179 was equipped with one set of these in 1951 and retained them until 1954. This went unnoticed even by the most observant as there was not much obvious difference between these bogies and their Glasgow counterparts.

The General Manager's report for the year ending 31st May, 1952 commented that the underframes for the six new bodies had still to be delivered but one year later he was able to confirm that delivery had taken place. Construction was due to commence shortly. The underframes were supplied by R. Y. Pickering & Co. Ltd., and differed only in minor detail from the pre-war examples. These underframes were to remain within the bodyshop at Coplawhill for many months but the first car, 1393, finally emerged in July 1954. The external appearance differed little in profile from a pre-war Mark I but was much tidier with the flush-mounted glazing. The 'CORPORATION TRANSPORT' illuminated panels were omitted. The interior lighting was extremely bright, being of Mark II Coronation style, and the internal and external cabin doors were dispensed with.

The headlamps also changed from pre-war standard to duplicate the detail of the Mark II with chromium plated bezel. The interior was utilitarian compared even with the Cunarders. Ceilings were plain enamelled white and side lining panels were brown painted plywood. Handrails were painted brass instead of chromium plated or covered with decorative plastic. On the other hand, the seats reverted completely to pre-war standards with cream excelloid-covered frames in both decks on 1393-1396. Despite a general scaling down in finish, the result was still appreciably more appealing than the contemporary Corporation bus. Like the bus, though, the heaters were omitted. The half-drop windows at the front of both decks were replaced by a single sheet of glass for the driver's cabin and by a fixed pane with access flap to the bow rope upstairs. The visors above the cabin windows were omitted, heralding the removal of these from all pre-war cars shortly afterwards.

1393 acquired the bogies formerly used on 1179. The Lightweight bogies have been quoted in official records as being of 4'-10" wheelbase. Cunarder pattern Maley & Taunton air brakes were fitted and motors were GEC WT184 of 35 hp. Metropolitan-Vickers remote control was installed. The new cars — all despatched to Newlands Depot — were fast and comfortable. Slight differences could be detected internally. 1397 had non-standard seat backs omitting the depression mid-way across the top rail. Both 1397 and 1398 had dark red trim on the tubular frames instead of cream employed on the earlier cars.

Late in 1954, a new body to the same general design was constructed for 1279 which had been burned to the frames at Renfrew Ferry. The new body was 1279's third and could be distinguished from 1393-98 by the retention of Mark I pattern

Two of the 1954 Coronations were given over completely to advertising the virtues of electricity (2 car sides, 2 dash panels and 16 windows being used). 1394 – the other was 1398 – is shown at Park Road Terminus. ***D. E. Sinclair***

headlamps and the omission of any plastic finish to the seat frames. 1279 then returned to Elderslie Depot.

In the following year, 1255, the last rebuild, was also given a new body, replacing that which caught fire in Coplawhill. Distinctive features were confined to the interior where white plastic panels were provided for the ceilings in both decks. These remained pure white to the end while the others had become nicotine brown. They were carefully removed from the body before despatch to the scrap merchant. The seating from this car and 1398 was retained and sent to the Crich Tramway Museum for their 1282.

The expenditure on each new car compared with the ultimate cost of the Cunarders was:

	Cunarder	*6 Trams*
Body	£3110	£2560
Bogies/Air Brakes	£1960	£1388
Painting	£170	£244
Motor equipment and Magnetic Brakes	£1680	£1136
Wiring	£280	£377
Bow Collector	£20	£10
	£7220	£5714

The cost of the bogies included purchase second hand and overhaul in Glasgow.

In service, these cars with Liverpool equipment seemed generally to be less reliable and they were, of course, non standard. The only difficulties peculiar to them related to their behaviour in extremely cold weather when they lost all braking, track, wheel, magnetic and AEB. After some experiments where cars were left exposed in depot yards all night with platform doors left open, it was found that there were low points in the air piping system where condensation gathered and froze. Repositioning of the automatic and auxiliary valves beneath the longitudinal seats and elimination of the dip in the pipework in a vulnerable position cured the problem.

During 1961, the opportunity was taken to re-equip the 6 cars with Glasgow bogies and motors which had by then become available. The process had not been completed before the Dalmarnock Depot fire destroyed four members of the class.

A letter was received from Liverpool Corporation Passenger Transport Department in November 1955 indicating that 39 bogie tramcars had become redundant following conversion of further services to bus operation. After receipt of the second batch of Green Goddess cars from Liverpool, it had been made plain by GCT that they would not be interested in any more offers. Liverpool's General Manager had more discussions with Mr. Fitzpayne on this matter, culminating in the further offer, although he admitted that the best trams were being retained and the 39 were those in need of most attention. Mr. Fitzpayne went so far as to have estimates prepared for the construction of further 1393-style bodies for use on the ex-Liverpool bogies as he was unable to recommend purchase of the Liverpool bodies. Allowing for increased costs, the price per new body was estimated at £6946. Discussions took place in the Transport Committee but, by this time, the writing was on the wall. No new tramcars were built and any further victims of street accidents requiring major rebuilding were scrapped or cannibalised.

Car Number	Date to Service	Depot (New)	Depot (1961)	Code	Withdrawn	Remarks
1393	5/7/54	n	x	F	17/4/61	Glasgow bogies/motors fitted 14/3/61
1394	4/8/54	n	x		2/10/62	Glasgow bogies/motors ex-1206, fitted 5/6/61
1395	27/8/54	n	x	F	3/5/61	Glasgow bogies/motors ex-1167, fitted 13/3/61
1396	24/9/54	n	x	F	14/4/61	
1397	1/10/54	n	x	F	6/4/61	Non-standard seat frames
1398	7/10/54	n	x		26/11/62	Received 1395's acquired bogies after 3/5/61

Glasgow motors were BTH 109 AW
Ex-Liverpool motors were GEC WT184

1393 received ex-Liverpool equipment which had been operated in Mark I Coronation Car No. 1179 from 11/10/51.
'F' indicates destroyed by fire at Dalmarnock Depot, 1961.

The 1954 Coronation Mark I cars used the basic body shell of the pre-war design but simplified the ventilation and glazing detail to produce a tram which still looked modern by contemporary standards. 1395 is on service 14 in Shawlands. R. F. Mack

Just how the 1954 Coronations blended with their pre-war sisters can be seen in this view of 1393 being followed by 1193 and 1211. 1193 has already received flush mounted glazing to the upper saloon due to corrosion of the original window pans.

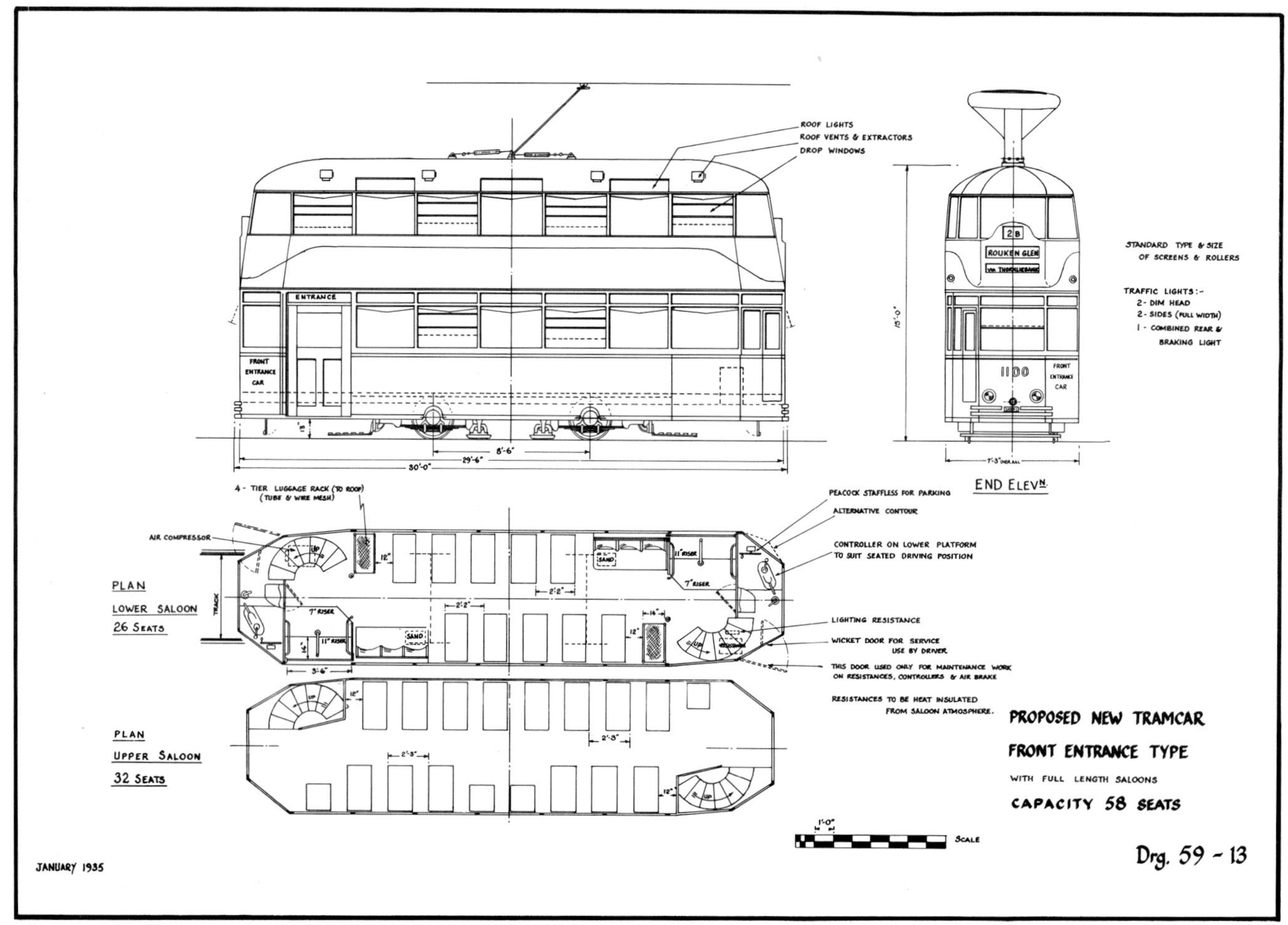

This line drawing was one of several - probably prepared for illustrative purposes - in January 1935. Various combinations of entrance and exits were shown in various positions. The styling owes a little to contemporary practice in Sunderland and to the Cowieson-bodied Corporation Buses of the time. The seating capacity could have been increased by up to ten. The number '1100' is purely coincidental!

1163 is about to swing round from Sauchiehall Street into Renfield Street. By 1960 the appearance of even these trams was beginning to deteriorate. This was one of the curves which prevented operation of the ex-Liverpool cars beyond their selected services.
W.D.McMillan

999, for many years a Maryhill car, was a familiar servant on the busy 18 service operated by that depot from Springburn to Burnside, with its easy-to-remember number. It is seen leading at least four other Standard trams down to the foot of Hope Street in 1957.
W.D.McMillan

108 head west along a quiet Argyle Street. The break in the granite sets in the foreground indicates lifting of track in Oswald Street. Someone has forgotten to change the rear destination display ..... *W.D. McMillan*

Gleaming with new paint is 1269 passing Anderston in 1958. If any area has changed beyond all recognition it is here, ravaged by the Clydeside Expressway and the Kingston Bridge approaches. There is no habitation to use the unfinished big dipper-like elevated pedestrian pathways. *W.D. McMillan*

CHAPTER 15

The Ex-Liverpool 'Green Goddesses'

THE EX-LIVERPOOL TRAMCARS: 1006-1016, 1018-1038, 1041-1049, 1052-1056

The purchase of forty six of Liverpool's streamlined bogie tramcars should be seen in context. No decision had been taken by 1953 to implement a general run-down of the Glasgow system, despite some individual cut-backs and substitutions. Scrapping of elderly vehicles which had commenced in the late 1930s had been matched generally by the introduction of modern trams or trolleybuses but the one hundred post-war 'Cunarders' had taken nearly four years to be placed in service at considerable expense. There was a decided lack of choice in firms willing to submit tenders for modern equipment. During this time the Liverpool system (formerly one of the most progressive in the country) was being run down towards abandonment to the extent that even their modern vehicles were starting to become redundant.

The illustration of these two Liverpool cars undergoing overhaul prior to entering service illustrates differences in the bodywork which depended on the amount of rebuilding accorded them in Liverpool. 931 became Glasgow 1011 with substantially improved appearance in Glasgow's attractive livery.
R. R. Clark/STMS Collection

Having been unsuccessful in obtaining permission to obtain either new trucks or bogies or bodies to mount on them and despite continual warnings about the increasing average age of the fleet and deteriorating overall condition, the idea to purchase second hand trams from Liverpool seems to have emerged from the 'old boy network'. The Liverpool streamliners were 36'-0" long as opposed to the 34'-0" of the Coronation Mark I and 34'-5¾" for the Mark II, both of which were tapered to suit Glasgow's limited clearance. On the instructions of the General Manager, the GCT Civil Engineer examined all routes as to their suitability for operating Liverpool trams. With only ¼" to 1'-0" drawings to work from, confirmation was received that service 15 would accommodate them except for difficulties with lifeguard 'feelers' at the Canal Bridge in Coatbridge. Service 29 was also suitable, at that time running from Anderston Cross to Broomhouse as was service 34 from Anderston Cross to Auchenshuggle, with some limited clearances at Kent Street. Depot access to Partick and Coatbridge was insufficient to permit stabling in their accommodation. These views were confirmed in correspondence dated 30th March, 1953.

By 13th May, 1953 Mr. Fitzpayne officially advised the Town Clerk at the City Chambers that Liverpool Corporation had twenty four tramcars available and recommended purchase at £500 each *delivered*. It was estimated then that a further £100 would require to be expended to make them fit for service in Glasgow. These trams were the survivors of the complete batch of 25 supplied with Maley & Taunton Swing Link Bogies and GEC WT184 motors. They were the only trams in Liverpool with these bogies and therefore less standard with the remainder of the fleet then extant. Mr. Fitzpayne indicated that the length would limit these cars to operation on seven of the existing routes but that they could in the first instance take the place of the maximum traction cars. The date given by Liverpool officials for the availability of these trams was the beginning of June. With limited accommodation in Liverpool, it was important that the Transport Committee in Glasgow should make an early decision. Acceptance of the offer from Liverpool was recommended by the Committee on 1st June with a price agreed at £500 per vehicle, delivered. Approval by the full Glasgow Corporation was given on 11th June. Liverpool Corporation agreed to let the matter rest between the General Managers and Transport Committee Chairman in each city. The book value of the trams had been written down in Liverpool to £471 each. Mr. Fitzpayne was at pains to stress that the purchase price really did reflect the true value of the trams to Glasgow Corporation Transport.

Some concern was later expressed in Liverpool when it emerged that the transportation costs considerably exceeded the difference between £471 and £500. Comparison between quotations and the costs in transferring London trams to Leeds proved to be invalid due to the differences in profile and the necessity to remove the bogies from the Liverpool bodies to permit clearance beneath a low bridge at Kendal. A pair of bogies was requested in advance for overhaul at Coplawhill to enable prompt entry into service to be achieved.

Supporters of the Glasgow and Liverpool systems would each claim that *their* modern trams were the ultimate in Great Britain and it is only right that this should be so. Invidious comparisons have frequently been made but tend to be based on the condition of the Coronation fleet versus the condition of the Liverpool streamliners post World War II. There is no doubt that the Liverpool trams suffered more than some from the rigours of war. The design of the bogie streamliner had — like Glasgow's — emerged from late 1920s experience with bogie trams after being traditionally wed to the standard four wheeled car. The design of their subsequent bogie cars went through a rounding-off process in appearance through heavyweight structure to the lightweight design of their 'Liners' (never referred to as anything else in Glasgow other than 'Green Goddesses'). There was a divergence from the Glasgow policy of retaining structural strength with long-term service in view, to abandonment of strengthening bulkheads, insufficient structural cantilevering of platforms and employment of three-dimensional panelling and curved glazing. The design was superb in appearance when pristine — but those examples which arrived in Glasgow were not pristine. The interior finish was functional if not luxurious and seating for 78 was provided, 34 below and 44 above.

The first Liverpool tram to arrive was 927 and the second, 942. It was 942 which entered service first numbered 1006 as a replacement car. Such was the condition of 927 that it was not placed in service until numbers 1006-1023 had been filled by other Green Goddesses, thus becoming 1024.

Clearance tests were carried out over much of the system, including the Paisley and Barrhead services, but the ex-Liverpool fleet was allocated to Maryhill Depot for the lengthened 29 service from Milngavie to Tollcross.

1011 was one of the Maley & Taunton first batch of ex-Liverpool cars. This was placed in service with little alteration until more refurbishing was found necessary. 1011 retained rain guttering around the top of the upper deck windows. ***G.C.T.***

Initially, the alterations carried out in Glasgow were limited to regauging, fitting of bow collectors, new lifeguards, removal of collision fenders to gain additional clearance, fitting of external mirrors and trafficators. 1006 and 1007 ran initially without trafficators. Entry to service of 1030 — the last of the Maley & Taunton cars — was achieved in April 1954. The number 1017 had been retained by the Transport Department's School Car.

After some cable fires, it was decided to re-wire completely the entire class, commencing with 1008. At this time the lighting was changed to 'Cunarder' pattern and bow-change access windows installed at the ends of the upper saloon. Glasgow standard coupler pockets were also fitted at this time. The repainting work was confined to the areas affected by these alterations and many were not again to receive a full repaint.

Late in February 1954 details were received concerning a further 22 Green Goddesses which would be available by the end of March and it was agreed to confirm arrangements between the Liverpool and Glasgow undertakings in order to preserve continuity of deliveries. A plea was made for a better price to be negotiated if only to offset the high transportation costs but the Corporation of Liverpool was very much in the hands of Glasgow officials and no concession was achieved. The second batch of trams was very similar but mounted on EMB Lightweight bogies or Heavyweight 'Jo'burg' pattern. The bodies were slightly older than on the Maley & Taunton cars but the bogies were more akin to those familiar in Glasgow Corporation's workshops. Mr. Fitzpayne indicated that the Liverpool trams had not exactly been free from trouble, explaining about the re-wiring, re-lighting and fitting of new axleboxes.

For the record, the incidence of withdrawals from service due to defects was 82% greater than with Coronation cars and withdrawals due to electrical faults was 175% more than on Coronation cars. The motors were particularly troublesome and arrangements were made with the General Electric Company to incorporate two extra brush-holders in each motor and to decrease the gap between the armature and pole pieces. The costs were:—

Fitting Standard equipment to cars	£90 0 0
Re-wiring, fitting new light shades and resistor	£468 0 0
Fitting new brush-holders and altering armature gap	£86 0 0
	£644 0 0

By February 1955, the cost of modifications to ex-Liverpool trams had increased to £1250 per vehicle.

GCT must still have judged their purchases to be a sound investment and the second batch of 22 started to arrive soon after 1030 was placed in service. Their entry to service was not as regular as with the Maley & Taunton cars due to a back-log of work at Coplawhill. Many were stored in Newlands Depot complete with Liverpool livery and when they were eventually ready for service they included from the outset all the alterations carried out to the first 24 trams. Not all the Liverpool trams were fitted with Automatic Emergency Braking (AEB) equipment when delivered.

Ex-Liverpool 1016 contrasts with the angular lines of an adjacent Glasgow Standard Car in Hope Street not long after the Liverpool product was placed in service. Note that while Glasgow's modern trams generally sported streamlined livery styling, the Liverpool cars did not. ***R. R. Clark/STMS Collection***

Some had this fitted when in Glasgow with parts supplied from Liverpool.

Notwithstanding all the problems which obtained, GCT was in further correspondence with Liverpool Corporation Passenger Transport in March and April 1955 to discuss 'the question of the purchase of the remaining Liverpool tramcars', and a visit was arranged for 25th March, 1955.

Investigations took place in Glasgow with a view to operating the 'Baby Grand' (ie four wheeled version) of the Green Goddesses over the Glasgow track configuration. These trams were newer, 33'-10" long — only 2" shorter than the Mark I Coronation — yet mounted on EMB swing axle 9'-0" wheelbase trucks. It was felt necessary to have the wheelbase shortened to be suitable for the Glasgow track but this would only be proved by actual operation. Nothing came from this except subsequent purchases of spare parts such as magnetic brake shoes and curved glasses. The purchase of a further 39 bogie streamliners was considered in November 1955 but they were admitted by their operator to be in inferior condition (see also Chapter 14).

Admitting that the remedial work dealt with in Glasgow was to an extent 'cosmetic', it was unfortunate that the case history for these trams displayed such frequent visits to Coplawhill with outage times well above average for the rest of the fleet. If they were a burden to the maintenance staff, the opinions of the operating personnel were also soured before long. There was nowhere for the conductor to stand clear of passenger circulation. Suggestions came from the Unions concerned that the Contactor cabinets should be re-sited to create a recess for the conductor and that the seating should be staggered and upgraded to Coronation car standard to facilitate fare collection. This was dismissed by senior management as such alterations would have cost more than the purchase price of the vehicle. Eventually a compromise was reached when most cars had the Liverpool seats removed and replaced with seats from scrapped Glasgow Standard trams. The opportunity was taken to provide increased circulation area in the centre of the lower saloon by placing two single seats almost opposite each other.

Other alterations involved the removal of the windscreen droplight and substitution with a smaller fixed pane. On some cars, difficulties had been experienced in preventing water ingress around the lower edges of the cabin curved glazing and this was substituted with flat glass. Most had the gaps filled with Densyltape — unsightly but effective when the life of the car concerned was finite and predictable.

Car 1042 was involved in a serious accident in August 1957 and after receipt of estimated costs it was decided to scrap the car and retain all equipment for spares. The bodywork was in poor condition before damage was sustained and it would have cost £450 to repair the wear and tear in addition to the £500 required to put right the accident damage. Scrapping was finally completed in June 1958.

Although 1056 had entered service as recently as May 1956, 1042's demise was the start of a gradual but relentless depletion of the fleet of Green Goddesses. They frequently had to be baled out — and were outlived — by the Standard and Maximum Traction cars they were intended to replace.

1038 was mounted on E.M.B. 'Lightweight' bogies similar to those employed in Coronation Mark I cars. The problems experienced with the Liverpool cars centred round their over-light bodywork with insufficient strengthening. Note the angled vestibule glazing which attempted to cure water ingress due to body movement. *Struan J. T. Robertson*

By 1954, 1017 was being used for shunting duties and is seen here towing Liverpool 877 (later to become Glasgow 1045) for storage in Newlands Depot pending refurbishing for further service in Glasgow. 1017 never lost the white collision fenders after the Second World War - proof that the car was not repainted after 1945! *R. J. S. Wiseman*

1037 rounds the curve from Moir Street in July 1955. The destination and 'via' apertures had been exchanged quite early on. *R. J. S. Wiseman*

1007 (and 1006) when first placed in service had no trafficators. The Glasgow livery enhanced the appearance of these trams to a considerable extent. *R. J. S. Wiseman*

1055 (formerly Liverpool 869) was one of the second batch mounted on E.M.B. 'Heavyweight' bogies. Note the fitting of a fixed one-piece windscreen and access to the bow rope from the upper saloon. 1055 is once more 869 and preserved at the National Tramway Museum. *Author*

Parkhead Depot eventually took a share in operation and they also appeared on service 15. Although some incorporated '30' on their number screens, none ventured beyond the 15/29 services other than on special tours or emergency towing/pushing expeditions to foreign depots. The Maryhill-Parkhead depot allocations were very fluid.

Part of the fascination of these imports was not their speed but that hardly any two were identical. This was doubtless a function of how much rebuilding had had to be undertaken in each tram in Liverpool in the 1940s. Fortunately one survives, 1055, now Liverpool 869 once more. This was rescued, patiently and thoroughly rebuilt by supporters in Liverpool and despatched to the Crich Tramway Museum to show ultimately what Liverpool held in such high esteem.

CODE:

V	Slotted vents in roof dome.
G	Fitted with seats ex-standard cars.
W	One-piece windscreen
O	Mounted on original bogies
R	Rebuilt vestibules omitting curved glass
m	Maryhill Depot
k	Parkhead Depot
MT	Maley & Taunton Swing Link Bogies, 4'-2" wheelbase.
EL	EMB Co. Ltd., Lightweight Bogies, 4'-10" wheelbase
EH	EMB Co. Ltd., Heavyweight Radial Arm Bogies, 'Jo'burg' Pattern, 4'-10" wheelbase.

Weight of Cars — 16¾ tons.

Dimensions: 36'-0" long x 7'-3" wide.

All cars originally had side destination boxes located above the lower saloon window adjacent to the platform. 1006 and 1026 had twin apertures. These had fallen into disuse in Liverpool and were either over-painted or removed prior to arriving in Glasgow. They were not used in Glasgow either.

Liverpool No.	Glasgow No.	Built	Delivered to Glasgow	To Service Glasgow	Depot	Withdrawn from Service	Bogies	Motors	Code	Remarks
942	1006	11/37	9/53	10/53	m	10/59	MT	WT184	VWG	Half-drop Windows
934	1007	11/36	9/53	10/53	m	9/59	MT	WT184	WG	Sliding Windows
938	1008	12/36	10/53	10/53	m	2/59	MT	WT184	WGO	Half-drop Windows
935	1009	12/36	10/53	11/53	m	4/59	MT	WT184	WG	Half-drop Windows
930	1010	11/36	10/53	11/53	m	6/59	MT	WT184	WG	Sliding Windows
931	1011	11/36	10/53	11/53	m	2/59	MT	WT184	WG	Half-drop Windows/Rain Gutters
923	1012	10/36	11/53	11/53	m	3/60	MT	WT184	WGO	Half-drop Windows/Rain Gutters
928	1013	10/36	11/53	12/53	m	3/59	MT	WT184		Half-drop Windows
932	1014	11/36	11/53	12/53	m	10/59	MT	WT184	WG	Sliding Windows
940	1015	12/36	11/53	12/53	m	6/59	MT	WT184		Half-drop Windows
921	1016	9/36	11/53	12/53	m	3/60	MT	WT184	WGO	Half-drop Windows
922	1018	10/36	12/53	12/53	m	5/59	MT	WT184	W	Sliding Windows
926	1019	10/36	12/53	1/54	m	11/59	MT	WT184	W	Half-drop Windows
937	1020	12/36	12/53	1/54	m	10/58	MT	WT184	RWGO	Sliding Windows
936	1021	12/36	12/53	1/54	m	2/60	MT	WT184	WG	Sliding Windows
918	1022	9/36	1/54	2/53	m	5/59	MT	WT184		Sliding Windows
939	1023	12/36	1/54	2/54	m	8/59	MT	WT184	GO	Half-drop Windows
927	1024	11/36	9/53	2/54	m	6/58	MT	WT184	WG	Half-drop Windows
925	1025	10/36	1/54	2/54	m	3/60	MT	WT184	WGO	Half-drop Windows
941	1026	10/37	2/54	3/54	m	9/59	MT	WT184	VGO	Half-drop Windows
924	1027	10/36	2/54	3/54	m	8/59	MT	WT184	G	Sliding Windows/Rain Gutters
933	1028	11/36	3/54	3/54	m	1/59	MT	WT184	WG	Sliding Windows
929	1029	10/36	3/54	4/54	m	5/59	MT	WT184	WGO	Half-drop Windows/Rain Gutters
919	1030	9/36	3/54	4/54	m	2/60	MT	WT184	RGO	Half-drop Windows/Rain Gutters
899	1031	10/36	7/54	9/54	m	2/60	EL	WT184	GW	Sliding Windows
901	1032	10/36	7/54	12/54	m	4/60	EL	WT184	W	Half-drop Windows/Non standard Seats
881	1033	7/36	8/54	1/55	m	3/60	EL	WT184	W	Sliding Windows
885	1034	7/36	6/54	4/55	m	2/59	EL	WT184	W	Sliding Windows
902	1035	10/36	7/54	5/55	m	7/59	EL	WT184	WG	Sliding Windows
891	1036	8/36	6/54	5/55	m	7/60	EL	WT184	W	Sliding Windows
880	1037	7/36	9/54	5/55	m	3/59	EH	WT184	WG	Sliding Windows
883	1038	7/36	8/54	5/55	m	6/59	EL	WT184	RGW	Sliding Windows
878	1041	7/36	5/54	6/55	m	4/59	EH	WT184	W	Half-drop Windows
886	1042	8/36	8/54	6/55	m	8/57	EL	WT184	W	Sliding Windows
903	1043	11/36	10/54	6/55	m	3/59	EL	WT184		Half-drop Windows/Rain Gutters
874	1044	6/36	9/54	7/55	k	2/59	EH	WT184		Sliding Windows
877	1045	6/36	9/54	7/55	k	10/59	EH	WT184	WG	Sliding Windows
875	1046	6/36	11/54	7/55	k	10/58	EH	WT184	WG	Sliding Windows
871	1047	6/36	8/54	8/55	k	3/59	EH	WT184	WG	Sliding Windows
887	1048	8/36	10/54	8/55	k	10/59	EL	WT184	WG	Sliding Windows
893	1049	9/36	9/54	8/55	k	6/59	EL	WT184	WG	Sliding Windows
897	1052	10/36	10/54	9/55	k	12/59	EL	WT184	WG	Half-drop Windows
884	1053	7/36	6/54	9/55	k	7/59	EL	WT184	WG	Half-drop Windows
890	1054	8/36	5/54	10/55	k	8/59	EL	WT184	WG	Half-drop Windows
869	1055	6/36	5/54	11/55	k	6/60	EH	WT184	W	Sliding Windows
904	1056	11/36	11/54	5/56	k	11/59	EL	WT184	WG	Sliding Windows

Cars with Half-drop Windows had steel (or originally glass) rain-shields over all main windows.

1047 and 1013 are at Broomhouse terminus. 1047 displays the smaller one-piece windscreen eventually fitted to all ex-Liverpool cars. 1013's was altered later. ***R. F. Mack***

1046 is shown operating on service 15 – the only other domain of the Liverpool cars apart from service 29. This photograph was taken in April 1958 and soon after this the appearance of these cars began to deteriorate noticeably. ***R. J. S. Wiseman***

CHAPTER 16

The Works Cars

WORKS CAR FLEET

With such an extensive fleet of trams to service and such a large network of track, overhead and mains cabling distribution to maintain, it is hardly surprising that the Glasgow Corporation Tramways system should require a considerable number of vehicles for its Works Fleet. Being its own generator of electricity until as late as 1958, it was logical — and good accounting practice — that these vehicles should be railed and electrically powered. Many were former passenger trams relegated to less glamorous use but others were purpose made.

Each department of the Tramways Department had its own fleet of vehicles separately numbered and prefixed with 'No.'. It is reasonably certain that the electric fleet and the non-electric fleet in each department were also differentiated by being placed in a separate numbering series. The Permanent Way Department had two electric fleets, Water Cars and others.

The Mains Department had its own series of numbers 'No. 1-No. 3' and, for some unaccountable reason, No. 20(I) appears. It is not known why the gap existed and it is possible that the vacant numbers were used by other sundry vehicles which were not electrically powered. It has been suggested that 'No. 20'(I) could have been a conversion from an electrified Horse Car but its very existence is questioned and what is listed in the tables as 'No. 20'(II) and ex-Paisley District 39 may in fact be the first (and only) No. 20. Indeed converted Horse Car '120' may have retained its capital stock number for a while just to add to the confusion before becoming 'No. 2'.

Cable Laying Car No. 1 at work in its original form at some now unrecognisable extension. No. 1 was purpose made and not converted from an erstwhile passenger car. Huge cable drums could be accommodated at the other end and the car had its own small four-wheeled trailer. ***G.C.T.***

Room & Kitchen Car 672 was converted into Mains Department testing car No. 3. In order to facilitate carriage of the heavy rotary converter equipment, the car was given four motors, one per axle. Following the intervention of the STMS in 1951, the car is once again 672 in the Glasgow Museum of Transport. ***G.C.T.***

The Water Tanks were also numbered in their own series from No. 1 to No. 9. Originally they were simply large rivetted water tanks mounted on open platformed underframes, in turn mounted on 6'-0" wheelbase 21E J. G. Brill trucks or Mountain & Gibson 21EM trucks. Later the platforms acquired roofs while remaining unvestibuled. In the 1930s, those destined to survive long enough acquired vestibules and post World War II most were re-trucked with roller bearing axle boxes and 'doctored' Regen BT-H 101J motors and OK45B controllers. By the 1940s, only four were in constant use. Their gross weight was nearly 15½ tons with 5½ tons of this relating to the water in a full tank. When latterly fitted with air brakes the air compressor was also used to apply scrubbing stones to even out track corrugations with the addition of water. The cars were used during night service operation and wore 2" off the scrubbing stones each shift. Their maximum speed with pressure on the scrubbing stones was only 15 mph which was latterly incompatible with service speeds for daytime use.

The original water cars had no cabin roofs or vestibules although these features were progressively fitted. Spare trolley masts, trucks and controllers were used to construct these cars. By the time they were scrapped hardly any of the original equipment remained. ***G.C.T.***

The first generation of sand and sett cars used bogies and electrical equipment from redundant Room & Kitchen cars with magnetic brakes added. No. 4 is seen being loaded in the Tramways Department siding at Custom House Quay. ***G.C.T.***

Other Permanent Way vehicles were numbered in a third series 'No. 1-No. 9'. 'No. 1' and 'No. 2' were Tool Vans. No record exists at all of 'No. 3' in this series but a photograph survives to prove that it was a bogie flat wagon manufactured out of redundant equipment from ex-'Room & Kitchen' cars 666-685 and similar to sister vehicles 'No. 4'-'No. 10' but with a much lower dash panel. 'No. 1' owed its ancestry to Room & Kitchen construction while 'No. 2' had been an electrified Horse Car in earlier life. The designation of the open wagons varies over their years of existence from 'Sand and Sett Wagon' or 'Mineral Wagon' to (latterly) 'Muck Wagon'. Only one survived the Second World War. To confuse matters completely, there is also record of Tool Van No. 7 (see Tables for information).

The combined numbering system appears to have emerged with the acquisition of rolling stock from the Airdrie and Paisley systems. Some of the latter's open top cars had recently been rebuilt but, despite being in sound condition, were too tall to accommodate a standard Glasgow top cover. When they became redundant, the opportunity was taken to convert them into new Tool Vans and to convert an ex-Airdrie & Coatbridge tram into an overhead inspection vehicle. The ex-Mains Department series remained 'No. 1'-'No. 3'. The surviving open wagons, from the Permanent Way series became 'No. 4'-'No. 6' and 'No. 8'-'No. 10', while their Tool Cars 'No. 1' & 'No. 2' became 'No. 21' and 'No. 22' respectively, Tool Car 'No. 7' becoming 'No. 23' (I). There was no No. 7 in the combined fleet! The Water Tanks had ten added to their original numbers becoming 'No. 11-No. 19' and the number 'No. 20' was filled by an ex-Paisley car (39) which had never been numbered into the Glasgow Corporation Tramways passenger stock series.

During the late 1930s the original open mineral wagons were replaced by new construction taking Brill 21E 7'-0" wheelbase trucks rendered surplus from Semi-High Speed Standard trams then undergoing further modernisation during Phase IV status. These new wagons thus acquired BT-H B18 controllers and Westinghouse 323V motors. Vestibuling was fitted to the Water Tank cars first; the new open wagons had them when built and most of the Tool Vans noted in the Tables were equipped around 1938.

Some duplication in numbering persisted even after the renumbering had occurred. A new Tool Van, 'No. 22' was constructed with Standard Car lower saloon (wide) body and round dashes in 1938 and appears to have co-existed with the converted

No. 38 was one of two sand cars specially-built with low cab roofs so that they could be driven into the sand drier building. Photographed in 1958, the original Brill truck has been replaced with ex-Regen equipment. These two cars were the only works cars to be seen regularly in daylight. ***R. J. S. Wiseman***

Mains Department Tool Car No. 20 was once Paisley & District 39, never acquiring a capital stock number in the passenger fleet. When the Permanent Way Dept. Tool Cars were vestibuled in the 1930s the same luxury was not accorded to No. 20. Note the front lifeguard tied up with rope! R. R. Clark/STMS Collection

electrified Horse Car of the same number at least for a short time. The first No. 23 was scrapped in November 1938 to be replaced by a new Van with identical body and semi-high speed truck/motors to No. 22(II). This was renumbered 'No. 23A' when a third 'No. 23' appeared as 'No. 23B' in November 1952 — an ex-Regen Standard tram 814, cut down and converted for use as a Tool Van. The latter two only co-existed for two years and when 'No. 23A' was scrapped, 'No. 23B' became — simply — 'No. 23'. For those who have stayed the course thus far, the story now becomes less complicated . . .

Water Tank 'No. 14' (ex 'No. 4') was equipped with an 8'-0" wheelbase GCT/Brush 21E type truck in 1951 but this was rapidly removed when it was found that the scrubbing stones fouled the track grooves on curves due to the extended wheelbase. However, as noted in the Tables, most surviving Works cars had new trucks and equipment fitted during the 1950s to the extent that the standard Permanent Way Department motors and controllers became ex-Regen BT-H 101J 60 hp motors and BT-H OK45B controllers. Trucks were either 7'-0" or 8'-0" wheelbase as appropriate and had an assortment of roller bearing axle boxes of various makers — Hoffmann, Bock, Skefko or Ransome & Marles. The Regen motors had been doctored and modified to normal fields and control.

Although GCT had two decorated cars numbered in passenger stock (1008 and 1073), the works fleet contained a further example, No. 50 — the 'Kelvin Hall Car'—a Hexagonal Dash Body with 8'-0" wheelbase GCT/Brush truck having GEC WT28 motors, EE. CDB2 controllers and no air brakes. Several other members of the fleet occasionally found themselves partially dismantled to form the basis of floats or sometimes something more exotic like a gondola, a modern house, a thatched cottage, the Queen Mary or The Comet. Latterly, the liberal application of light bulbs sufficed to promote special campaigns and events.

The normal livery was originally crimson lake or dark brown, fully lined out in yellow edged with red with fine inner white lining. Lettering was yellow. After the 1930s, all lining was omitted and ultimately the lettering was dispensed with too.

In addition to the electrified vehicles, there were other non-powered ancillary vehicles such as Salt Wagon trailers (42 in number) mounted on ex-Horse Car trucks, together with rail carriers, grinders, crane jibs or flat trucks utilising redundant Room & Kitchen Car bogies or Standard Car trucks.

Following conversion to bow collector operation, towers were constructed on each car to accommodate standard bows, except on selected cars which had extra long armed bows to permit operation on the Duntocher service.

It was this section of track in Govan which dictated that the track gauge in Glasgow would be the non-standard 4'-7¾". This enabled railway goods wagons to gain access to Stephen's and Fairfield's Shipyards from goods yards. With their different wheel profiles these wagons ran on their flanges. Fairfield's Electric Loco is seen passing Standard Car 42. A. K. Terry

The 1959 Scottish Industries Exhibition provided a last excuse for an illuminated car. Works car No. 27, ex-1005 (I) performed on this occasion. D. E. Sinclair

Original Number	Ultimate Number	Ex-Fleet Number	Date New	Type	Equipment	Depots	Withdrawal Date	Remarks
No. 1	No. 1	New	—/05	Mains Dept. Cable Layer & Withdrawer	Brill 21E truck, 6'-0" wb B18 controllers, 2 x GE58 motors at 30 hp each	x	Sold 10/62	Large van housing cable drums. Preserved at National Tramway Museum, Crich. Had illuminated destination box displaying 'Cable Car'
No. 2	No. 2	ch120	8/12	Mains Dept. Tool Van	Ditto, but with 2 x WH49B motors at 30 hp each	.x	2/59	Remained unvestibuled. Acted as mobile workshop for cable, section boxes and traction phone repairs
No. 3	No. 3	672	9/08	Mains Test Car	2 x GCT equal wheel bogies 4'-0" wb, B18 controllers, 4 x WH49B motors at 30 hp each	x	10/53	Converted Room & Kitchen car. Stored and restored 1959-62 for display in Glasgow Museum of Transport
No. 3	—	?	5/06	Mineral Wagon	Ditto, but with WH controllers Ditto	?	?	Scrapped by 1925 Open wagon using equipment ex-Room & Kitchen car(s)
No. 4	No. 4	?	8/06?	Mineral Wagon	Ditto	?	By 11/38	Ditto
No. 5	No. 5	?	10/07?	Mineral Wagon	Ditto	?	6/38	Ditto
No. 6	No. 6	?	10/07?	Mineral Wagon	Ditto	l	9/49	Ditto
No. 7?	No. 7	?	?	Mineral Wagon	Ditto	?	11/38	
No. 7?	No.23(i)	ch86	4/13	Tool Van P.W. Dept.	EEC 'Preston' compensating truck, 6'-0" wb, B18 controllers 2 x WH49B motors at 30 hp each truck later as 'No. 2'	b	11/38	Remained unvestibuled 'Preston' truck exchanged c1930 See footnote
No. 8	No. 8	?	6/14	Sand/Sett Wagon	As mineral wagon No. 3	?	5/38	As Mineral Wagon No. 3
No. 9	No. 9	679	—/16	Sand/Sett Wagon	Ditto	?	12/38	Ditto. Decorated Car 'Queen Mary' in 1937
No. 10	No. 10	670	7/20	Sand/Sett Wagon	Ditto	l	4/39	As Mineral Wagon No. 3
No. 1	No. 11	New	4/07	Water Tank /Scrub Car	Brill 21E truck, 6'-0" wb, WH controllers, 2 x WH 49B motors at 30 hp each; later 2 x WH220 motors at 45 hp each	l	12/38	Platforms roofed c1908 Air brakes and compressed air operation of scrubbing gear c1933
No. 2	No. 12	New	4/07	Water Tank /Scrub Car	Ditto, but with 2 x GE203L motors at 30 hp each, later WH323V and finally WH220 at 45 hp each	b	12/38	Ditto
No. 3	No. 13	New	4/07	Water Tank /Scrub Car	Ditto, but with 2 x WH220 motors at 45 hp each	b	12/38	Ditto. Decorated Car, 1937 'Thatched Cottage'
No. 4	No. 14	New	4/07	Water Tank /Scrub Car	M&G 21EM truck, 6'-0" wb, WH controllers, 2 x GE57 motors at 30 hp each. Later (12/51) GCT/Brush 21E pattern, 7'-0" wb OK45B controllers and BT-H 101J motors at 60 hp each	b	c1957	Ditto Water Tank No. 11 See text for further details

Original Number	Ultimate Number	Ex-Fleet Number	Date New	Type	Equipment	Depots	Withdrawal Date	Remarks
No. 5	No. 15	New	4/07	Water Tank /Scrub Car	Ditto, but with B18 controllers and Witting motors at 30 hp each, later 323V motors at 45 hp each then with GCT/Brush 21E pattern truck as No. 14	b y	7/58	Ditto Water Tank No. 11. Vestibuled 7/34. Had GE58 motors prior to 1936?
No. 6	No. 16	New	4/07	Water Tank /Scrub Car	Ditto, upgraded as Water Car No. 14 with ex-Regen equipment	l y	Sold 10/62	Ditto, vestibuled 9/35 Upgraded 11/53
No. 7	No. 17	New	5/07	Water Tank /Scrub Car	Ditto, but not re-trucked or re-equipped	n	3/30	Ditto, but unvestibuled. Scrapped at Newlands Depot
—	No. 17	New	4/31	Water Tank /Scrub Car	Replacement, with Brush 21E pattern truck, 6'-0" wb, 2 x WH220 motors at 45 hp each, ? controllers	l	11/38	Ditto Water Tank No. 11 Vestibuled 2/34
No. 8	No. 18	New	7/07	Water Car Weed Killer Car	Brill 21E truck, 6'-0" wb, B18 controllers, 2 x WH49B motors at 30 hp each, later WH220 and then WH323V at 45 hp latterly (5/53) upgrading as water tank No. 14 with ex-Regen equipment	d l y	4/60	Ditto, vestibuled 5/28 Dismantled and converted to 'Comet' 1937 Converted to weed killer car 7/37. Retained offside and nearside access to each cab
No. 9	No. 19	New	7/07	Water Tank /Scrub Car	Ditto water car No. 18	b y	Sold 12/63	Ditto, vestibuled 8/36, no nearside access to cabins
No. 20?	No. 20(i)	ch?	12/03	Mains Dept. Tool Van	Brill 21E truck, 6'-0" wb with 2 x GE58? motors at 30 hp each and B18? controllers	?	?	This car may actually have been converted horse car '120' which retained its number for some time before being transferred from passenger stock, albeit used by Mains Dept.
No. 20	No. 20(ii)	Paisley 39	3/25	Mains Dept. Tool Van	Brush A-A truck 6'-0" wb, B13, then B18 controllers, 2 x GE58 motors at 30 hp each, later 49B	x	2/59	Never acquired number in GCT Passenger stock prior to conversion. Remained unvesti-buled
No. 1	No. 21	New	12/03	Welders Tool Van	Brill 21E truck, 6'-0" wb, B18 controllers, 2 x GE58 motors at 30 hp each, later upgraded with ex-Regen equipment as No. 14	l y	Sold 10/62	Resembled half 'Room & Kitchen' car Built from spare parts Vestibuled 10/39. See footnote. On display at National Tramway Museum
No. 2	No. 22(i)	ch31	1/06	Tool Van P.W. Dept.	Ditto, but with 2 x WH49B motors at 30 hp each. Not upgraded	b	11/38?	
—	No. 22(ii)	New	c9/38	Tool Van P.W. Dept. Mobile Squad	Brill 21E truck, 7'-0" wb, B18 controllers, 2 x WH323V motors at 45 hp each. Later upgraded with 7'-0" wb GCT/Brush 21E truck and ex-Regen equipment	b y	Sold 10/62	336-317 type body, vestibuled 8/38 Sold to National Tramway Museum for parts
No. 23(ii)	No. 23A	New	10/38	Tool Van P.W. Dept.	Ditto, but originally with 2 x WH220 motors, ditto	?	11/54	Ditto, vestibuled 8/38 Renumbered No. 23A, 11/52
No. 23B	No. 23	814	11/52	Tool Van P.W. Dept. Closure Car	Equipped with GCT/Brush 8'-0" wb 21E truck and ex-Regen equipment from outset	b y	8/62	Renumbered No. 23 in 11/54 Ex-Monitor Roof round dash Standard car
—	No. 24	1076	10/24	Overhead Inspection Car	Brush? truck 6'-0" wb ? controllers and 2 x Brush 1002 motors at 30 hp each	n	12/38	Ex-Airdrie & Coatbridge open top car.

1008 was numbered in Capital Stock unlike the Kelvin Hall Car 'No. 50'. This view was taken at the time of the 1937 Coronation celebrations. *G.C.T.*

Photographed in the Newlands Depot forecourt, the Kelvin Hall Car No. 50 advertising the annual Carnival had modern equipment but lacked air brakes. *G.C.T.*

The Coronation of King George VI provided an excuse in 1937 for the 'launching' of two tramway department floats. One was a representation of the Queen Mary based on bogie Mineral Wagon No. 9 contrasting with The Comet mounted on Water Tank No. 18. This was not the first reproduction of The Comet, nor the most ambitious. *G.C.T.*

Original Number	Ultimate Number	Ex-Fleet Number	Date New	Type	Equipment	Depots	Withdrawal Date	Remarks
—	No. 25	Paisley 40	3/24	Mineral Wagon	HN 21E truck, 6'-0" wb, B18 controllers, 2 x GE58 motors at 30 hp each. Later 2 x WH49B upgraded with ex-Regen equipment as No. 21.	b	8/58	Truck & equipment, only, from Paisley District 40. Body scrapped without acquiring GCT number in capital stock
—	No. 26	1021	5/33	Tool Van Mobile Squad	Brush A-A truck 6'-0" wb B18 controllers and 2 x GE58 motors at 30 hp each	b y	3/59	Vestibuled 9/38. Received Glasgow style dashes. Retained bulkhead double sliding doors
—	No. 27	1005	1/34	Tool Van Rail Car	Brill 21E truck, 7'-0" wb, B18 controllers, 2 x WH49B motors at 30 hp each. Later upgraded as per No. 21	b y	Sold 10/62	Vestibuled 9/38 Illuminating car 1959. Sold for parts
—	No. 28	1003	2/34	Tool Van Rail Car (Spare)	Originally as No. 26 Later upgraded as No. 21	b y	3/58	Vestibuled 9/38
—	No. 29	1007	6/34	Tool Van Thermit Welding	Ditto	b y	7/59	Ditto
—	No. 30	1026	6/34	Tool Van (Spare)	Ditto but not re-equipped or re-trucked	b y	7/59	Ditto
—	No. 31	1004	9/34	Tool Van Thermit Welding	Ditto, No. 27	b y	12/60	Ditto
—	No. 32	1002	11/34	Tool Van (Spare)	Ditto, No. 28	b y	7/50	Ditto
—	No. 33	New	5/37	Sett Wagon	Brill 21E truck, 7'- 0" wb, B18 controllers and 2 x WH323V motors at 45 hp each, later re-equipped & re-trucked as per No. 27	b n	7/59	
—	No. 34	New	7/37	Sett Wagon	Ditto	b n	3/58	Original truck ex-car 756
—	No. 35	New	8/37	Sett Wagon	Ditto	b n	7/59	Original truck ex-car 906
—	No. 36	New	10/37	Sett Wagon	Ditto	b n	8/58	Original truck ex-car 771 Illuminated car 1957
—	No. 37	New	11/37	Sett Wagon	Ditto	b n	8/59	Original truck ex-car 791
—	No. 38	New	5/39	Sand Drier Car	Ditto, but re-equipped with 8'-0" wb truck	l	12/58	Special low roof cabs
—	No. 39	New	9/39	Sand Drier Car	Ditto	l	12/59	Ditto
—	No. 40	722	11/54	Tool Van Points Repair	Ditto No. 23B	b y	Sold 10/62	Ex-Standard car, Round Dash Monitor Roof, 722
—	No. 50	New	c1930	Decorated Car Kelvin Hall Car	GCT/Brush 21E truck, 8'-0" wb 2 x GEC motors at 60 hp each. EE controllers. No air brakes	n	1/49	Hex-dash body. Destroyed Newlands Depot fire 11/4/48

Original Number	Ultimate Number	Ex-Fleet Number	Date New	Type	Equipment	Depots	Withdrawal Date	Remarks
—	No. 51	Paisley 51	c1908	Sand/Sett Wagon	HN 21E truck, 6'-0" wb, B18 controllers, 2 x GE58 motors at 30 hp each, later re-trucked and re-equipped as No. 21	b n	8/59	Ex-Paisley District multi-purpose works car totally rebuilt by PD, then again by GCT
—	No. 10	Paisley 50	c1905	Scrub Car	Brush A-A truck, 6'-0" wb B18 controllers, 2 x GE58 motors at 30 hp each, later 2 x WH323V at 45 hp each. Latterly re-trucked and re-equipped as No. 21	b n	Sold 10/62	Sold for parts at National Tramway Museum

Numbers between No. 41 and No. 49 plus Nos. 52-100 not used.

Footnotes:

(1) Pinkston Power Station was owned and operated by GCT and had its own fleet. This comprised of two locomotive cranes which lifted coal wagons off the track and tipped coal out of them. Although condemned in the early 1940s they remained in use until a new wagon tipping plant was installed c1953. In addition, an ordinary electric locomotive was purchased from Fairfield's in 1940 for shunting purposes and continued in use after the sale of the power station to the South of Scotland Electricity Board until conversion of the Power Station to oil burning.
The Pinkston Fleet had the only standard 4'-8½" gauge vehicles owned by GCT as opposed to the 4'-7¾" of the trams.

(2) Ex-Paisley Cars 1001, 1029, 1034, 1045 and 1047 were used as P.W. employees' cars while remaining in passenger stock, 1933-1938.
1029 was latterly used as a Tool Van (without rebuilding) 1042 used as P.W. Employees' 'Sleeping Car' 1932/33.

(3) Re Tool Cars Nos. 1 & 7 (original numbers) Permanent Way Fleet. The alternative theory is that original numbers No. 1 and No. 2 were former Electrified Horse Cars 31 and 86 which became No. 22 and No. 23 with No. 21 being built new in 1920 from ex-Room & Kitchen car parts either ex-stores or dismantled from bodies still extant. Information to confirm either option put forward is inconclusive.

(4) Decorated Cars
In addition to those indicated above either purpose-built or adapted for special events, GCT had two others numbered in the passenger stock series.
1073 ex-Airdrie and Coatbridge car (see chapter 5) converted to Decorated Car 12/27, scrapped 1/35.
1008 ex-Paisley District car (see Chapter 4) converted to Decorated Car 9/34, scrapped after Newlands Depot fire 1/49 (see also Appendix ii)

(5) For details of Parcels Cars and Ticket Box Car, see Chapter 2.

(6) For details of Motor School Car, see Chapter 4.

No. 21 can best be described as 'quaint'. It was constructed from Room & Kitchen car parts but unlikely to have origins in any one example of these. Despatched to the Crich Museum it served there for a while as bookshop and is now on display beside the Town End terminus. *R. R. Clark/STMS Collection*

Time was when the essential accompaniment to any nocturnal track repairs was the Tool Van complete with stove and smoke screen. It was most unusual for this night-time ritual to be observed in broad daylight. *R. R. Clark/STMS Collection*

The Permanent Way Department's heavy-duty Mineral Wagons based on ex-Room & Kitchen cars' equipment made suitable patriotic decorated cars during the 1914-1918 War. These were regularly repainted, exhorting Glaswegians to charitable deeds. *GCT.*

Before special floats were constructed or purpose-built illuminated or decorated cars were placed in service it was normal to use spare Phase I open toppers for special occasions. This is 690 bedecked for the jubilee of the Loch Katrine water supply scheme for the City of Glasgow. *G.C.T.*

1937 also saw contrasting decorated floats representing land-based subjects. Developments in housing were represented by a Thatched Cottage mounted on Water Tank No. 13 and a modern villa built round the Kelvin Hall Car, No. 50. *G.C.T.*

The first of the 1954 Coronation Cars, 1393, heads for Rouken Glen in May 1959 with Shawlands Cross in the distance. The simplification in Mark I design did little to reduce the attractive appearance of these cars — especially when freshly painted.
W.D.McMillan

Cunarder 1337 and A141 were photographed outside the Pollokshaws Burgh Hall on 10th May 1959. By this time the Corporation buses were beginning to look better cared for than the trams.
W.D. McMillan

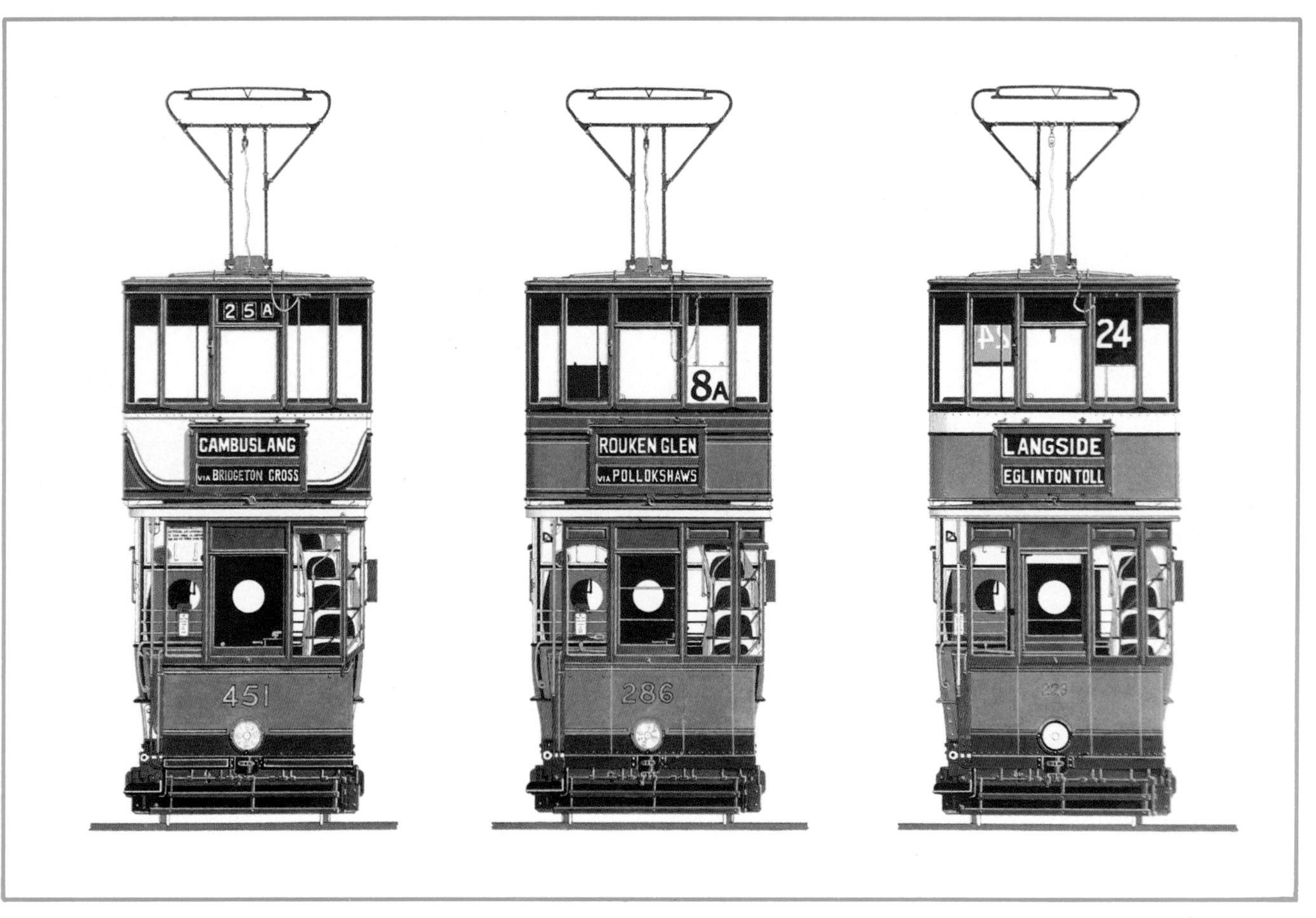

Various experimental liveries have been applied to Standard trams over the years without any lasting impression. 451 has 1936-style streamlining, 286 displays red service colouring over bus green while 223 is all cadmium. *Drawings: Author.*

Coronation trams have not escaped experimental livery styles. 1143 shows the first attempt at a standard livery, 1278 has the 1949 experimental red while 1239 has a gold visor. *Drawings: Author*

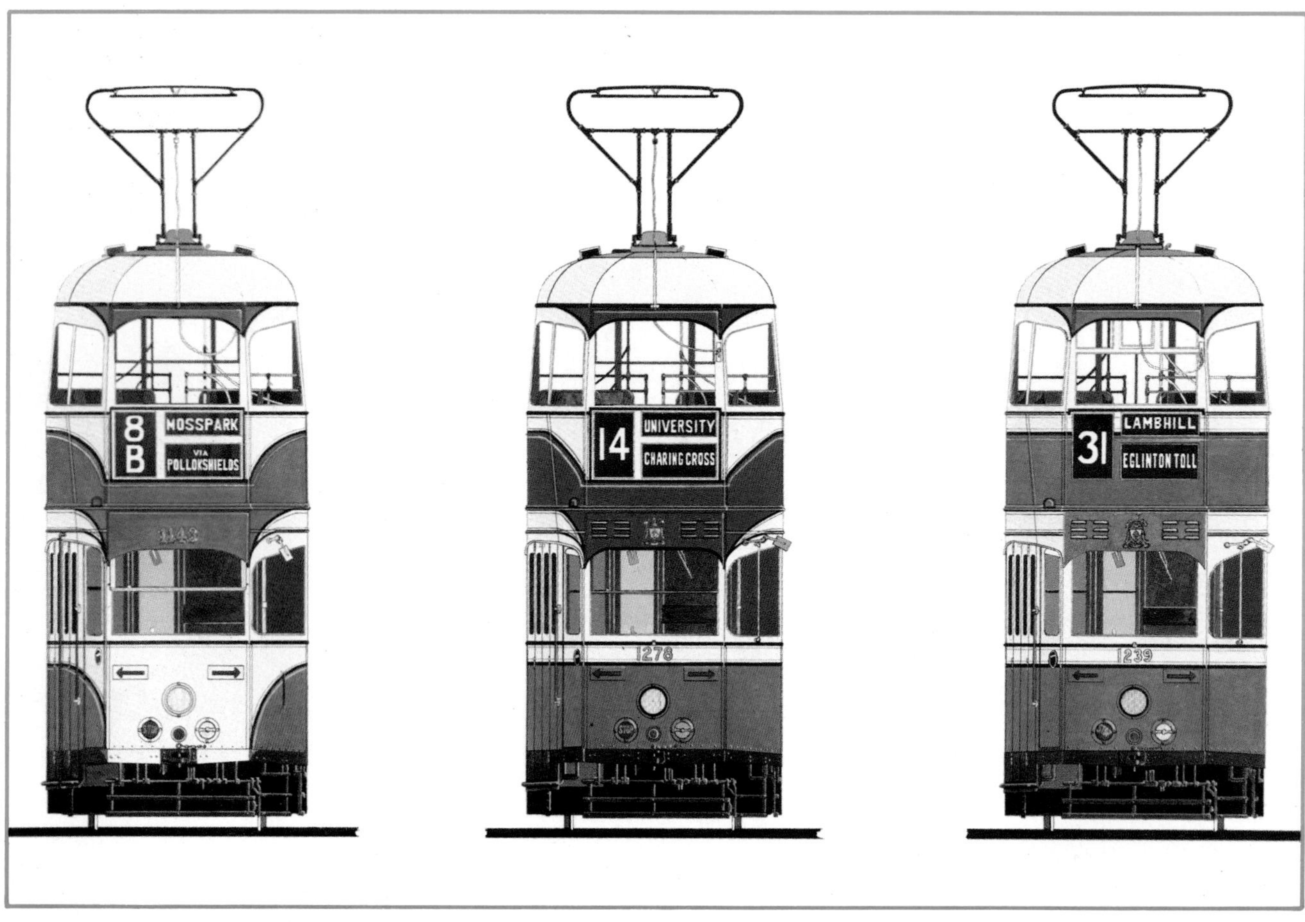

Printed on Trulux Gloss 115 G.S.M.

CHAPTER 17

The Livery of Glasgow Corporation Tramcars

THE LIVERY OF GLASGOW'S TRAMS

By the mid 1930s the route colour concept was becoming increasingly difficult to adhere to and the first experiments to eliminate its use centred round car 451 (red) and 215 (green)-shown here. Both were painted in streamlined style and additionally 215 had an extra-large service number box.
Dr. J. G. Stewart

The style of painting adopted for the electric trams in Glasgow was highly distinctive, if not unique, and owed a lot to Trans-Atlantic practice as will be seen. What is not perhaps appreciated by those who remember only the declining years is that the specification applied was of the highest quality and that — as a result — only accident-damaged cars had required to be repainted by World War I. By this time, many of the fleet had seen intensive city use for nearly fifteen years. When cars were converted from open top to having top covers, the original portions not undergoing alteration were 'flatted' and revarnished. That this could suffice is explained by the stringent specification and quality control maintained at the Coplawhill Carworks.

In 1908, Mr. John Ferguson, Chief Engineer, set out his views on various aspects of Car Building. His opinions on painting and varnishing set high standards which were maintained relentlessly. It was his view that the life of a car depended not so much on the frequency of attention to its paint surface but mainly on the quality of the original job. While other tasks could be speeded up by putting extra pressure on staff, similar practices with painting operations compromised the durability of the work. There was ample evidence of this in Glasgow. Mr. John Young had been most anxious to have the first double decker, 686, available for the inauguration of the first electrified service on 18th October, 1898 and, for the three weeks previous to this, painters worked night and day to achieve their deadline. The finished result was most pleasing, but after six months work it all had to be scraped down and repainted. Similarly, the Gloucester-built cars 901-980 arrived in Glasgow looking no different in quality to the home-built cars. However, as soon as the twelve months guarantee period expired, these too had to be scraped down. Normally this task is nasty to execute and time consuming to complete, but in the case of these cars, all that had to be done was to put an old plane at one end of the panels underneath the surface and push it from one end to the other. The paint easily stripped right off down to the filling.

All told, Glasgow trams received 18 coats of paint and varnish in the following order:—

Two coats of priming were first applied, made of genuine white lead, thinned with turpentine, with a little gold size and driers.

Then came six coats of filling, made up of seven parts of filling worked into a paste with turpentine, with two parts of white lead in oil, two parts varnish and two parts of gold size.

Two coats of staining were then applied, made up of Indian Red, gold size and turpentine. This was allowed to dry thoroughtly before rubbing down to a perfectly smooth finish. After this, the first coat of ground colour was brushed on, rubbed down again and a second coat of ground colour was applied. Then paint of the ultimate panel colour or general woodwork colour was brushed on in two coats, followed by a third with more varnish added. Lining and transfers were added to this and the job completed with three coats of best finishing body varnish. The cost confirmed for this in 1908 was £9 0s 0d for materials and £16 2s 6d for labour! The total cost then for a complete top covered tram inclusive of all oncosts was £632 7s 5d.

The National Tramway Museum at Crich recently rebuilt one of these following traditional practice as near as availability of materials and labour would allow. Car 812 cost over £50,000 to restore. Such is inflation.

The finished result was splendid. Basically, the Glasgow Corporation Tramways colour scheme was cadmium orange and ivory with the orange applied to the main lower saloon side panels, only, at the outset. Lower saloon window framing was always ivory and this colour was also used at first for the dash panels up to Car 698. Latterly all cars, commencing with 699, had plum/brown dashes which had the virtue of being less prone to disfigurement by mud splashes from other users of the indifferent road surfaces of the time. The brown dashes were retained for the Unobtrusive Top Covered cars and all surviving open top cars right up to 1923/24 by which time the standard colour for dashes had long since become cadmium orange.

When top covers were constructed, these employed durable varnished teak bulkheads and window frames but it was the upper deck side panels which gave the Glasgow trams their best remembered and most distinctive feature. The Glasgow Tramway & Omnibus Company had introduced the service colour differentiation to the city. They used the upper sides for advertising but painted the lower panels red, white, blue, green, brown, yellow or Menzies Tartan to identify the service. When Glasgow Corporation commenced operation with their own cars in 1894 they transferred the colours to the upper panels, retaining red, white, blue, yellow and green. The G.T & O. Co. retained brown for their competing horse buses. These colours were transferred to the electric cars and were carefully selected to be capable of identification by the colour blind. The blue was

328 is a wide-bodied Round-Dash Standard tram once mounted on a Mountain & Gibson Radial truck. It is shown in 1938 at Scotstoun in a short-lived experimental livery with upper deck side panels in bus green surmounted by a narrow band of route colour red.
W. Fisher, Courtesy D. W. Fisher

prussian, red slightly darker than post office red, yellow was chrome yellow and the green was fairly close to the Verona green which has seen use with Strathclyde, West Yorkshire & Merseyside Passenger Transport Executives. The colour bands were copiously lined-out with Greek corner patterns and formed into panels. The yellow and white trams used black and red lining while the others used black and white. In both cases, the black was thicker and was also used for panel edging. On top covered cars the colour band was separated from the varnished teak window frames by a band of ivory with thick orange lining similar to the concave panel below the lower deck main side panelling.

The rocker (or concave) panels also featured an inner fine black line and this detail had originally been applied to the earliest cars with ivory dashes. Destination boxes and slip boards were painted to match the colours on the top deck sides. Lettering on the slip-boards was white except on the yellow and white cars where black letters were used.

Lining on the lower deck comprised black fine lining, picking out the pillars and window tops (retained until the last) and aluminium edged black for the cadmium panels. Aluminium was also used for the fleet numbers and GLASGOW CORPORATION concave panels inscription and full Greek corner patterns were used. Gold and silver had been found to react unfavourably with the polluted atmosphere in Glasgow at the time which probably explains why cars with brown dashes used yellow edged with red instead of gold.

Flooring and roofs were battleship grey. Controllers, handbrake columns and seat-framing were black. Staircase treads and handrails were maroon and dash inner sides were khaki. The service colouring was carried round the upper deck exterior bulkheads when the cars were Phase II or Phase III and this proved invaluable for checking original colours as latterly these were over-painted brown on modernisation to Phase IV. Trucks and handrails were painted maroon. The trucks and collision fenders were ornately lined out in black and white similarly to detail on the contemporary Caledonian Railway locomotives. Staircase stringers were ivory edged orange and black while the trolleys were also black. This was Glasgow Corporation Tramways ornate yet honest and colourful livery, surviving right until 1936 when the first rumblings of discontent were heard. The undiluted livery was also applied to the Maximum Traction cars new in 1928/29 but — after all — these were 'Standard Double Bogie' cars having no obvious external appearance of modernity.

No doubt the senior staff of tramway undertakings liaised then as bus operators do now and an amicable relationship grew between the Glasgow and Sheffield undertakings which — among other things — resulted in staff from Sheffield being despatched to Coplawhill to see how things were done there. Particular attention was paid to the painting of the Glasgow cars. The Sheffield staff could not compare the construction or artistry of style of the Glasgow trams with their own (*well, really!*), but had the greatest admiration for the organisation of the paint shop and methods adopted. They were experiencing problems at the time with their colour of blue and, perhaps as a result of advice received in Glasgow, lightened this shade on later construction.

By May 1936 a shortage of available cars had arisen and depot foremen were having to resort to sending out cars of whatever colour they had available whether or not the colour was appropriate to the service being operated. This caused confusion among the public. Dalmarnock Depot was notoriously short of white cars and used to send out red ones with white slip boards.

It was therefore suggested that a uniform colour should be adopted and a service numbering system introduced with a large number screen prominently displayed. This was actually tried on Car 215 in 1936 which was painted in a style reminiscent of Sunderland's modern cars with the green service colour downswept at the ends. It was fitted with a large number screen aperture mounted centrally above the drop-light in the upper vestibules which displaced the digital head-code screens. Car 451 was painted in this style but retained the red service colour band. It was not fitted with a new service number display. These experiments came to nothing at the time on Standard cars as — no doubt — attention was being concentrated on the construction of the new Experimental Saloon Car 1141, but similar styling soon appeared on locally built Cowieson bodied Corporation buses.

A portent of what was to follow could be seen on 1141 when the car first appeared. Gone was the service colouring to be replaced by the same green as had been used on the Corporation Buses since 1928. Known, logically enough, as 'bus green', it had less blue pigment and more yellow, being not unlike contemporary Southdown buses. This was downswept at the ends in similar style to 215 and 451. The cadmium yellow or orange which had origins in USA was replaced by a more distinctly orange colour — slightly darker. The green panels were lined in gold, edged in black and the orange panels lined in white. The rest of the car was cream lined in black and picked out with fine orange lining

The upper saloons in most older cars (and the lower saloons, too, in many) acquired a dark-stained varnish finish known at Coplawhill as 'glossy dirt' but to enthusiasts as 'treacle'. It is evident in this view. The seat handles of this pattern indicate this was one of the later modernised cars. ***G.C.T.***

The Second World War saw the return of female staff to conducting and-later-driving duties. This young lady demonstrates her right turn signalling on a Hex-Dash Standard tram on which the first simplification of lining treatment can be noted. ***Thomson Publications***

below the lower saloon windows or fine green lining elsewhere. The bogies and lifeguards were plain maroon. This styling was slightly simplified in later Coronation car repaints when the white lining on the orange panels was omitted and the fleet number transfers were changed from gold, double blue shaded, to aluminium with plain black edging.

The Standard Cars then came in for some attention. Around forty cars were placed in service with the usual main service colour panels painted in lined bus green and the upper ivory band displaced by the appropriate service colour. The Greek corner patterns and panelled effect were omitted and the cream upper deck corner pillars were lost in encircling bands of colour. The slip boards were retained just at first after the introduction of a service numbering system in May 1938 but were soon dispensed with to save on maintenance costs. The orange colour was extended down over the concave panels and, although the aluminium lining was retained, the corner detail became quarter-circular concave instead of a full Greek corner pattern. Strangely, the Maximum Traction Cars retained a simplified form of Greek corner pattern and panelling with upper deck cream corner pillars until after 1946. This even included those which had been repainted before the war in bus green.

From 1938, trucks were unlined maroon but, as cars received partial repaints, many combinations of styles existed until around 1946. The bus green plus service colour combination was not deemed successful. Some were more pleasing to the eye than others but the combination of bus green with service colour green surmounted by brown window frames was too unrelieved. The forty cars were repainted in bus green with ivory band above and a start was also made in repainting the white and service colour green cars. The Semi-High Speed Standard cars were not destined to last long and tended to lag behind in the repainting programme; hence the last service colour green and white cars in 1942 were of this type.

To achieve further economies, the aluminium lining was omitted from around 1940. Initially, yellow or red lining was used, edged in black and applied by hand, but this was substituted by pale green. The first examples had three horizontal bands applied the full length of the concave panels instead of 'GLASGOW CORPORATION' lettering. This had decorative motifs at the extremities but was labour intensive and was soon replaced by a green/black lining application at the top and bottom of the orange panels. By this time, the large aluminium edged black fleet numbers were being replaced by smaller green edged black numbers. (At first the green numbers were also large.) Until around 1944, the upper panels were still lined out, although unpanelled, but 998 heralded the final simplification by omitting all decorative lining on the cream and main colour panels, retaining only the black edging. This form, in all remaining colours, survived into the era of exterior adverts and red, yellow and blue cars all carried advertising from 1950 until 1952.

By November 1946 there were 158 (52) blue cars, 474 (19) green cars, 276 (10) red and 123 (10) yellow. The numbers in brackets are those remaining Semi-High Speed Cars and the high number of blue cars of this type will be noted.

This situation can be explained in that their only all-day duty was the former very long service from Renfrew Ferry to Milngavie which required blue cars. By 1946, however, the Semi-High Speed cars were used on special workings and peak hour extras. Newlands Depot, for instance, operated them at rush hours on the 3 service to Mosspark, providing the spectacle of blue cars where none normally ventured and all this led to further confusion.

The General Manager reported that white, as a service colour, had been discontinued because appearances could not be kept up and recommended that service numbers be standardised, all repaints and new cars should be in bus green and orange, coloured screens should be used when these became available and side destination boxes with service numbers should be fitted to all cars.

Of the four Coronation Mark I & II cars which entered service with red upper panels, 1278 was the shortest lived and most elusive, nearly escaping Bob Clark's camera as it scurried up Renfield Street past the Odeon Cinema. Note the treatment of the downward sweep of the red band compared with green cars.
R. R. Clark/STMS Collection

A front view of early Cunarder 1296 shows the reason for mounting the fleet number at high level. The 'L' plate and candle lamp holder occupies the dash panel between trafficators. This was modified and mounted higher when the fleet numbers were resited in conventional positions from 1301 onwards.
R. R. Clark/STMS Collection

In May 1949, the matter came up yet again when the Tramways Engineer was called on to explain that it was no longer possible to guarantee all cars on one service would be of the same colour. There had previously been 20 services but then there were 38. He suggested a compromise whereby white could be reintroduced as a 'neutral' colour for specials. He followed up with a suggestion that the colours could be reintroduced and re-allocated on an 'arterial road' basis. This would have involved most of the Coronation trams being repainted red, with some white and a few retained as green. A start was actually made in pursuing this when five Mark I and one Mark II Coronation cars were actually repainted with red substituting green. Only four entered service and even they did not survive long in this attractive style. The Traffic Superintendent was quite sure that numbers were much less confusing than colours. He emphasised that the new sodium exterior lighting in Fenwick Road effectively neutralised the colours in any case. The Tramways Engineer explained that if re-colouring of the trams was to be undertaken it could not be completed in less than two years. Standard Cars took 113 hours to paint while Coronations took 157. A complete strip down would be required as some finishing paints were incompatible with other manufacturers' undercoats. With this ammunition, the General Manager finally killed off any revival of service colours in April 1950 in his recommendation to the Transport Committee and a start was made in repainting all remaining non-bus green trams commencing with Red Car 200 in December 1950.

The Cunarder or Mark II Coronations had their own livery variations which are outlined in the Chapter devoted to them. The ex-Liverpool Cars, Lightweight Cars and 1100 were all painted in Coronation Mark I style but with straight green bands around the upper deck.

Although retaining more distinctive upper deck lining than Standard cars, the Maximum Traction fleet acquired the standard, simplified, livery in time for the appearance of exterior advertising. Here is Pickering bodied 1122 at Anderston Cross.
Parr/STMS Collection

The interiors of the Standard cars were functional. From the 1920s, the woodwork of the older cars — and later some of the newer ones and Maximum Traction Cars — had become painted near ebony coloured. This was known among paintshop staff as 'glossy dirt' and by enthusiasts as, simply, 'treacle'. Birds Eye maple panels were used for lower saloon ceilings, ornately lined out and decorated, and this was used also for ceiling linings in the upper saloon of some of the Unobtrusive Top Covered Cars. During the 1930s all these panels in the lower saloon were stripped down and repolished to provide an appearance identical to that achieved in the National Tramway Museum's excellently restored car 812. Upper saloon ceilings were latterly painted white and the zinc perforated ventilator shields aluminium.

Around 150 Standard trams of all types were repainted from around 1952 with the upper interior panels of the top deck painted cream, initially lined out in orange. This was pleasing to the eye when new but was not very durable.

The Coronation Mark I cars altered very little except to lose some of their more opulent features. The inlaid Alhambrinal panelling tended to become greasy and was almost impossible to restore. By 1952, a start was made in overpainting the green and brown embossed decorative flashes in cream. The leaf green frames of the lamp fittings in the top deck were repainted brown and all lower and bulkhead panels painted gloss brown.

The preserved tramcars have been depicted in different styles:

22	White	Phase III	1920s
488	Bus Green	Phase IV	1950s
585	Blue	Phase IV	1930s
672	White	As Built	1898
779	Red	Phase II	1910
812	Yellow	Phase IV	1930s
1088	Blue	Phase IV	1930s
1089	—	Single Decker	1951
1100	Bus Green	As Rebuilt	1950s
1115	Red	Max. Traction	1930s
1173	Bus Green	Mk. I Coronation	1938
1245	Bus Green	Mk. I Coronation	1950s
1274	Bus Green	Mk. I Coronation	1950s
1282	Bus Green	Mk. I Coronation	1952
1297	Bus Green	Mk. I Coronation	1953
1392	Bus Green	Mk. I Coronation	1957

Summary of Standard Trams Painted in Dual Colour Scheme, 1938.

Car	Colour	Date
584	Green	11/6/38
328	Red	18/6/38
140	Blue	25/6/38
143	Yellow	2/7/38
633	Green	9/7/38
180	Blue	9/7/38
585	Green	9/7/38
530	Yellow	15/7/38
644	Green	15/7/38
433	Red	15/7/38
232	Yellow	15/7/38
642	Blue	15/7/38
208	Green	15/7/38
471	Blue	6/8/38
295	Yellow	6/8/38
412	Red	6/8/38
404	Red	6/8/38
215	Green	6/8/38
105	Green	6/8/38
387	Green	6/8/38
598	Red	13/8/38
491	Green	13/8/38
312	Yellow	13/8/38
385	White	13/8/38
286	Red	13/8/38
151	Yellow	13/8/38
157	Yellow	13/8/38

The Scottish Industries Exhibition at the Kelvin Hall in 1959 guaranteed much traffic for trams running along Dumbarton Road. 1251 leads other transport in this busy scene. By this time advert blank panels were being painted out. ***W. A. C. Smith***

1003 represented the closest adherance to the brief given to the G.C.T. tram designers who were to incorporate existing equipment in their design solution. 1003's truck came from 413 and the seats were ex-scrapped Semi-High Speed trams. This was the only 'Lightweight' car to acquire advert blank panels.
R. R. Clark/STMS Collection

The normal photographic credit would read 'Photo: Courtesy A. K. Terry. However this view of 1100 in final condition ought to read 'Photo and Tram'; 'Courtesy A. K. Terry'. Against all odds Keith Terry secured for posterity this unusual Glasgow tram. It can now be viewed alongside some of the fruits of his other rescue efforts at the National Tramway Museum. 1100 carried a quasi-modern car livery.

Experimental Lining—lower panels (omitting 'GLASGOW CORPORATION') May 1940.
Yellow lines No. 467
Red lines No. 505
Green lines Nos. 42, 51, 180, 211, 232, 235, 300, 315, 328, 466, 476, 890.
All-over Wartime Grey livery Car 288 only
Orange upper deck Car 223 only.
Last white car 954 (1942) Last green car 962 (1942)
Last blue car 929 (1954)
Last red car 746 (1952) Last yellow car 942 (1953)

Advertisements were originally sign-written and applied both to car sides and dash panels. These were later changed — commencing with those on the dashes — to paper bills, to enable football pools promoters or newspapers to achieve topicality by regularly changing information. Exhibitions and cinemas also took advantage of this facility which tended to disfigure rather than enhance the apperance of the trams.

88 is seen at Darnley, location of Glasgow's longest-ever running road works, just after being repainted in 1955. The appearance was neat and a surprising amount of lining-out was retained until the end. K. MacKay

1001 was for six years allocated to Elderslie Depot and performed solely on Paisley local services. This is 1956/57 and the car displays evidence of spasmodic use with dust and dirt streaking from the roof down the car sides after exposure to rain. Note the upper saloon end half-drop windows have been replaced. There are two city crests visible, of differing sizes. K. MacKay

CHAPTER 18

Maintenance of Rolling Stock

The following text is the reproduction of a paper read to the Municipal Tramways Association (incorporated) Managers' Section on 15th June 1922 by Alexander Gerrard, Works Manager, Glasgow Corporation Tramways.

It gives an insight to the problems and scope of maintaining a very standardised fleet of tramcars in the years following the First World War and is included without editing or alteration in any way.

MAINTENANCE OF ROLLING STOCK

This subject must be so familiar to the members of the Association that it is doubtful whether any new matter can be introduced. Every tramway undertaking has its own method of inspecting and maintaining its rolling stock; one system may differ slightly from another, yet both be equally efficient. This paper will outline the system adopted by Glasgow, so that members may compare it with their own. If it is the means of raising a useful discussion, its purpose will have been fulfilled. Generally speaking, the overhauling and repairing of cars is carried out at the workshops, where the great bulk of the skilled tradesmen are employed. Only routine work and incidental repairs are carried out at the depots, the staff of which is employed at night, and is mostly unskilled and semi-skilled.

ROUTINE OF DEPOT WORK

Daily inspection of—

- Trucks, including hand and magnetic brakes.
- Trolley heads, wheels, contacts, etc.
- Bells, pushes, and batteries.
- Lamps and switches.
- Lifeguards.
- Car bodies generally.

Bi-weekly inspection of—

- Controllers (contacts and fingers cleaned and lubricated).

Weekly inspection of—

- Commutators, brush holders, and brushes.
- Lubrication of axle bearings.

Fortnightly inspection of—

- Lubrication of armature bearings.

Monthly inspection of—

- Armature clearance of Westinghouse No. 323 ventilated motors. Cars equipped with this type of motor are not sent to the works for periodical inspection every 3,000 miles, as are cars fitted with the old type of motor, but are being kept out for a longer period, which has not yet been definitely decided upon.

Equipment generally renewed at the depots include—

Brake shoes and chains	
Controller fingers and contacts	
Trolley wheels and pins	
Carbon brushes	Wear and
Dry cells	tear
Lamps	

Equipment frequently renewed at depots—

Brake spindles	
Controllers, switches	Defects and
Fuse block, brush holders	Accidents
Trolley poles	
Lifeguards	
Pilot boards	
Odd panes of glass	

Truckmen examine all the trucks each night for loose parts, also take up the wear of the brake shoes and replace those worn out. They also inspect the wheels, and report loose or worn-out tyres. Two men attend to 40 cars.

Controllermen clean the contacts and fingers twice per week, see that all is in good order and well lubricated, and once per week they inspect the commutators, brush holders, and carbon brushes. Any commutator requiring burnishing is attended to, and where they find the mica high they report same. One controllerman attends to 30 cars.

Trolley poles and wheels are inspected nightly. One man attends to 100 cars.

Lubrication—One man attends to 60 cars.

In addition to routine work, there is always the question of defects and accidents. Accidents affecting lifeguards, pilot boards, trolley poles, and glass (where there is no damaged woodwork) are generally replaced by the depot staff; but, as the staff is very limited, it cannot afford to devote much time to any particular car, otherwise the remainder would not get their proper share of attention. The foreman must promptly decide whether he can afford the time to deal with the case or send it to the works for repair. When controllers, switches, fuse blocks, brake spindles, trolley poles, or brush holders break down, or get into a condition which would entail some considerable time to put right, they are replaced, and the defective article is sent to the works for repair. Power cables breaking down receive a temporary repair, which keeps the car in service until it is going to the works for some other purpose. The defective cable is then made good by the electrical staff.

The depot staff pass on to the works all cars which have been damaged by collision, also all cars suffering from defective armatures, field coils, rheostats, wheels, axles, bearings, gear wheels, pinions, gear cases, hand-brake levers, magnetic brakes, and, of course, all cars requiring attention to defective woodwork, sheet-iron work, or paint work.

The erecting shop at the Coplawhill Carworks where all the Corporation-built trams were assembled. This photograph was taken in 1899, before the Paintshop was built to the left and track was extended over the Pollokshields East railway bridge. The electric tram is 702. ***G.C.T.***

CAR WORKS Six-Weekly Inspection and Overhaul

The great majority of the cars on this system are equipped with Westinghouse 49B or similarly-rated motors, and all cars thus equipped are sent to the works for overhaul every six weeks or thereby; to be precise, the mileage between overhauls is as near 3,000 as possible. Larger motors, such as the Westinghouse No. 220, are allowed to run 7,000 miles. The term 'six-weekly overhaul', was applied to this inspection when it was inaugurated some twenty-one years ago. At that time the motors were opened up for inspection every six weeks, but after a little experience it was decided to make the inspection after a specified mileage of 3,000 had been run. A note is forwarded weekly from the rolling stock department, in the Head Office, to the depot foremen, notifying them of the cars which are due for overhaul the following week, and detailing the mileage run by each car. The foreman then select the cars in the order of their mileage, as far as possible. The average mileage of cars sent to works for week ending 29th April, 1922 was 3,720.

This inspection covers motors, gearing, gear cases, trucks, brake spindles, and automatic switches. The motors and gear cases are opened up, motor axle bearings and oil wells lowered.

ARMATURES are carefully examined for defects, such as flats on commutators, defective or high mica, worn-out commutators, open circuits, broken steel bands, burnt hoods, burnt string bands, and oil-throwers unscrewing and becoming liable to jam the armatures.

If all is well with the armatures, the carbon dust is blown out from the inside of same by compressed air, and the commutator is burnished up. Minor faults discovered on the armature are rectified at once, and the armature goes out on the same car; but, should defects be revealed which will take a few hours to rectify, a fresh armature is supplied. No delay can be tolerated on this job, as the fitter and his handyman are working on bonus and are overhauling three cars per day.

Clearance between armature and pole pieces is examined, and if found necessary, the bearings are renewed. If clearance is found to be all right, the oil grooves in the bearings are cleaned out, and allowed to go out for another 3,000 miles.

BRUSH HOLDERS are examined for broken springs or defective insulation, and made good.

FIELD COILS and leads, also armature leads, are examined, and if found defective are repaired or replaced.

GEAR WHEELS and pinions are examined to see that all nuts and lock washers are in their places, and also for fractured or damaged teeth. The gear wheel is also examined, to see if it is fast on the axle. If there is any sign of movement, the car is held up and handed over to the Engineering Department for attention. The condition of the bearings is also a vital factor in the life of gearing. In order to obtain long life, the wheel and pinion must be kept deep in mesh, and this cannot be obtained if undue wear is tolerated in the bearings. The replacement of gear wheels on this system has been very small. Only some 400 have been replaced since the system was inaugurated. For the year ending 29th April, 1922, the number of gear wheels scrapped was 40, representing rather more than 2 per cent, per annum, and of that number only 24 were actually worn out. Of the others, 10 were rejected for broken or damaged teeth; 5 were cracked through the boss, and 1 through the rim.

GEAR CASES –The top half is carefully examined to see if it is tight on its support. The oil in the bottom half of the case is examined to see if there is anything foreign in it, such as a lock washer or split pin, or parts of same. The case is then filled with oil.

The syphon pads in oil-well are cleaned or renewed; the wells are then filled with fresh oil.

BOLTS –The bolts are all examined for signs of screw being overhauled. The motor cases and gear cases are then ready for closing up.

TRUCK –The truck is then examined for broken semi-elliptic or spiral springs, broken brace brackets, or loose bolts. Anything found defective is made good.

The brake spindle handle is taken off, the ratchet, spring, and top end of spindle examined, and any defect made good.

BODY DEFECTS —While the fitter is engaged overhauling the motors, the coachbuilder is busy making good minor defects, such as renewing pilot boards, lifeguards, platform steps, commode handles, stair-ascending rails, vestibule, mirror and ventilator frames and glasses, all broken glass in body and top cover, also repairing defective end-window shutters and rolling shutters over staircases, and all subsidiary repairs that accumulate in the course of six weeks, but which are not demanding immediate attention, are attended to when the car is in the works for its periodical inspection and overhaul. An order accompanies each car to the works, specifying all the defects known to the depot foremen. The various shop foremen then receive an order calling their attention to defects appertaining to their department.

On turning to the appended list showing the nature of repairs executed on the cars, we find that during the twelve months ending 29th April, 1922, 6317 cars passed through the shops for six-weekly overhaul, and of that number 3753 required something about the motors, truck, or body repaired or replaced. One outstanding feature in connection with this inspection is the number of minor defects revealed in the armatures. On referring to Items 49 and 50, it will be seen that 1691 armatures which came into the works in apparently good order were found to have minor defects. These were attended to, and thereby prevented from developing into something much more serious.

GENERAL OVERHAUL

Fourteen cars per week are being sent in for general overhaul. The normal period allowed for this work is three weeks. Should there be any abnormal work to be done, such as renewing corner pillars on the top cover, the cars affected are sent in a few days in advance, so that this work may be carried out at a special stance alongside a high working platform. These cars are then ready to take their places along with the others for general overhaul.

The first job is to uncouple the cable connections and remove the lifeguards, then lift the bodies from the truck and deposit them on trestles in an adjoining lye. The time required for this operation is, roughly, fifteen minutes per car. The whole fourteen cars are handled, their bodies and trucks placed in their respective stances in less than three hours.

TRUCK OVERHAUL –A fitter and his helper overhaul two trucks per week, on a bonus scheme. They undertake all the ordinary routine work about the truck, strip it down to the frame, despatch the wheels to the turning lathe, the semi-elliptic springs to the smithy, the armatures to the electric shop, and all

Inside the erecting shop at Coplawhill in 1900 with Phase I Standard trams under construction, including the experimental 770 with reversed stairs. In the foreground, right, can be seen platform collision fenders, trolley standards, axle boxes for Room & Kitchen car bogies and a wireplough lifeguard in front of the array of belt-driven machinery. ***G.C.T.***

defective or worn-out brake parts or other truck accessories are thrown out, either to be made good by the engineering department or scrapped. All the springs and other small parts are taken away by painters' labourers, cleaned in hot water, dried, and painted. The inside of the truck frame and all other parts of same, where the paintwork has been damaged, are coated with grey paint made from white lead.

Before the wheels are despatched the fitter closely examines his gear wheels to see if the two halves are biting the axle. If the two faces will not allow a five-thousandth feeler to pass between them, one of the halves is sent to the planing machine to have $\frac{1}{16}$ inch removed from the face. Of course, the cut of $\frac{1}{16}$ inch removed at the boss tapers out to nothing at the periphery of the wheel. After the gear wheel has been removed, the axle is carefully examined for fracture. The motor cases, being open for removal of armatures and brush holders, are thoroughly cleaned out, and coated with insulating varnish.

The fitter then makes good all armature and motor axle bearings, overhauls both hand and magnetic brake, renews (if necessary) axle and thrust brasses, and makes fast the top half of his gear cases. Having two trucks to work upon is a great advantage to him, as, after stripping the first truck and despatching his wheels and armatures, etc., for attention, he turns to his second truck and strips it down. By that time the wheels, etc., have been returned for the first truck, and he starts to reassemble it. The result is that the first lot of trucks are ready for their bodies on Friday morning and the second lot on Saturday forenoon. The fourteen cars are then ready to move into the paint shop. Odd jobs, such as squaring the truck, fitting diagonal braces, renewing defective end sills, brake hanger brackets, pilot board brackets, etc., are looked after by other fitters.

ARMATURES, FIELD COILS, BRUSH HOLDERS, AND MAGNETIC BRAKES—After the motor cases have been opened, the armatures are taken out and tested for insulation. If found good the commutators are turned up, and if the micas are hard they are recessed. The armatures are then coated with waterproof insulating varnish. The brush holders are taken away and renovated. The armature and field-coil leads are renewed, if found defective. The field coils are tested for insulation and ohmic value. The brake magnet coils are also tested for insulation and ohmic value.

CAR BODY OVERHAUL— While the fitters are busy overhauling the truck, the coachbuilders, electricians, tinsmiths, and painters are looking after their particular work on the bodies.

The coachbuilders' inspection and overhaul include the following:—

Platforms set up, all decayed flooring and bulkheads renewed, platform-step brackets set up and steps renewed (if necessary), stairs overhauled and fitted with new stringers, risers, steps and treads where required, canopies, bends, ribs, and cleading made good where necessary, roll-top shutters and garden seats overhauled, doors overhauled, all slack glasses re-rubbered, ventilator frames and glasses overhauled, vestibule frames and glasses overhauled, lifeguards taken down and refitted with new parts where required, lathing and wearing boards renewed. All furnishings inspected and made good.

In order to facilitate the work of maintaining the cars, the Stores Department carry a stock of every part of the body, machined and ready to take the place of the damaged or decayed part. The machine work is carried to the point of boring and countersinking the screw holes. Lathing and wearing boards, when issued to the coachbuilder, are cut to a length, bevelled, coated with paint, and all screw holes bored.

SHEET-IRON WORK— The tinsmiths renovate the dashes, end destination sheets, and ventilating ducts on roof of top cover. Dashes which are slightly dinged are made good in position, but if they are out of shape they are removed from the car, and, if necessary, flattened out and re-rolled into shape again.

ELECTRICAL WORK—The controllers, automatic and canopy switches, also bells, are taken off and sent to the electric shop for overhaul. After being overhauled the auto switches are tested, and set to blow at 200 amps, for the 30 hp motors, and at 250 amps for the

40 hp. The rheostats are tested for insulation and ohmic value. The trolley poles and bases are removed from the cars, the poles going to the electric shop and the bases to the engineers' shop for overhaul. These are returned and refitted to the car before the end of the week.

All power and brake cables are examined and made good, also all lighting and bell wires, switches, lamp holders, and pushes.

When the car comes out of the paint shop, the controllers, power switches, bells, etc., are refitted. The car is then tested for direction on each motor singly, then on both motors, also electric brake, before being passed.

PAINT WORK— As the cars vary in age, generally speaking so does the condition of the paint work. Some of them are passing through the shops for the first time after only sixteen months' service; others have twenty years' continuous work. Some have pushed their way through traffic since their last general overhaul, and have met with no accidents; but, on the other hand, we find a fair percentage which have not been so fortunate. Their dashes are dented and patched-looking, and their panels show marks where they have been torn and then touched up. We find that the paint work on the top cover suffers much more from the sun than does the paint on the lower part of the body. Probably 25 per cent of the cars passing through for general overhaul require the panels and end sheets of the top cover repainted. On some of them the colour is faded, but not cracked; on others we find the varnish perished and showing deep cracks right through the paint as far as the filling.

As the renovating of the paint work extends over two weeks—the first week by semi-skilled men and the second week by skilled men—it might be advisable to note the nature of work done by both classes of men.

The labourers thoroughly clean the under-framing, flooring, hatches, heel boards, inside of dashes and end destination sheets, deck rails, seat legs, etc., and give them all a coat of paint.

DASHES—All damaged paint on the dash is scraped off, then sand-papered, and gets two coats of ground colour. Any depressions are filled up with putty.

PANELS—All cracks in the varnish on the main panels are faced out, and any part of the panel which has been scraped or torn by colliding with other vehicles is sand-papered, and then coated with priming and filled with putty. If the concave or end panels or under side of canopies are discoloured, they are sand-papered, and get one coat of ground colour. If the paint on the panels of the top cover is faded, but not cracked, it is sand-papered and gets one coat of ground colour. If, however, the varnish is perished and the paint cracked, it is treated with ammonia, and the paint removed with a scraper. The filling below the paint is, of course, not touched. The panels are then rubbed down with pumicestone and water, and get one coat of priming and two coats of ground colour.

All the cleaning, rough painting, scraping, and removing of paint by ammonia, patching with putty, coating with priming and ground colour, as described above, is done by unskilled and semi-skilled men during the first week, while the car body and truck are in the general overhaul shop. On Saturday forenoon the shift is made; those fourteen cars are moved into the paint shop, where the skilled painter gets a week to do his part.

When the painter receives the car, it has a coat of many colours. It is often a very scarred-looking vehicle. It may show many white patches on the main panels, and one or both of the dashes may have been off and through the rolls; its top-cover panel and end sheets may have been faded, and are handed over to him with a coat of ground colour. However, he has signed a contract to turn the car out in good shape, and, no matter how much or how little there is to do, the car is ready for removal from the paint shop at the end of the week.

Dealing with a car in the condition mentioned above as a typical job, the painter first flattens with ground pumice and water the whole outside of the car; the scars on the main panels and dashes where putty is shown are faced down and touched up with ground colour and colour until they match the main body. The whole panel is then coated with varnish colour. Where the whole dash or part of same has been scraped and got two coats of ground colour from the semi-skilled man, it gets other two coats of colour and one coat of varnish colour from the painter. If the top-cover panels, end or concave panels come into the paint shop in ground colour, they get one coat of colour and one of varnish colour, and are then picked out and lined, ready for varnish. The stairs, front and back, get two coats of straw colour, and the sheet-steel stringers are touched up if required. Truck frames and platform angles get one coat of brown paint and one coat of varnish colour lake, then lined, ready for varnish.

VARNISHING—The main panels and dashes get two coats of varnish. All the rest of the body, including the top cover and stairs, also the truck, only get one coat of varnish; that is, if the old varnish has not been disturbed, there is only one fresh coat put on, but if the old paint has been removed and fresh coats put on, it gets two coats of varnish.

INSIDE OF CAR BODY AND TOP COVER— The inside of both are thoroughly washed down with hot water and soda. The painter then touches up and varnishes everything below the window-sills, including seats, back rests, heel boards, etc. The polisher looks after everything above the window sills, including end casings. The painter finishes off his job on Saturday by coating the roof, the middle-deck floor, the body flooring, hatches, and platforms with a coat of grey paint. In order to allow the varnish to be thoroughly hard before going into service, the cars are kept in the works another week after leaving the paint shop. During that week all the electrical fittings, such as controllers, automatic switches, etc., are brought back and reconnected to the car. The coachbuilder also finishes off his work, re-erects the lifeguards, trims the feelers to within 3½ inches of the rail, and the point of the tray to a similar distance. The tension spring is adjusted so that there is a downward pressure of 50 lbs on the rail, at the point of the tray, when the life-guard is released.

DAMAGED CARS—All damaged cars are sent to the works for repair, unless the damage is very trivial and can be attended to in the depot. It is difficult to estimate the number of men to hold in readiness to cope with this class of work, as it fluctuates very much, so the men who attend to damages must have a stand-by job to turn to when the damages are light. When dealing with damaged cars, it is well to note that the advent of the vestibule front has brought a tremendous amount of work in its train. It is estimated that after a car has been fitted with a vestibule front it requires to go to the works for repair at least five times as often as it did before being thus fitted. A car without a vestibule may get four or five bumps before it gets one sufficiently heavy to call for attention at the works, but once a car has been fitted with a glass front the least bump shivers the glass and breaks the vestibule framing.

From the appended list, Item 8, it will be seen that for the year there were only 97 cars sent in for repairs to lower dashes. This item appertains to cars still unfitted with vestibules. As against that we find from Items 9, 10 and 11 that there were 687 cars sent in for repairs to dash and vestibule, vestibule framing, and glass. In addition to this, there were 1,171 panes of glass fitted to vestibules in the depots. These figures show that the damage to vestibule cars is out of all proportion to the number of cars running, which a year ago was, roughly, 500 cars fitted with vestibules against 420 unfitted, and today there are, roughly, 600 fitted against 350 not fitted.

TRUCK REPAIRS—The engineering department looks after the re-wheeling of all cars which are sent to the works between general overhaul, also all odd jobs, such as renewing of gear wheels, replacing defective gear cases or broken truck end sills, renewing broken axle boxes or any job which necessitates lifting the body from the truck.

RE-WHEELING—The number of cars sent in for tyres to be turned up or renewed averages about 8 per week; that is, in addition to the 14 cars per week which have their wheels attended to when passing through for general overhaul. This means that over 1,000 sets of wheels are passing through the lathe per annum. The average time taken to turn up one pair of wheels is 1½ hours. The squad of two fitters and one handyman re-wheel a truck in 7½ hours. After the body has been replaced on the truck, the car is handed over to the overhaul department, and its motors are subjected to the usual six-weekly inspection, so that when the re-wheeled car leaves the works it is all in order for another 3,000 miles. This system has the advantage of placing the responsibility on one foreman of seeing that all cars leaving the works are in good running order.

In connection with re-wheeling, it may be stated that cars are not sent to works for re-wheeling until they have run at least 3,000 miles since last at works, unless absolutely necessary, such as cases of broken axles, flats skidded on tyres, loose or burst tyres, etc.

RE-TYRING—The time taken to bore out one pair of tyres ready for the wheels averages about two hours. The tyres are expanded by gas; the wheel is then lowered into the tyre, which is immediately cooled by water until it clings to the wheel. Both tyres are being dealt with at the same time, so that after the first tyre is shrunk the second wheel is dropped into the other tyre. The number of tyres renewed for the year ending 29th April, 1922 was 1,424. The average mileage of tyres for the five years ending 31st May, 1921, was 76,000.

COST OF TURNING WHEELS–As to the re-tyring of wheels, it is interesting to look into the cost of turning up old tyres, and thereby ascertain at what diameter they ought to be scrapped, in the event of their getting out of shape. In 1914, also in 1919, we very carefully went into the cost of turning up wheels, also renewing of tyres, and, although the wages in 1919 were nearly three times as great as during 1914, the result was the same—viz., that 29¾ inches was the economical limit at which it paid to strip the wheels from a car and have them turned up again. Dealing with tyres as used in Glasgow, 31¾ inches outside and 26$^{11}/_{16}$ inches inside diameter, we find that 28½ inches is about the minimum that the tyre can safely be worn down to. This means that the total available wear is 3¼ inches, or 1⅝ inches radial wear. Taking the 1919 figures, we find that it cost some £28 2s 8d to re-tyre a car, or £7 0s 8d per tyre. The above figure is equal to 10s 9d per ⅛ inch radial wear. If we assume that a set of wheels come into the works at 29¾ inches for turning up, and after being machined they go out at 29½ inches, there remains only ½ inch radial wear, the value of which is equal to 10s 9d x 4 = £2 3s per tyre, against which we find that it cost £9 3s 9d to turn up the set of wheels, equal to £2 5s 11d per tyre.

The figures shown above for re-tyring and turning up of old tyres includes every item of expenditure incurred from the time the car enters the works until it leaves again, such as breaking the electrical connections between body and truck, removing life-guards, lifting body from truck, transporting the truck to the re-wheeling department, dropping the wheels out of the truck and transporting them to and from the lathe, re-fitting the wheels to the truck again, etc.

Glasgow Corporation Tramways achieved a remarkably high degree of standardisation during the pre 1920s period. But there were differences. Mountain & Gibson were given an order for 100 21EM trunks and these operated alongside the otherwise omnipresent Brill 21EM. The detailed differences between the two can be examined: the upper view shows the 21E with the 21EM below. G.C.T.

Therefore it appears as if it does not pay to turn up wheels at or below 29¾ inches. They ought to be kept in service as long as possible, and then scrapped.

The following instruction is issued to depot foremen for their guidance:—

NOTICE TO DEPOT FOREMEN

STEEL TYRES—Depot foremen will please note that it has been found to be unprofitable to turn up tyres after they have worn to 29½ inches diameter, owing to the fact that the value of the available metal left for wear is less than the cost of turning up the tyres. They will therefore arrange that when tyres have reached this diameter they will not be turned up, but run as long as possible with safety, and then scrapped.

AXLE EXAMINATION—Every time an axle comes into the engineering department, either for wheels to be turned up or re-tyred, the gear wheel is stripped off and the axle examined for fracture. Should a fracture be found, the wheels are pressed off and the axle scrapped. During the past year the number of axles scrapped was 103. Of these, 12 were broken, 76 were found to be fractured, 9 bent, 4 had torn journals, and 2 had worn journals.

Item No.		*No. of Cars*	
1.	Cars inspected (six-weekly overhaul, including re-wheeled cars)	6,317	
2.	Cars overhauled (yearly)	690	
3.	Cars repaired (only)	1,260	
4.	Total cars passed through works	8,267	8,267
5.	Cars repaired (from six-weekly inspection)	3,753	
6.	Cars re-wheeled	417	
7.	Cars for upper dash repairs	24	
8.	Cars for lower dash repairs	97	
9.	Cars for dash and vestibule repairs	162	} 687
10.	Cars for vestibule frame repairs	173	}
11.	Cars for vestibule glass repairs	352	}
12.	Cars for glass, other than vestibule	203	
13.	Cars for canopy repairs	75	
14.	Cars for upper roof repairs	152	
15.	Cars for pillar and rail repairs (top cover)	155	
16.	Cars for pillar and rail repairs (body)	13	
17.	Cars for panelling (body and top cover, including water rail)	111	
18.	Cars for body fittings, seats, casings, doors, etc.	543	
19.	Cars for hood and roll-top repairs	192	
20.	Cars for handrail repairs	96	
21.	Cars for subsidiary body repairs	495	
22.	Cars for underframing and packing bar	21	
23.	Cars for platform and stair damage, including angle iron, etc.	125	
24.	Cars for platform step repairs	396	
25.	Cars for lifeguard and pilot board	111	
26.	Cars for axle box repairs	50	
27.	Cars for axle box spring repairs	397	
28.	Cars for semi-elliptic spring repairs	180	
29.	Cars for spring post repairs	17	

Item No.		*No. of Cars*
30.	Cars for horn block and side repairs	1
31.	Cars for truck cross iron repairs	75
32.	Cars for hand brake repairs	299
33.	Cars for magnetic brake repairs	77
34.	Cars for motor case repairs	65
35.	Cars for gear case repairs	74
36.	Cars for gear wheel repairs	123
37.	Cars for subsidiary truck repairs	63
38.	Cars for power and brake cable repairs	250
39.	Cars for lighting and bell wiring, fittings, etc.	57
40.	Cars for electrical equipment, including brush holders, solenoid device, lightning arresters, fuse box, etc.	214
41.	Cars for automatic switches changed)	69
42.	Cars for rheostats (changed or repaired)	42
43.	Cars for trolley pole (only) repairs	21
44.	Cars for trolley base or base and pole repairs	51
45.	Number of field coils changed	448
46.	Number of controllers changed (from six-weekly inspection)	59
47.	Number of controllers repaired and out on same car	104
48.	Number of armatures changed (from six-weekly inspection)	810
49.	Number of armatures repaired, including commutators turned out in same car again	1,221
50.	Number of armatures with string bands renewed only, and out in same car again	470
51.	Number of armatures fitted with new commutators	109
52.	Number of armatures re-wound	304
53.	Number of armatures repaired (heavy jobs)	44
54.	Number of armatures repaired (light jobs)	442
55.	Number of armatures with spindles renewed	25
56.	Number of armatures with sleeves fitted	103
57.	Number of controllers overhauled from general overhaul	1,371
58.	Number of controllers repaired and overhauled from general stores and own stocks	126
59.	Number of field coils scrapped	140
60.	Number of tyres scrapped	1,424
61.	Number of wheels scrapped	14
62.	Number of axles scrapped	103
63.	Number of gear wheels scrapped	40
64.	Number of pinions scrapped	206
65.	Number of axle boxes scrapped	80
66.	Number of top gear cases scrapped	23
67.	Number of bottom gear cases scrapped	15

29th May, 1922

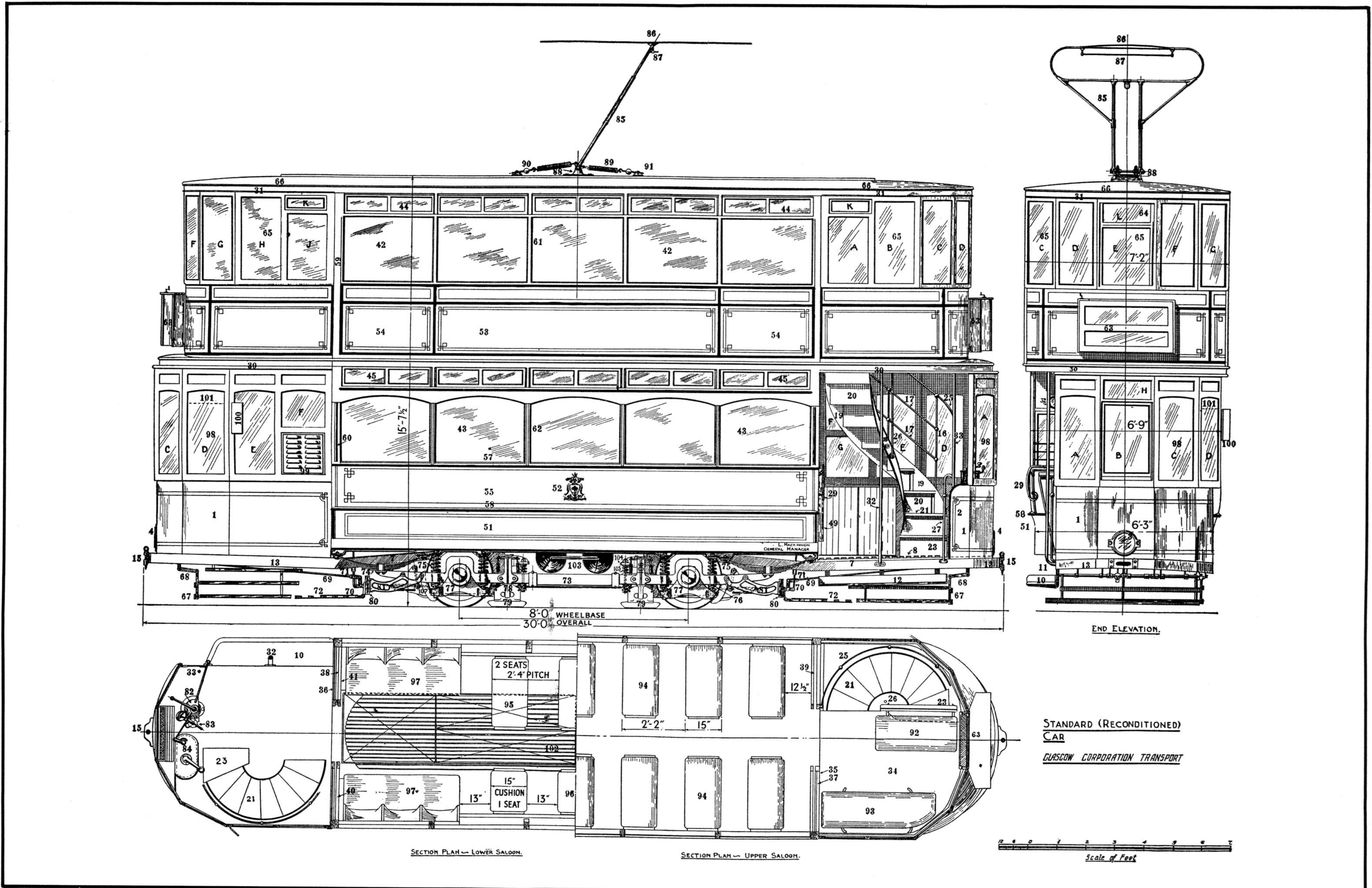

End Elevation.
8'-0" Wheelbase
30'-0" Overall
L. Mackinnon General Manager
2 Seats 2'-4" Pitch
15" Cushion 1 Seat
Section Plan — Lower Saloon.
Section Plan — Upper Saloon.
Standard (Reconditioned) Car
Glasgow Corporation Transport
Scale of Feet

LIST OF COMPONENT PARTS

STANDARD RE-CONDITIONED TRAM

To be used in conjunction with diagram of Corporation Tram

1. Dash.
2. Dash Beading.
3. Dash Light Glass.
4. Dash Light Brass Frame.
5. Dash Light Casting.
6. Dash Light Reflector.
7. Platform Bearers.
8. Platform Wearing Strips.
9. Platform Packing Piece Under End Sill.
10. Platform Step.
11. Platform Step Brackets.
12. Platform Step Toeplate.
13. Platform Angle Iron.
14. Platform Bearer Cross Beam.
15. Draw Bracket.
16. Stair Stanchion.
17. Stair Rail (½ inch Round).
18. Stair Stringer (Inside).
19. Stair Stringer (Outside).
20. Stair Riser.
21. Stair Tread (Wood).
22. Stair Tread (Wearing Plate).
23. Stair Loose Box Step.
24. Stair Fillets.
25. Stair Rail (Outside).
26. Stair Ascending Rail (Inside).
27. Dash Hand Rail.
28. Dash Hand Bracket.
29. Commode Handle.
30. Canopy Bend (Driver's Vestibule).
31. Canopy Bend (Top Deck Vestibule).
32. Canopy Rod.
33. Canopy Support.
34. Canopy Flooring.
35. Headstock Panel (Upper Deck).
36. Headstock Panel (Lower Deck).
37. Bulkhead Fixed Glass (Upper Deck).
38. Bulkhead Fixed Glass (Lower Deck).
39. Bulkhead Hinged Casement and Glass (Upper Deck).
40. Bulkhead Hinged Casement and Glass (Lower Deck).
41. Inside Drop Shutter for End Pane (Lower Deck).
42. Side Glass (Upper Deck).
43. Side Glass (Lower Deck).
44. Ventilator Frame and Glass (Upper Deck).
45. Ventilator Frame and Glass (Lower Deck).
46. Door Glass.
47. Door Woodwork.
48. Window Guards.
49. Ticket (Used) Box (Large).
50. Ticket (Used) Box (Small).
51. Concave Side Panel.
52. Coat of Arms.
53. Main Side Panel (Upper Deck).
54. Short Side Panel (Upper Deck).
55. Main Side Panel (Lower Deck).
56. Drip Rail.
57. Window Rail.
58. Waist Rail.
59. Corner Pillar (Upper Deck).
60. Corner Pillar (Lower Deck).
61. Intermediate Side Pillar (Upper Deck).
62. Intermediate Side Pillar (Lower Deck).
63. Destination and Route Indicator.
64. Route Number Indicator.
65. Complete Vestibule (Upper Deck) containing Fixed Frames and Glass marked "A," "B," "C," "D," "F," "G," "H," "J," and "L," and Drop Light Frame and Glass marked "E," also Hinged Ventilator Frames and Glass marked "K."
66. Canopy (Upper Deck).
67. Life-Guard Feeler.
68. Life-Guard Feeler Bell Crank.
69. Life-Guard Feeler Connecting Rod to Pilot Board Crank-shaft.
70. Life-Guard Pilot Board Crank-shaft.
71. Life-Guard Connecting Rod Pilot Board Crank-shaft to Car Body.
72. Life-Guard Tray.
73. Main Truck Frame.
74. Semi-elliptical Truck Springs.
75. Spiral Truck Springs.
76. Axle Box Springs.
77. Axle Box.
78. Magnetic Brake Horn Block Guides.
79. Magnetic Brake Magnets and Shoes.
80. Pilot Board.
81. Pilot Board Brackets.
82. Hand Brake Handle and Column.
83. Air Brake Control Gauge.
84. Controller.
85. Bow Collector (Complete).
86. Bow Collector Skid Plate.
87. Bow Collector Skid Plate Counter Balance.
88. Bow Collector Base.
89. Bow Collector Springs.
90. Bow Collector Insulators.
91. Bow Collector Spring Anchor Brackets.
92. Short Seat on Canopy.
93. Long Seat on Canopy.
94. Seats (Upper Deck).
95. Double Seats (Lower Deck).
96. Single Seats (Lower Deck).
97. Longitudinal Seats (Lower Deck).
98. Complete Vestibule containing Frames and Glass marked "A," "B" (Drop Light), "C," "D," "E," "F," "G," and "H."
99. Louvred or Grilled Ventilator for Rheostat.
100. Driver's Mirror.
101. Special Route Slip Board.
102. Floor Hatches (Lower Deck).
103. Compressed Air Reservoirs.
104. Motor Suspension Bar.
105. Motor Suspension Springs.
106. Magnetic Brake Suspension Brackets.
107. Brake Blocks (Air Brake System).

The Tramways Department Motor School contained a complete framework of a Phase I open top Standard car which remained there until the end. The 6′-0′′ wheelbase truck was salvaged for preserved Phase II car 779. With the benefit of hindsight, it is a pity that the framework was not panelled and completed to produce a Phase I tram for posterity. *G.C.T.*

The erecting shop at Coplawhill in 1930 was still a hive of activity during the modernisation era. Centred in the photograph is the first 334 to the right of 282. Note the new 8′-0′′ wheelbase truck frames ready for assembly in the foreground. *G.C.T.*

CHAPTER 19

Etcetera

ETCETERA

Film actor Michael Caine — as many are aware — takes pleasure in collecting useless information and then impressing his friends with it, adding 'not a lot of people know that . . .' Piecing together the pieces of the story of the Glasgow Tramcar has been like assembling a jigsaw puzzle. Inevitably, some pieces remain to be filled. On the other hand there are some left over which could not be slotted logically into the preceding Chapters. They probably come into Michael Caine's orbit. You, too, can impress your friends . . .

For instance, when the author and Dr. Struan Robertson were cataloguing the collection of tramways drawings now in the possession of the Glasgow Museum of Transport, they came across a general arrangement drawing of a Barrow-in-Furness single-deck bogie tramcar. This was puzzling. After all, there was very little which the mighty Glasgow system could learn from the humble Barrow-in-Furness except, perhaps, how to run trams with less current consumption per mile than anyone else. The existence of the drawing was put to the back of one's mind until, years later, examination of the ledgers for the financial years 1919-20 and 1920-21 revealed that the Coplawhill Carworks had in fact rebuilt Barrow-in-Furness tramcar No. 24 and two sets of maximum traction bogies. No. 24 had been built by Brush in 1912 and the bogies are thought to have been of Mountain & Gibson origin. It was unheard of for Glasgow to have involved itself in this way with another system and it must remain a matter of speculation as to why this liaison was established. On New Year's Day 1920 the Barrow-in-Furness Corporation had acquired a very run down undertaking from the British Electric Traction Company and presumably what they acquired was in such dire need of major repair or rebuilding that it was beyond their resources at the time.

There may have been an element of persuasion from the Board of Trade which resulted in the Glasgow involvement, although one would have thought that Manchester was nearer to Barrow and better equipped to deal with maximum traction trucks, so there could have been an arrangement concluded at a more personal level. It is certain that GCT's involvement had been set up prior to Barrow Corporation's acquisition of their tramway system.

Glasgow's neighbouring tramways with physical rail connections were the Paisley District Tramways, acquired by GCT in 1923, and the Lanarkshire Tramways Company. The latter was the largest tramway company in Scotland and continued to undertake substantial modernisation until the 1920s when they built the prototype of their 'N' class cars, No. 77. This looked very much like a Phase III Glasgow Standard Hexagonal Dash car of the time. Not having the neatness in detail of the Glasgow design, it was more advanced technically, incorporating many features which were not to appear in Glasgow until the modernisation to Phase IV standards. Friendly approaches had been made from Lanarkshire with regard to inter-working of their trams with Glasgow but GCT cast them aside. They said that the swivel head trolleys of Lanarkshire were incompatible with Glasgow's fixed head, or Estler pattern. One cannot help feeling that this could have been resolved if there had been a will. Notwithstanding this, Lanarkshire No. 77 made the return trip to Coplawhill to undergo a tilt test accompanied by its designer Mr. H. C. H. Moller who had picked up many ideas on tramcar design from that source. GCT never allowed Lanarkshire the opportunity to operate in its territory when it could not reciprocate. Do times really change in all things?

The only other 'foreign' visitors to the Glasgow system were Paisley District Nos. 51 and 52 but there was nothing 'cloak-and-dagger' about this. Both these trams were assembled in the Motherwell Depot of the Lanarkshire Tramways Company from parts delivered there by Hurst, Nelson Ltd., also of Motherwell.

They were then delivered under their own power via the Cambuslang link through Glasgow to the Paisley Depot and Workshop at Elderslie. This was the only instance of such a delivery throughout the Clyde Valley conurbation. Indeed, subsequently even the Lanarkshire system received new trams from Motherwell by railway! This historic drive over three systems' tracks was duly photographed in Trongate, Glasgow early one morning in 1908.

It has been seen how successful the design of the Mark I Coronation tram was from all viewpoints. Mr. Fitzpayne once conceded that the Mark II version could not excel it. It is interesting to note that today's operator of both versions, the National Tramway Museum at Crich, who have undertaken considerable rebuilding on both their 1282 and 1297, hold a different view. While admitting the quality of specification, comfort and finish on the Mark I 1282, they point out that the Mark II version is better thought out with regard to accident repairs, routine maintenance and accessibility. This was, of course, precisely what the designers set out to achieve. Be that as it may, a letter was received from the General Manager of Aberdeen Corporation Tramways in 1945 enquiring whether, in the event of Glasgow Corporation Transport building car bodies in the near future, it would be possible to incorporate provision for 20 car bodies for bogies being supplied to Aberdeen via the EMB Co. Ltd. Unfortunately there was no provision in the Corporation Tramways Acts under which this proposal could be undertaken, and the vision of Coronation Mark I (or even Mark II) trams in Aberdeen remains a matter for the imagination. The order was eventually undertaken by R. Y. Pickering Co. Ltd., of Wishaw who nearly became involved in concluding the Cunarder order for Glasgow due to difficulties which obtained in Coplawhill. When these very bogie cars were offered to Glasgow Corporation Transport on December 9th, 1957 the offer was politely refused.

In a large system like Glasgow's, it was important to keep control of the use of materials and component parts. In order that records could be maintained and the movement of equipment tracked or monitored, nearly everything was given a number. Not only was the car body numbered uniquely but also controllers, resistances, motors, switches, etc. The one component most noticed by the observer was the truck. Each truck or bogie had a cast brass plate mounted on one side. Centred on this plate was the truck number flanked on each side by space to stamp or emboss the dates of overhaul. Until the early 1950s a system of one tram-one truck had been adhered to but after that it was decided to marry the best bodies to the best trucks and it became very difficult to detect any order in the system. The inside framed bogies used for 1005 and the Cunarders had the truck numbering plates attached to the truck end sills; hence they were only seen from the inspection pits or when the body was removed. Some trucks lost their number plates, a few were mounted upside down which made matters most confusing when 866 should have been 998!

Throughout this book there have been references to tramcars which have been preserved. The various colours and periods depicted are listed in Chapter 17. They can be viewed at the following museums.

The Glasgow Museum of Transport (static exhibits)
Cars 543 (Horse drawn) 672, 779, 1088, 1089, 1173 and 1392.

The National Tramway Museum, Crich, Derbyshire (operating museum).
22, 812, 1100, 1115, 1282, 1297, Works Cars No. 1, No. 21 and Paisley District 68 (ex. GCT 1068).

The Science Museum, South Kensington, London. (static exhibit).
585.

The East Anglia Transport Museum, Lowestoft. (operating museum).
1245.

The Seashore Trolley Museum, Kennebunkport, Maine, USA. (operating museum).
1274.

Paris. A.M.T.U.I.R., Paris Transport Museum, Avenue Sainté Marie. (static exhibit)
488.

In addition, The National Tramway Museum has Liverpool 869 which operated in Glasgow from 1955-1960 as 1055.

By any standards, this is a considerable number of trams still to exist. No doubt the survival of the Glasgow system until 1962 ensured that the enthusiasts, who by then had the Crich Museum as a potential home for their purchases, would dip their hands into their pockets to ensure preservation of their favourite type of species. However, these survivors are a lasting tribute to the builders and operators of the Glasgow Corporation Tramways.

By 1913 most cars running along St. Vincent Place were evidently top covered with each one in immaculate condition looking as if they were ex-works. Before long the First World War would tarnish this image. 250 is a red car. ***T. & R. Annan***

Service 6 provided a link from west of Partick with Sauchiehall Street but did not operate on a close headway. Nonetheless the photographer's wait for 648 was well rewarded by its shining appearance in Parliamentary Road. ***R. J. S. Wiseman***

Single track sections in Glasgow were very few indeed. 1166 leaves one such section in Coustonholm Road. This provided a short cut from Pollokshaws for Newlands Depot trams. The abandoned rails in the foreground formerly served the original depot in Pollokshaws. ***R. F. Mack***

APPENDIX (i)

SUMMARY OF CONTROLLERS, MOTORS AND TRUCKS IN STOCK AS AT OCTOBER 1951

NUMBER OF TRAMS OWNED — 1164

CONTROLLERS: (Car Sets)		
Metro-Vic OK23B, OK26B, OK20B	=	479
English Electric CDB2 Form F	=	399
British Thomson-Houston Master Controllers	=	153
		(includes 1100)
Metro-Vick Master Controllers	=	98
		(1391/2 not complete)
British Thomson-Houston OK45B (Regen)	=	24
British Thomson-Houston B18	=	7
Crompton Parkinson Master (1002)	=	1
Crompton Parkinson Vambac (1005)	=	1
GEC Master (1004)	=	1
GEC KH8 (1089)	=	1
	Total	1164

MOTORS: (Car Sets)		
MV101DR	=	481
		(including 6 and 1001)
DK105/24	=	97
GEC WT28	=	301
		(including 1003)
BT-H 101J (converted)	=	24
WH323V (Semi-High Speed Cars)	=	7
BT-H 264 (1089)	=	1
BT-H 109AW (Mk I Coronations)	=	150
MV109AW (1141 & 1142)	=	2
MV109AR (Mk II Coronations)	=	98
CP (1002)	=	1
CP (Vambac) (1005)	=	1
GEC WT283 (1004)	=	1
	Total	1164

TRUCKS: (Car Sets)		
M. & T. 596 5'-0" wb	=	98
EMB Lightweight 4'-9" wb	=	151
M. & T. Swing Link 4'-2" wb	=	1
GCT/Brush 21E, 8'-0" wb	=	840
J. G. Brill 21E, 7'-0" wb	=	7
Kilmarnock Max-Traction 4'-6" wb	=	50
Hurst Nelson Max Traction 4'-2" wb	=	2
M. & T. 8'-6" wb	=	2
GCT/Brush 21E, 8'-6" wb	=	1
EMB Swing Axle 8'-6" wb	=	10
M. & T. HS44 6'-0" wb	=	1
J. G. Brill 77E1 5'-4" wb	=	1
	Total	1164

As at October 1951
From total of 1164:—

(1) To be scrapped immediately	=	35 tramcars
(2) In bad condition	=	21 tramcars
(3) In fair condition	=	487 tramcars
(4) In good condition	=	311 tramcars
(5) In very good condition	=	310 tramcars

APPENDIX (ii)

Schedule of Tramcars Damaged or Destroyed in Fire at Newlands Depot 11/4/48

No. 1 Lye		
1 Tower Wagon		—destroyed
1 Decorated Car	No. 50	—destroyed
1 Decorated Car	1008	—destroyed
1 Standard Tramcar	513	—destroyed
1 Standard Tramcar	985	—seriously damaged (but not repaired)
1 Standard Tramcar	211	—damaged
No. 2 Lye		
1 Standard Tramcar	261	—destroyed
1 Standard Tramcar	55	—destroyed
1 Coronation Tramcar	1148	—destroyed
1 Standard Tramcar	656	—damaged (slight)
No. 3 Lye		
1 Horse Tramcar	543	—damaged
1 Permanent Way Trailer	——	—damaged
1 Tower Wagon	——	—destroyed
1 Coronation Tramcar	1239	—destroyed
1 Coronation Tramcar	1272	—damaged (serious)
No. 4 Lye		
1 Coronation Tramcar	1241	—damaged (serious)
1 Experimental Tramcar	6	—damaged (serious) (rebodied)
1 Coronation Tramcar	1141	—damaged (serious) (rebodied)
1 Experimental Tramcar	1003	—damaged
No. 5 Lye		
1 Coronation Tramcar	1173	—damaged (slight)
1 Coronation Tramcar	1176	—damaged (slight)
1 Coronation Tramcar	1177	—damaged (slight)
Total number of trams damaged/destroyed =		16
Total miscellaneous destroyed =		6
Total		22

APPENDIX (iii)

Schedule of Tramcars Destroyed in Fire at Dalmarnock Depot 22/3/61

108	1207	1316*	1344	1370
169	1208	1323	1345*	1376*
283	1210	1324	1346	1386
500	1214	1325	1347*	1387*
526	1216	1326	1353	1388
1153	1227	1331	1354*	1391
1156*	1229	1333	1357	1393
1157*	1233	1334	1365	1395*
1159	1244	1335	1368	1396
1204	1251	1337*	1369	1397
			Total	50

Car 1202 was scorched but returned to service.

Car 108 had been earmarked for preservation, its place taken by 22.

Car 526 had been earmarked for preservation, its place taken by 585.

This fire caused the return to service of Car 488, already repainted for the Paris Museum, together with 76, 1051, 585 (and 1088 which had been in storage awaiting restoration).

* indicates material salvaged.

APPENDIX (iv)

The scrapping of Glasgow Corporation's Electric Tramcars started with the converted horse cars and redundant Room & Kitchen single deckers from around 1907 through the 1920s to the small cars acquired from the Airdrie & Coatbridge and Paisley systems in the 1930s. It was 1939 before a real start was made in disposal of ageing Standard cars and this process was interrupted by the Second World War. Before this time most of the scrapping involved dismantling at the depots or at Coplawhill Carworks. Newlands Depot played a significant part in this process, after Dalmarnock and Langside. After hostilities ceased in 1945, scrapping recommenced as soon as conditions were favourable and nearly all this work was undertaken at Elderslie Depot until it was closed along with the Paisley services in May 1957. The last tram scrapped there was 847.

After this scrapping was — for a while — put out to tender.

(a) 50 Cars were sold to Connell's of Coatbridge between June and October, 1957. Nos. 1, 19, 120, 175, 197, 201, 241, 251, 252, 263, 285, 317, 319, 321, 348, 352, 353, 354, 355, 369, 374, 392, 393, 410, 443, 450, 453, 456, 461, 492, 503, 523, 562, 566, 568, 609, 629, 653, 683, 684, 696, 697, 726, 752, 780, 798, 870, 872, 891, 995.

(b) No. 1042 was dismantled at the Carworks.

(c) 25 Cars were sold to Bird's Commercial Vehicles, Stratford on Avon, January, 1958.
Nos. 20, 149, 200, 206, 214, (226), 253, (329), 430, 434, 486, 490, 528, 580, 639, 679, (713), 810 (839), 850, 876, 928, 986 (994), 999.

(d) In April 1958 a further 50 cars were sold.
2 cars to Arnott-Young, Old Kilpatrick,Nos. 340 and 402 and 48 cars to Connell's of Coatbridge. Nos.29, 31, 33, 43, 78, 105, 163, 174, 182, 193, 199, 208, 210, 228, 242, 256, 265, 266, 272, 273, 279, 293, 303, 304, 306, 318, 322, 326, 331, 358, 359, 378, 422, 471, 538, 549, 555, 602, 610, 612, 626, 660, 670, 673, 831, 833, 904, 917.

(e) In August 1958 a further 50 cars were sold to Connell's
Nos. 10, 28, 32, 57, 58, 101, 104, 122, 129, 152, 157, 161, 167, 173, 181, 202, 213, 222, 223, 238, 277, 291, 323, 325, 344, 364, 367, 368, 381, 411, 418, 451, 455, 457, 462, 495, 517, 540, 570, 574, 576, 604, 617, 625, 678, 680, 808, 813, 895, 909.

(f) A further 55 cars were sold to Connell's in November 1958.
Nos. 14, 25, 38, 44, 53, 67, 70, 88, 99, 107, 123, 125, 127, 135, 137, 164, 166, 185, 186, 196, 207, 212, 216, 225, 240, 254, 264, 274, 278, 301, 314, 315, 338, 341, 384, 398, 401, 409, 438, 463, 465, 497, 621, 675, 705, 729, 832, 889, 939, 942.

(g) The last cars sold for scrap to Connell's were Nos. 6, 1001, 1002, 1003 and 1004 in February 1959.
Thereafter all remaining cars were dismantled at the Carworks. Some were disposed of by the Transport Department, others were sold in component parts to scrap merchants.
Cars indicated ( ) were scrapped at GCT's coup at Colston but this practice stopped due to local residents' complaints of environmental pollution.
Remainder in section(c) believed to have been re-sold to Connell's by Bird's Commercial Vehicles.

APPENDIX (v)

THE RISE AND FALL OF THE GLASGOW STANDARD TRAMCAR

The following lists the numbers of standard trams in existence during their period of operation. Included are the single decker standard cars converted in 1939. Excluded are 142 after 1927 and the ex-Paisley standard cars 1053-1072.

Year	*Number of Cars*	*Year*	*Number of Cars*
1898	2	1928 & 1929	1003
1899	41	1930-1932	1002
1900	287	1933-1938	1001
1901	442	1939	970
1902	472	1940	967
1903	530	1941-1947	965
1904	542	1948	957
1905	621	1949	925
1906 & 1907	644	1950	871
1908	645	1951	833
1909	690	1952	801
1910	694	1953	756
1911	695	1954	706
1912	771	1955	663
1913	842	1956	563
1914	843	1957	484
1915	850	1958	304
1916	851	1959	110
1917 & 1918	854	1960	18
1919	856	1961	6
1920	913	1962	6
1921	942	1963 to date	5
1922	966		
1923	994		
1924-1927	1004		

Figures are for years ending 31st December

488 was the tram which went to Paris. The vessel conveying the car sailed right up the River Seine and this limited its size and the dimensions within which 488 had to conform. Hence certain sizeable portions had to be removed. Notice the sponsor's advertising on the car sides. One wonders if the re-assured Customs officials in France really did say 'That will do nicely!'

The Glasgow Herald

In re-reading the finished text of this book I have become aware of an inconsistency in terminology. Sometimes I refer to the 'tramcar', sometimes 'tram' but most often 'car'. I have made no attempt to change this–it says something in itself: there really was no need to differentiate in Glasgow between motor-cars and tram-cars. Cars (not 'caurs', please . . .) could only refer to the latter–the People's car. The Glasgow public adored them, defended them. They transcended all class distinctions–trams were as much at home in Pollokshields as in Parkhead. Their like will never be seen again.

Ian G. McM. Stewart.

THE END